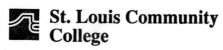

Henry Steele Commager

Henry Steele

Commager

Midcentury Liberalism

and the History of the

Present

Neil Jumonville

The University of

North Carolina Press

Chapel Hill & London

© 1999 The University of North Carolina Press

All rights reserved

Set in Minion type by Keystone Typesetting, Inc.

Manufactured in the United States of America

The paper in this book meets the guidelines for permanence
and durability of the Committee on Production Guidelines for
Book Longevity of the Council on Library Resources.

Library of Congress Cataloging-in-Publication Data

Jumonville, Neil.

Henry Steele Commager: midcentury liberalism and the history
of the present / Neil Jumonville.

   p.   cm.

Includes bibliographical references (p.   ) and index.

ISBN 0-8708-2448-8 (alk. paper)

1. Commager, Henry Steele, 1902–1998. 2. Historians—United States—
Biography. 3. Political activists—United States—Biography. 4. Historians—
United States—History—20th century. 5. Liberalism—United States—
History—20th century. 6. United States—Intellectual life—20th century.
I. Title.

E175.5.C73J86   1999

973.9′092—dc21   98-14589

             CIP

To the memory of

GEORGE A. RAWLYK

Canadian historian, intellectual,

mentor, friend

Officially I am a teacher of English literature, but
in reality my business in life is to wage war on the
crude and selfish materialism that is biting so deeply
into our national life and character.
—Vernon Parrington

I like the dreams of the future better than the
history of the past.
—Thomas Jefferson

Contents

Illustrations

Preface

This book is first a story about a historian and political activist, an individual with human strengths and weaknesses who made an important contribution to the national political and intellectual culture. Whatever else this volume is about, I hope that story itself is not lost. But there are several themes that I address most thoroughly in my account of Henry Steele Commager's life, and for me they structure what the book is about.

First, I've employed Commager's career to explore the relationship between the midcentury generation of scholars and the late-century (baby boomer) generation in the university. As a midcentury intellectual historian and American studies figure, Commager serves as a particularly good figure through which to assess the cultural wars that have torn the nation in the 1980s and 1990s. Every young generation distinguishes itself by symbolically slaying the generation before it, and it is fitting that Commager's crowd fell under the knife a quarter century ago. But the time to reassess our midcentury culture is upon us, and no figure holds a more central vantage from which to view the struggle than Commager. I suggest that my generation (I was born in 1952) has underestimated and misunderstood the contribution of midcentury liberals and that we should incorporate more of their ideas and commitments into our own cultural agenda. The record of the generational battles involving Commager is the history of the cultural feuds still with us today, and that is the most important reason I have chosen to subtitle the book *Midcentury Liberalism and the History of the Present*.

Second, because Commager's involvement in civic issues covered the century so widely and prominently, I have used him to chart the course of twentieth-century American liberalism with all its ironies, contradictions, and good intentions. Especially in the last half of the century, conservatives accused liberals of being leftists, and leftists accused liberals of being cold war conservatives who abandoned affirmative action. I suggest that liberals, caught in the middle (and how much glory is there in the middle of anything?), held to the beneficial principles of intellectual freedom, pragmatism, democratic toleration, and cultural diversity.

Finally, I've used the example of Commager to ask whether the intellectual life is compatible with scholarly life. Can an intellectual (who writes as a partisan generalist for the wide public on contemporary issues) still operate as a scholar (who is a "neutral" archival academic who writes for his or her professional peers)?

Our histories and accounts of American intellectual life seldom include consideration of historians. We are likely to hear about the political and cultural activism of journalists, lawyers, literary critics, and sociologists, but rarely historians. And historians have no one to blame but themselves—not only because they write many of the accounts and could well include those from their own discipline but also because historians as a rule have shied away from contemporary public enthusiasms and have had less impact on political life than they could have.

More than other scholars, historians have been threatened by partisanship and the present because they have been afraid that they would be mistaken for journalists and lose their special responsibility to interpret the past. Unlike historians, sociologists and literary critics have no need to fear losing their scholarly identities by addressing matters of contemporary debate, because the present is part of their professional assignment.

Still, over the course of the twentieth century, a handful of historians have resisted the pressure to remain exclusively within the scholarly corral. Commager, Charles Beard, Allan Nevins, C. Vann Woodward, and Arthur Schlesinger Jr., among others, have been activist intellectuals in addition to producing prolific professional scholarship. Yet, with a few notable exceptions, their intellectual contributions have been ignored as though their scholarly output is all that is fair to assess. Those who write the record of our political culture consider it an insult to describe historians in any role other than as professional and nonpartisan historians.[1]

Yet these politically active historians have added to the record of our intellectual life as much as other activist thinkers—for example, sociologists such as Daniel Bell or Nathan Glazer and literary critics such as Alfred Kazin or Edmund Wilson. The activist identities of American historians should not be ignored. Overlooking their activism will make them no better historians, but it will prevent us from adding the necessary complexity to our intellectual record.

Commager is a natural figure to use for this reevaluation of civically involved historians. Born in 1902, his life and intellectual activity spanned the century as few have. He corresponded with a wide array of important public figures—presidents, senators, intellectuals—and traded ideas with the most important historians in America and England. Commager wrote or edited more than forty books. While still in midcareer he was honored as an early Pitt Professor of American History at Cambridge University and Harmsworth Professor at Oxford. By 1978 he held forty-three honorary degrees and the Gold Medal of the American Academy of Arts and Letters.

As few have been able to do in the past half century, Commager brought together the two worlds of scholarship and public intellectual activity. Like Reinhold Niebuhr, Commager was one of the activist liberal intellectuals who helped define his generation. Instead of a dry academic figure, an isolated professor and teacher, Commager was an almost frenetic intellectual and political activist whose opinions, both when profound and ordinary, were constantly before the public. His example is another reason for the subtitle of this book: Commager thought a scholar should participate as much in the history of the present as in that of the past.

So let me pose my third theme again. Is the intellectual life compatible with scholarly life? Can an intellectual also operate as an effective scholar? As Commager's life shows, there is a danger to a historian's scholarly work if the broader and shallower approach (in the best sense) of the intellectual is simply extended to the professional work of the scholar. But a historian can be both an intellectual and a scholar if he or she takes care to separate those functions and not wear both hats for the same project. In fact, I would go even further. Historians *must* reach out and engage the wider public in a dialogue about historical issues if history as a field is to continue to have relevance in our national culture. Like the example of the tree that falls in the forest unheard, if historians are not read by the public, then what they write no longer carries on the function of history.

Acknowledgments

There are several key individuals whose help made this book a possibility. Mary Powlesland Commager, the second wife of Henry Steele Commager, reconciled herself to my wish to write about her husband and did all she could to assist me. In the summer of 1991 she invited me to come to Amherst and begin arranging her husband's unorganized papers, which were not yet housed in the Robert Frost Library at Amherst College but were still in boxes and on shelves in his office. Without access to those papers and the privilege of quoting from them, I could not have written this book. In addition to putting up with me during several interviews of her husband, she invited me to lunch at the family home to talk with him and through her graciousness allowed me to see a personal side of Commager that otherwise would have eluded me.

The help given me by William Leuchtenburg (from broad ideas to the details of copyediting) demonstrates how much graciousness still exists within the scholarly world. Although he didn't know me, he allowed me to encroach on his time throughout the project, answered my inquiries with the greatest care and gravity, and read the entire manuscript at a late stage and commented on it thoroughly. In addition, he sent me selections from his correspondence with Commager, from which I benefited. If Commager had done nothing else in his career except produce a scholar the quality of Leuchtenburg, the profession would owe him its thanks.

Harold Hyman, another noted scholar whom Commager mentored, also read the entire manuscript. During a busy period, Hyman went through the manuscript line by line, correcting factual and grammatical mistakes. When I revised my writing, I followed his suggestions closely.

Gregory Mark Pfitzer, the biographer of Samuel Eliot Morison, knew about plans for this volume before anyone else. As we were leaving graduate school in 1987, he was already helping me frame my inquiry for what I hoped would become a book on Commager. Since that time he has given me countless hours of advice, provided materials, and allowed me to check my ideas against him. At an early stage, when help was in short supply, Pfitzer read several of the chapters and gave me the benefit of his scholarly judgment. In addition, he has been my friend in the field of history with whom I've most shared the joys of common interests: historiography and intellectual and cultural history.

At an early stage of my research, Merle Curti, in his mid-nineties and living in a retirement home, walked in the dead of winter to the State Historical Society of Wisconsin to have an archivist send me letters relevant to Commager from both the Curti and the Alexander Meiklejohn Papers. In addition, Curti carried on a correspondence with me that would have fatigued a man half his age. I will always admire his enthusiasm and graciousness toward younger scholars.

Daniel Aaron, at whose knee in graduate school I learned much of what I know about the history of American ideas, provided me a copy of his correspondence with Henry Nash Smith. Because the two of them were among the earliest doctoral students in American Studies, those letters provided me a valuable glance at the early days of the movement with which Commager became associated.

Lisa Commager, Henry's daughter, read portions of the manuscript, fielded questions by letter and phone, lent me family photos, and invited me to dinner, during which we talked very informally about the family. Getting to know her has been an added benefit of this project.

The Columbia University Library allowed me to read through the papers of Allan Nevins, and the Columbia University Oral History Research Office permitted me to read through the oral histories of Commager and Nevins. Meredith Mayer and Anne Loftis, daughters of Allan Nevins, read part of the manuscript, gave me useful advice, and allowed me permission to quote from their father's letters and papers.

The administration of Florida State University, which is committed to faculty research, and Richard Greaves, chair of the Department of History, provided me with separate grants to fund a research trip in 1991 and to help locate and acquire photos for this book in 1996. In addition, I was allowed a research schedule that permitted this volume to be finished.

One of the heaviest burdens of my research fell on the librarians at Strozier Library at Florida State University. Reference librarians such as Greg Toole were endlessly patient with my requests and graciously lent me their scholarly expertise. The librarians in Strozier's interlibrary loan department were true professionals, occasionally pursuing several avenues to secure material I thought impossible to obtain. Representative of their effort was Ann Spangler's series of contacts with Columbia University Library that finally produced several copies of the Columbia University catalogue from the 1940s and 1950s.

In the autumn of 1963, the Columbia Broadcasting System (CBS) aired a long conversation between Commager and Nevins on American historiography. Thirty years later it was nearly impossible to find a copy. Toni Gavin at CBS, William Bridegam, librarian of Amherst College, and Vicky Bernal of the Florida State University Department of History went out of their way to make sure I got a copy of the film.

Daniel Horowitz was the first to read the entire manuscript and give me important conceptual advice on it, which made the book more coherent. Former Commager students or colleagues who were kind enough to read portions of the manuscript and offer their comments include Milton Cantor, Leonard Levy, and August Meier. Others who read portions of the book and gave advice are Irene Balderston, John Diggins, Annette Ansley Jumonville, Robert Jumonville, Milli Laughlin, Jeff Pasley, and George Rawlyk.

A group of people, some of them former students or colleagues of Commager, were kind enough to answer letters and in many cases to provide recollections or stories, some of which I used. These include Jacques Barzun, Patrick Boarman, Daniel Boorstin, William F. Buckley Jr., Milton Cantor, Merle Curti, John Diggins, John Hope Franklin, George M. Fredrickson, John Garraty, Theodore Greene, Allen Guttmann, Hugh Hawkins, Harold Hyman, Alfred Kazin, James Kloppenberg, Christopher Lasch, William Leuchtenburg, Leonard Levy, Leo Marx, August Meier, Arthur Schlesinger Jr., Robert Skotheim, John Thomas, and C. Vann Woodward.

Those who also provided help on this book include Robert Commagere, Brian Hurlbert, Russell Sizemore, Alan Steinweis, David Crist, and Michael Wreszin. The students in my graduate seminars on American historiography at Florida State University contributed more than they know to this volume.

During the years that I wrote this book, Bill Edmonds at the *Tallahassee Democrat* allowed me to write a monthly column for his intellectually lively op-ed page, and from month to month he worked tirelessly to place it on the national Knight-Ridder wire. That experience gave me a useful glimpse into the dual life of scholarship and journalism that Commager experienced.

For six years before publication, Lewis Bateman, at the University of North Carolina Press, supported and encouraged the concept of this book. I hope there is a special room in heaven for editors like him who work on behalf of books about ideas. Thanks also to Pamela Upton and Nancy Malone for their editorial help.

I would like to acknowledge the example of historians such as John Diggins and Peter Novick, whose books make it easier for younger historians to imagine what work can be done. They, and others like them, provide what Van Wyck Brooks once called a "windshield" for those who follow them.

My mother, Annette Ansley Jumonville, remains interested in my work, which is rewarding to me. She never failed to support this volume and inquire about its progress, although she would rather it had been about humor.

Finally, a special thanks to Karen Marie Jumonville for the most meaningful help with this project: wandering with me down the paths of this particular project with patience and enthusiasm.

I

Intellectuals and Historians

CHAPTER 1

The Formation of a
Public Intellectual,
1902-1932

In 1964 a classroom of Los Angeles high school seniors studying American government decided to compose a letter to the historian Henry Steele Commager. Addressing the sixty-one-year-old Amherst College professor as one "of the more prominent citizens of the world," because he was "one of those who 'make the news,'" the young students asked if he would be willing to reveal the "real person" inside himself instead of the "image" the public saw. Did he have one primary goal that he had pursued in life? Had his fame come with a "special loneliness"?[1]

Flattered, Commager replied that he had "no personal experience with fame." But what about his goals? He admitted he had "a deeply ingrained antipathy to abstract questions" such as theirs, because abstract inquiries usually hide what is really being sought: in this case, a curiosity about his moral values, purpose in life, or philosophy of history. There is no reason to assume, he warned the students, that young people, starting out as he once had, harbored such values, purposes, or philosophies. No, he told them, these "are not things that a normal young person deliberately adopts, any more than a normal young person deliberately decides what is the purpose of love before he falls in love, or what is the purpose of children before he has a family. Philosophies of life, if there are really such things, are things that develop with life, and usually only after most of life is over."

The high schoolers had prompted a candid response from him, and his characterization of himself as far more pragmatic than theoretical was true —both in his approach to life and in his historical scholarship. Commager never became as interested in theory as some others in his profession did, despite being an intellectual historian—a historian of ideas. While he was fascinated with political conflict and the struggle for cultural power, he avoided abstract explanations of those battles.

So Commager's young correspondents, he suggested, should "distrust men of maxims," those of "great moral generalizations," those with "one overriding 'goal' in life." Actually, he advised, because goals emerge from "deep drives in character or in the subconscious," most people are unaware of those distant marks on the horizon. And that is how it should be, for "the important things are not to be achieved by setting out for them. . . . They are by products. Those who say I will achieve happiness, don't. Happiness is something that comes, sometimes, as a by product of your work or your other activities. . . . Success is something that comes when you stop thinking about it and think about the job you are doing." His young admirers from Los Angeles, he concluded, should "stop thinking about these broad and windy things, and address yourselves to doing a good piece of work at whatever you are working at: your studies, the peace corps, raising corn, whatever it is."[2]

Perhaps his modest and practical response deflated or disappointed his eager fans, for he presented himself as a humble worker merely doing his daily task. But while Commager thought more about fame than he indicated to the students, he was probably surprised, as an academic figure, to be declared famous by adolescents a continent away. His notoriety had grown over the decades, he knew, but he still harbored insecurities from his past.

Commager, for example, thought his physical appearance an obstacle rather than an asset. He was of medium height, and as the *New York Times* remarked, he had "that tough little bantamweight look," that " 'feel'—as the boys along Jacobs Beach say—of a fellow who once boxed."[3] While he was not heavy, he was stocky like an athlete, and even into his twilight years he was described as "that old pug-nosed historian" who "moves on his feet like a boxer."[4]

The fighter image described not his personality, which was friendly and witty, if sometimes sarcastic, but rather his slightly off-center jaw, a square chin that appeared to have absorbed a blow from the right that pushed it permanently to the left. As a consequence, his face resembled a trapezoid that was longer on the left side, a side whose angular thrust and denser mass seemed softly to crowd his left eye, which was occasionally pinched into a half squint. Yet for all this, Commager was ruggedly handsome, similar to Peter Falk's television detective Columbo.

Family and close friends knew Henry as "Felix" (happy), the affectionate nickname given him by his first wife, Evan, who intended it to convey his cheerful personality. Driven by his wry perceptions of the world around him, he often made humorous comments about events or figures that delighted his companions. He loved life, and he raced through it at blinding speed, which added significantly to the disarray of his days. His schedule was enough for a half-dozen people: teaching, writing newspaper and magazine columns, editing a series of books, collaborating on textbooks, doing research on his historical projects, flying here for political lectures or there to give the government historical advice, being interviewed by reporters, doing a radio talk show, being filmed for a special program for the Columbia Broadcasting Service (CBS) or the Public Broadcasting Service (PBS), giving congressional testimony. When time permitted he loved attending concerts. He relished eating good food, which was one reason he belonged to several prestigious clubs and traveled to Europe by ship.

When the Los Angeles students wrote him in 1964, Commager lived in the small New England town of Amherst, Massachusetts, in a spacious white colonial house owned by the college and just one-half mile down the road south of campus. Yes, he was successful by most standards. Evan wrote children's books, and his son, Steele, was a professor of classics at Columbia. Nell, his oldest daughter, had graduated from Barnard College and married the historian Christopher Lasch. Lisa, the youngest in the family, had just graduated from Radcliffe.

Still, that high school seniors would see an academic figure, a historian, as a prominent citizen of the world is surprising. Most scholars, certainly most professional historians, are usually considered by the general public to be irrelevant, at best assumed to be scribbling away in talmudic isolation in a dusty wing of some library. That teenagers in California in the mid-1960s had such a different impression of Commager, that they saw him as a newsmaker, suggests the degree to which he pursued a career very different from most of his professional colleagues.

Within a handful of years straddling the start of the twentieth century, Pittsburgh, carved into the timber of the western foothills of the Allegheny Mountains, was the birthplace of several individuals who would later become prominent essayists. When Henry Steele Commager was born there on October 25, 1902, he joined Kenneth Burke and Malcolm Cowley, who were only a few years older. As Cowley grew and finally left Pittsburgh, he continued to draw great sustenance from his memories of his Pennsylvania childhood.[5] Unlike Cowley, as the young Commager matured he gladly left the memories of his childhood behind him. "The remembrance of things past is a fitful affair," he later admitted wistfully.[6]

The lineage of the Commager family wound back to the mid-1600s, when Henry's French Huguenot ancestors lived in the little farming village of Lafitole in the Upper Pyrenees. In the first years of the nineteenth century, his great-great-grandfather Gerard Jean Commagere of Lancaster, Pennsylvania, married Abigail Steel.[7] Their son, Henry Steel Commagere, moved to Toledo, Ohio, in 1827 at age twelve, and at that spot where one could stand in Ohio and throw a rock into either Michigan or Lake Erie, the family became settled and expanded.[8] In 1841 Commagere entered the law offices of Young and Waite to study law, then established a prosperous law practice in Toledo. Morrison Waite, under whom he studied, went on to become the seventh chief justice of the U.S. Supreme Court. Somewhere between 1843 and 1846 Henry Steel Commagere dropped the final *e* from his last name. In 1854 he campaigned unsuccessfully as the district's Democratic candidate for Congress, and later he earned a name as a celebrated Civil War officer in the 67th and then the 184th Ohio Infantry, attaining the rank of brevet brigadier general.[9]

His son David Hedges Commager, born in 1848, became a judge and local official in Toledo and followed his father Henry Steel into the Union army. David's son James Williams Commager was born in 1875 in Toledo and married Anna Elizabeth Dan in about 1897. James and Anna had three sons, the youngest of whom was born two years after the turn of the century as Henry Irving Commager (and who later changed his middle name to Steele). Although his brothers, Roger and James, had been born in Toledo, by the time Henry was born the family had moved to Pittsburgh.[10]

Henry lived in Pittsburgh during his "tender years," probably until he was six or seven years old. "My only recollection of the place," he wrote to a friend while in college, "is the fearsome colored quarter, and my firm belief that a negro man would cut my throat with a razor if he felt so inclined." Attending Pittsburgh Pirates baseball games was his favorite diversion, and even into graduate school he kept "a fondness for the Pirates" and followed their progress.[11] Then, when Henry was still a child, the Commagers moved from Pittsburgh back down the slopes of the Alleghenies to Toledo, to their family roots. Still in grammar school, Henry was transplanted to the heartland, the home of the great Progressive historians Vernon Parrington, Charles Beard, and Frederick Jackson Turner.

But for Commager it was not a Midwest full of promise, for the young boy's family began to fall apart around him. His parents had divorced, and the three boys lived with their mother in modest circumstances, as she tried to sell encyclopedias and make ends meet as best she could. Then, worse, when Henry was nine years old his mother died. Consequently, his two brothers went to live with an uncle in Syracuse. Young Henry, who was more active than most adults appreciated, was sent to live in Chicago with Adam Dan, his maternal grandfather, a well-known Danish Lutheran minister who was knighted by the king of Denmark.[12]

Adam Dan had been born Niels Pedersen in Odense, Denmark, in 1848, but as a youth he had changed his name. As a young man Dan published several collections of poetry in Denmark on themes of religion and patriotism (he later published novels and songs, as well) and was said to be "in a class by himself." After training to go to Africa as a missionary, Dan was stopped by illness, and at age twenty he went instead to Syria as a missionary for two years to teach in an orphanage. Then in 1871 he received a call to become one of the first four ordained Danish Lutheran ministers to be sent to the United States. His congregation was located in Racine, Wisconsin. The next year Dan met with an associate in Wisconsin and formed the Church Mission Society, which in 1874 was renamed the Danish Lutheran Evangelical Church in America. At the same time he became the first editor of the *Kirkelig Samler*, the Church newspaper.[13]

As a prominent literary and religious figure in the Danish American community, Dan opposed the Americanization of Danish immigrants. "When we make it one of the aims, or almost the chief aim of life to become Americanized," he told his followers, "we sterilize ourselves and become incapable of enriching the life of the community. We become mere empty vessels waiting to be filled with something we naively call Americanism, but which in many cases is only a barbaric hodge-podge of English-Irish-German-and nonsense. The American smiles at us, and we interpret his smile as applause!"[14]

During the late nineteenth and early twentieth centuries, the Danish Lutheran Church in the United States split into two factions. The first, to which Dan subscribed, followed the path of the Danish Bishop N. F. S. Gruntvig, who stressed Danish nationalism and language, claimed that Denmark was God's chosen country, and emphasized the objective side of Christianity. The second faction was inspired by Vilhelm Beck, was not nearly so nationalistic, and was a pietistic Inner Mission movement. So Dan was promoting the Gruntvigian nationalist philosophy by resisting the Americanization of Danish immigrants.[15]

An equally important feature of Gruntvig's philosophy was that, unlike the more pietistic Lutherans, he saw great value in human action on earth.

Adam Dan,
Henry Steele Commager's
maternal grandfather.
(Courtesy of Danes Worldwide Archives)

This commitment led Gruntvig and his followers such as Adam Dan to become involved in cultural and political matters, value democracy, and concern themselves with education for the common person. Because of their democratic reform convictions, Adam Dan and other Gruntvigian Lutherans became known as political liberals and dissenters.[16]

After serving congregations in California, Iowa, Minnesota, and Boston, Dan settled into his final pastorate in Chicago in 1902. Within a decade, Dan became guardian of his grandson Henry. There in the house on Chicago's East 64th Street the young Commager was raised by Dan, now in his sixties, who was still busy enough to have competing demands on his attention. Under the influence of his grandfather's nationalism, Commager forged a strong bond with his Danish lineage.[17]

As a young member of his new family, Henry accompanied Pastor Dan and his wife on family occasions. On September 12, 1912, for example, just six weeks before his tenth birthday, he went with the Dans to a wedding in Chicago. Georg Lindegaard, a Danish immigrant, was marrying his fiancée, Aedelborg. The Dans were witnesses at the ceremony and afterward were invited with Henry to the couple's newly rented apartment for the wedding dinner. The story of the dinner was passed down for generations in the Lindegaard family, retold every September. "World Series time was near and 'Little Henry' could not contain himself and no one could shut him up!" The groom, Georg Lindegaard, "was a 'greenhorn' and did not understand baseball, but by the time his wedding evening was over he not only knew about everything from a bunt to a homerun but the name of every player in both leagues and what each had done during the season."[18]

By the age of fifteen Henry was expected to earn his own living.[19] Only two decades after Theodore Dreiser wrote *Sister Carrie*, the young Commager was buffeted by the same cold winds of ill fortune in Chicago that initially greeted Carrie Meeber on her arrival in the city.

While in high school he felt the first stirrings of an interest in politics. "My instincts," he reported, "from the very beginning were with democracy. They were passionately for Woodrow Wilson. When I was too young to know why, I was passionate for Woodrow Wilson. And the excitement about the League of Nations."[20]

Commager was lucky to have one of the finest universities in the nation across town. As City College allowed a quality education to those poor but bright New Yorkers such as Sidney Hook, Daniel Bell, Irving Howe, and Alfred Kazin, who could not afford to travel to Harvard or Yale, so the University of Chicago allowed Commager to study under some of the best minds in the country without the expense of leaving the city.

During the autumn months of 1918, just before his sixteenth birthday, he secured a job working in the University of Chicago library. Spending forty to fifty hours a week there was how he supported himself and put himself through college. Occasionally he opened the university library in the morning. "I came in the back way," he remarked about his introduction to campus. "Not as a regular member of the university, but as a librarian, earning my living."[21] But who was to know or care how he entered? Here he was at a great, effervescent center of learning, walking the library once occupied by Thorstein Veblen, John Dewey, John Broadus Watson, and other iconoclastic radicals in the Chicago tradition. And, because Commager had to support himself at such a young age, he developed a practical orientation that prompted him to sympathize with the pragmatic philosophy of Dewey.

Majoring in history and minoring in political science and American literature, he ignored freshman courses and plunged straight into upper-

Henry Steele Commager
at age fourteen.
(Courtesy of Lisa Commager)

division history classes, including those taught by Andrew McLaughlin and William Dodd. When he finished his undergraduate work with a bachelor of philosophy degree in 1923, the young Commager thought seriously of law school. After all, his ancestors had been members of the bar: his great-grandfather Henry Steel Commagere was a law partner of Chief Justice Morrison Waite, and his grandfather David Hedges Commager was a federal judge. But Henry decided that history graduate school at Chicago would be easier than law school to handle with his schedule, and he later remarked that he entered the study of law by the side door of constitutional history.[22]

Part of the reason he chose constitutional history was the presence of Andrew McLaughlin, who, Commager claimed, influenced him more than any other teacher. McLaughlin was born in Illinois at the beginning of the Civil War and earned a bachelor's degree in classics and then a law degree from the University of Michigan. In 1887 McLaughlin began teaching history at Michigan, and from 1898 to 1914 he served as an editor of the *American Historical Review*. Then in 1906 he replaced J. Franklin Jameson as the head of the department of history at University of Chicago.[23] While Commager was a student at Chicago, McLaughlin was writing *Steps in the Development of American Democracy* (1920) and *The Foundations of American Constitutionalism* (1932). In 1936 he was awarded the Pulitzer Prize for his *Constitutional History of the United States*.[24]

But the ideas that he imparted to Commager are most easily found in the address he gave as the president of the American Historical Association in 1914. McLaughlin told the gathering of historians that real history was more about tracing changes in national character and spirit than about cold political facts or military events. Vigorous history needed to be institutional and intellectual in outlook.[25] Scholars needed to acknowledge that America had "a particular destiny" and "a mission" and that it had animating enthusiasms. As though it were psychiatry for the culture at large, McLaughlin noted that "one duty of historical study and writing is to help make a nation conscious of its most real self, by bringing before it its own activity and the evidences of its own psychology." McLaughlin wondered "whether a nation can ever become truly great without intense self-consciousness and self-appreciation."[26]

So historians were not to be embarrassed by their optimism about America. McLaughlin admitted that he was calling for "nationalism in a real spiritual sense." Further, a historian was obligated to find the character, the spiritual core of nation, because "a community without the possession of a common domain is not a community at all."[27] Consider, then, how well McLaughlin's ideas fit with the beliefs promoted by Adam Dan during Commager's youth. Both McLaughlin and Dan stressed cultural nationalism, the common bonding, character, and domain of a people (American or Danish American) and the overriding importance of ideas and intellectual and institutional history. It is little wonder that Commager, as he matured, became an intellectual historian in the American character school.

But McLaughlin's influence on Commager went beyond his formal scholarship. At the *American Historical Review* McLaughlin's colleagues noted that he "strongly believed that the continuance of a democratic society depended upon a willingness of each of its members to render public service and to inform himself of the debt which his generation owed to its predecessors." That is, McLaughlin thought historians had a civic duty to their fellow citizens, and he passed that conviction on to his students. He was not an Olympian and detached scholar. Instead, "he made the past serve both his own day and their future."[28]

It also is easy to see the influence of William Dodd on the impressionable Commager. Born in North Carolina in 1869, Dodd received his Ph.D. from the University of Leipzig in 1899, where he wrote a dissertation entitled "Thomas Jefferson's Rückkehr zur Politik, 1796," (Thomas Jefferson's Return to Politics, 1796) and then went on to become a noted historian of the American South. Dodd arrived at the University of Chicago in 1908, two years after McLaughlin.[29]

At one point, Dodd was the only professor in the country who concentrated all his teaching on the South, and consequently Chicago was recognized as a leader in that field. Dodd was ashamed of the southern treatment of blacks, and so in his work he tried to avoid the issue by arguing that the South would have abolished slavery on its own in due time. He portrayed the South as the land of Jefferson rather than Calhoun, a place where small farmers took central stage and tried to resist the political and social corruption brought by the planters and the slave system.[30]

Most important for the young Commager, Dodd was a model of active public involvement by an engaged intellectual. Even more than McLaughlin, Dodd felt that it was important for historians to involve themselves in public affairs, and Dodd appreciated the University of Chicago's emphasis on useful scholarship. (Albion Small, dean of the Graduate School of Arts and Literature, recommended the "marriage of thought with action.") Slowly Dodd began to focus his energy on writing for the general public. For example, he wrote book reviews for the *Chicago Evening Post* and essays for the *Nation*. He looked to history for current lessons, and in his own work he found that captains of industry in the Progressive period were little different from the greedy slave owners. His civic enthusiasm gradually turned him from scholarship to public affairs. As a young professor in Virginia he fought the Virginia Democratic bosses, in 1908 wrote letters of campaign advice to William Jennings Bryan, later had dinner at the White House with Teddy Roosevelt, and made campaign speeches for Wilson in 1912. During World War I he served, with McLaughlin, Charles Beard, and others, on the history subcommittee of the Committee on Public Information, known as the Creel Committee.[31]

What has been remarked about Dodd could as easily be said later of Commager: that he was "less interested in supplying reformers with 'scientific' observations than in working directly for social action." While most liberal scholars preferred expert testimony to more direct campaigning on public issues, Dodd found unappealing the "Wisconsin Idea" of the expert who served on commissions or dispensed advice while wearing a lab coat. Instead, he wanted, as a Jeffersonian, to help promote an earlier condition of society in which the citizens rather than the interests ruled.[32]

Consequently, it was characteristic of Dodd that in 1932 he wrote articles supporting Franklin Roosevelt's early New Deal ideas. As a result, in 1933 Roosevelt appointed him ambassador to Germany on the advice of his secretary of commerce, Daniel Roper, who had worked with Dodd on Wilson's 1916 campaign and who told FDR that "Dodd would be astute in handling diplomatic duties and, when conferences grew tense, he would turn the tide by quoting Jefferson." Dodd, who had studied in Germany and appreciated its people, was convinced that he was being sent to Berlin to promote democracy.[33]

In response to the growth of Nazism, Dodd campaigned for collective military security measures among the Western democracies and consequently became estranged from German officials. But his liberal outlook offended some at home as well. In the spring of 1937 his Jeffersonianism and populism prompted him to charge that "there are individuals of great wealth who wish a dictatorship and are ready to help a Huey Long. There are politicians who think they may gain powers like those exercised in Europe." Although it was hardly an irresponsible charge, several senators demanded that he be replaced. Secretary of State Cordell Hull agreed, remarking that Dodd was "somewhat insane" on subjects such as Jeffersonian democracy and world peace. At the end of 1937 Dodd left his diplomatic position.[34]

During the mid-1920s Commager studied under Dodd and, when a graduate student, worked as his assistant. Although this was well before Dodd's diplomatic adventure, Dodd was already an active civic participant and a proponent of historians' public roles. Commager saw firsthand his professor's contributions to public debate, was drawn to his activist example, and decided to fashion himself at least partly in his image.

At the university Commager wrote his master's thesis on the treaty between the United States and England concerning ownership of the Oregon region, which allowed him to mix American and European perspectives and avoid provinciality. The United States didn't win the bargaining on Oregon because of strength, he found; instead, England lost it because of the weakness inflicted on it by a number of distracting problems at home that rendered the government less eager for an international struggle. Although he would later become known as an intellectual historian, his master's thesis, which was accepted in 1924, was a standard political history written in a straightforward manner.[35]

After deciding to continue in the Ph.D. program at Chicago, Commager arranged to spend the following academic year studying at the University of Copenhagen. There he would be in a proper location to research his dissertation, which would analyze the eighteenth-century political reform movement in Denmark led by Johann Friedrich Struensee. After spending the fall semester in Copenhagen, Commager decided to visit Professor Paul Darmstadter in Göttingen, Germany. Darmstadter was one of those rare non-American historians of the United States. He had traveled around the United States, married his wife in New York, written U.S. history, and served as a major in the German army in World War I. Intrigued, Commager paid him a call in Göttingen. The Darmstadter family liked him so well that he was invited to stay. So Commager remained there for the winter and most of the spring, working on his Struensee material, which he had carried with him, and taking a class from Darmstadter at the University of Göttingen.

Commager usually functioned as a member of the Darmstadter family, carrying their bags of groceries home from shopping trips, riffling through Darmstadter's personal library of over twenty-five hundred volumes, or engaging his love of music by playing the work of Paderewski on the piano in his room. Despite his own Danish heritage, Commager reported that he preferred the Germans to the Danes, and felt more at ease in the smaller town of Göttingen, even though it meant sacrificing the greater cultural opportunities of Copenhagen.[36]

At the young and eager age of twenty-two, traveling and living on his own in Europe, Commager's exhilaration and sense of humor were evident. He wrote repeatedly to his friend in chemistry at Harvard, Hans Duus, and the letters reveal a good-natured and self-confident young man. Wistfully poking fun at himself for being too responsible, he complained to Duus that "it is ever my fate to go thru life unappreciated by any except elderly ladies and fond mothers who realize that I am harmless and will be good company for their sons and safe company for their daughters." And he lost doubly. "As the sons detect moral guidance and the modern daughter doesn't always want safe company," Commager noted, "I am deservedly odious to all of my own age." It could be different of course. "By being as wicked as I know how to be and as sophisticated as I could be, I could become very popular, but all the mothers would forbid their children to go out with me. You see," he told Duus, "this is a very tragic dilemma. H.I.C., the story of a frustrated soul."[37]

Further, Commager bragged repeatedly, and for humorous effect, about his use of the practice—still known to graduate students and faculty members alike—of skimming books or reading reviews instead of carefully and methodically reading entire works. "Verily, verily, I say unto you, I am the loadstone," he told Duus, with an assurance that his friend could follow his literary advice. "If you think this is because I've read a lot and separated the chaff from the wheat, you're wrong. For the last six years I've read nothing but book reviews," and before that it was Horatio Alger books, Commager joked. "But this has no bearing on my qualifications as a literary oracle."[38] Then several months later, explaining to Duus that he had accidentally become interested in a book and finished it, he boasted that "I always discuss books without reading them; it's a way we have at Chicago."[39]

On another occasion, Commager asked Duus not to forward books that had arrived in the United States for him. "I shall never read them anyway," he crowed. "I purchased them for effect and out of conceit. They are in French and will look imposing on my shelves, as will some of the German books I am getting here. I shall read the English translations however, and then talk about them glibly. This is what all scholars do but very few are honest enough to admit it."[40]

His wittiest professional quackery was advice to Duus about how to write an efficient book review. After leafing through Darmstadter's collection of the *American Historical Review*, which Commager considered the best journal in the field, he told Duus that all book reviews were innocuous and not worth their effort. "There is an unvarying formula," he instructed his friend, "and I guarantee to write an 800 word review of any book within 12 hours."

First, from the book's dust jacket copy you talk about the title and author. You note that the book and its style are fair, "point out typographical errors at great length," discuss the bibliography, "noting with sorrow" its missing monographs, and "end up by saying that all students of the period are under debt to the author for his piece of research." He assured Duus that this latter compliment is "bunk because students of the period do their own research and no one else cares to read the book as it is too dull."[41]

Despite his humorous posing, Commager remained intellectually energetic and politically curious in Europe. Darmstadter's collection of American books was impressive, and the young boarder enjoyed sampling them. Yet he also witnessed Europe's poverty. After watching a protest march in Copenhagen, he reported that "you never saw such a bedraggled Communist parade" since "the poor chaps had been rained on for an hour or so." Obviously he sympathized with those Danish workers. He confided to Duus that "this damn lock out is ruinous for a lot of these chaps. I should think some of them would get radical and do something reckless. Blow up the roof of Marmor Kirken or something like that." Visiting Scotland, he was distressed in Edinburgh by the "frightful slums" and "the most ghastly wreckage of humanity that I've seen anywhere."[42]

If the young Commager had not earlier felt his attachment to his homeland, he, like Malcolm Cowley and the other self-conscious expatriates his age who were beginning to be called the Lost Generation, found an imaginative connection to America while in Europe. A few years younger than the literary exiles, Commager narrowly missed involvement in World War I and the disorientation that it produced.

Fatigued by the alienation and anti-intellectualism at home, Cowley and the others fled to Europe to be nourished by what they considered to be real culture. But while there they found America instead. "These young Americans," Cowley reported, "had begun by discovering a crazy Europe in which the intellectuals of their own middle class were more defeated and demoralized than those at home. . . . Having registered this impression, the exiles were ready to find that their own nation had every attribute they had been taught to admire in those of Europe." The realization slowly grew. "Some of the exiles," Cowley confessed, "had reached a turning point in their adventure and were preparing to embark on a voyage of rediscovery."[43]

Commager showed little of the dissatisfaction with the United States that propelled Hemingway, Dos Passos, Hart Crane, and others across the Atlantic. Besides, at heart he was a historian, and although he was strongly interested in literature, he also once described himself as a "lawyer manqué."[44] So he took a scholarly route to his writing and was not in Europe for the same reason as Cowley.

Still, Commager's year in Europe reaffirmed his cultural tie with America. Some of the European scenery had reminded him of the Adirondacks in New York. "It made me long for Cranberry Lake and Blue Mountain and other of my loves," he wrote Duus from the ship as he crossed for home.[45] In early June 1925, when the ship docked and Commager went by rail on the Empire Express up the Hudson, he was even more spiritually moved by the presence of his native land around him. "After this absence," he affirmed to his friend from aboard the train, "I find a good deal of imagination in these lovely American hills and the quiet beauty of the river."[46]

It was true, he admitted, that he hadn't been eager to get back, but now that he witnessed the country he felt its strong impact. "I am inordinately proud of some aspects of the U.S.—some parts of its scenery,—some of its small towns, some of its people,—as if I were responsible for them or owned them," he wrote Duus. "You have noted, sometimes with a rather surprisingly uncomprehending sarcasm, my enthusiasms for American colleges and universities: I have other enthusiasms of the same provincial nature."[47]

The roots of his tie to American studies and character studies were evident from these early years. Raised, as he was, under the committed Gruntvigian nationalism of his grandfather, it is hardly surprising that Commager revealed his own nationalist enthusiasm. True, it was hardly the Danish nationalism of Pastor Dan. But if it was only a growing passion for America, still it was nationalism that bore a resemblance to his grandfather's commitments.

His return to Chicago in the summer of 1925 allowed him to renew his relationship with Dodd, and his estimation of his mentor continued to grow warmly. When Duus criticized a Dodd article on Jefferson that Commager had recommended, Commager quickly jumped to the defense of both Jefferson and Dodd and demonstrated that he was a disciple of both. "Certainly there was never in this country a statesman of more talent, more genius, more admirable versatility than Jefferson," he told Duus. "His constant and intelligent interest in science; his scientific experiments, his scientific agriculture, his ideals in the foundation of the University of Virginia, and his architectural designs for that place . . . the list is almost endless. For sheer versatility and alertness of mind, this country has seldom seen Jefferson's equal in any walk of life."[48]

In addition Commager worked with Dodd closely during the summer on two volumes of the Wilson papers and felt a firmer appreciation of Wilson and "the tragedy of his career." At the same time during the summer months he was working forty-five hours a week at the library and assisting in a course on contemporary American literature. As he approached and then passed his twenty-third birthday in the fall of 1925, he thought more seriously about finding an academic job. His department "gently urged" him not to expect a job at Chicago. Instead he was told of a possibility at New York University (NYU), and while he realized the benefits of being in "hailing distance of Columbia," he preferred the idea of other options he was pursuing at the University of Minnesota and at Cornell or even staying on another year at Chicago to finish his dissertation. He even briefly thought of enrolling at Duke Law School, but because they gave no scholarships he discarded the idea.[49]

Finally in the spring of 1926 Commager wrote his friend Duus and told him that he had accepted an instructorship at NYU in American history.[50] So his time in the Midwest was now ending. As a child he had been brought to Chicago under the most somber conditions. With help from Pastor Dan and a strong ambition, effort, and perseverance on his own part, he was now turning eastward again under more promising circumstances.

At the end of his first academic year in New York in the spring of 1927, Commager published his master's thesis on the Oregon question in the *Oregon Historical Quarterly*.[51] But one of the important tasks he faced immediately, in addition to the burden of preparing his lectures and teaching classes, was to finish his dissertation. In the summer before he left for the East he had confided to Duus that he had lost interest in eighteenth-century Denmark and Struensee. "I may be forced to turn him over to you for a musical comedy" or, perhaps more fitting, "a tragedy," Commager told his friend. If he had it to do over again, he would now plan a dissertation on Henry Adams. "He is big enough for it," he reported.[52]

As his choice of Struensee as a dissertation topic revealed, Commager began very early his lifelong fascination with Enlightenment thought, of which Jefferson was an important American figure. When it was completed, his dissertation was more of an analysis of the eighteenth-century reform movement in Denmark than a biographical study of Struensee. Originally the physician of King Christian VII, Struensee was a bourgeois reformer who rose to power when the king lost his sanity in 1768. To evaluate the changes in Danish government and society during this period, Commager wrote chapters on the reforms in administration, civil service, land ownership, finance, commerce, the judiciary, public health, education, journalism, and religion. Written in graceful prose, most of his dissertation was conventional political and cultural history, with Commager guardedly sympathetic to Struensee's influence. For example, the Danish physician was in favor of land reform, and his sympathies were with the peasants. But although he instituted some useful reforms, Commager concluded that they weren't radical or particularly significant and were measures to which the previous administration was already committed.[53]

As one might expect from his background in constitutional history, Commager was most adept in his chapter on reforms in the judiciary. Yet even this early in his career he had begun to realize some of the problems of intellectual history. He admitted, for example, that he wasn't sure how much Struensee was influenced by the Enlightenment in other cultures when he moved to stop torture in the legal process in Denmark. "In the realm of history," Commager told his readers, "there is nothing more difficult to evaluate that the actual influence of an idea."[54]

As his comment about Henry Adams indicated, Commager's fascination with Europe had declined during his last year at the University of Chicago under the influence of Dodd, McLaughlin, and his employment in the course on American literature. So it was fitting that he filled an Americanist position at NYU. But he would not teach American history in a vacuum. Having done much of his work and research on a European topic, Commager, who would later be accused of having a parochial fascination with America, was actually better equipped and more eager to make comparative connections than were most of his Americanist colleagues.

Despite the fact that he wrote a study of European history when he already thought of himself as an Americanist, Commager won the Herbert Baxter Adams Prize in 1929 for the year's most distinguished first book (as it was never published, in this case a dissertation) in European history. That honor, in addition to having his master's thesis published in the *Oregon Historical Quarterly*, freed him from feeling as though he had to prove himself as a technically competent historian. Now he could write what he really wanted to: "interesting intellectual history and the interpretation of history." He felt free to pursue his inclination to speak to broader issues: "I didn't have to prove anything anymore," he remembered later. "I could write articles."[55]

In September 1926, Commager began his position at NYU's Washington Square campus in Greenwich Village. Two years later in the autumn of 1928, the start of Commager's third academic year, Allan Nevins began teaching at Columbia University, a short subway ride uptown on the West Side IRT line from NYU. The two didn't meet until Commager enthusiastically reviewed Nevins's *Grover Cleveland* in 1932.[56] From that moment on the eve of the New Deal, their lives and reputations became entwined, and they slowly developed into best friends and close professional colleagues, until finally, at Nevins's death in 1971, many would have thought that the names Commager and Nevins belonged in the same sentence.

Nevins, who was twelve years older than Commager, was born in 1890 in the small farming community of Camp Point in west central Illinois, about twenty-five miles east of the Mississippi River and about the same distance north of Hannibal, Missouri, where Mark Twain spent much of his childhood. During his early years, Nevins, as the fourth of five children, helped work the 220-acre family farm that raised corn and hogs, wheat and oats, and turnips and clover. It was a farm started by his paternal grandfather, John Nevin (no final *s*), a Scottish immigrant who "took pride in his little farm and found in it a much-prized independence."[57]

Young Allan didn't like the drudgery of farmwork, but his father, who was "endlessly industrious, had Scotch Presbyterian ideas about the disciplinary value of toil." Although often it was "a harsh, grim life," it also had compensations such as independence, self-sufficiency, and a tightly knit "Swiss Family Robinson quality." As a boy Nevins enjoyed butchering hogs before winter, and with a shotgun he hunted pigeons, squirrels, quail, and rabbit to eat. His father declined to buy a car and continued to use horse-drawn machinery on the farm.[58]

Both parents were religious, and the children were required to attend Presbyterian services. No cards or Sunday sports were allowed, their language was monitored, and Nevins's mother, who led the local chapter of the Women's Christian Temperance Union, outlawed liquor in the home. "While family life in town is subject to centrifugal forces," Nevins later recalled, "ours were centripetal." His father carried frugality almost to excess, proclaiming his chosen three great watchwords: "Liberty, equality, and frugality."[59]

Nevins overcame his poor farm schooling by taking advantage of his literate family and village. His parents had five hundred books, many of them classics. Four families in town, including the Nevinses, formed an informal club, in which each subscribed to one of either *McClure's, Cosmopolitan, Harper's*, or *Century* and then exchanged them.[60] So Nevins had the pleasure of intelligent magazines as well as books that helped to reduce the distance between Camp Point and the intellectual centers of culture.

When Nevins graduated from high school in 1908, he already intended to go into journalism. At the University of Illinois he distinguished himself immediately as a good writer. The English department became his intellectual center, and he ignored history courses almost entirely. History, he thought, was "limited and dull" and beneath English literature. Continuing the work ethic he learned on the farm, Nevins made the most of his school opportunities and was elected to Phi Beta Kappa.[61]

When Paul Elmer More, the noted literary critic and editor of the *Nation* magazine, came to speak at the university during Nevins's senior year, the young collegian was associate editor of the *Illini*, the school paper. Professor Stuart Sherman of the English department, who admired Nevins and wrote for the *Nation*, made More promise that when Nevins graduated he would be given a try as an editorial writer at the New York magazine.[62]

Nevins received his bachelor's degree in 1912, and a year later he moved to the Morningside Heights neighborhood in New York City, the upper Westside area whose western border was the Hudson River. Morningside Heights was a collection of brownstones, walk-ups, and ten-story apartment buildings that climbed gradually up a low hill from the West Nineties in Manhattan before it descended steeply into the southern border of West Harlem at 125th Street. The crest of the Heights at 116th Street was adorned by Columbia University, whose libraries Nevins planned to use for his editorials at his new job at the *Nation*. There on the low uptown Manhattan hill, whose relative quiet he appreciated for its distance from downtown, Nevins knew Carl Van Doren, who had graduated five years before him at the University of Illinois.[63]

In New York, he landed in a more complex and interesting journalistic position than he might have expected. Nevins reported to work on the tenth floor of the eleven-story building on Vesey Street in southern Manhattan, located near City Hall Park and the Woolworth Tower, then the city's tallest building, and from his vantage point he could look south over the courtyard of St. Paul's Chapel where President George Washington had worshiped. When Nevins arrived he learned that the *Nation* magazine, the liberal weekly that had been started by E. L. Godkin in 1865, had since the early 1880s shared its high-windowed offices with the *Evening Post* newspaper. The two publications employed separate editors, but according to Nevins, "the editorials of the *Post* were simply lifted into the columns of the *Nation.*" So, in essence, he "worked for both publications simultaneously."[64]

His willingness to put in the extra work on researching political and historical details continued to serve Nevins well as years passed. And the enthusiastic work ethic he had learned on the farm was noticed by his colleagues. Stanley West, an associate of his, used to say that "the staff on the *Evening Post* spent much of its time trying to prevent Allan Nevins from writing the entire paper."[65]

Then, at a literary gathering Nevins met Mary Richardson, who had come to the party with her mother, Anna Steese Richardson, the associate editor of *Woman's Home Companion*. At the end of 1916 Allan and Mary were married at the Richardson family home on Long Island Sound in Larchmont, New York.[66]

When the conservative Republican Cyrus Curtis bought the *Evening Post* in 1923 to add to his *Saturday Evening Post, Ladies' Home Journal*, and *Philadelphia Public Ledger*, Nevins left. He had worked there for a decade and had prospered but realized that he was not in sympathy with its new political incarnation. The *New York Herald* offered to raise his one-hundred-dollar weekly salary by fifty, and Nevins accepted. His new offices were near his old. The *Herald* and the *Evening Sun* were located in large rooms on the mezzanine floor of "what had once been the huge department store of A. T. Stewart, at the corner of Chambers Street and Broadway, a stone edifice of eight stories" from which the editors gazed out on City Hall and its park.[67]

In 1923 Nevins left the *Herald* and took a job at the *Evening Sun*, where he continued to write editorials but also was made literary editor. Nearly every day he wrote a literary column, and each Saturday he was responsible for assembling several pages of book reviews. He loved the work and made important friendships with people such as the historian James Truslow Adams and the journalist William Allen White. Later that year, when Walter Lippmann offered him an editorial job at the *New York World*, Nevins accepted.[68] During the mid-1920s, he came to identify his very soul with the *World*. He loved the paper, loved journalism, and identified the two with each other. "It is a curious fact," Nevins noted respectfully, "that in our headlong, mutable American civilization one of the best repositories of tradition should be found here and there in a newspaper. Universities, churches, parties are not more mindful of a continuing heritage than the finest of these publications which are born anew every morning."[69]

Yet, while Nevins cared deeply about journalism, since college he had felt a growing desire to write books of history. A reason that he was so happy at the *World* was that Lippmann, unlike most editors, encouraged him to pursue his books. Along with Nevins's *World* colleague Claude Bowers, whose work on Jefferson and Hamilton was so appreciated by Commager while he was in graduate school in this period, he shared an expanding interest in history.

"He and I would sometimes race in the afternoon to finish our work by four o'clock," Nevins recalled about Bowers, so that together they could catch the subway from the City Hall station, ride uptown to the New York Public Library, and work in the special collections room on manuscripts and rare books. The room closed at five. "We would reach it by half-past four, frantically copy all we could by five, and then busy ourselves in other parts of the building."[70]

By 1928, after five years at the *World* and still only thirty-eight years old, Nevins had already published eight books. These volumes were compiled or written in the cracks in a journalistic schedule that was so busy that he was suspected of writing those newspapers alone. This developing split in his interests and the increasing demands on his time presented a problem. With a growing commitment to writing history, Nevins gradually became impatient with the lack of research time available in a newspaper job. Regularly getting to a manuscript collection for its last half hour of operation he found unworkable. "Academic writers," he complained later, "seldom comprehend the handicaps of newspapermen. We had no funds for research; we worked six days a week and our labor was often harassing; we thought the month's vacation offered by the *World* generous—on other papers I had gotten two weeks, and one year on the *Post* I took no vacation at all."[71]

So Nevins was receptive when his notable collection of history books caught the attention of those at Cornell who were looking to fill an American history position in 1927. The next year, he was hired to teach history at Columbia in the mornings and to work again at the *World*, under Lippmann, in the afternoons.[72] When the *World* finally went out of business early in 1931, Nevins was at last relieved of his journalistic duties and accepted a full-time position at Columbia as DeWitt Clinton Professor of History, beginning that period which some observers of the university have called "the Nevins era."[73] Now, confined to a university chair, he found it even more important to reach, through his histories, a semblance of that same audience with which he had communicated as a journalist.

Well before Commager left Chicago for New York he was engaged imaginatively in the literary life that awaited him. In the spring of 1926 he described for his friend Hans Duus several good articles in the *Forum* and the *American Mercury*, noting the books he would buy based on their reviews.[74]

When after his second year at New York University, in the summer of 1928, Commager married Evan Carroll of South Carolina, he found that his financial resources were stretched even thinner. So he made a virtue of necessity and turned toward outside literary pursuits for extra money. Because of his growing journalistic interests, perhaps he would have become involved in reviewing and essay writing anyway. Commager had arrived at NYU at an annual salary of two thousand dollars, and when he married he was making only slightly more. So almost immediately he did a book of translations and started reviewing books to enrich his finances.[75] Although perhaps he didn't realize it fully at the moment, from this point in his life Commager began increasingly to function as a public intellectual.

The distinction between scholars and intellectuals has been made frequently in the recent past. A scholar writes for his or her professional peers and usually in books instead of essays, operates within the academic conventions of peer-reviewed publishing, pursues archival research instead of contemporary political and social issues, and aims for objectivity or neutrality rather than partisanship. An intellectual, however, is one who writes for the general educated public instead of experts and addresses issues of contemporary social or political importance as an activist. Typically an intellectual appears as a reviewer or essayist in periodicals, often employs an interdisciplinary approach, usually is thought of as a critic in the broad sense of the term, and is partisan rather than neutral.[76] Commager, soon after he was married, began to gravitate toward the intellectual community and function.

Interacting with the world of journalism was a heady and exciting experience for him, especially in New York. Henry and Evan lived in Greenwich Village, and he got caught up in the literary and publishing life very quickly. "I started reviewing for the *Herald Tribune*," Commager remembered later. "I reviewed probably more history books than anybody else in those days. Almost every week I reviewed either for the *Tribune* or the *Times*." He wrote journalistic reviews for the general public, not scholarly reviews for a small group of peers. "They paid all of fifteen dollars per review in those days, which was very good. . . . And it was fun reviewing," he admitted. "And I got to know everybody. The writers and the publishers and the editors, and [got] caught up in the literary life, such as it was, and it was all very exciting for a youngster in his late twenties, early thirties, to be part of the intellectual life of the Village."[77]

In 1932, after he favorably reviewed Nevins's new *Grover Cleveland: A*

Study in Courage, Commager was contacted by the author. It was a fitting reason to make contact with each other. Here were two historians involved in journalism, one of whose scholarly achievements had been reviewed by the other in a newspaper. Nevins was now forty-four and Commager thirty-two. Sensing their similarities, the Commagers invited the Nevinses to tea.

Evan Commager and Mary Nevins became friends quickly, as did their husbands. Allan invited Henry to the quarterly dinners given at Columbia where papers were read and discussed. The Nevinses had since sold their house on Long Island and moved to 147th Street and Riverside Drive in Manhattan, where they purchased a small brownstone near the Hudson River, a mile and a half north of Columbia and bordering Harlem. After he met Commager, Nevins bought the brownstone across the street from his own and convinced Henry and Evan to move there from the Village. As Commager noted, "We could, as it were, look at each other from our study windows. His was upstairs and mine was upstairs."[78]

Although he had entertained strong doubts about moving to New York from Chicago, Commager found it increasingly fascinating. Because he and Evan liked it so well, they decided to turn down a job offer at Johns Hopkins in order to stay at NYU and in New York. After Hopkins made the offer, NYU doubled his salary, and suddenly Commager felt quite well off, as though he could now begin to buy books and live the life that suited him.[79]

Yet the gratification he found in the success of his literary journalism is what bound him to New York more than anything else. In the winter of 1928–29, during his third year in New York, Commager walked into the books office of the *Herald Tribune* carrying a letter of introduction from Lincoln Colcord. "His first review was so good," the editors there later confirmed, "that he was given twenty-four more books to review before the end of the year, and he reviewed 234 books for the *Herald Tribune* within the next decade—lending distinction to its pages." Others who reviewed for the *Herald Tribune* between its founding in 1924 and World War II included Ellen Glasgow, Sinclair Lewis, Katherine Anne Porter, Robert Benchley, Arthur Schlesinger Sr., Carl Van Vechten, Van Wyck Brooks, Malcolm Cowley, Charles Beard, Samuel Eliot Morison, Bertrand Russell, and Alfred Kazin.[80]

Nevins, who knew literary journalism as well as anyone in the country, respected his friend's work. "The value of his great body of book-reviewing (for years he was a main pillar of *Books*) lay beyond the moment," he remarked about Commager. "It gave him, as such work gave John Fiske and James Truslow Adams, familiarity with a tremendous number of books old and new, so that he became one of our best-read historians. At the same time it gave him the capacity to distill into a thousand words the essence of a thoughtful volume, just as his essays on current affairs helped him to an analytical mastery of complex political and social developments."[81]

A close friendship quickly grew between Commager and Nevins. It represented their shared respect for the combination of history and journalism in the same career. The alliance of the two writers also illustrated their common dedication to an activist public life.

What influences led Commager to the intellectually activist career that was so different from most of his colleagues? Like some other historians, he later was swayed by events such as the New Deal and World War II, and he was even more influenced by McCarthyism and the Vietnam War. Yet as important as these events were to his political development, Commager showed unmistakable activist traits well before these events occurred. Years prior to the New Deal, he was already writing for the *New York Times* and the *Herald Tribune* and was beginning to function as the sort of public intellectual for which he later became so recognized.

Further, when so many of his fellow historians also experienced the New Deal and other major occurrences, why was it that Commager followed such a comparatively unique path within the discipline of history? At least part of the answer, as he acknowledged himself, is that when he was young several important mentors influenced his ideas and encouraged his partisanship. In addition to the activist model provided firsthand by his grandfather Adam Dan, Commager was shaped by William Dodd and Andrew McLaughlin at the University of Chicago. Finally, Commager found inspiration in activist models from the past such as Thomas Jefferson, Theodore Parker, and Vernon Parrington.

So, despite his fascination for literary journalism, beginning in the 1930s Commager wrote with an even more eager enthusiasm on political topics. That writing marked the beginning of his activist career.

CHAPTER 2

Philosophy Teaching by Experience, 1928-1936

While Commager's scholarly ties in the late 1920s and early 1930s were mostly in New York, at NYU and Columbia, he also was loosely tied by friendships to other universities. When Samuel Eliot Morison was already an established and respected member of the Harvard history department in the late 1920s, for example, Commager came into contact with him. The two were from different worlds: Commager was yet a beginning professor at NYU who had just finished his doctoral dissertation, a young man new to the East Coast with a fine educational pedigree but from a rather inauspicious background, whereas Morison had achieved wide recognition, paraded himself in a New England patrician manner, and had impressive family and social connections.

Despite the difference in their stature and station, Morison invited Commager to help him write *The Growth of the American Republic*, which became the most important American history textbook in the middle decades of the twentieth century. It is unclear how the two scholars met and why Morison was willing to take on an unknown associate in the project. Perhaps they came into contact when each of them had an article published next to the other's in the *Oregon Historical Quarterly* in March 1927.[1] Maybe Morison saw there, in a condensation of Commager's master's thesis, a clear mind at work or the ability to summarize and transform a complex debate into an interesting story. Morison was committed to reaching the larger public with narrative history, and he might have noticed the same about Commager.

In the years surrounding World War I, when Nevins was involved as a journalist at the *New York Post* and Commager was still in high school, Morison was already performing in the dual role of scholarly historian and public intellectual that his younger colleagues would later follow. Although Morison was well respected in academic circles, observers described him as "a political idealist who took an intense, even partisan, interest in public affairs." In the atmosphere of Progressivism, Morison became involved in municipal community work, helped draft a housing code for Boston, campaigned against teacher loyalty oaths, and labored to elect local politicians.[2]

But like many other Progressives, by the end of World War I Morison was frustrated by the small amount reformers and the war itself had been able to accomplish during the previous few years. Consequently, he became disillusioned with politics and began to retreat from his public activism. By the time he met Commager, Morison had already abandoned the role of civic intellectual, an identity that his young associate was just beginning to adopt.[3]

Before the end of World War I Morison had written his books in an orthodox scholarly prose, but increasingly he had trouble executing his role as an author. In the summer of 1920 his editor at Houghton Mifflin was drumming his fingers impatiently, waiting for a general history of Massachusetts that Morison had promised. Facing this obstacle, Morison remembered the admonishment of his friend Albert Beveridge that "the trouble with you professors is that you write for each other. I write for people almost completely ignorant of American history." Taking Beveridge's advice, Morison proposed to Houghton Mifflin that he instead do a maritime history of the New England area aimed toward popular consumption. The result was *The Maritime History of Massachusetts, 1783–1860* (1921), written, according to Morison, "in one swoop, on a wave of euphoria."[4] So by the time Morison and Commager formed their partnership on the *Growth of the American Republic*, Morison was already a historian who wrote well and narratively for the general public, and Commager had ambitions to follow suit.

Clearly Morison always considered himself the commanding officer of his friendship with Commager, although the old sailor signed most of his letters "Affectionately, Sam," was godfather to Commager's daughter Lisa, offered to take his son, Steele, cruising, and sent gifts to his children. Some of Morison's formality with Commager, as with others, was simply the New England social distance apparent in many families that have been rooted there for several generations, and it was combined with the patrician self-conception that, for example, prompted Morison to complain that it was difficult to keep a maid past early June.[5]

Morison's rigidity wasn't lost on Commager, although it didn't bother him. Neither of them had much enthusiasm for going to academic conferences and avoided them when possible. But later Commager was known to reenact, in a playful demonstration of his friend's reticence, Morison stiffly marching back and forth at a cocktail party at the annual convention of the American Historical Association, of which Morison was president at the time. Commager's Morison, asked what he is doing, replies, "I'm mixing."[6]

So in 1928 Morison made Commager, "then a young and unknown scholar," a collaborator on *The Growth of the American Republic* (GAR).[7] They were an odd pair. During the decades of their work on the project and its many editions, Morison was always more conservative than Commager, less a public activist than his younger colleague, always more eager to get new revisions finished quickly to make money, and therefore forever nagging and fussing at him to focus more attention on the volume. Much of their correspondence consisted of Morison scolding him for ignoring his responsibilities on the project and Commager good-naturedly changing the subject or making friendly excuses. "I don't accuse you of not answering letters," Morison told him with typical frustration, "but of not answering what I put into my letters."[8] They ignored their very different intellectual outlooks: for example, that Morison strongly disliked John Dewey, whereas Commager was one of his disciples.[9] Despite significantly different work habits, values, and ideological commitments, the two historians were tied together on the GAR by their common respect for the literary grace and broad vision that elevates the best historical writing.

The Growth of the American Republic was an outshoot of Morison's *Oxford History of the United States*, which he had written when he was teaching in England. Oxford University Press suggested that he revise and condense it; it seems that Morison revised some of the earlier book to constitute the antebellum chapters of the GAR, and Commager was conscripted to write those chapters on the Civil War and after. "He is a Middle-Westerner of the post-war [World War I] generation, with Southern affiliations [Evan's family]; I, a New England historian approaching middle age, with Oxonian and Pacific Coast affiliations," Morison acknowledged about some of the differences in their backgrounds and outlooks. "This book, therefore, represents the work of two men whose paths crossed only very recently, and the fusion of two points of view. We hope that, as in a pair of field glasses, the fusion may create an image at once sharp and solid."[10] The first edition of the book appeared in one volume in 1930 priced at six dollars. The second edition in 1937 was issued in two volumes at eight dollars and fifty cents, and the successive revisions remained two volumes but at a progressively more expensive price.[11]

Henry Steele Commager (back row, fourth from left) and the New York University history department in 1927. (Courtesy of New York University Archives)

It was in the survey texts that he helped write—*The Growth of the American Republic* with Morison and later *The Pocket History of the United States* with Nevins—that Commager did some of the most impressive writing of his career. Commager rose to his most commanding vision and his most graceful prose when he was challenged with summing up broad tendencies or movements of history. His tone alternated between intelligent discussion, useful reporting, wistfully elegiac scenes, and proud assertions, frequently bound by an overconfident optimism, all in a lyrical prose. But even at the end of the 1920s, when he was adding his chapters to the Morison project, Commager was enough of a dissenter, enough of a critical observer of American politics, that his additions to the volume had more bite than might have been expected.

A representative example, in this regard, is his discussion of the frontier. Yes, Commager painted vivid and dramatic pictures of the West. The "turbulent, heterogeneous throng of miners" drawn to the West "first revealed to the nation the resources and possibilities of this country." Soon "the roaring towns of Virginia City, Austin and White Pine sprang up in the desert wastes, the Territory of Nevada was carved out of California and Utah, and ten thousand men were digging frantically in the bowels of the earth for the precious yellow stuff." After the miners came the cattle kings, who produced "one of the most dramatic shifts in the screen-picture of the West." It wasn't long before cattle drives were mounted in which "35,000 longhorns pounded up clouds of dust all along the famous Chisholm trail, across the Red and Arkansas rivers and into the land of the Five Nations, to Abilene, Kansas." Ultimately, what finally "marked the end of the picturesque mining and cattle kingdoms, and of the old, romantic, 'wild west,' was the irresistible pressure of the farmers, swarming by the hundreds of thousands out onto the High Plains and into the mountain valleys, subduing this wilderness of prairie and mountain land to cultivation and civilization."[12] Commager could write, arranging words as if he were writing literature instead of history, and could sweep the reader along with him in his imaginative reconstruction of America.

But this robust accounting of the progress of America was not all there was to Commager's history. In the same chapter on the West, he introduced a strong criticism of U.S. Indian policy. The white treatment of Native Americans was a scandal. "It is," he wrote with regret, "a tale of intermittent and barbarous warfare, of broken pacts and broken promises, of greed and selfishness and corruption and maladministration, of alternating aggression and vacillation, on the part of the whites, of courageous defense, despair, blind savagery and inevitable defeat for the Indians." While Commager advised that the "sober historian" should ignore the myths surrounding the "noble redman" and also the "bitterly prejudiced interpretation of Indian character by frontiersmen," he subscribed to President Hayes's eloquent condemnation of government betrayal, mistreatment, and robbery of Native Americans, and he quoted Hayes at length.[13]

One of the most impressive chapters Commager contributed to the GAR addressed "arts and letters," the intellectual life of the nation. Remember that the young historian, only twenty-seven years old when he wrote this material, had been trained in European history at the University of Chicago and had taught American history at NYU for only four years when he turned himself to the job of helping Morison construct the book. A chapter on American intellectual life seems a natural and simple task in the late twentieth century, but in 1929, when Commager was drafting his ideas, there were few precedents for that kind of work.[14]

Vernon Parrington's *Main Currents in American Thought*, one of the first sustained analyses of American culture, had been published only two years earlier. During the teens and twenties, few people were writing the history of American cultural life. There was Van Wyck Brooks, whose *America's Coming-of-Age* was published in 1915. Arthur Lovejoy at Johns Hopkins wrote on ideas, but not on American intellectual history. Parrington's only real predecessors were Edward Eggleston, Moses Coit Tyler, and Barrett Wendell, and Eggleston and Tyler wrote only on the colonial period. None of them achieved great recognition or produced a following.[15]

So in the late twenties when the young Commager, only recently employed in the field of American history, shaped a chapter for the *Growth of
the American Republic* that addressed American intellectual life, it was a
precocious move. Its style represented the best and worst of his work. The
strength of his account was its well-written and broad-ranging description
of literature and journalism, art, architecture, education, and leisure. Who
would expect a young historian, at the end of the 1920s, to attempt to
categorize into schools, movements, or important tendencies such un-
charted areas as American literature or architecture—not to mention the
intellectually peripheral areas of journalism and leisure? As became his
trademark, Commager unearthed minor figures he considered important in
each field, and this added a depth and richness to his portrait, even when his
judgments have not withstood later fashions and assessments.

If the breadth of his vision stands as part of Commager's strength, it also
is part of his weakness. In painting his canvas with broad strokes and popu-
lating his portrait with a crowd of figures, he produced an effect similar to
Whitman's style of cataloguing in his poetry. Where Whitman would make a
point or suggest an image and then have a list of examples, so Commager
would offer a shard of analysis and then append to that realization a long
and dense bibliographic essay that would drag the tip of his analysis beneath
the waves. Only the essays he wrote for journals and magazines escaped this
limitation.

During this period, as the Great Depression expanded and Franklin Roosevelt's New Deal rose to counter it, Commager continued to write for
periodicals, dedicating himself to journalism and scholarship both. But in
the surrounding atmosphere of strong ideological turmoil, from what political outlook would he write his articles? In a decade in which communists,
socialists, liberals, and conservatives—factions and splinter outlooks too
numerous to catalogue—all argued strongly for their separate solutions,
toward which section of the political spectrum would he gravitate? What
part of the ideological matrix would he defend?

If, as a young man, Commager's earliest political sympathies were for
Woodrow Wilson and the Democratic Party, his greatest allegiance as he
matured was to Jefferson. Yes, as president, Jefferson had his problems—
such as contradicting his small-government philosophy during the acquisition of Louisiana and the embargo of British goods—Commager admitted
to his friend Hans Duus, but still his example loomed as a beneficial presence over early American culture. "Certainly there was never in this country

a statesman of more talent, more genius, more admirable versatility than Jefferson," he told Duus. "His constant and intelligent interest in science; his scientific experiments, his scientific agriculture, his ideals in the foundation of the University of Virginia, and his architectural designs for that place . . . the list is almost endless. For sheer versatility and alertness of mind, this country has seldom seen Jefferson's equal in any walk of life."[16]

Jefferson's rival Alexander Hamilton, however, "was a much overpraised individual." Although Commager admitted that "Hamilton was possibly the most brilliant intellect of his age, possibly of America," he assured Duus that Hamilton "was quite out of spirit with the whole trend of that nascent nation which he, strangely enough, did so much to make and to maintain. He was essentially a class-legislator."[17]

When Claude Bowers, Nevins's associate at the *World*, published his *Jefferson and Hamilton: The Struggle for Democracy in America* in 1925, Commager read it in Chicago and wrote Duus that it was "absolutely fascinating" and the best that had been written on the period. "Bowers is an out and out Jeffersonian, for which thank God," he wrote, "and this is the cleverest defense of Jefferson I have seen in so short a compass."[18]

Commager enjoyed politics as a young man and later claimed to have voted for Robert La Follette, the Progressive Party candidate in the 1924 presidential election. Yet three times he wrote to his aunt in Syracuse suggesting that John W. Davis, the Democratic nominee, was her best vote. She chose Coolidge instead, and throwing up his hands, Commager admitted to Hans Duus that "I know when I'm licked."[19]

The Coolidge administration, he believed, represented a pendulum swing toward reaction, his fellow citizens were "primarily interested in prosperity, autos and the radio," and the Democratic Party was leaderless and could not unite on important policies. Finally, Commager complained about "how ineffectual the representations and convictions of academic men, of learned men, are. It is not true in other democracies."[20]

Beginning in the early 1930s in New York, while he was teaching at NYU, Commager began writing for *Current History*, a publication of the *New York Times*. This marked the beginning of his close publishing relationship with the *Times*, which lasted throughout his career. The ink was barely dry on the legislation from Roosevelt's First Hundred Days in 1933 when Commager jumped into print in *Current History* to defend the New Deal from its conservative critics. With amused contempt, he dismissed those who accused FDR of mounting a dictatorship, for the New Deal was "neither the scuttling of democracy nor the surrender to socialism nor the application of fascism, but merely the repudiation of obsolete shibboleths of individualism and *laissez-faire* and a full-throated assertion of the right and purpose of democratic society to readjust its legal machinery to the demands of a new order."[21]

Laissez-faire fit the open frontier lifestyle of earlier American centuries, Commager acknowledged, but it had been captured as an ideology of selfish corporate greed in recent times and was now only a perversion of its former liberal integrity. Already as early as the Populist and Progressive periods, Americans had "substituted doctrines of social welfare for those of selfish aggrandizement." But it was the First Hundred Days that marked "the legislative repudiation of *laissez-faire* and the advent of a new ideology." True, there was a government partnership with business now being forged, but instead of fascism or socialism it was intended to create "a wholesome capitalist economy."[22]

An essay in *Current History* the following year contained the heart of Commager's developing political philosophy. Again he attacked conservative critics of the New Deal, who now characterized Roosevelt's policies as dangerous social and economic regimentation. Yes, he admitted, part of FDR's program was "to regiment certain heretofore irresponsible industries" in order "to bring some order out of industrial, financial, and agricultural chaos." But why worry? Why, he asked, is governmental regulation any more threatening than self-regulation? Why is a government action more threatening than a corporate measure? "Why are gentlemen's agreements, pooling agreements, trusts, cooperatives, labor unions and similar agencies expressions of American individualism and in the American tradition," he wondered, "but codes, enacted by the agents of the people at large, contrary to American tradition and to the spirit of the Constitution, and examples of regimentation?"[23]

More fundamental, he asked, why did the critics of the New Deal assume that there was an inherent conflict between law and liberty? "Historically at least," he reminded the critics, "law and liberty are not antagonistic but compatible." Instead of threatening rights and liberties, regimentation preserves them from destruction. A similar misperception, he reported, was held by those who saw a meaningful difference between the democratic ideals of Jefferson and Wilson, only because Jefferson spoke on behalf of small government and Wilson saw a need for the regulation of some areas of economic life.[24]

In terms reminiscent of John Winthrop and John Cotton in the seventeenth century, Alexander Hamilton in the eighteenth, and Abraham Lincoln in the nineteenth, Commager told the conservatives that "whether our approach is historical, pragmatic or moral, we are led irresistibly to the conclusion that it is *law* that makes us free." As he would continue to shape this theme throughout his career, Commager advanced the idea that, if framed and handled properly, there was no necessary conflict between the demands of freedom and order. Those worried about New Deal regimentation, he counseled, should remember that "experience proves that the real danger to our liberties has come not from the governments, but from lawless and irresponsible privileged groups who will not discipline themselves and who must be forced to submit to collective regimentation."[25]

Nevins, who during the thirties also wrote several articles supporting the New Deal, agreed with Commager that more regulation would not damage liberty. "The American people," Nevins noted, "are a singularly hard people to regiment." Besides, as he pointed out, the New Deal "is not a piece of regimentation forced by the government on the people; it is an act that the people forced upon the government." Further, economic and social stability could not be achieved during the depression without planning and "without replacing some of our old rage for individualistic freedom by a new rage for social justice, even if it lessens freedom."[26]

Just as Commager had seen the New Deal as a battle between the old commitments to laissez-faire and a newer dedication to orchestrating life, Nevins assured his readers that "America has indeed come to a parting of the ways . . . between two radically different philosophies of government . . . and that since Mr. Roosevelt entered upon the Presidency with his amazing program this choice can no more be evaded than the choice between slavery and emancipation could be evaded once Lincoln had entered the Presidency." Nevins later admitted that the goal of the New Deal "was not always clear to me, and its methods were sometimes dubious, but it embodied our best hope not alone of recovery, but of regeneration. . . . It was exhilarating."[27]

When Commager began writing in defense of the New Deal for *Current History* in the thirties, his articles not only marked him as a Jeffersonian liberal but also showed his lack of interest in socialist solutions. Asked later why he never moved to the socialist left during the depression as did so many other intellectuals of his generation, he replied that he found socialism boring and it never really engaged him. Never, Commager admitted, had he read Karl Marx's *Capital* or any of the important leftist literature. The policies and ambitions of the New Deal and Franklin Roosevelt were where he felt comfortable.[28] Commager said simply that he was a Jeffersonian, and Jeffersonians did not become communists.

The term "Jeffersonian" is one of protean vagueness. By it, Commager meant that he was particularly committed to civil liberties, the benefits of dissent, intellectual freedom, competition, individual opportunity, and an uncensored marketplace of ideas. Commager's Jeffersonian pronouncements also were his recognition, well before those characteristics surfaced in him publicly, that he was already vigilant about issues of free speech before McCarthyism made such caution fashionable.

Yet what Commager failed to acknowledge when he described himself as a Jeffersonian was the extent to which his political outlook was also strongly Hamiltonian. All modern social liberals (not individualistic classical liberals) since the time of Theodore Roosevelt and Herbert Croly early in the twentieth century have been at least partly Hamiltonians. All have agreed with Croly that their mission was to create Jeffersonian ends (decentralism, small government, and individual freedom) through Hamiltonian means (centralism, active government, and social and economic planning).[29] Like other twentieth-century Democratic liberals, Commager, while proclaiming himself a Jeffersonian, lobbied strongly for a centrally orchestrated welfare state, argued that civil rights and other problems were best handled at the national level instead of by state governments, and campaigned vigorously, before the 1960s, for a strong presidency.

While Commager acknowledged his admiration for Franklin Roosevelt, he argued later that FDR wasn't Hamiltonian because Hamilton's policies weren't egalitarian and he did not care about the common person. According to Commager, Hoover, not FDR, was the Hamiltonian because Hoover didn't care about common people.[30] But equality and concern for the common masses weren't nearly as central to Hamiltonians as the size and activism of government, the strength of the presidency, and an emphasis on an organic instead of individualistic conception of society.

Demonstrating the pragmatic approach he so admired in John Dewey, in 1937 Commager told readers of the New York Times Magazine that the proper amount of government power exercised by state and nation should be a matter of experience instead of doctrine. The mix should result from "sociological experiment." Looking to experience should quiet fears that the national government during the New Deal was growing too large, because government expansion was caused by the growth of the nation's population and economy instead of the ambitions of political leaders. Greater national government power was needed to regulate national corporations and problems. To assuage uneasy citizens, Commager noted that states had actually gained power because there had been "an enormous growth of the power of all governments."[31]

Yes, there had been a greater "centralization of power" during the New Deal, he admitted, and it had been "inspired by a different philosophy" that "insisted that if there is to be regimentation, the representatives of the nation, not of business, command the regiments." Demonstrating his Hamiltonian, republican sympathy for orchestrated social goals, Commager told his readers that "the determination of the allocation of powers rests not alone upon considerations of efficiency but even more emphatically upon considerations of larger social welfare and liberty."[32]

Allan Nevins agreed with his friend about the virtues of a limited Hamiltonian approach to government. While Jefferson's democratic ideas were "broad" and "humane," they were also "faulty." Jefferson, Nevins reported, "did not realize, as Hamilton realized, that liberty and democracy are bound to suffer if they do not have a strong government to protect them. A powerful central government, fortunately for the American democracy, was set up despite Jefferson and in defiance of his wishes."[33]

Although Commager throughout his life remained an enthusiastic champion of Jeffersonianism, his analysis of the New Deal in the early 1930s betrayed the extent to which he had already blended with Jefferson's ideas a strong respect for Hamiltonian centralization and active government. Having assisted William Dodd with the Woodrow Wilson volumes as a graduate student, what other conception of political organization would one expect of Commager except that hybrid of Jeffersonianism and Hamiltonianism forged by Croly, Teddy Roosevelt, and Wilson during the Progressive period?

Commager's mix of political thought was flexible and pragmatic instead of rigidly fixed. On matters of intellectual freedom and government abridgments of civil rights, he was clearly more Jeffersonian. On the need for society to organize and orchestrate itself for the greatest social good, under the leadership of its elected national government, he was decidedly more Hamiltonian. In this respect, Commager was already a twentieth-century liberal, one who would become increasingly insistent, impatient, and radical. Meanwhile, his friend Nevins, who in addition to embracing Hamiltonian centralization also harbored a growing respect for the accomplishments of American business, slowly moved toward the more conservative end of the liberal spectrum.

Yet another strong feature of Commager's intellectual values was his sympathy for moral dissent, prompted by the liberal Danish Lutheran reform beliefs of his grandfather Pastor Dan and represented by his first book, *Theodore Parker* (1936). As he once noted about himself: "From childhood my sympathies have always gone to the come-outers and the dissenters and the non-conformists, to the Struensees or the Voltaires or the Jeffersons or the Gruntvigs or the Parringtons or whatever it might be. Right down the line, so far as I know." Although he insisted that this "doesn't mean I don't understand and admire a Hamilton or understand and admire a Burke," he admitted that "it's an interesting index in character to find out who you admire, who you want to live with. I want to live with Gruntvig, not Kierkegaard, with Jefferson, not Hamilton, or with Tom Paine, not Burke."[34]

In the example of the New England Transcendentalist minister Theodore Parker, Commager found an illustration of moral dissent that caught his imagination. He was drawn to Parker's life of "the scholar who is also active, the activist who is also a scholar." In our own contemporary parlance, he was fascinated with Parker's ability to mix the roles of the intellectual (an activism on matters of contemporary public importance) and the scholar (a more neutral and detached writer for a smaller group of professional colleagues). Commager's own desire to have a foot in each camp, to be an activist, partisan intellectual at the same time that he was a respected, objective scholar, also prompted his lifelong interest in the eighteenth century, because the Enlightenment demonstrated that the "learned world seemed to have time for both activism and politics." So when Commager began focusing his scholarly energies around research for a book on Parker in the early thirties, as he later acknowledged, "this was autobiography I was writing. This was what I wanted to be and in a way what I was." His project was an attempt to combine scholarship with a devotion to moral welfare.[35]

Merle Curti, the intellectual historian who was then teaching at Smith College in Northampton, Massachusetts, and who later in the decade would become his colleague at Columbia, wrote to Commager at NYU in 1933 and complimented him on a magazine piece on Parker. Commager thanked him for the "gracious letter" and acknowledged that he had "all of the research and some of the thinking already done" on a Parker biography, which he hoped to write that year. "My interest," he affirmed to Curti, "is, like yours, in the secular rather than the religious field." In addition to his research on Parker, he told Curti that he was also undertaking an expedition to the William Jennings Bryan manuscripts in Washington.[36]

When *Theodore Parker* was published in 1936, there were autobiographical insights in it, indeed. Parker, much like Commager, worried "that as a lawyer I might have been more useful" and in other moods confided that "there is a pulse in my heart that beats wildly for the stir and noise and tumult and dust of a literary course." Although Commager was a devout Jeffersonian democrat and believed in majority rule, like Parker, Emerson, and Thoreau he believed there were times when the majority had to be spoken against by an individual who was protecting an important moral principle. As Parker counseled, "In all good works, in all reforms, he [such an individual] must lead the way. Neither Church nor State, neither laws nor opinion, could impose on him; he was no apologist, but a judge." In this sense of wearing the judicial robes of moral and political principle, Commager had found his way back to the practice of law.[37]

Parker's talent for bringing his scholarship to the democratic mass of people in an activist and understandable form evoked Commager's constant admiration throughout the book. It was a model he hoped to follow. "Nor did he doubt his ability to read the future, or his duty to announce it," he wrote of Parker. "That was the business of the scholar in the Republic (the transcendental scholar)—to realize, to embrace the future." The Boston cleric knew that the Old World scholar depended on aristocratic or government patronage and served the few, rather than society at large. But in the American New World, Commager wrote, "the greatest scholar was the most democratic, here the man of learning spoke to the whole of the people, not to an exclusive segment."[38]

Parker's commitment to interacting with the great national congregation in the realm of ideas instead of protecting himself in his scholarly sanctuary caught Commager's imagination. Surely it reminded him of his grandfather Adam Dan's activist Gruntvigian convictions. The scholar in this republic, Commager wrote about Parker's example, "is not a slave to the past but master of the present and prophet of the future; he is to play his part in the making of a new world." The Transcendentalist minister was unable to convince himself that writing scholarly articles fulfilled his entire duty. "He had developed a talent for the popularization of learning," Commager noted about Parker, "and he rationalized it into a duty."[39] Commager might easily have aimed the remark at himself.

Although Parker was a minister, he felt that historians had a similar responsibility, and Commager wanted his fellow historians to heed Parker's advice. "In telling what has been," Parker suggested, "the historian is also to tell what ought to be, for he is to pass judgment on events, and try counsels by their causes first and their consequences not less. When all these things are told, history ceases to be a mere panorama of events; it becomes philosophy teaching by experience, and has a profound meaning and awakens a deep interest, while it tells the lessons of the past for the warning of the present and the edification of the future."[40] The historian should not remain comfortably turned to the past but needed to confront the present and then turn his or her face to the harsh weather of the future.

What political stance did this activist role require? Did dissent, skepticism, moral principle, iconoclasm, and activism require the historian to secede from the mainstream—perhaps join the socialist left in the thirties? In his portrayal of Parker, the liberal but moderate Commager emphasized that a healthy dissent was important but that it might be done from within the mainstream structure of society. Parker's fellow Transcendentalist minister Octavius Brooks Frothingham had announced that "he that rejects the church must not belong to it. If he wishes to throw stones at the windows, he must go outside." Commager countered that "Parker might retort that sometimes it was necessary to throw stones through windows in order to let in light and air, and that the thing could be done from within just as well as from without."[41]

From the first page, his book on Parker was a well-crafted work with an unassuming literary grace. With the memory of his Grandfather Dan's literary success before him, Commager from the beginning was committed to producing fluent and interesting prose. Unlike so many other authors, Commager took time to set his sentences so they flowed with an elegant ease. The story, the actual narrative of Parker's life, was highlighted rather than lost amid the historian's other duties. Nor was he willing to ignore the natural drama of Parker's life. Drama was built into the story intentionally, as when Commager, full of theatrical asides and parenthetical comments to the reader, recounts for several pages Parker's appearance at Faneuil Hall in Boston in protest of the Fugitive Slave Law—when Parker addressed his Massachusetts audience as "fellow subjects of Virginia."[42]

The stagecraft was apparent in his rendition of Boston judge Edward Loring's ruling on an escaped slave, an account in which Commager, to produce a more intimate sense of action, alternated between third- and second-person narrative, as he did occasionally. So within the space of a page the reader finds a transition from "but Loring thought otherwise, and he ruled against the prisoner on every point," to "that decision cost you dear, Judge Loring. The women of Woburn sent you thirty pieces of silver, and you could travel the length of the Cape by the light of your burning effigies." The shift to the second person not only allows the reader access to the narrative, of course, but makes the historian a participant in the action.[43]

Occasionally, Commager did well juxtaposing conflicting ideas and allowing them to reveal their differences in action. He showed, albeit briefly, the disagreements between abolitionists such as Theodore Weld, Lewis Tappan, and William Lloyd Garrison. Similarly, Commager pointed out, in Parker's abolitionist agenda, the connections between antinomianism, nullification, and a priori thinking. And Commager, if only hesitantly, was willing now and then to question and challenge the principals of his study, as when he pointed out that Parker's abolitionism was mounted in complete ignorance of the South and that his thinking was absolutist instead of appropriately pragmatic.[44]

When issued, *Theodore Parker* was welcomed respectfully but not as enthusiastically as Commager would have wished. Yes, C. Hartley Grattan acknowledged in the *New York Times Book Review* that Parker was a welcome figure for a depression generation "which is witnessing a rebirth of the American spirit of rebellion against existing social conditions and a revival of the passion for reform." Sure, Merle Curti in the *New England Quarterly* affirmed that the book was an "objective" and "living" biography. True, Newton Arvin in the *New Republic* reported that it was "a literary scandal" that it had taken so long for a biography of Parker to appear and that it was fortunate Commager was such a good scholar and writer.[45]

But these and other reviewers found the book lacking interpretation and critical evaluation. It was no surprise that they found interpretation missing, because Commager announced in his preface that he had no interest "in passing judgment on Parker or in stating the verdict of history upon the movements in which he so energetically participated." Instead, he would give us "Parker and his contemporaries as they appeared to themselves," rather than Commager's reaction to those careers. "It would be easy enough, and dangerous, too," he told his readers, "to say, Here history has proved him right, here wrong, here his judgment has been vindicated, here impeached. It is better that the reader should have the satisfaction of doing this for himself."[46]

Few observers were impressed with Commager's decision. His friend Merle Curti had already "thought of writing a biography of Theodore Parker and had read a lot of his writing" and at the suggestion of Samuel Eliot Morison wrote a review of Commager's book for the *New England Quarterly*.[47] There, Curti reported that Parker himself "would not have been satisfied with this biography," because it was written "without reference to any social responsibility or any broadly functional conception of scholarship beyond accurately setting down facts in an aesthetically satisfying way." Curti wondered what had happened to Commager's admiration for Parker's statements that "the historian is also to tell what ought to be, for he is to pass judgment on events" and that the lessons of the past are to inform the present and future. "Mr. Commager believes, apparently, that the historian and biographer have no business with any of this," Curti concluded. "It would, indeed, be hard to imagine a more decisive repudiation of Parker's tenets than one finds in this, the most recent and the best biography of him."[48]

Grattan agreed. "It is always wise to avoid criticizing a man for not doing what he has said he has not attempted," he noted in the *Times*, "but in this instance I strongly feel that Professor Commager has defaulted the fundamental task of the biographer and historian." In the *New Republic*, Arvin

Merle Curti in 1944,
about a decade after he
first met Commager.
(Associated Press;
courtesy of Library of Congress)

suggested that "a biographer to whom the exploitation of slave labor is not a question of right and wrong" will "fail, too, to throw into full relief the qualities in Theodore Parker that make him seem an authentic 'ancestor' to American radicals today."[49]

In the *Nation*, John Chamberlain, who was then a Trotskyist and a regular reviewer for the *New York Times*, was even tougher on Commager. Yes, the book was fascinating and conveyed Parker's energy, so it succeeded as art, but because it never evaluated how the energy was used, it failed as criticism. Chamberlain suggested that "it might be called an example of the roar-machine theory of biography: so many degrees registered of intellectual intensity, of moral passion, of querulousness, of Yankee colloquialism," but no room for judgment. Chamberlain was disappointed at "Mr. Commager's profession of temporary agnosticism in the face of the social forces that moved Parker." Van Wyck Brooks, he noted, had more substance on the antislavery writers in the sixteen pages devoted to the issue in *The Flowering of New England* than in all of Commager's book, mostly because Brooks was willing to advance an interpretation.[50]

The tragedy, Chamberlain reported, was that Commager missed the opportunity to draw a parallel between Parker's opposition to slavery in the South and America's resistance to Hitler's Germany as Chamberlain wrote in the mid-1930s. Similarly, Parker's fight for economic justice shared continuities with the labor union struggles of John L. Lewis during the depression. "Now, as before," Chamberlain pointed out, "two imperialisms, running on irresistible momentum, face collision. There is much to be learned from the life of Parker that has contemporary application. One wishes that Mr. Commager had drawn the parallels; one wishes that he had more curiosity about the approximate laws of history."[51]

There are other serious weaknesses of the volume that the reviewers failed to note. On the whole the book skates along the surface of ideas without ever penetrating into them deeply, and the reader is often left with an abstract and disorienting study that a lack of dates and firm chronology in the story only magnifies. Commager excelled at description, language, and anecdote, much like the later Van Wyck Brooks, but he failed to pause long enough in his narrative to grapple with ideas sufficiently, never stopping to explain or analyze them. Because he rarely gave a person's ideas more than a line or two before he dismissed them from the stage with a clever aside or a witticism, the thinkers in his study are image instead of substance. Too frequently he was willing to substitute a string of unanswered questions in place of hard analysis and real ideas.

Often, for example in his chapter entitled "West Roxbury," Commager wrote of intellectuals as someone might write about those who attended a dinner at a social club: listing who spoke with whom but not covering in any detail the important ideas exchanged and transformed. Because his intellectual appetites were so broad, he read so widely, and he remembered so well, Commager's prose was stacked with names in almost a catalogue fashion, producing paragraphs that look like the lists in Walt Whitman's poetry. The lists themselves were not fatal. There's a place for them. But he so seldom went beyond them very deeply or spent time with any figure long enough to understand them in an important way. Commager's quick mind was often good at making connections but seldom adept at explaining and analyzing an idea in depth.

Further, Commager's work was needlessly one-dimensional. Partly because he was not a contentious person himself and never cared for staged polemics, Commager usually failed to properly construct a conflict of ideas in his writing. Parker's antagonists were present in the book, but usually not in any real sense where intellectual repartee was visible. The give-and-take of intellectual battle never caught Commager's imagination. He usually made his own case on the ground of important principle and then rushed out of the political arena to his next appointment without waiting to hear the response of his antagonists.

That pattern was duplicated in his books, where he often appeared as a cheerleader for one side but recorded no chant in reply. One hand clapped. Consequently, it was nearly impossible for him to sketch, let alone examine in detail, the contradictions and ironies in the ideas of his principals. That weakness was magnified in *Theodore Parker*, as the reviewers suggested, by his decision to write the book from Parker's perspective, not from his own. It gave the book an exhortatory instead of investigative accent. Because Commager preferred a general rather than an analytically specific focus, the book often seems to be a picture of everyone it mentions, and then finally no one.

But the many virtues of *Theodore Parker* and Commager's historical style should not be lost in the book's deficiencies. The study was written gracefully as a work of literature as well as history, and Commager took pride in a craftsmanship that most historians had abandoned in favor of other values. For example, of a book that Parker reviewed, Commager wrote that "Parker attacked it like a pirate, struck it fore and aft, boarded it, slashed its rigging and toppled its masts, and made its master walk the plank." On another occasion in the story Commager told his readers, "It was on Friday morning, the second of June, that Loring read his decision, and the word flew over Massachusetts and darkened the skies like an eclipse."[52] Such writing adorns every page.

Further, some chapters, such as "The Unitarian Controversy," bear a stronger presence of ideas than others. And even when analysis remains in the background in his work, the reader is treated to an encyclopedic knowledge of connecting books, thoughts, figures, and movements. Commager's appetite for knowing the topography of American intellectual life made him, as he referred to Parker, an "intellectual gourmand."[53] It is fundamentally important for viable democratic cultures to have intellectual historians such as Commager who are literate enough to elevate social discourse, appealing enough to be read by the general public, and broadly knowledgeable enough to describe trends in thought and indicate their interconnections.

Commager's *Theodore Parker* remains important for the interconnected sense of culture it brings to antebellum New England. In providing the story and folklore of the past, Commager also was a twentieth-century version of the historian George Bancroft. In *Theodore Parker*, Commager, like Bancroft, promoted a pride in American cultural history, but unlike the earlier historian, Commager still criticized America's weak points and supported its dissenters.

As did Van Wyck Brooks in his *Makers and Finders* series, which was started at the same time as Commager's book (Brooks's *The Flowering of New England* was published the same year as *Theodore Parker*), Commager wove together the story of thinkers knowing one another, interacting with one another, living lives in a common community where they bumped into one another. This kind of cultural and intellectual history provides the texture of the past and a model for future thinkers to emulate. The historian William Leuchtenburg, as a graduate student in a Commager colloquium, witnessed "the lilt in his voice and the sheer pleasure on his face when he marveled at the way Brooks would have one character encounter another on a New England street. Henry gave every indication that was the way he wanted to write, the way he thought history should be written."[54]

Here is a reason not to forget Commager and his circle of friends and colleagues who felt as he did about the importance of narrative history, writing for the public, and becoming involved in civic matters. Remembering their interactions, disagreements, discussions, and common projects, we understand better the context of what important intellectual figures such as Morison, Nevins, and Commager were trying to accomplish. But even more important, as in a Brooks portrait, attention to these writers and the larger group they represent allows us to see the process of culture in progress—in this case, the construction of a literate cultural history—and witness it as a collective endeavor that transcends the effort of one individual.

Put simply, the complaint filed most by reviewers against *Theodore Parker* was that Commager had not been Parringtonian enough. As narrowly orthodox as many professional historians were about the need to remain neutral and objective, even they thought he had been too detached and Olympian. Considering Commager's own description of his intellectual value system and commitments, his failure to write a more openly partisan or at least a confidently interpretive account of Parker is curious.

After all, it was Parrington, Commager admitted, who was one of the first to prompt his interest in the moral passion, political activism, and cultural erudition that Parker represented.[55] Because Parrington's first two volumes of *Main Currents in American Thought* were published in 1927, when Commager was in his first year at NYU and just beginning to write seriously, his influence is hardly surprising. So deeply did Parrington leave his imprint on him that Commager told the readers of his *American Mind* that his "deepest intellectual debt is to Vernon Louis Parrington whose great study of American thought has long been an inspiration and whose disciple I gladly acknowledge myself."[56]

Parrington never tried to hide his own partisanship. "The point of view from which I have endeavored to evaluate the materials," he disclosed in his first volume, "is liberal rather than conservative, Jeffersonian rather than

Federalistic; and very likely in my search I have found what I went forth to find, as others have discovered what they were seeking." His audience was left to determine for itself whether his advocacy had distorted his interpretation, but he never denied his agenda. As he told a correspondent in 1908, "Officially I am a teacher of English literature, but in reality my business in life is to wage war on the crude and selfish materialism that is biting so deeply into our national life and character."[57]

In the war Parrington waged, he understood that the enemy wasn't personal evil but rather economic and social conditions and the cultural environment. This belief Parrington had adopted from the work of Hippolyte Taine, the nineteenth-century French historian. The Puritan theocrat John Cotton, for example, "was the child of a generation reared under the shadow of absolutism," and so "the age was more to blame than the man." The same with John Winthrop, whose "political bias was unconsciously shaped by his experience" as a Jacobean judge "which he brought to New England as a legacy from an autocratic past." For Parrington, political and intellectual revolutions "were psychological explosions, resulting from irritations commonly economic in origin."[58]

History, as Parrington saw it, was a struggle that connected battles in the past with those in the present, so that historical events described by the historian were simply other ways of writing about political and social battles that sweep around us today and carry on into the future. Therefore, seventeenth-century Puritanism "was the ecclesiastical form of a struggle, which, shifting later to the field of politics and then to economics, is still raging about us. The long battle is still far from being won."[59]

So Roger Williams, Parrington's brave and democratic Puritan seeker, was not trapped by his seventeenth-century confinements. No, "he was contemporary with successive generations of prophets from his own days to ours. His hospitable mind anticipated a surprising number of the idealisms of the future," and he was forerunner of Ralph Waldo Emerson, William Ellery Channing, Thomas Paine, and others. "Democrat and Christian," Parrington said of Williams, "the generation to which he belongs is not yet born. . . . He lived and dreamed in a future he was not to see, impatient to bring to men a heaven they were unready for."[60]

In his writing Parrington emerged as a partisan advocate of liberal historical figures. He accused the conservative colonial governor of Massachusetts Thomas Hutchinson of operating from an "economic class interest," but he had no similar suspicions of Samuel Adams's liberal radicalism. Hutchinson "hardened early, and thereafter he was incapable of changing his views or liberalizing his sympathies," but Parrington considered it a beneficial mark of character when Sam Adams hardened early into a radical and would not change his outlook. "To stimulate what we call today class consciousness," he said of Adams's work, "was a necessary preliminary to a democratic psychology," so what had been reprehensible in Hutchinson was admirable in Adams.[61]

Yet Parrington was far less one-sided and dogmatic than he is usually assumed to be, often by those who have not yet found the time to read him. Although he disapproved of John Cotton's theocratic conservatism, for example, he painted a gracious portrait of Cotton and gave him credit for being a "social revolutionary" who would "refashion society upon ethical rather than economic lines." Parrington was nearly always more balanced in his accounts than his reputation suggests. Still speaking of Cotton, for example, he quotes a state paper of his and then notes about the Puritan leader that this passage "quite evidently, is the negation of democracy, and it has been freely charged against his reputation by later critics. But in fairness it must be added, that it is equally the negation of the principle of hereditary aristocracy; and to reject the latter was a severer test of his integrity than to deny the former."[62] The famed partisanship of Parrington, that is, was a flexible and cordial one.

It has been fashionable in the last half of the twentieth century to dismiss Parrington's enthusiasms, along with his history, as naïve and embarrassing. There are modifications that one would make in Parrington's emphases—especially his oversimplified separation of history into rich, elitist, and conservative bad figures against the common, little, and democratic good people. Yet the historical profession, not to mention its audience, has been weaker for having driven Parrington from its polite company. His works have strengths seldom found in succeeding generations of more scientifically professional historians. Parrington had talents that many of his successors, those who have smirked at his reputation, would be lucky to recover for themselves.

Throughout, Parrington's history is written imaginatively, gracefully, and lyrically, as one might expect from a professor of literature. His literary polish and dexterity added to instead of subtracted from the clarity of his ideas. And although he was a literary historian, he was one of the first to take the history of American religious, literary, political, economic, and social ideas seriously and look for their interconnections.

Commager was not alone among his generation of historians in his respect for Parrington. As several studies revealed, from the 1930s to the early 1950s Parrington's *Main Currents* was among the most respected works in the field. One of Commager's associates who most shared his enthusiasm for

Parrington was Merle Curti, whose *Growth of American Thought* (1943) was chosen by historians as the best book to appear between 1936 and 1950.[63]

In the 1930s Curti considered himself a socialist influenced by Marxism. He was also a strong advocate of Charles Beard's work, an enthusiasm that Commager never shared with Curti. Actually, Curti was so taken with Beard that he wanted to write his biography but was forced to abandon it because Beard had destroyed most of his personal papers.[64]

Yet, if Commager and Curti admired Parrington, Commager knew that his friend Allan Nevins "had less passion for Parrington than I had, because he wasn't as interested in style, and I was seduced by Parrington's stylistic genius." But even though he was not as enthusiastic as Commager about Parrington, Nevins did believe that some political or moral advocacy was important in historians' work. According to Commager, Nevins knew "that scholars could take care of themselves. They would either accept it or they wouldn't accept it. [Parrington] wasn't trying to seduce them or fool them or mislead them. . . . And besides, in a great university, enough people had other views, and there were enough books in the library that didn't agree."[65]

Commager agreed. "I think there's nothing in the world wrong with partisanship," he maintained, "because it is so obvious it doesn't seduce any intelligent man. In fact, it's counter-productive. You begin to suspect anyone who's an ardent partisan." So, he claimed, "I don't mind reading Parrington's partisanship. It didn't persuade me that Hamilton was a bad man, for example. It made me reconsider, and maybe made me more ready to defend Hamilton than I otherwise would have been." Further, in Commager's opinion, one "must" put political opinions in history. "We do this in all of life, as far as I know, without imposing our views on others." To encounter political advocacy in a historical work was a necessary and beneficial intellectual invigoration instead of a danger. "So that I think," Commager concluded, "there's a great deal of unnecessary fuss, furor, about partisanship or subjectivity."[66]

Besides, Commager must have noticed the similarities between Parrington and himself that fostered a kinship there. Both were midwesterners and had some nostalgia for the heartland, even though Parrington's experience there had been less urban than his own. Parrington noted that Hamlin Garland's *Son of the Middle Border* (1917) captured "truly the life that I knew and lived; every detail of discomfort and ugliness and rebellion which he sets down vividly I can match from my own experiences."[67] Commager, who had his own ugly and discomforting memories of his midwestern childhood, was drawn to the more positive picture of "idyllic" simplicity and community in Garland's book. In 1926, when Commager was only twenty-four years old, he told his friend Hans Duus that *Son of the Middle Border* was "one of my very favorite books, and I think one of the classics of our literature." Garland, Commager reported, "was the first of the young rebels, of the realists in our literature, and gave a very bitter picture of farm life in the nineties. . . . But age has invested this epic of Garland's with a very rich charm."[68]

Moreover, Commager shared Parrington's commitment to the fusion of history and literature, and the synthesis of intellectual activism with scholarly soundness. "We may begin as critics," Parrington once wrote, "but we end up as historians."[69] Commager might have said it just the opposite, given that he began as a historian and then ventured from there into literary journalism and criticism. But no matter which of the two elements were given precedence, Parrington and Commager shared them.

In addition, Commager and Parrington were both Jeffersonians. Richard Hofstadter said of Parrington's politics that while "he remained much more the Jeffersonian liberal than the Marxist, he seems to have arrived at a generous, undoctrinaire, ecumenical radicalism which, seeing no enemies on the left, reached out to embrace many varieties of protest that were hospitable in spirit even if not quite congenial in doctrine." Commager would fit quite comfortably under that same description. There was also in Parrington's outlook, according to Hofstadter, an old, nearly anarchist's fear of the coercive state. Despite Commager's persistent Hamiltonian urges, he too, like Parrington, was a strong Jeffersonian in his opposition to state control of ideas or political powers of the people. This side of Commager was apparent in his long-standing identification with the American Civil Liberties Union and his leadership on issues of intellectual freedom.[70]

But, all of these similarities acknowledged, was Commager really a Parringtonian? If so, then why wasn't he more aggressively interpretive, in his *Theodore Parker*, as many of his reviewers pointed out? The reality is that Commager was a Parringtonian only in his intellectual civic activism, his public involvement in contemporary political issues, but not in his scholarship. In his scholarship he operated by a different principle. As Commager said on several occasions, "I have long subscribed to George Macaulay Trevelyan's sagacious dictum that philosophy is not something you take to the study of history, but something which, if you are lucky, you carry away from that study."[71] It is hard, that is, to conceive a less Parringtonian conception of the historian's approach than the one Commager employed—despite the fact that he claimed he was Parrington's disciple.

Even though Commager was an antibusiness liberal in the reform tradition, his scholarly work was far less political than his reputation suggested.

Perhaps he was more a product of 1920s values, when he came to political maturity, than of those of the 1930s. Commager was closer in age to Malcolm Cowley and the Lost Generation than to Richard Hofstadter, Daniel Bell, and those who came of age during the socialism of the 1930s. So perhaps the Lost Generation's dictum of "art for art's sake" became with Commager "the past for its own sake" more than he would have liked to admit.[72]

Unless we are willing to see him as less of a Parringtonian partisan than he claimed he was, we are left with a troubling dilemma: Commager argued against historians acting as strong moral judges in their work. "If he sets up as a judge," Commager counseled about the historian, "he changes the whole pattern of his intellectual and professional role from one dedicated to objective inquiry to one devoted to prosecution or defense." Can anyone imagine Parrington writing against advocacy this way? In fact, Commager was more explicit. Historians were biased, so, he asked, "can we really trust Carlyle on Cromwell . . . or Vernon Parrington on John Marshall?" Commager answered his question: "Clearly we cannot."[73]

Sure, all historians judge their principals unconsciously, but they should not try to increase that tendency. "Is there not, indeed," he asked, "some danger that if the historian continually usurps the role of judge . . . that if the historian insists on treating his readers as morally incompetent, they may turn away from history altogether to some more mature form of literature?" Instead, historians should give their readers the material to judge for themselves. Then, in true Jeffersonian fashion of free inquiry and debate, "errors will be corrected; wrong opinions will be set right. For every historian who defends British policy in Ireland there will be one to expose it and reprobate it."[74]

Yes, there was some role for professional judgment by the historian, but a modest one. After a sufficient cleansing of his or her ideological lenses, after winnowing the facts and placing them in position, the historian may advance a discreet judgment on her or his subject—but not a preconceived indictment.[75]

Based on these opinions, it is more apparent why neither *Theodore Parker* nor any of Commager's other scholarly books were very partisan in a Parringtonian sense. *Theodore Parker* was written by a historian who followed Trevelyan's advice not to force a philosophy on the subject but to let it be the result. This outlook was much more consistent with the Jeffersonian marketplace of ideas than with Parringtonian advocacy, and it must be said that Commager was always much more a Jeffersonian than a Parringtonian, despite his occasional suggestions to the contrary. And his Jeffersonian reformism was always more consistent with the ideas he learned from Adam Dan, Andrew McLaughlin, and William Dodd.

Still, if Commager didn't practice Parrington's advocacy in his historical scholarship, partisanship hardly was absent from his work altogether. Instead, Commager's political views appeared in his publicly activist, journalistic writings on the New Deal, McCarthyism, intellectual freedom, the Vietnam War, and other problems of the post–World War II period. This writing is best represented in his *Freedom, Loyalty, Dissent* (1954), *Freedom and Order* (1966), and *The Defeat of America* (1974), books that have collected the best of his political and cultural essays.

It was in his articles for the *New York Times Magazine* and the *Saturday Review of Literature*, for the *New York Review of Books* and *Harper's*, for the *Nation* and the *New Republic*, that he exercised the advocacy that he pared from his historical scholarship. It was in these essays for the general public that he allowed himself the reformist partisanship passed to him by Dan, McLaughlin, Dodd—and, yes, even Parrington. Here in Commager's generalist essays, both the activist and literary influences of his mentors are evident. And despite Commager's impressive scholarly production, these generalist articles from a public intellectual share an equal place in his permanent legacy.

CHAPTER 3

Columbia and New York

in the Forties,

1938-1950

In 1938, two years after his *Theodore Parker* was published, Commager was invited to move 110 blocks uptown from New York University and join the history department at Columbia. His academic career had been blessed. Beginning as an instructor at NYU in 1926 with his dissertation on Struensee not yet finished, by 1931 he was already a full professor at age twenty-nine. After a dozen years in the field, after *The Growth of the American Republic* and *Theodore Parker*, Commager was prominent enough to be romanced by other departments.

Columbia, on the eve of World War II, was not quite the university it would become in the next two decades, but it was the major university in the nation's most exciting city, and it had an impressive tradition behind it. Intellectual and scholarly weight had been provided to the school in the early part of the century by the presence on the faculty of James Harvey Robinson (1895–1919) in history, Charles Beard (1904–17) in political science, and John Dewey (1904–30) in philosophy.

When Commager arrived on campus in 1939 and moved into the history department's quarters arranged on the sixth floor of Fayerweather Hall, Columbia was beginning to be an even more interesting university. Lionel Trilling, who had done his graduate work on campus and then started as an instructor in 1931, was one building away in the English department, where he was promoted to assistant professor the year Henry moved into Fayerweather Hall. Robert Merton was hired by the sociology department in 1941 and within a dozen or so years had helped build a department that included such faculty and graduate students as C. Wright Mills, Daniel Bell, Seymour Martin Lipset, Nathan Glazer, Lewis Coser, and Paul Lazarsfeld. Across the street at Union Theological Seminary, Reinhold Niebuhr had made Morningside Heights the center of gravity of American Protestant thought since he arrived in 1928.

And who knew what kind of intellectual activity might be found among the undergraduates on campus during Commager's early years? Jack Kerouac appeared as a freshman on campus the year after Henry began, and such diverse undergraduate literary personalities as Allen Ginsberg and Norman Podhoretz studied there in the forties.

Meanwhile the history department was building itself into one of the most exciting groups on campus and perhaps the most impressive department in the country. Nevins, of course, had been DeWitt Clinton Professor of History since he left the *World* in 1931. Jacques Barzun had studied at Columbia during the 1920s, earned his Ph.D. in 1932, was a member of the history faculty as an assistant professor when Commager arrived, and continued to teach there for the rest of his career.

In 1937 Merle Curti had arrived, although he was affiliated with Teacher's College at Columbia, across 120th Street, rather than with the history department proper. Curti and Commager had known each other for several years, although Curti felt he never knew Henry as well as he wished. They met in the manuscript division of the Library of Congress, while each was using the Robert Rantoul Papers, they "may have had lunch together at the nearby Methodist Building cafeteria," and then they corresponded about Theodore Parker in 1933. Curti later reviewed Commager's book on Parker, and although it wasn't the most favorable assessment of the volume, the two remained friends, especially from 1938 when Commager arrived at Columbia until 1942 when Curti left New York. When Curti visited the Commagers for dinner he found himself "enchanted" by Evan and concluded that their "marriage was the most enduring romantic one among my acquaintances."[1]

In 1942 Curti accepted a job at the University of Wisconsin, and thanked Commager for his "hand" in the offer. While Curti was excited about the move, he confessed that he would miss Henry, who he had seen more "than any of the Columbia historians." Two years later Curti was again thanking Henry for the role he suspected Nevins and Commager played in the award of a Pulitzer Prize for his *Growth of American Thought* (1943).[2]

Although Commager had helped Curti land in Madison, almost immediately Columbia tried to lure him back. When Curti declined, Commager told him he was sorry that he wouldn't be in the next office so the two of them could "discuss the affairs of the universe, or only of the American mind." Columbia was looking for someone "primarily in intellectual history or, if that does not work out, in south and west, which we have long neglected here." A few days later he admitted his own ambivalence toward assuming the intellectual history leadership in the department. "What we need," he told Curti, "is someone who can really take hold of intellectual history and develop this place as a center for the study of Am. civilization. I'd like to try it myself, but I don't want to quit constitutional history, and I'm no good as an organizer or administrator anyway, or even as a salesman."[3]

This was likely the job that Richard Hofstadter assumed in 1946. Hofstadter and Commager corresponded throughout the early 1940s, with the younger historian telling Commager that he had enjoyed working with him in the summer of 1942, explaining that at the University of Maryland he was teaching a history of ideas course, inquiring about how to get the Book of the Month Club to hire him as a reviewer, and asking Commager to write recommendations on his behalf. Finally in April 1945 Hofstadter wrote him that he was in Buffalo with his ill wife, who soon died. He told Commager that the department at Maryland had been very kind to him, providing him indefinite leave with pay while other faculty picked up his load. When he returned to Maryland, he explained, he felt committed to working off that debt. A year later he accepted a job offer from Columbia.[4]

Commager liked his younger colleague, but they weren't close. Hofstadter had a historical outlook different from that represented in Fayerweather. Intellectually, Hofstadter was far closer to the critical socialist heritage of the New York Intellectuals gathered around *Partisan Review* and *Commentary* than he was to the midwestern Progressive dissent in which Commager had been nurtured. Commager paid tribute to Parrington, while Hofstadter used Parrington as an example of the soft thinking and intellectual simplicities of the previous generation. Further, by teaching an interdisciplinary faculty seminar in the 1950s on McCarthyism with sociologists Bell and Lipset and through his friendship with sociologist Mills, Hofstadter became more interested in sociological perspectives on intellectual history. Hofstadter also had been influenced by Reinhold Niebuhr's *The Irony of American History* (1952) and by the associated "tragic view of life" that had colored the work of many of the New York Intellectuals.[5] He was in a different intellectual orbit from Commager and the others in the department.

Socially, Hofstadter and Commager were no closer. When Hofstadter arrived on campus he went his own way. Representative of that independence was that Hofstadter took an office not in Fayerweather, with the rest of the history department, but in Hamilton Hall, several buildings away, where undergraduate affairs were housed.[6]

Dumas Malone, an interpreter of Jefferson, arrived in the department in 1945, after teaching at the University of Virginia, editing the *Dictionary of American Biography*, and serving as the director of Harvard University Press. Malone's presence strengthened Columbia's offerings in southern intellectual history.

When Richard Morris was hired in 1946, Henry found a friend and collaborator. He took up residence in the office next to Commager's, and together they coedited several projects. Morris, who was brought on board to teach colonial and constitutional-legal history, "was a New York Jew, one wholly, wholesomely, and permanently proud of his heritage." With a "clipped, staccato speaking style," Morris earned a reputation as a tough and demanding teacher. While some found him "hard-driving" and "abrasive," he was also a role model for ambitious graduate students, "especially among the military veteran–second generation immigrant group."[7]

Morris, like his colleagues, was aware of the intellectual weight of the Columbia historians and Commager's contribution to their reputation. "Those were the days when giants bestrode the sixth floor," Morris remarked of Fayerweather, "and Henry Commager walked with giant strides. On the Columbia campus Commager stood out almost like a historic landmark. One might just as well imagine Columbia without the Low Library or St. Paul's Chapel."[8]

And Commager himself? When he arrived at Columbia he immediately assumed control of the graduate seminars in American history.[9] While some of his colleagues later complained that he did not read students' papers closely enough or give students all the time he should have, Commager remained a popular and legendary speaker.[10] His talents at lecturing, often without notes, left students and colleagues stunned. Because he was an energetic reader of literature and history, in his classes he often handed students a daunting list of suggested books. His course Studies in Recent American History at Columbia came with a single-spaced reading list of three and a half pages. Among the densely packed group of authors, students were encouraged to read Schlesinger Sr. and Lewis Mumford on the city, Claude Bowers on Progressivism, and Washington Gladden and Walter Rauschenbusch on the social gospel; they should absorb John Chamberlain, Morris Hillquit, and Vernon Parrington and understand Walter Weyl, George Santayana, and Herbert Croly. Students should read about the West of Walter Prescott Webb, Hamlin Garland, and Willa Cather; study the autobiographies of Bryan, La Follette, and Lincoln Steffens; read Nevins on

Cleveland, Curti on peace movements, and Jacob Riis on the less fortunate; and contemplate literary works by Abraham Cahan, Sherwood Anderson, Edith Wharton, Booth Tarkington, Theodore Dreiser, and Frank Norris.[11]

Students wanted to associate with Commager, but some also feared him. It was said that when graduate students chose the time for their oral exams, some intentionally marked slots when he would be busy teaching. "His very sniff," Morris remembered about his friend's role as an orals examiner, "would send shivers up the spines of candidates" because they knew it "was a portent of some very searching questions to come."[12]

In Fayerweather Commager could be seen with "suit rumpled, locks tousled, a gently sardonic smile twisting his mouth to one side, one arm piled high with books, the other clutching an assortment of mail, *Congressional Records*, and at least one nice fat dissertation." But usually he was working like a demon in his office next to Morris's, "punching away furiously on his antique portable the first and final draft of still another brilliant essay for the *Sunday Times*," using no notes and pulling all of the quotes and allusions from memory. Books were piled everywhere and rose to the ceiling in Commager's cluttered rectangular office. Few ever accused him of a talent for organization. Boxes of books and manuscripts were strewn about, urged up against the walls or into corners. A large oak desk near the window was buried under a confusion of letters and typescripts. Legend has it that it once took him two years to find beneath the pile on the table a book manuscript sent to him by an author in his *New American Nation* series.[13]

In the forties Commager was already recognized as an important presence on the Columbia campus, a scholar and intellectual of international reputation, a figure whose writing added public visibility to the department, a friendly if busy character around the university whose idiosyncrasies were reassuring and colorful.

During the same years, about the time he arrived at Columbia, Commager moved from being simply a recognized professor to being viewed as a much more major public figure as well. He also became known as a widely read intellectual who wrote for the general press, a figure who belonged to social clubs and was recognized as a member of the literati.

Some observers thought Commager had a passion for literary celebrity and social advancement. If so, he would not have been the first intellectual with such ambitions. And who would count it a fault if it didn't decrease the attention he paid to his formal historical scholarship or spread him so thin that it turned him into a lightweight? Some of Commager's associates thought of him in much the same way that Hofstadter once described the historian Charles Beard: "To a remarkable degree he enjoyed both the benign stance of the sage and the more heady pleasures of the gadfly."[14]

Finding himself in New York City as a young man only fired his literary and social ambitions and introduced him to those with similar outlooks, among them fellow Columbia history professor Jacques Barzun, for example, about whom Nevins and Commager had different estimations. Workaholic that he was, Nevins was suspicious of Barzun's elegance, his writing about music, and the fact that he was a social figure, and he wondered whether Barzun was a gifted historian or merely a dilettante. Nevins had similar hesitations about Morison's social standing. But Commager felt differently. As he described himself, Commager "fell in love with Jacques from the beginning. I like that kind of elegance, and I shared his passion for music and everything else. So I ardently championed Jacques Barzun."[15]

This was part of a fundamental difference between Nevins and Commager. Allan cared little about money and would take the subway, whereas Henry would take a taxi. Allan would eat at the Horn and Hardhart automat (sandwiches from a machine), whereas Henry preferred to eat at the Century Club. Partly these habits resulted from different calculations about what was best for their work. Valuing a solitary and rigorous scholarship above the life of an interactive and social intellectual, Nevins hated to waste time and consequently didn't want to get caught in long-winded conversations.[16] Choosing the intellectual over the scholarly life, Commager found much of use in conversations and debates over contemporary issues.

Consequently Commager joined several clubs that had more to do with social than intellectual rank. In New York he belonged to the Century Club, in Boston it was St. Botolph's, and in London he was a member of the Athenaeum.[17] Already by 1944 he was successful in promoting for membership in the Century such of his friends as Denis Brogan, a colleague at Cambridge University who had a similar interest in questions of the American character and identity.[18] Commager's membership in the Century Club, which had a racially restrictive policy, was not lost on his doctoral student August Meier, who considered it an indication that his adviser was not a leader in civil rights issues. Yet Meier also noticed that Commager wanted to host a dinner for Max Lerner at the Century Club, even though Lerner as a Jew could not be a member.[19]

To satisfy his literary leanings Commager fraternized with such people as the publisher Bennett Cerf or the magazine editor and historian Bernard DeVoto. In addition Henry and Evan socialized with those connected to newspaper journalism such as the *New York Herald Tribune*'s book editor

Irita Van Doren, with whom he had established a "tradition that involves a lunch at the Gotham."[20]

Commager wrote for the newspaper and magazine press for several reasons. It fit his conception of history as a public civic discussion that educated and helped society, and it fulfilled his desire to communicate with a larger public as had earlier heroes of his such as Francis Parkman or George Trevelyan. Commager also appreciated the attention and celebrity journalism brought him. Always a little unsure of his social status, perhaps because of the instability of his family when he was young, the recognition brought by his writing for the public elevated his social rank. Writing for the *Atlantic* or the *Herald Tribune* gave him a cachet that substituted for the family lineage he saw in Samuel Eliot Morison and others around him.[21]

Further, Commager was driven to write for the general press at least partly for financial reasons. With a family to support, frequent travel to Europe and a house in England, real estate in Vermont, and club memberships and restaurant bills, he found his Columbia salary anemic. So he supplemented his salary by writing. His close relationship with the *New York Times Magazine* and the *Saturday Review* was partly because they paid well. When asked why he never wrote for *Partisan Review*, political considerations aside, he responded, Did they pay?[22]

Because they were eager to print his pieces, Commager wrote frequently for the *New York Times Magazine* from the late 1930s to the late 1960s. Sometimes it seemed as though he appeared there twice a month; rarely did he write for them less than several times a year. Lester Markel, the Sunday editor (who Commager once jokingly referred to as the Stalin of the magazine), told him that the *Times* couldn't get "too much Commager," but he frequently became irate with Commager's tendency to be late with an article or not answer his letters. On one occasion Markel remarked with a strained smile that he was hesitant to assign him a particular article "because Commager has let too many of Markel's good ideas die by the wayside."[23] This was a frustration Markel shared with Morison and Nevins, who experienced Commager's disappearing act when they were trying to finish manuscript revisions on their respective textbook collaborations with him.

For the same reasons that he wrote for the *New York Times Magazine*, Commager agreed in the early forties to write a regular column for Scholastic Publications, which published several magazines aimed at middle school and high school students. During most of the decade his short analytic commentaries, pieces that gave a historical perspective on contemporary problems, appeared every couple of weeks in *Senior Scholastic*. The publisher paid him eight hundred dollars for thirty-two articles in the academic year 1942–43 and offered him five hundred dollars for sixteen articles the following year. Social studies teachers benefited by historical pieces that touched on current issues, and Kenneth Gould, editor at Scholastic Publications, reminded Commager that "the effect of the war upon our institutions" was very timely. For Commager's analysis of such American institutions as constitutions, political parties, the courts, the church, schools, business, labor, the press, libraries, and women (which Commager changed from the family), he was instructed to provide "ample emphasis on the native roots of our institutions in the 18th and 19th centuries, while at the same time giving full attention to their present place in our civilization."[24]

Although his columns were aimed at high school readers, they were far more sophisticated than might have been expected. Part of Commager's success in all aspects of his career, of course, resulted from his talent at making important concepts and relationships easy and interesting for the general reader—whether in his high school pieces, his *New York Times Magazine* articles, his survey textbooks, or his public talks. In his *Senior Scholastic* work, as in his other, similar performances, he presented engaging and provocative ideas without sacrificing analysis.

On Morningside Heights Commager's closest companion was Allan Nevins, with whom he had already shared a half-dozen years of friendship by the time Henry arrived at Columbia. When, almost nightly, Allan phoned Henry, he began the conversation by asking, "Is this the great savant?" Those close to Nevins believed he had no more valued friend in his lifetime.[25]

Yet, like Commager's relationship with Morison, his friendship with Allan was never perfectly equal, although it was compatible. Throughout their years as friends, Nevins was always the senior partner in their firm. Constantly, but particularly when Allan was out of town, he asked Henry to do him favors or run errands for him. It would have been hard for him to find a less suitable errand boy than Commager, for Henry was always engaged in a dozen matters at once: teaching, traveling, lecturing, writing books, writing articles for magazines, giving interviews, bolting for a lunch date at one of his clubs. Yet Henry rarely complained about Nevins nagging him like a parent about unfinished chores. "Don't grumble too much," Allan replied from Chicago when once Henry did balk. "Just remember that I was the main instrument in getting you into Columbia, and that this is the first time I've demanded a lecture. I'll repay you in the future."[26]

In the 1940s Allan had already reached full stride in a prolific and influential scholarly career. "I am no longer a journalist—I am a historian," he wrote

Henry from his summer home in Vermont in 1941, and during that decade he rose in prominence in the discipline.[27] Yet he was more than merely a scholar who produced books. In addition he conspired to transform the entire field for the better.

"We can recall him looking out from his eyrie on the sixth floor of Fayerweather Hall," Henry later remembered about his friend's ambitious vision, "that vast book-lined and paper-strewn room where the very air vibrated with his energetic presence—looking out not merely over the campus of Columbia University but over the whole broad realm of history and planning forays and excursions to assure its prosperity and its triumph."[28] By the time Commager was taken aboard by Columbia at the end of the thirties, Nevins already was working to reshape the profession of history as it was practiced in the United States.

In 1938 Nevins and a few other prominent historians suggested that the American Historical Association (AHA) should help institutionalize a new historical publication for the democratic public. Led by Harvard's Frederick Merk, the AHA rejected Nevins's proposal partly because it seemed financially risky and partly because it was afraid of associating itself with a potentially slick, commercial, and unsophisticated magazine whose standards might be difficult to control. Although Allan accused his opponents of an undemocratic snobbism, even some of his supporters—such as Conyers Read and Carl Becker—acknowledged that, because it was so glossy (it was to be issued by Conde Nast, *Vogue*'s publisher), Allan's proposed magazine would be too expensive for all but the rich. *American Heritage*, the publication Nevins's imagined, didn't see the light of day until 1954.

Undeterred, Nevins the next year founded the Society of American Historians (SAH), an invitation-only group made up of those who wrote history for the general public yet maintained an elevated standard. Although he drafted many amateur historians into its ranks, individuals of the caliber of Douglas Southall Freeman, Nevins also filled its membership with scholars of literary talent such as Commager, Morison, Becker, Read, Crane Brinton, Schlesinger, Ralph Henry Gabriel, and more than twenty past and future presidents of the AHA. As with his magazine proposal, when he founded the SAH, Nevins was forced to withstand criticism. Charles and Mary Beard, for example, first signed on and then quit—partly because of the antagonism prompted by an article Nevins published in the *Saturday Review of Literature* in February 1939.[29]

Historians in the 1930s, Nevins complained in his magazine piece, had none of the wide reading public enjoyed earlier by James Truslow Adams, Vernon Parrington, or Van Wyck Brooks. Echoing Brooks's own earlier call in *America's Coming-of-Age* (1915) for a middle ground in culture between highbrow and lowbrow, Nevins worried that the writing of history was now polarized between the scholars (he called them "dryasdust" pedants) on one side and the popularizers on the other. History would regain its audience only if a middle ground could be established where the analysis and ideas of the scholars could be combined with the imagination and literary skill of the popularizers. Still, Nevins made it clear that the scholars were a greater threat than the popularizers, and he charged that "by far the larger number of our best historical writers are still to be found outside academic lines."[30] It is no surprise, considering his attack on academic history, that those on campus dismissed Nevins and the Society of American Historians as a group of journalists. Although his antagonists questioned the motives for his proposals, Nevins seems to have been inspired by a sincere wish to have history become a vehicle of broadly democratic discussion and enlightenment.

In keeping with these activist visions within the profession, in the late 1940s at Columbia Nevins organized the first oral history archives in the United States, certainly one of the most important moves he ever made. The first interview was conducted on May 18, 1948. Nevins not only orchestrated the fund-raising but also handled some of the first interviews.[31] Other universities and organizations slowly followed Columbia's lead in oral history, which grew in the last half the twentieth century into an important and widespread resource for historians. Together, Nevins and Commager worked to help secure a bequest to Columbia from Frederick Bancroft (or, as Henry later put it, "cajoling old Frederick Bancroft out of his millions"), which helped underwrite the oral history project.[32] Despite Commager's offhand comment, he and Nevins knew that on weekends when they weren't in Washington with Bancroft, representatives of Yale or Harvard probably were. Nevins remarked that Bancroft had likely so enjoyed the company of these scholars that he postponed his decision as long as possible.[33]

If Nevins performed an entrepreneurial role in the field of history, identifying needs and building the necessary institutions, it fit well with his interest in business history. In his opinion, the important role of business in shaping American culture and politics had been overlooked unjustifiably by his colleagues. While he was still pursuing a double life as a journalist and historian in 1929, two years before he took the position at Columbia, Nevins was already fretting about the omission of business history from historians' interests. "It is lamentable that so little has been done for the history of American business," he scolded his colleagues, "a subject whose romantic and almost epic possibilities" had not been sufficiently pursued.[34]

That business history had not caught on in the United States, that the

Allan Nevins in the late 1920s, when he and Commager met and became best friends.
(Courtesy of Library of Congress)

"superior enterprise" of our "merchant princes" or "courageous importers and traders" had not yet appeared on the pages of American historical chronicles, "was not merely capricious or accidental." No, Nevins charged in 1953, there was a "social prejudice" among historians, an Old World conviction that the tradesman stood in rank beneath "the warrior, the churchman, and the statesman." Further, historians saw business as vile, greedy, and antisocial. "Business was sordid," Nevins admitted, "and in part anti-social," so it was right that historians had focused on the darker side of business. But the time had arrived when the record needed to be made complete about the influence of business on the development of American society, and it could not be done so long as it was a topic that was too embarrassing to address directly. In a remarkable comment, even considering the context of the economic optimism and conservatism of the early fifties, Allan claimed that "it is impossible to write the history of the period since 1865 in the United States—of what is now nearly the whole past century—without giving business history a fundamental position; for it is more important to the development of the republic, and to an understanding of our civilization, than our political history or intellectual history."[35]

Consequently Nevins turned his own considerable energies to ushering business leaders onto the stage of American historical accounts. In the words of one historian, Nevins's "heroes were the conservative Grover Cleveland, the reformist but wealthy ironmaker Abram Hewitt, the traditionalist Hamilton Fish, and the super-entrepreneur John D. Rockefeller."[36] Nevins's works on these figures, like his accounts of Henry Ford and Eli Whitney, were respectful. William Leuchtenburg was a graduate student in Nevins's big lecture course on the United States since 1877, a course he later found himself teaching. "We all thought of him as very conservative, an apologist for capitalism, and not only because of his books such as his biography of Rockefeller," Leuchtenburg recalled. "One especially vivid memory is of him saying in a lecture that it was capitalists who had made possible victory in World War II. If it were not for big businessmen, he said, there would be two storm troopers standing beside him as he lectured at that moment."[37]

Nevins's admiration for the contributions of business leaders arose from similar characteristics within himself. Commager recognized in Nevins "that single-minded practicality which had no time for academic dalliance but concentrated on getting results." Another observer remembered "Allan's hurried pace across the campus, weighted down with two armfuls of books and portable typewriter to boot."[38] Should anyone expect any different from a man who had been raised on a farm, working fourteen hours a day?

But as Nevins's friend the Civil War historian Bruce Catton knew, his preoccupation with work did not entirely rule out extending himself to friends. "He was one of the busiest of living men," Catton acknowledged of Nevins, "but he was never too busy to give help to someone else. If you had a problem, you could lay it in front of him, certain that he would give it as much time as you needed, certain also that in the end he would strike a light to illumine the path you had to follow. To be sure, the moment he felt that he had done all he could do for you, he became very busy again. He had no time to spare; he would jump up, slip into his coat before you quite realized that the consultation was over, and go out of there, coattails adrift in the breeze. He was all yours as long as you needed him, but he had no time for small talk."[39]

In the midst of his frenetic life in the mid-1940s, Commager also found time to give the James W. Richards Lectures in History at the University of Virginia, which, when revised and compiled, became one of the most highly regarded books of his entire career, *Majority Rule and Minority Rights*. In this 1943 volume, Commager's tone was much more critically analytic than in his *Theodore Parker* seven years earlier or in his contributions to *The Growth of the American Republic*. In *Majority Rule*, as in his articles for the general press, Commager was, as Nevins later remarked, much more openly partisan, which brought out the best of his critical spirit and analysis.[40] So when he spoke of America in *Majority Rule*, it was not in the epic tones of an American studies writer. Instead, he described an American experience that produced the tangible if conflicting doctrines of majority rule and limited government.[41]

In this provocative little volume, Commager denigrated the widespread belief in America that there was a danger of a tyranny of the majority. This undemocratic conviction had many proponents: those who were "misleading" such as Tocqueville; such conservatives as John Adams, Alexander Hamilton, John Calhoun, Daniel Webster, and Joseph Story; and a more recent but less distinguished "motley group" including William Graham Sumner, Henry Cabot Lodge, H. L. Mencken, and Nevins's friend Walter Lippmann.[42]

The early hero in the volume is Jefferson, who Commager portrays as the defender of the great majority. Yet Commager was forced to admit that even Jefferson, in his response to the Alien and Sedition Acts, was quite afraid of the malevolent power of the majority in matters of intellectual and political freedom, which prompted the statesman to draft the Kentucky Resolutions to limit the power of political majorities. With Lincoln, who Commager quotes as saying that a majority "is the only true sovereign of the people," his memory is less acute.[43] Lincoln was no majoritarian: he was unwilling to support Stephen Douglas's call for majority rule in the western territories on the issue of slavery. Despite Commager's portrayal of him, Lincoln stood in that long line of American thinkers, from John Winthrop to Emerson and Thoreau, who rejected the majoritarian idea that moral right and wrong could be decided by a show of hands.

Commager found judicial review, the evaluation by the courts of the constitutionality and legality of the actions of other branches of the government, to be profoundly undemocratic. This process of court review became, in his volume, representative of the harm done to the political process by the exercise of minority instead of majority power. Commager found himself persuaded by those who argued that "there is really more justification for legislative or executive than for judicial determination of the law, for the decision of the political branches is subject to popular referendum, that of the judicial is not."[44]

Each time a court overturns a legislative act, Commager warned, it is rejecting a law that was reached by a majority vote both "for its wisdom" and its constitutionality. So why have "the one non-elective and non-removable element in the government" overrule the "two elective and removable branches" that the people have ratified themselves? Actually judicial review, he charged, seldom rests on legal insight. Instead, "for the most part judicial rejection of legislative acts has not been an exercise of learning but of discretion."[45] The judiciary has claimed for itself the right to determine the interests of society.

Although court review has been granted the appearance of operating behind a sacred veil of erudition, in reality "questions that have evoked judicial nullification of majority will have turned on considerations of policy rather than of law." Commager concluded that "almost every instance of judicial nullification of congressional acts appears, now, to have been a mistaken one." Further, conservatives and liberals have been equally blind to this fact, since each side complains when court decisions go against them but honors the process when it vindicates their policy choices.[46]

Yes, minority rights are important, Commager acknowledged, but "it is a characteristic of almost every anti-democratic philosophy that it purports to serve the welfare of the people but refuses to trust the judgment of the people on questions affecting their welfare." So Americans needed to realize that "the checks and balances of democratic politics" often "enable the minority to delay and defeat the majority." The important question, as Commager framed it, is whether these safeguards are necessary to protect minority rights or whether the majority will usually behave itself.[47] The answer he found was different from that proposed by those who had come of age in the last half of the twentieth century—those who had a sharpened sense of commitment to a multicultural society based around the preservation and rights of subcultures and ethnic identities.

Again it was Jefferson who Commager revived, this time as a model supporter of majority rule. Wasn't it Jefferson, after all, who endorsed Shays' Rebellion as proof that the people had enough liberty? "If the happiness of the mass of the people can be secured at the expense of a little tempest now and then," the Virginia statesman said in defense of the majority, "it will be a precious purchase." Further, Jefferson shuddered, "God forbid we should ever be twenty years without such a rebellion."[48]

Commager admitted that majorities in the South (and he should have said in the North) had oppressed blacks, and he acknowledged that this was hard to reconcile with his assurances about majority rule. In addition, the courts had done well evaluating laws addressing censorship, antievolution education, anticommunism, the flag salute, and similar issues. "It is here, if anywhere," he explained, "that judicial review has justified itself." Perhaps, he suggested with his partisanship showing, judicial review of economic matters (which had benefited conservatives) should be discontinued, but court review of civil liberties (which had benefited liberals) should be encouraged.[49]

And, Commager asked, his political commitments intruding further, why should we value "the technical question of constitutionality" higher than simple political wisdom? Since "much that is highly illiberal would be clearly constitutional," liberals needed to design a different attack. "The real battles of liberalism are not to be won in any court," he told his readers. "If we make constitutionality the test of civil rights legislation we are pretty sure to lose our case," because crafty conservatives would merely design their laws accordingly.[50]

But wouldn't a system of real majority rule oppress minorities? Wouldn't blacks, women, and other disfranchised groups be left with an intolerable lack of rights and protections in society? Commager answered that traditionally liberalism had put too much emphasis on "the individual or minority interest in minority rights." Instead, majorities had to be taught their interest in maintaining a society in which all the diverse subcultures and groups had equal rights. "The real task confronting us," he decided, "is to make clear to majorities that the interest of the whole of society is at stake in questions such as those raised by these hapless victims of legislation." Those in a majority needed a diverse multicultural society. This educational job was to be performed by institutions such as schools, churches, the press, and political parties.[51] So majorities could and should rule but needed to realize that their interests extended beyond themselves and that the majority had a genuine self-interest in protecting a diverse society.

Curiously, only four years before *Majority Rule* was published, Commager had praised judicial review in a *New York Times Magazine* article on John Marshall. The conservative Supreme Court justice "developed the doctrine of judicial review," and his opinions equated property interests with national interests and identified "business enterprise and business expansion with nationalism and constitutionalism." According to Commager, "Marshall's ultimate achievement" was actually "a very great one, and this notwithstanding the limitations of his learning and the illiberal slant of his mind."[52]

Why would a liberal like Commager be attracted to the likes of Marshall at the end of the thirties? The depression was still suffocating America, and the organizing power of the New Deal—an organizing impulse that could draw on the example of the nationalism and strong government Marshall embodied—seemed even more vital at the end of the decade. Marshall's unifying nationalism, represented by a strong judiciary that ruled on the common values that bound society, was also important for liberals during the thirties because there was a profound identity crisis in the country as the culture, under the pressure of the economic crisis at home and the threat from a rising fascism abroad, seemed as if it might wobble dangerously out of control. The need for a binding cultural nationalism is one of the reasons that liberals founded the American studies movement in the mid-1930s and turned toward studies of the American character. And, finally, as the prospect of global war appeared on the horizon, liberals realized in Marshall's nationalism a model of social and economic organization that might help them prepare for the approaching ordeal. As Commager phrased it, although Marshall was a conservative, he "helped to liberate the forces making for national growth and to strengthen national sentiment against the dark days of secession and war that were ahead."[53] Commager's lesson was not lost on liberals during the year of the Nazi-Soviet Pact.

But as the example of *Majority Rule* shows, Commager's romance with Marshall soon dissipated. He reverted to the lessons he had learned at the University of Chicago, where Andrew McLaughlin had taught his classes that constitutional history, contrary to Marshall, was not "judicial pronouncements, but great controversies, discussed and rediscussed by statesmen and the common people."[54] Motivated during World War II more by a desire to promote democracy than order or minority protections, Commager wrote *Majority Rule* and even explained the issues to his high school audience in his regular column in *Senior Scholastic*. He told his young readers that the Supreme Court's ruling that a local school could require school children to salute the American flag was "mistaken" and would likely "do more harm than good." But the correct response should not be to appeal to the courts to change the policy but to encourage public opinion to change so it would ask the legislature to alter the law. As in *Majority Rule*, Commager's sympathy was for legislative action because it is more democratic and participatory than judiciary action. "Has not the majority, in a democratic system, the right to make experiments, even to make mistakes?" he asked his high schoolers about the flag salute case. "And can we not trust our legislature to correct their mistakes? Is there, indeed, any hope for democracy if it is to depend, always, on correction from the judiciary?"[55]

Majority Rule struck a sympathetic chord in the liberal community and received a friendlier reception than most of his other books. Richard Hofstadter made his "historiography seminar students read it as a model of analysis," telling Commager that "judicial review has been one of my little peeves for years and I think you've made a swell statement of the case against it."[56] Sidney Hook, reviewing the volume for the *Nation*, found it "eloquent, forthright, and cogent." Pragmatist that Hook was, he emphasized that the process of democracy was a more significant value to protect than any simple piece of legislation that a majority decided on. Hardened by years of

Henry Steele Commager in the 1940s. (Courtesy of Lisa Commager)

Far Left infighting, Hook was sensitive to the threats to the democratic process of free inquiry and choice, and while he joined Commager in a fear of minority rule by the judiciary, Hook was more worried about protecting the intellectual freedom and voice of the majority.[57]

The subject of the tensions between the majority and minorities in America was not simply a casual interest of Commager's. In the 1950s he was still working to convince his fellow citizens that Felix Frankfurter, like Jefferson, was right to respect the democratic process of legislatures more than the edicts of the judiciary.[58] When in 1966 he wrote that "the place of judicial review in a democracy" had remained a central interest of his, Commager was acknowledging, twenty-three years after *Majority Rule and Minority Rights*, the continuing importance of that conflict in *Freedom and Order*, his major collection of essays on politics from the two decades following World War II.[59] Commager's curiosity about the bond that glued society together into a majority with at least a partly shared identity, as well as his worry about the problems that this bond created for minorities, prompted his long-standing investigation of the work of Tocqueville. This curiosity also provoked his fascination with character, in *The American Mind* (1950), as an expression of the identity and bonding values that the majority shared.

With his increasing visibility as an interpreter of American intellectual history, Commager in the early 1940s was invited to become a contributor to *The Literary History of the United States* (1948). Edited by Robert Spiller, Thomas H. Johnson, and a handful of others, the massive volume formed an assessment of the American cultural past and served as a benchmark from which other interpretations might depart. Spiller was a professor of literature at Swarthmore College and shortly would become one of the leading figures in the new American studies movement. Johnson taught literature at the Lawrenceville School in New Jersey and was a scholar who had compiled a multivolume collection of Puritan writings with Perry Miller, produced compilations of the poems of Emily Dickinson and Edward Taylor, and edited a collection of Jonathan Edwards's writings.

In early 1943 Commager agreed to write a section of the *Literary History of the United States* on the interaction of American history and ideas from 1890 to 1940, but in the end he fashioned a piece on reform in the Progressive period—perhaps because Spiller rearranged the assignments. Before he began the editors told him that the book was "a collaboration by a group of historical critics; not a collection of monographs by specialists." The volume was aimed at "the intelligent general reader" and needed to be interesting, so it "should be written in clear, rapid English." This was to be no detached and formalistic literary account but rather literary history with the emphasis on history, on "historical contexts." The project was intended to create a canon of works that intellectual historians and literary critics agreed were important to the American cultural experience and were "worthy of preservation."[60]

Although Spiller and Johnson taught literature and the volume was proclaimed a literary history, historians played a prominent role in the project. Johnson himself was a member of the Society of American Historians, the organization started by Nevins which promoted better, less technical writing and which welcomed nonacademic historians. Explaining to Commager the makeup of a gathering of contributors in New York, Spiller told him that "it should look more like a meeting of the Society of American Historians than of the Modern Language Association."[61] His comment revealed the extent to which the *Literary History of the United States* had been designed as a fusion of history and literature in the midcentury American studies, contextualist approach. The other contributors showed the interdisciplinary company Commager kept: Nevins, Curti, Henry Nash Smith, Henry Seidel Canby, Howard Mumford Jones, Joseph Wood Krutch, F. O. Matthiessen, Kenneth Murdock, Malcolm Cowley, Tremaine McDowell, Eric Goldman, Ralph Henry Gabriel, and Spiller, among others.

Commager's essay betrayed some of the weaknesses of his approach, particularly his habit of racing too quickly, with almost bibliographic brevity, over important figures or ideas. When it came time to address seminal thinkers in the period, he noted in an offhand manner that "Veblen was profound but scarcely constructive, and Lester Ward, who was constructive, was largely neglected. Holmes, greatest of American jurists, had no confidence in abstract notions of the Law or Justice and no faith in reform, but merely an unassailable conviction that he was not God, and that in a democracy people had a right to make fools of themselves."[62] Even if we acknowledge that in a survey such as *Literary History of the United States* an author must be concise, it is hardly worth introducing a figure if so little is said that he or she is given no substance.

Like his treatment of individual thinkers, Commager's portrayal of movements lacked sufficient depth. "Armies of reformers advanced upon the battlements of vested interests, bands of humanitarians waged guerrilla warfare upon every form of social injustice, visionaries imagined felicitous Utopias and some even indulged in them, less felicitously," he explained about the Progressives. "There was a youthful ardor to weed out abuses, democratize government, redistribute property, humanize industry, improve the lot of the workingman and the farmer, rescue the victims of social injustice, elevate the moral tone of society. It was the day of the music makers and the dreamers of dreams, of world seekers—though rarely of world forsakers."[63]

But there was also a critical edge to his portrayal of the Progressives. "There was much ado about the maldistribution of wealth," Commager complained, "but no attack upon wealth itself," nor any realistic "recognition of the economic basis of politics." Labor in the period was opportunistic without ultimate ends. Only a few of the muckrakers were driven by high ideals. Even Ida Tarbell, for example, wrote an admiring biography of the industrialist Elbert Gary. Commager listed children's reformers who ended up opposing the New Deal, crusaders against insurance fraud who celebrated Andrew Carnegie, and leaders in race relations who opposed the nomination of Brandeis to the Supreme Court. While Commager recognized in the Progressives a kinship with his own rather optimistic reformist tendencies, clear enough in his proud portrayal of their accomplishments, his frustration with their unwillingness to pursue their agenda far enough sharpened the edge of his criticism toward the entire period.[64]

In the 1940s Allan Nevins agreed to edit for Yale University Press eight volumes to be added to their Yale Chronicles of American History Series, and he was to choose the appropriate authors. Naturally, Nevins enlisted Commager to write one of the volumes, and because Henry currently was interested in the American character, he set about writing what would become his best-known book, *The American Mind*.[65] When Commager submitted the manuscript to Yale in 1947, he received a discouraging letter from Arthur Brook, head of the press. Nevins quickly interceded from England and told his colleague to ignore Brook. The real problem was that the book was too scholarly and profound and would be "above the heads of the average college undergraduate, though the exceptional undergraduate may well get from it intellectual inspiration that he will remember all his life." If only Commager would cut some of the chapters in two, making twice as many, and rewrite it slightly for a more general audience, it would be perfect. "It is your best book," his friend assured him, "and I think it will make your reputation as a critic (in the Arnoldian or Paul Elmer Moreian sense) as you have long since made your reputation as a historian."[66]

The next summer Nevins wrote an angry letter to Commager from his retreat in Windham, Vermont. Nevins had run into Brook in New York and heard that Henry had sent the press director a rude letter. Couldn't he have used some courtesy? Nevins asked. Yale had some rights in the book given that the Press had suggested it to Commager, and only a little cooperation was wanted. Originally Henry had signed to write "a cultural history of the recent past" in two volumes, but instead of this easy assignment he launched himself on "a long and brilliant volume of essays" that exceeded the acceptable length. So Nevins had encouraged Yale to write a new contract for the two volumes for the Chronicles series, plus a more popular, one-volume trade edition. Henry was now interested only in the trade book and had ignored the two scholarly volumes he owed the Press, and other completed books were being held up so that all could be issued together.

Further, Nevins accused him of being obstinate about well-intentioned criticism. The book was too scholarly, even for someone like Nevins. Its style needed to be simplified. Parts of the book, he told Commager, "read as if you were writing for Harold J. Laski and Felix Frankfurter instead of the general body of intelligent readers." Its lack of chronology made it accessible only to experts.

In a far less defensible request, Nevins asked him to conform to accepted standards of taste. Why did he need to include material that he and Morison would omit from *The Growth of the American Republic*? "Suppose you said to Sam Morison, 'We must have a section entitled "Abnormal Sexuality in American Fiction and Poetry," in which we shall discuss in the frankest language possible all the literature of incest, homosexuality, abnormal perversion, and Krafft-Ebbing impulses.' I would be much astonished if Sam did not protest." Even if Morison didn't raise his voice, publishers and educational authorities would. Because volumes in the Chronicles series were essentially textbooks, Nevins agreed to print anything that Commager would also use in the GAR. In addition, Nevins asked him to delete "expressions that will offend Catholics *unnecessarily*. So, too, with expressions that would unnecessarily offend Protestants, such as the statement that their clergy are intellectually inferior to the Catholic clergy (which I think untrue anyhow)."[67]

Nevins assured him that "we are not trying to censor you," but of course this was precisely what they were attempting to do. Not only was the request distasteful from one friend to another, it was inexcusable from one historian to another. Because the Chronicles were intended for all faiths and impressionable youth, Nevins explained, "great care and conservatism must be exercised in dealing with matters which impinge on religion and morals. The world would be intolerable if we all insisted on thrusting our views on such matters before those to whom we know they would be offensive. I don't think it cowardice which makes the Saturday Evening Post abstain from publishing articles on 'The Homosexual Problem in the United States'; I think it is good taste and good sense." Commager refused to concede. When

The American Mind was published his discussion of sexuality remained, although by now it seems hopelessly prudish instead of radical.[68]

This showed dramatically the difference between the two prominent Columbia historians. Nevins was a conservative, and Commager was not. Henry believed in the importance of dissent, debate, and disagreement, saying publicly what others did not accept. How else would the world change? How else would a historian influence his or her readers? How else could history be written honestly and with absolute integrity? How else could Jeffersonian intellectual freedom be preserved? Nevins apparently saw a different role for history and historians.

Commager's *American Mind* was an ambitious book. Contrary to Nevins's memory it encompassed the period from the 1880s to World War II. It was constructed as an intellectual history that discussed literature, philosophy, sociology, economics, historical thought, political theory, law, and architecture. But underlying the interdisciplinary inquiries was a curiosity about the American character. Like Henry Adam's *History of the United States of America during the Administrations of Jefferson and Madison*, which began with chapters analyzing the American mind in 1800 and ended with a chapter on the American character in 1817, Commager began with a chapter on the nineteenth-century American and ended with a chapter on the twentieth-century counterpart. Taking soundings like this at two distant points was a strategy used by Adams and Commager to detect a direction of change along the way and allow themselves to extrapolate a general tendency in the evolution of character. Throughout the volume Commager was sensitive to Americans' beliefs in the exceptionalism, mission, and destiny of the nation, and in his formulations he echoed those convictions himself.

Although it was published at midcentury, *The American Mind* was prompted by the same conviction that the liberal Left felt in the 1930s: that in a disorienting period of crisis, America needed to find and confirm rather than lose its best traits and values, its best identity and character. As the ideological crises of the 1930s evolved into the precipitous cold war of the later 1940s, it was still important for the American studies movement to concentrate on character, myth, and symbol. "The iron compulsion of events forced, temporarily, a reconsideration of basic assumptions, a restatement of traditional doctrines, and a revival of philosophical inquiries," Commager told the book's readers. "History searched out the nature of democracy and the mainsprings of the American national character in an effort to invoke the virtues of the past to justify the defense of the present."[69]

When Commager turned his efforts to writing on the American character and intellectual history in *The American Mind*, more than anything else he addressed the advent and development of pragmatism. His book was part of a wave of interest in pragmatism at midcentury. Richard Hofstadter, for example, had cited the pragmatic influence of Lester Ward in his *Social Darwinism in American Thought* (1944), and Morton White in 1949 had published his study of the impact of pragmatism on American ideas in his *Social Thought in America: The Revolt against Formalism*. Perry Miller, a few years after Commager's book appeared, edited a small volume of pieces, *American Thought: Civil War to World War I*, that traced the growth and manifestation of pragmatism in various disciplines of American ideas.[70] This period of the 1940s and 1950s was a time when much of the intellectual community was swinging from a dependence on ideological constructions to a more pragmatically based approach to analysis and ideas. Witness, for example, the dramatic shift in this period, the critical (important) crossing in critical (analytic) assumptions, from the ideological to the pragmatic within the New York Intellectuals.[71]

Involved in the same project as White, Hofstadter, and Miller, Commager described the "watershed" between the nineteenth- and twentieth-century outlooks. The old nineteenth-century "block-universe," as William James had called it, was an a priori thought system based on faith or supposition that came as one absolutist, inseparable belief unit. The new twentieth-century pragmatic and tentative universe was characterized by testing, doubt, scientific method, free will, open debate, empirical observation, partial solutions, and analysis of the consequences of actions. The old Newtonian universe had been reformed by evolution and economic and psychological forces.[72]

White's term for this revolution was the revolt against "formalism." It was the same shift from stasis to dynamism in the world that was lamented by Henry Adams and witnessed by Theodore Dreiser's Frank Cowperwood and Carrie Meeber. It was a changeover led in economics by Thorstein Veblen; in history by James Harvey Robinson, Charles Beard, and Carl Becker; in philosophy by Charles Sanders Peirce, William James, and John Dewey; in sociology by Lester Ward and E. A. Ross; and in law by Oliver Wendell Holmes Jr., Roscoe Pound, and Louis Brandeis.[73]

With the pragmatic agenda Commager had set for himself, it was hardly a surprise that his *American Mind* sported as a frontispiece, sternly surveying the rest of the book, a painting of William James. It was James as a dissenter that Commager admired. "That pragmatism challenged authority, dissolved institutions, destroyed security, cannot be denied," Commager announced happily, "for James himself admitted that he was 'willing that there should be real losses and real losers, and no total preservation of all that is.' It provided a convenient rationalization, if not the inspiration, for the attack on the State, the Law, Sovereignty, and many other concepts which had enjoyed the finality of Euclidian axioms and which had served to foreclose rather than provoke inquiry."[74]

So pragmatism was just the sort of radicalism that dissenters needed, and McCarthyist suspicions be damned. At midcentury it was not only intellectual repression, conformity, and political totalitarianism that needed to be fought. The conservative and a priori philosophical assumptions that allowed bad ideas to rule also needed to be attacked. A tentative and dissenting pragmatic outlook was not only the approach Commager wanted to help promote in the world. Pragmatism was also one of the tools, the weapons, that needed to be used to create the new world.

The book's weakness, as with much of Commager's scholarly work, is its encyclopedic breadth at the expense of analytic depth. Although he announced that it was "an interpretation rather than a detailed chronicle," it read more as chronicle than interpretation.[75] Much of the book is so general that it inspires challenge instead of confidence. It depends too often on summaries instead of careful and precise delineations. His final pages are devoted to a list of questions about American thought that he leaves unanswered. Worst, the questions address matters that he has earlier claimed to answer in the book, so it undermines what authority he has built.

Together with his earlier *Theodore Parker*, this book showed Commager to be a historical counterpart to Van Wyck Brooks, a historical person of letters who was interested in anecdote, description, and narrative. But because Commager rushed through catalogues of individuals who represented each tendency, the reader is whipped by an unending list of names like grains of sand in the wind until the trail can no longer be found. While there was more interpretation in this outing than in *Theodore Parker*, still he often sped breezily though a crowd of thinkers with only a tip of the hat.

Moreover, for someone who once thought of writing a dissertation on Henry Adams, Commager was often strikingly optimistic in his account of American thought. Yes, sometimes he expressed discouragement in his volume with the progress of America.[76] But frequently, in his celebration of New over Old World values, he adopted the tone of George Bancroft. Clearly, Commager was more optimistic in 1950 than he would be amid the problems that beset America twenty years later.

The book achieved an instant popular celebrity when it was published, but it received mixed reviews. In the *Saturday Review*, for which Commager wrote regularly, Dixon Wecter praised it warmly as a worthwhile successor to Parrington's work. Morton White, then an assistant professor of philosophy at Harvard, claimed in the *New Republic* that it was "a courageous book" and maintained that Commager had "bravely exposed himself to snipers of all varieties—from those who will shake their heads at his philosophic interpretations to those who will be horrified by his sociological bravado and his literary taste." Not least, White admired the courage it took to stand up for Parrington in what he considered an anti-Parringtonian atmosphere. Commager's critics, White predicted, "will be taking potshots at him from their comfortable holes and nests, venturing nothing and losing nothing." Yes, there were problems with the book, but it had the virtue of "richness and breadth."[77]

Arthur Schlesinger Jr. was more ambivalent about the volume. Although Commager had never written with such "felicity and charm," with such "wit and urbanity and penetrating insight," the book hardly justified its title. To construct a book demonstrating the existence of American exceptionalism and character "would involve a much more systematic comparative study of ideas and behavior, particularly as between the United States and Western Europe." Richard M. Weaver, although he appreciated the book, thought that it was caught in several contradictions. Foremost among these was that in the volume Commager proclaimed an optimism of destiny and progress but then had to admit that in many areas (such as popular culture, degraded politicians, and poor industrial craftsmanship) the nation had devolved from an earlier standard.[78]

The review that most wounded Commager appeared anonymously in the *New Yorker*.[79] The book was a "high, daring dive," said the reviewer, that "hits the water in one of the most resounding belly-whoppers that the academic swimming hole has seen in years." Commager had depended too much on casual observations that could not be demonstrated, such as his statement that " 'the American had spacious ideas, his imagination roamed a continent, and he was impatient with petty transactions, hesitations, and timidities.' " Although the book was competent, the critic concluded that Commager's "outstanding achievement is that he never comes up with a single really fresh or striking idea" in the entire volume.[80]

Time magazine was no easier on him. In a disdainful review wrapped around his photo, readers were advised that "Commager's fast look through the library stacks results in just what might have been expected: an academic catchall of social, literary and economic interpretations that illustrate the American mind less than they indicate Professor Commager's lack of time." Because he was a public intellectual who lectured, wrote for Sunday newspaper supplements, and advised government, *Time* suggested he was a dilettante. Real historians, the magazine predicted, would find Commager's observations routine, while the layperson would turn to works that employed more direct evidence.[81]

So the forties were an important period for Commager's scholarly development. With his elevation to a respected position on the notable Columbia faculty, his status as a highly regarded historian was confirmed. The slim *Majority Rule and Minority Rights*, Commager's most analytically rigorous book, fueled his developing commitment to analyze the tensions between freedom and order and between the rights of majorities and those of minorities. The analysis of these political tensions marked the beginning of his lifelong fascination with Tocqueville and his increased interest and participation in the civil liberties battles that became so central to his career. Further, Commager was invited to contribute to *The Literary History of the United States*, the benchmark intellectual history of his generation. His essay in this volume helped lead him into the kind of broad intellectual approach that nearly immediately showed itself in the work for which he is best known: *The American Mind*, published in 1950.

Choosing to write as a character historian in *The American Mind* instead of operating with a more specialized focus such as constitutional history, Commager ran contrary to the newer trends in history after World War II. Although he remained a prominent historian, he was not considered to be working at the forefront of his field. Gradually, younger historians began to consider him passé. Their evaluation of him would have been similar to what he wrote of Sinclair Lewis in *The American Mind*. "He belonged to that school of historians content with description and not curious to know the causes of things," Commager remarked about the novelist. "Sooner or later he turned his searchlight on almost every aspect of American society and on almost every problem that engaged public attention, but a searchlight illumines only the surface of what it touches. He left few areas of American life unexplored but none surveyed, few issues unprobed but none explained."[82]

Yet the strength of *The American Mind* derived from Commager's broad curiosity and wide-ranging knowledge, so evident in his mastery of minor novelists and poets who escaped even the attention of literature professors. Further, he showed an ability to trace the influence of such thinkers as Lester Ward, who foreshadowed the pragmatic revolution, to twentieth-century figures such as Louis Brandeis and Frank Lloyd Wright who applied the ideas of that revolution.

Despite his book's weaknesses, Commager was more courageous and ambitious than many subsequent intellectual historians. Intellectual history since the 1960s, for the most part, has been built around multiple biographies, short sketches within a book about a collection of individuals. That strategy is more precise and allows a more confident interpretation. Commager, by contrast, tried to catch the general sweep of tendencies and focus on those ideas to a greater extent than he did on individuals. His approach can produce a less assured and more vulnerable study, in which he skates on thin ice, but while it is less specific, it is also braver than a cautious history.

II

Freedom and the
American Century

CHAPTER 4

Protecting Liberalism in
World War II,
1939-1947

If, in the 1940s, Commager was drawn to writing in periodicals, there were important reasons. With the rise of Nazi Germany in the late 1930s, the future of democracy was in danger. Intellectual activists, public commentators—whether or not they were also professional scholars—had an important role to play in the protection of intellectual freedom. Historians, in Commager's view, should earn no exemption from this task.

Although not central to his writing, foreign policy had been an interest of his for at least fifteen years before World War II. The diplomatic conflict between the United States and Britain over the Oregon territory was the subject of his thesis and his first scholarly article. Yet it was not until the end of the thirties that Commager, like the rest of the nation, awoke to the increasing urgency of global affairs. Like many in this period, he had learned the lesson of World War I that the United States should not waltz into conflict with idealistic illusions or with the idea that a war was naturally an "irrepressible" and unavoidable conflict.[1]

But some wars were more imperative. On the front page of the *New York Times Magazine* on New Year's Day 1939, under a drawing of a torch-bearing Roman warrior battling a Nazi beast, Commager launched a series of articles encouraging America to defend democracy in the world. For the next two years he took it as his responsibility to nudge his fellow citizens to prepare for a battle to defend free institutions.

Yet it was not war that Commager encouraged but measures by which America could do the most to ensure democracy short of military conflict. The solution was to meet the challenge in the realm of philosophy and economic and social policy instead of building a stronger military machine. Already wary of strident anticommunism in 1939, he now saw fascist Germany replacing the Soviet Union as an example that could be used to attack civil liberties in the United States. But democracy was vulnerable only if it failed "to fulfill its promises." If Americans employed "the weapons of fascism or communism" to fight the enemy—if, that is, overheated anticommunism or superpatriotism overrode civil liberties at home—then we would have allowed ourselves to be defeated without a fight. So censorship, oppression, Red-baiting, witch-hunting, or promoting the Ku Klux Klan or Blackshirts were all "treasonable" offenses. Invoking Jefferson, Commager warned that the inescapable "duty of democracy is to remain democratic" and that "every act of suppression is a confession of guilt."[2]

Commager's pursuit of a moral and philosophical rather than a military answer to the conflict with totalitarianism was characteristic of the longing in America for community, identity, and democracy (both political and economic) during the 1930s. This national thirst for community fueled the American studies movement in the mid-1930s and its search for an American character and mind that could bind a confused and centrifugal society together.

In the summer of 1940 Commager took another step out into the public arena on behalf of war preparation when he agreed to allow a letter to be sent out above his name for membership in the Committee to Defend America by Aiding the Allies (CDAAA). Directed nationally by William Allen White, the committee chose Commager as a respected figure to sign the letter that would be mailed out to members of the history profession to try to form a subcommittee of historians within the larger organization. The committee's program, as suggested in the letter, called for open American sympathy for the Allies, the sale to the Allies of war planes and other weapons, a provision of surplus agricultural commodities, and a ban against the sale of weapons to Axis nations.[3]

On the committee's letterhead were listed an impressive, if incompatible, group of American intellectuals, including Van Wyck Brooks, Archibald MacLeish, and Lewis Mumford, who considered themselves on the liberal left but who were seen by many as patriotic cultural conservatives. There were more convincing conservatives such as Columbia president Nicholas Murray Butler and Johns Hopkins historian Arthur Lovejoy. Also listed was Dean Acheson, rather early in his career.

Perhaps the most interesting members were Freda Kirchwey, editor of the *Nation*, and Frederick Schuman, a leftist from Williams College who later played a minor role in the contested Waldorf Conference in 1949, whose participants anticommunists accused of being soft on communism. Both Kirchwey and Schuman would later be called fellow travelers by anticommunists such as Sidney Hook.[4] Kirchwey, Schuman, and other leftists supported the Committee to Defend America because of their antifascism (despite the Nazi-Soviet Pact) and their desire to protect the Soviet experiment from the ravages of Hitler's ambitions.

Reinhold Niebuhr and Max Lerner were also listed on the letterhead, representative of those who were in the orbit of the New York Intellectuals. And Commager was on the list. So a wide spectrum of political beliefs existed in the committee, showing the common resolve much of the American intellectual community was forming on this issue in 1940—although adherents of each different political tendency had their own separate reasons for supporting the committee's agenda.

By the early 1940s, even before the entry of the United States into the war, Commager had already committed himself to what would become the axioms of midcentury liberalism: interventionism on behalf of democratic freedom, and a strong presidency to achieve that goal. It was an ethic that he would support only for two decades. Later, in the 1960s, in the shadow of Vietnam and domestic unrest in the nation, Commager would abandon both sides of the doctrine. Especially after the Kennedy presidency, American intervention in global matters appeared arrogant and self-serving, and Congress would seem a much safer and more democratic architect for policy than a potentially reckless executive.

Yet in October 1940 Commager was explaining in the *New York Times Magazine* the case for interventionism and moral leadership that Henry Luce echoed four months later in his *Life* editorial "The American Century." The isolationist ideas of the previous two decades, Commager found, "curiously dovetail" with Hitler's assurances that European antagonisms were no threat to the United States. America could not let the disillusionment from the end of World War I continue to infect it as it faced a rising Nazi power.[5]

If Commager encouraged the population to repudiate isolationism, he tried to soften the request by pretending it was hardly a reversal. Isolationism had not really been the tradition of the United States, because "roughly since the Eighteen Nineties, the United States has been a world power" involved in affairs around the globe. It was only after World War I that the virus of isolationism attacked the national body and infirmity caused the United States to further "the debacle of Europe." Sadly, the United States refused "responsibility for the new world order that should have been constructed," staging a "philosophical and cultural repudiation of that Old World of which we are inextricably a part."[6] This final comment was ironic, as a rejection of the Old World was a central feature of those writers who Commager and the American studies movement spent so much time celebrating at midcentury.

A few months later he assured his readers that although a strong presidency was required to carry out an active international role, a powerful executive was no threat to the country. Actually, he affirmed, "with the single exception of Polk, all the 'strong' Presidents were 'great' Presidents, and all the 'great' Presidents were 'strong' Presidents." Was Lincoln a threat to our political freedom? No. Yet Lincoln, who "himself admitted that he had gone pretty far," knew "that it was better to save the Union without a Constitution than the Constitution without a Union." Conversely, the period of congressional control produced only disastrous results such as Reconstruction. Similarly, Commager advocated strong executive leadership to guide the country through the war. "American liberties, American democracy, what we call the American way of life," he concluded, "have not only survived the growth of Presidential power but have, in the past, flourished under it."[7] Later, after 1965, he must have blanched when he remembered promoting this opinion.

Where did Commager's opinions on the war stand in relation to others in the intellectual community? After their fears that war would create a powerful American state became eclipsed by the prospect of totalitarian threats abroad, most conservatives left the isolationism of the interwar years and quickly subscribed to the antifascist and then, after the war, the anticommunist crusade. Liberals, of whom Commager might serve as representative, joined the war effort early because they had fewer fears of a large American state to impede their enthusiasm. Surprisingly, even many radicals and socialists came to support the war. The prospect of supporting a capitalist power in the war prolonged the hesitation of some socialists to support the United States, but the Moscow Trials and the Nazi-Soviet Pact in the 1930s had ruined American radicals' romance with the Soviet Union and much of the Far Left anyway, leaving them free to support American involvement.

Within the profession of history there was a division over the war, although it was more pronounced at first. Especially before Pearl Harbor, the isolationists could count the support of such historians as Charles Beard, Merrill Jensen, William Hesseltine, Fred Shannon, Thomas Cochran, Frank Freidel, Henry May, and Commager's friend Merle Curti.[8] Like many other observers, Curti worried that an overheated war patriotism was silencing scholarship as it had in World War I.[9] "Being somewhat a pacifist I came, in contrast with Commager, slowly and reluctantly to see the need of armed intervention if Hitlerism was to be destroyed," Curti later recalled. "I remembered the eminent historians who came to regret their urgency in pushing American intervention in the Great War and who subsequently looked on their writing as propaganda."[10] Yet Curti finally became reconciled to the war effort.

Opposed to the isolationists were interventionists within the literary-historical community such as Nevins, Archibald MacLeish, Van Wyck Brooks, Lewis Mumford, Bernard DeVoto, Howard Mumford Jones, and Waldo Frank.[11] MacLeish and Brooks, who had claimed that the isolationists were, in MacLeish's words, "irresponsibles," had infuriated those isolationists in the Beard-Curti camp and in the *Partisan Review* circle.

Following his involvement with the Committee to Defend America by Aiding the Allies in 1940, Commager became even more publicly active in his support for the Allied cause in the war. Precedent existed for this kind of involvement by historians he respected. Andrew McLaughlin, the professor of constitutional history who so influenced him at the University of Chicago, had enthusiastically supported the Allied effort during World War I, had written for the Committee on Public Information, and had lectured in England promoting democracy and criticizing German autocracy.[12] Samuel Eliot Morison, Commager's collaborator on *The Growth of the American Republic*, had joined the staff of Woodrow Wilson's inquiry committee during World War I and wrote position papers proposing solutions to border disputes in Europe. Early in 1919 Morison got himself appointed to the Russian division of the U.S. delegation to the Paris peace talks. More than two decades later, in the spring of 1942, Morison convinced Franklin Roosevelt to appoint him to a Navy position to write the official history of naval operations in World War II.[13] Commager's future friend Barbara Tuchman began working for the Office of War Information in New York in 1943.[14]

In October 1943, at the request of General Henry H. Arnold, chief of the Army Air Forces, a group of nine historians were assembled under the auspices of the War Department to predict from the evidence of the past and present how well the Nazi's military power would be able to withstand the Allied assault. Commager was among them. Others in the circle were Major Frank Monaghan, who had been a professor of history at Yale and who gathered the group; Carl Becker from Cornell, Arthur Cole of Western Reserve University, Louis Gottschalk of the University of Chicago, and Elias

Lowe of Princeton; Dumas Malone, Commager's colleague at Columbia; Bernadotte Schmidt of the University of Chicago; and J. Duane Squires of Colby Junior College. The historians read secret reports and plans and listened to dozens of witnesses before filing their prediction in January 1944. The War Department later called the report "a remarkably accurate forecast of the things that ultimately came to pass."[15] During the late autumn, as the report was being fashioned, Commager commuted from New York to Washington two or three days a week in his position as special consultant, and the War Department arranged a room for him and "good priority on plane transportation."[16]

In addition, beginning in 1943 Commager advised the War Department on how it should organize the production of its internal war history. Apparently Arthur Schlesinger Jr., Archibald MacLeish, Allan Nevins, Guy Stanton Ford, Conyers Read, and others were also interviewed for suggestions about how to set up the military history. The recommendation that emerged from these interviews was that a historical branch should be formed in the Military Intelligence Division of the War Department.[17] Retired Brigadier General Oliver Spaulding filed a dissenting opinion, arguing that a separate division did not need to be set up, because the Army War College could do the work, but he lost.[18] Commager was one of a half-dozen individuals appointed to the Historical Branch's Advisory Committee, which was split evenly between civilians and military officers.[19]

The British, Commager suggested from his position on the Advisory Committee, provided a good example of war history because they conceived of it "in a somewhat more comprehensive way than we do." With his extensive contacts in England, he was able to tell his colleagues on the Advisory Committee how the British orchestrated their own official historical work. The Americans, he advised, needed to translate the war record immediately into a rough narrative form that later could be improved on. These "first narratives" would function as the core of the project. Each military unit should have some trained historians to organize source material, as it is developed, into these first narratives. To aid the process, military leaders needed to submit monthly diaries.

The real history, of course, would have to be written over a longer span of time by future historians. The task of the Historical Branch of the War Department would be to preserve material and put the record into shape for subsequent historians. As Commager foresaw it, the War Department could publish a short popular history, a series of histories of special subjects for scholars, and a large multivolume official history after the war. During the production of these larger projects, the War Department might consider releasing some popular pamphlets, written more as public relations than real history, for immediate popular consumption.[20]

As a historian who already had sharpened his talents at addressing the general public in short pieces—whether high school students in his regular column or the educated citizenry in his *New York Times Magazine* articles— it is little wonder that Commager was asked by the government to provide a series of talks to be broadcast to Europeans on the shortwave radio. The Office of War Information (OWI) contacted him early in 1944 and asked him to record a half-dozen or more "nonpolitical talks" on how the president and vice president were elected in the American system. During the election year it would be useful for Europeans to know how the electoral college and other processes worked. Similarly, on the advice of Norman Cousins, editor of the *Saturday Review of Literature*, the OWI asked if they could combine two of Commager's *Senior Scholastic* high school columns into one piece for the OWI's magazine *USA*, a digest publication sent abroad.[21]

In the final year of the war the OWI continued to ask Commager for contributions. In August 1944 it requested that he take part in a radio program for the anniversary of the Atlantic Charter, which had been drawn up in August 1941 by Winston Churchill and Franklin Roosevelt. This occasion was an opportunity, he was told, to talk about the United Nations conferences that were beginning to shape the postwar world. Commager was assured that he had done "some of the best scripts we have ever had for overseas use." A few months later the OWI asked him to explain the tradition of American isolationism to the Europeans. In May 1945, three months before the atomic bombs were dropped on Japan, the OWI wondered whether he would do a talk suggesting that a constitutional government is not necessarily a democratic government—a point that had been made in David Rowe's book *China among the Powers*.[22]

After the war Commager continued to lend his services to the government. Into the 1950s he still served as a historical adviser. Further, he lectured to German prisoners of war at Fort Getty, Rhode Island; talked to Foreign Service trainees at the Department of State; wrote some ten-page biographies of famous American political people for *Amerika Illustrated*, a State Department publication for the Soviets; and as late as 1951 spoke to students at the Armed Forces Information School.[23]

With the immediate crisis of the war now in the past, it is not clear why he continued to scurry around giving talks, meeting government trainees, and writing biographical sketches for Soviet consumption, especially when that sort of work meant sacrificing his research time and scholarly productivity. One possibility is that Commager received greater personal or ideological satisfaction from his government work than from his scholarly endeavors. Another answer, for at least some of these projects, is that he did them to earn money. *Amerika Illustrated* paid him one hundred dollars an article, and he was unwilling to let them reprint without pay articles that he had already published elsewhere.[24]

Yet perhaps there was not an unbridgeable canyon between his scholarship and his public activity during and after the war. In the 1940s his study of American democracy that culminated in *Majority Rule and Minority Rights*, his inquiry into American ideas that found its way into *The Growth of the American Republic*, and his meditation on the American character that became the backbone of *The American Mind*—all served as the script for his speeches to Americans and the British about their duty to preserve democratic freedoms. Actually, the direction of learning here might be reversed; perhaps it was Commager's examination of the issues surrounding World War II and the need to support the Allies that led to the insights he wove into his books in the 1940s. As the *Saturday Review* remarked at the end of the decade, "*The American Mind*, his second work without collaborator, crystallizes his findings on the Yankee mainspring, so valuable to the OWI and, even now, the War Department, for which he went to Britain, France, and Belgium."[25]

Early in the 1940s, Commager and Nevins were able to collaborate on a project that they hoped would demonstrate the proper role of a historian. In 1942, shortly after Nevins had finished a year as Harmsworth Professor of American History at Oxford, the two friends published *The Pocket History of the United States*, a mass-market paperback issued by Pocket Books. Over the years the book appeared under a variety of titles with very little change in text except an occasional chapter appended to update it.

Both the U.S. State Department and the British government wanted an inexpensive book they could give away to the English people during the war, and when Nevins and Commager agreed to do it they were under great pressure to finish quickly. According to legend, the two men divided the work and wrote it in thirty days. Although the book was originally written for Pocket Books under the title *The Pocket History of the United States* and distributed free in England, it was published simultaneously in hardback for the U.S. market by Little, Brown under the title *America, the Story of a Free People*. Apparently the authors earned royalties only on the Little, Brown sales. Then, in 1945, as the war wound down, Random House released the book in its Modern Library series under the title *A Short History of the*

United States. By the time the fifth edition of the *Pocket History* was issued in 1967, the volume had already sold two million copies since its first edition in 1942 and now had chapters discussing the presidencies of Eisenhower, Kennedy, and Johnson.[26]

The five-hundred-page volume, which was compact for an entire American survey, was intended to remind the English (and perhaps other nations) at the beginning of World War II of America's commitment to democracy and liberty. The book was meant not only to reassure those nations worried about the future of liberty but also by example to encourage them to pursue their own commitment to freedom.

The preface, obviously written by Commager, was a tribute to the broad and resonant histories of the nineteenth century, the works of the grand narrative historians and their sweeping visions—a tribute to that style of American history that became so embattled in the last half of the twentieth century. In the span of only two and a half pages, he was able to summon the ghosts of some of the most eloquent and ardent, if also repudiated, historians of the American past. Invoking the tone of George Bancroft, Commager assured his readers that American history "recapitulates the history of the race." (By this he meant the human, not the Caucasian, race.) Like Francis Parkman in *France and England in North America*, Commager reported that on the North American continent the greatest forces of the modern world have battled one another in open view. Like others who wrote within the context of the American studies assumptions—historians and literary critics as diverse as Vernon Parrington, Perry Miller, and F. O. Matthiessen—Commager noted of the country that "from its earliest beginnings, its people have been conscious of a peculiar destiny, because upon it have been fastened the hopes and aspirations of the human race." Further, echoing Thomas Jefferson's defense of the "New World" in his *Notes on the State of Virginia* (1787), Commager insisted that Europeans were wrong in their assumption that America was "colorless and prosaic." Instead, he emphasized, it stood proudly, "wonderfully dramatic and picturesque and cast in a heroic mold," with ineffable natural beauty and talented leaders. The book, he admitted, was written to address the crisis of the war. As he explained, "To a generation engaged in a mighty struggle for liberty and democracy, there is something exhilarating in the story of the tenacious exaltation of liberty and the steady growth of democracy in the history of America."[27]

The epigraph to the volume, an excerpt from a poem by Stephen Vincent Benét, spoke of the common men who "made this thing, this dream," and assured readers that "it shall be sustained." The opening chapter, surely produced by Commager, upheld this optimism. The great North American heartland was a basin in which people from diverse backgrounds collected "on equal terms. It became a great pool in which a new democracy and a new American sentiment developed." That French and Mexican sovereignty over these western lands would dissipate when confronted by the British-American advance was "inevitable."[28]

Nevins, whose writing was more factual, direct, concise, and informative than Commager's, but not as imaginative, lyrical, or graceful, also was optimistic, although because his style was less effusive his optimism seemed more contained. While the Americans had many advantages over the British, Nevins explained in his chapter on the Revolution, their greatest was the leadership of those such as Washington. When finally the British were driven away, "the homely, hard-working farmers, shopkeepers, and artisans were free to create a civilization after their own hearts." In this new society "heredity, wealth, and privilege counted for less, and human equality for more"; now "the standards of culture and manners were temporarily lowered, but those of equity were raised."[29]

Commager, who followed with a chapter on the Constitution, announced that "it would have been difficult to assemble at a dinner table anywhere in the world in 1787 more talent and character; certainly no Old World group could have boasted more impressive figures" than those who gathered to rewrite the fundamental American legal blueprint. Yet the dissenter in him would not allow Commager to overlook the convention's political conservatism. Because Jefferson, Patrick Henry, Thomas Paine, Samuel Adams, and Christopher Gadsden were absent, Commager complained that "the radicals, in short, were not adequately represented."[30]

Nevins, who might have been expected to send his English readers a conservative account of the benefits of American business, instead wove a more ambivalent message about the late nineteenth century. Yes, business had produced a strong society, he acknowledged, but it had its dangers as well. The corporation's legal identity as a fictitious person allowed it to "enjoy all the legal advantages but escape most of the moral responsibilities of a human being." The growth of trusts had produced more efficiency, "but all at a heavy cost to society." So while Andrew Carnegie had called this system "triumphant democracy," Nevins pointed out that "others were quite willing to admit that it was triumphant, but not at all sure that it was democracy." What Nevins wrote concerning "the confusion in the American mind" about corporations, he might also have noted about himself. "Americans feared big business," he confided to the English, "but they admired it too."[31]

This message to the English and other readers of the volume was sent in the voice of the narrative historians, leavened with the analysis that was expected from professional historians by World War II. Those who want to witness the continued presence of literary grace and wide vision in American historiography in the 1940s need only read the final paragraph of Commager's chapter on the Constitution. So the volume that Nevins and Commager sent to England was not only a civics lesson during wartime on the benefits of democracy but also an example of the continuing ability of professional historians to communicate with the general public, the aptitude of certain scholars to orchestrate a public discourse that could be read by sophisticated historians and educated citizens alike, and the ongoing capability of some historians to address contemporary problems and issues by appealing to the example of the past.

An important bond between Commager, Nevins, and Morison was their common belief in the importance of maintaining narrative and literary qualities in historical writing. They opposed the movement in the discipline, over the course of the twentieth century, into a narrower, more specialized, and analytic focus and away from the nineteenth-century emphasis on history as literature and story. The profession of history, of course, had experienced only what other fields in the humanities and social sciences also had witnessed. A wave of intellectual specialization had swept through America accompanying the Industrial Revolution in the late nineteenth century, and fields that had once been populated by amateurs pursuing an avocation were increasingly made the province of professionals who earned money and were expected to carry credentials and uphold standards.

Not surprisingly, this gravitation toward specialization and expertise changed how history was written. No longer were dramatic narratives, engaging stories, grand themes, surrounding scenery, moral lessons, or literary flourish valued in the field. The need by the turn of the century, many historians believed, was for more modest but more reliable accounts, no matter that these works, these monographs, were often narrow, arcane, and poorly written. J. Franklin Jameson, one of the founders of the AHA, wrote in 1891 that it was "good second-class work" that history as a science now needed. He meant that history needed to become more technically proficient, better at its skill, and that, because it was a cumulative field, small bricks had to be formed before the larger structures could be built.[32]

Commager, Nevins, Morison, and others—some of the more prominent of them associated with the Society of American Historians, an organization that cared about readability—were not ready to wave good-bye to the benefits of historical narratives with literary integrity, works of the sort written by

Samuel Eliot Morison (center), holding the pennant in 1940 of the Harvard-Columbus Expedition that retraced Columbus's route. (Courtesy of Library of Congress)

Francis Parkman or William Prescott. The widespread publication of technical and jargonistic monographs had lost historians their audience, and history could not be a public discourse important to the civic culture unless it engaged in a dialogue with a democratic audience. If historians were occupied in an incestuous discussion only with those who had graduated from similar programs and held similar convictions, it was a waste of time. Sophisticated analysis did not need to be sacrificed on the literary altar; narrative and analytic interpretation were not mutually exclusive.[33]

Together Morison and Nevins, according to Commager, were America's two greatest narrative historians. He believed that Morison was a better writer than Nevins, although the latter had his individual strengths. "Morison is the successor of Parkman," Henry later explained. "Allan is the successor of a group of people like Rhodes, and Oberholzer. . . . Allan was not a conscious stylist as Sam Morison was, or as Parkman was. But how he admired these people."[34]

While Commager was probably not as strong a scholarly historian as either Nevins or Morison, he was a better writer for the general public on the broad themes that need to be addressed in history textbooks, a more lyrical, imaginative, and graceful writer than his two friends, who were eager to enroll him in their textbook projects. Though Commager was always the junior member of those relationships, both socially and as part of the textbook team, that seems never to have bothered him. His friendships with Nevins and Morison, under whatever circumstances, were a matter of great pride for him.

England, America's closest ally in the war, was a nation filled with significance for Commager, Morison, and Nevins. Morison, who was saturated nearly to caricature with New England style, might be forgiven for looking to England with such high regard, given that he was raised in its cultural shadow. Nevins, raised at a farm crossroads in Illinois, had to work harder to fall under England's spell. For Commager England seemed to signify the cultural nobility that his own broken family had lacked in his childhood.

Nevins once noted Henry's affinities, "including a strong Anglophilism in books, manners, and outlook."[35] Allan could not have exempted himself from that same inclination. At the first suggestion of war Nevins rushed to England as Harmsworth Professor of American History at Oxford during the winter and spring of 1941.[36] Naturally, few of Nevins's friends would have ignored the opportunity to travel to Europe during the war, not to mention fill a prestigious chair at Oxford. "I envy you having a good reason for going," Walter Lippmann assured him, "and so sharing in what I really believe to be the greatest human experience that men have passed through for many centuries."[37] While in Britain Nevins gave two courses at Trinity College, Oxford, one course at the University of Birmingham, and was scheduled to speak twice at the Royal Institution and at "various other places" as well.[38]

By the time Nevins arrived, Oxford had already been nearly abandoned by students and faculty who were enlisting in the military. Shortly "the British Ministry of Information asked me to come to its offices in London, and there requested of me that I give up to a considerable extent my teaching duties in Oxford and Birmingham, and devote myself to propagandist work for the British government," he noted. "That seemed to me a much more useful employment in wartime than mere teaching to slender audiences could possibly be, and I was therefore equipped with the proper credentials and sent out on the road."[39]

So to a large extent Nevins's Harmsworth year was spent outside the confines of Oxford, lecturing in various towns. There he told his British audiences that the United States was going to enter the war soon and help them, though he later admitted that his opinions were "quite without warrant." Nevins assured them about American strength and raw materials and "heartened them greatly by these discourses."[40]

When America finally joined the war, Nevins offered his services to the U.S. Office of War Information. That agency asked him to go to Australia and New Zealand to tell them of the American interest in their welfare and discuss the role that the United States was playing in the war, and he remained there eight months. In 1942 he returned to England to help the British secondary schools adopt an American studies curriculum.[41]

It was not only the immediate crisis of the war that sent Nevins to Britain, since after the conflict ended he continued his public activity there. In 1946 he went to London as a public affairs officer for the American embassy. It was important, he decided, to do something to prevent the British Labour Party, which was in power, from sympathizing too closely with the Soviets and distrusting the United States.[42] Nevins was obviously happy making a contribution to what he considered the health of the Western world at the dawn of the cold war, and he was especially pleased to provide this service in the Britain that he so admired.

For his part, Commager had fallen in love with Britain and its academic surroundings from an early age. When he was only twenty-two and traveling in Europe doing research for his doctoral dissertation, he was overwhelmed by the social gentility and intellectual polish of English university towns. To his friend Hans Duus he wrote that the few days he spent in Cambridge were "ecstasy piled on ecstasy." No week of his life had he enjoyed more. His first sight of the university "took my breath quite away." Oxford "was at a disadvantage" when Commager saw it because of the rainy weather. "On the whole I liked Cambridge in every way better than Oxford," he told his friend. The town, university buildings, and students all were better in Cambridge.[43]

Considering his youthful enthusiasm for Cambridge, it was fitting that in 1942 Commager was appointed lecturer in American history there, following by a year Nevins's pilgrimage to Britain. Commager's was "the first appointment in American history to be made at Cambridge," according to the *New York Times*. Like Nevins at Oxford the year before, while in England Commager was planning "to broadcast and make speeches for the British Ministry of Information."[44] Commager and Nevins had only recently finished their *Pocket History of the United States*, which was to be distributed free to British citizens as a guide to democratic life and a boost to democratic enthusiasms. Now the two friends made adjoining trips to the United Kingdom to lecture about American free institutions and the need for the British to be a strong bulwark defending democratic values from the forces of totalitarianism.

During his first appointment at Cambridge in 1942, Commager stayed at Peterhouse College and got on well there, forming a friendship with the Americanist Denis Brogan. Later, in 1944, Commager helped get Brogan membership in the Century Club in New York, and in return, when Commager was appointed Pitt Professor in 1947, Brogan arranged for him to stay at Peterhouse during his time in Cambridge. There was a shared fondness between them for the other's culture. "I'm as homesick for New York or at any rate USA," he complained to Commager, perhaps with some affectation, "as you two (or you all) are for Cambridge."[45]

The Commagers liked England enough that they bought a house in the little town of Linton, about ten miles southeast of Cambridge, where they could spend summers or such free time as they could make for themselves in their busy lives. Commager's embrace of Britain and its manners and values did not escape the notice of those in the wider circle of his friends. Leo Marx, the noted literary critic and American studies figure who taught with Commager at Amherst, referred to him as "an unrepentant Anglophile" who "loves British (patrician) manners (as seen by Henry James), British speech, writing, humor, and P. G. Wodehouse, [and] disdains most vulgar arriviste American academics and their petty concerns." William Leuchtenburg, Commager's student and then colleague at Columbia who went on to surpass him in reputation as an intellectual historian, acknowledged that "HSC was very much of an Oxbridge man in his manner. I often wondered about his background—how this man born in Pittsburgh came to have so much the air of a patrician at the Garrick, and I don't know the answer."[46]

Commager admitted that he performed as a propagandist during the war, a rather daring admission given that professional historians are counseled to be as objective and nonpartisan as possible. Yet it is difficult to ask historians not to have a public life. The roles of scholarly historian and partisan citizen ought to be able to be separated and available equally to someone such as Commager, so long as the two functions do not interfere with each other.

But with this distinction in mind, Commager probably did not emphasize enough that he spoke as a citizen instead of a professional historian. "However Commager saw his role in actively arguing for intervention in World War II and his intensive support of the Allied cause in the War itself," Merle Curti noted about this separation of functions, "his audiences no doubt heard him as a distinguished and scholarly historian" rather than a layperson. "I like to think of his role as that of an ardent citizen," Curti remarked charitably, "not that of a historian." Curti was being kind, as he was not as enthusiastic as Commager about U.S. involvement in the war or Commager's activist writing on its behalf.[47]

As Curti admitted with typical modesty, we evaluate whether scholarly propagandist efforts are good or not depending on whether we approve of the position being supported. Curti confessed that "when Commager took a leading part in condemning our Vietnam war and in publicizing the scandal of Watergate[,] I, somewhat inconsistently perhaps, applauded him. I overlooked the point that most of those who read what he wrote and heard what he said would have thought of him as a historian and that he probably thought of himself in that role."[48]

But Commager was not haunted by fears of having betrayed his professional function. Propaganda and partisanship had always been entwined with historical writing, he believed. Some propagandist history had been obnoxious or offensive—works produced by Nazi or Communist historians, for example. Many of the most respected volumes of classical history, however, were propaganda, as were "such major works as Charles A. Beard's studies of American foreign policy between the wars, or Parrington's brilliant *Main Currents of American Thought*, or Winston Churchill's *World Crisis*, but we do not really think the worse of them for that." While dishonesty would ruin a history, an activist enthusiasm would not. "Actually partisanship often adds zest to historical writing," he emphasized; "for partisanship is an expression of interest and excitement and passion, and these can stir the reader as judiciousness might not." Didn't Parrington prompt an unmatched interest in American literature, and didn't Churchill change the world with his volume?[49]

With his high school audience he was even clearer about the unthreatening function of propaganda. Information and propaganda were not different concepts, he instructed the readers of *Senior Scholastic* during the war. No, "the best propaganda is truth, and all information influences opinion." Sure, Hitler and Goebbels misused propaganda. "But propaganda as the presentation of information or of arguments designed to inspire support or to arouse fear is eminently respectable. It is, in fact, little more than good argument." As he reported to his young readers, Samuel Adams, Thomas Paine, Benjamin Franklin, and Harriet Beecher Stowe were all good propagandists.[50] To make it fit with his promotion of the Jeffersonian ideal of the free marketplace of ideas, Commager viewed propaganda as merely a strong opinion filed in favor of one side of an argument, designed, as an advocate's support or a lawyer's brief might be, to influence debate.

Neither Commager nor Nevins thirsted to punish the enemy after World War II. As the war finally neared its conclusion in Europe, Allan remarked to Henry, "What news!—and yet I shudder over the destruction in Germany."[51] Similarly, Commager demonstrated a conciliatory and evenhanded view of what should constitute American foreign policy.

Already by the early months of 1946 Commager had fashioned for the *Atlantic* a set of suggestions that became his personal blueprint for postwar U.S. policy abroad. The essay articulated the heart of the foreign policy values that he followed in his future pronouncements and battles over China, the Soviet Union, Cuba, Vietnam, and Nicaragua. Ostensibly an evaluation of U.S. arms policy, Commager's "Where Are We Headed?" set the tone for much of his later public writing.

In the wake of the war, Commager acknowledged, we had to decide whether we wanted a war or peace policy, and we had to accept the consequences of our choices, no matter how little choice we thought available. It is a principle of law and international relations, he reminded his readers, "that if we will the act—large-scale military preparedness, for example—we also will the consequences of the act. Our intentions are going to be judged by our conduct, not our conduct by our intentions."[52]

Consider our monopoly on the atomic bomb, he suggested. If the United States starts an arms race it can hardly be surprised if other nations join in. "However pure our motives or irreproachable our purposes," he warned, "we cannot maintain a double standard of international morality for ourselves and other countries." It was characteristic of Commager for the rest of his career to remind the nation frequently that it was pursuing a double standard in world affairs. Politicians should scrap the atomic bomb approach, he thought. Weapons of that magnitude were only "a confession of the bankruptcy of statesmanship." They would produce a catastrophe. Americans had not yet come to understand that atomic bombs were different from other weapons and had changed the concept of war itself. Traditional ideas of security and sovereignty were now unworkable. We were ignoring the United Nations and instead, with our arms race, were creating fear in other nations.[53]

Worse, our dependence on a monopoly on the atomic bomb and its technology would bring about a culture of secrecy and oppression. An atomic arms race "would require, to be effective, the rigorous control of every feature of the scientific and industrial life of the nation for military purposes," he cautioned. "It would require the subordination of all those values which we cherish to the values which we have heretofore held hateful." Instead, Commager suggested that we internationalize the bomb through an international atomic commission as had been recommended by the Moscow Conference.[54]

Our military goals should be met through the Security Council of the United Nations (UN). The United States should "abandon unilateral and informal meddling in the affairs of other nations or regions" and should let the UN or other international agencies perform that role. "Our own experience here is illuminating," he pointed out. "New York criticism of Alabama justice, for example, merely irritates the people of Alabama, but Supreme Court decisions are accepted as a matter of course." Twenty years later he might not have been so optimistic about the Court's welcome in Alabama.[55]

Yet Commager's point after the war was clear: the United States should avoid unilateral action in the world, but it did need to stay involved in an active manner. The time for isolationism was gone, smashed by the lessons of the past fifteen years, and U.S. leadership was now "a responsibility we cannot evade." But America needed to exercise that leadership under a system of global democracy and national self-determination, without double standards or unilateral action. It was a difficult set of requirements to follow, a confusing and hazardous role to perform, but one that Commager consistently demanded that the United States live up to and fulfill.[56]

In his collaborations with Morison and Nevins on two of midcentury's most highly regarded survey accounts of American history, Commager established himself as a talented narrative historian who could write for the general public and interested scholars alike. In those volumes he demonstrated his considerable ability to produce work in the new field of American intellectual history.

Yet the example of those historians he most respected (Parrington, Trevelyan, Churchill, Morison, Nevins) and those figures from his early life who had influenced him most (Adam Dan, William E. Dodd, Andrew McLaughlin) encouraged him to pay at least as much attention to his intellectual as to his scholarly function. When, in the forties, World War II and then the cold war grew into a threatening reality, Commager believed that it was his responsibility to use his voice to help defend democracy and shape national policy.

CHAPTER 5

Anticommunism and McCarthyism, 1945-1960

In the decade following the end of World War II, Commager was best known by the public as a vocal opponent of McCarthyism, and his struggle against McCarthyism as a civic intellectual helps illuminate some of the political and philosophical divisions in American liberalism at midcentury. It became particularly apparent, for example, that he held a more optimistic political view than many others in the liberal community and was more satisfied to talk about issues of freedom of speech rather than to discuss the benefits of various ideas and policies. As he demonstrated repeatedly during this period, he valued freedom for intellectual dissent more than national power and security derived from political toughness.

Yet why did an academic figure such as Commager, a member of that curiously detached profession of history, become so embroiled in political issues that he found himself the object of suspicion and criticism from friends and foes, publishers, writers, and colleagues? Why is it that one whose responsibility was to understand the remote past instead fought contemporary battles as a kind of unofficial leader against McCarthyism? Part of the answer, at least, resides in Commager's view of the relationship between the practice of history and American civic life. As a Jeffersonian liberal committed to civil liberties, the integrity of honest political dissent, intellectual freedom, and the benefits of an uncensored marketplace of ideas, Commager had a history of vigilance on issues of free speech before such became fashionable.

As far back as the late 1920s, when he was writing his doctoral dissertation, Commager admired Johann Struensee because he began his administration in September 1770 by outlawing censorship as part of the Enlightenment impulse in Denmark.[1] A decade later, in 1936 in his book *Theodore Parker*, Commager showed his respect for the New England reformer's opposition to the Sabbath laws. "The laws were innocuous enough, to be sure," he wrote about Parker's opinion of the statutes, "rarely observed, more rarely enforced, but even the mildest of laws represented an assertion of the authority of the State over the consciences of men." Both Parker and Commager believed, in Jefferson's words, that "it is error alone which needs the support of government. Truth can stand by itself."[2] The state had no business enforcing ideas.

Before the fight against intellectual repression became popular in the academic community, Commager worried about the dangers of excessive anticommunism. Well before World War II, on New Year's Day 1939, he warned that the idea of communism had become in America "merely a bugaboo with which professional patriots frightened old ladies, timid business men and Congressional committees."[3] Despite his strong opposition to totalitarianism during World War II, this statement is representative of what more strident anticommunists saw as his soft-headed refusal to worry about Soviet Communism.

While Commager was not portrayed as a pro-Soviet fellow traveler, he was outspoken enough against hard-line anticommunists that he was lumped by them with those called "anti-anticommunists." The "anti-antis" were thought to have been fooled either by Soviet professions of goodwill or by their own reliance on a utopian Jeffersonian belief that all points of view need to be heard and that, once heard, those opinions were no longer dangerous.

To argue the benefits of moderation rarely brings honor or fame to an intellectual. Yet moderation was the task Commager designed for himself: to defend the intelligent freedoms and rights associated with liberalism even though that effort might not vault him into the admiring eye of history. He thought of himself as a liberal rather than a leftist, and friends acknowledged that he was "against McCarthyism without having any particular identification with the organized left."[4]

A few months into 1939 Commager cautioned readers of the *New York Times Magazine* that the fundamental protections of the First Amendment were under attack by the radical forces of the Left and the Right. Radicals of the Left misunderstood Marx to say that the freedoms of the Bill of Rights were incompatible with economic and political justice. Radicals of the Right thought those same freedoms would limit the justifiable power of the state.

Still, Commager denounced the political fringes for undermining liberal rights, yet his own liberal tolerance prompted him to warn that if the American system persecuted these fringe dissenters it would destroy itself. Worse than the threat from domestic fascism and communism was a patriotic impulse that silenced criticism of the status quo, required conformity, demanded that teachers take loyalty oaths, considered foreigners a threat, decreed the Constitution exempt from criticism, branded pacifism as disloyalty, and refused fascism and communism a hearing. This malevolent patriotic doctrine, he warned, "denies freedom of speech to Socialists in one State, to Communists in another," and was the product of "those who believe that the way to fight anti-Americanism is to impose their own brand of Americanism on their fellow-citizens."[5] During the war Commager continued to campaign for toleration of dissent and unpopular ideas. Shortly after America entered the conflict he announced that it would be fatal if the war destroyed the freedom to criticize and disagree or led to the suppression of minorities.[6]

When it came time, in the late 1940s, to assess the culture of mid-twentieth-century America as he began to write his study of *The American Mind*, Commager pointed to intolerance as one of the prominent features. Yes, there was precedent for political repression (the Alien and Sedition Laws, for example), but it was only in the wake of World War I that intolerance received official approval in the United States. This new repression was characterized by "a certain moral flabbiness" and "a weakening of intellectual fibre" compared with the earlier forms. The intolerance of the Puritans and Jonathan Edwards was a scholarly undertaking, and those like John Calhoun made sure that proslavery and states' rights arguments were coherent. "The intolerance of the thirties and the forties," Commager sighed bitterly, "had not even the dignity of intelligence or accuracy, or of a moral purpose."[7]

With this history of defending dissent behind him, after World War II Commager increasingly moved into a public role as one of the leading voices in the intellectual community trying to quiet American fears of communism. In the autumn of 1945, only months after the end of World War II allowed Americans to celebrate an Allied victory over Germany and Japan, the hostility to the Soviets was much stronger than in the past, partly because the Soviets represented a much greater military threat. Alarmed by what he perceived as the growing stridency of American anticommunism, he became one of the most prominent academic intellectuals to campaign for a more moderate U.S. response to the Communist challenge. His civic leadership on this issue was recognized by the *New York Times*, which regularly reported on his activity.

In late October 1945, Commager spoke to three hundred Christian and Jewish scholars at the Institute for Religious and Social Studies at the Jewish Theological Seminary, a few blocks from Columbia University. Americans knew nothing of Russia's history in past centuries, he claimed, knew nothing of the "century of ignorance, oppression and poverty from which the Revolution came." Perhaps, he counseled his audience, Americans should apply a political golden rule to their evaluation of the Soviet Union. Europeans, after all, considered Americans quite radical long after our own Revolution had ended. So "it behooves us to attempt the same degree of understanding that we would have wished for ourselves."[8]

Within two years of the end of the war, a developing fear began to haunt Americans that communists inside U.S. borders might also threaten the nation. When Truman's executive order requiring loyalty oaths of federal employees was announced in 1947, Commager realized that the president might have designed it to bridle other more repressive measures, but he cautioned in the *Nation* that "as it stands it is an invitation to precisely that kind of witchhunting which is repugnant to our constitutional system." The program was "guilt by association with a vengeance," and yet guilt was no longer determined by personal acts but by sympathetic association with those assumed to be subversive.[9]

Typical of Commager's public activity on the issue of anticommunist repression was his appearance with three others the following year on the unrehearsed New York radio program *What's on Your Mind?* Along with A. J. Liebling of the *New Yorker*, newspaper editor Hodding Carter, and Seth Richardson, who was chair of the President's Loyalty Review Board, Commager was critical of the House Un-American Activities Committee (HUAC). He and the rest of the panel agreed with Richardson that HUAC's use of "klieg lights and a host of reporters" damaged civil rights, and Carter and Commager proposed that without HUAC there was already a sufficient number of laws on the books to keep the country from subversion. But dependence on laws to safeguard individual rights was not sufficient, Commager pointed out, and he urged that liberties be better ingrained through education of the public, press, and politicians.[10]

When Senator Joseph McCarthy burst into public view with a media spectacle in Wheeling, West Virginia, in February 1950, where he waved his alleged list of 205 known communists working in the U.S. State Department, Commager had already been resisting the roots of McCarthyism for more than a decade. Within days of McCarthy's Wheeling speech, Commager teamed up with former assistant secretary of state Adolph Berle Jr. to address 130 high school leaders at the Columbia College Forum on Democracy.

Under a photo of him standing with a foot propped on a bench while speaking to the students, the *New York Times* reported that Commager said loyalty oaths showed American insecurity. The United States had to encourage originality and criticism instead of conformity or it would be a second-rate nation whose second-rate institutions were stocked with people who did not read or question. He told the students that to learn by experience children should be exposed to dangerous political ideas just as they were exposed to other dangers.[11] A vaccination, after all, is nothing more than exposure to the disease it protects against.

Those conservative Americans who considered such statements by Commager evidence of his sympathy for Soviet Communism were probably not aware that in the late 1940s and early 1950s he was still advising the U.S. Army about the best way to write its military history, still promoting democracy by giving lectures to State Department trainees or to personnel at military bases for the Department of War, and still writing material for the State Department to use abroad as propaganda. As a front page article in the Sunday *New York Times* in early 1951 made clear, Commager was one of a few people selected by the State Department to help find ways to advertise the ideals of American democracy abroad. Commager joined Reinhold Niebuhr, Arthur Schlesinger Jr., and a handful of other intellectuals to discuss, allegedly without State Department intervention, questions such as how to expose the fallacies and errors of communism to those who would be confronted by it, what single attribute all non-Communist governments share, and how to shape democracy into a practical and exportable form so others could experience its concrete benefits instead of merely its abstractions. The participants asked themselves how to define "the essence of democracy" and how to distinguish communism from socialism.

Still, Commager had a habit of provoking conservatives. Trained in the art of communicating with the public by decades of writing for the general press and his lecture excursions around Britain and the United States during and after the war, he stood before one thousand faculty members and students at Barnard College in the fall of 1951 and charged that the loyalty oaths brought about by McCarthyism were "part of a rather fat-headed, feeble-minded, though not altogether depraved pattern peculiar to American life." If dissenters became afraid to speak, he reported to the sea of faces at Barnard, it would create a group of second-class citizens who would not utter their real opinions, even though the "only kind of advice a society needs is unpalatable advice."[12]

A few months later the Advertising Council asked him to appear as a member of an American Round Table panel of intellectuals and industry representatives at the Waldorf-Astoria in midtown New York. Speaking before one hundred American business leaders and a dozen French journalists, he presented his opinion about McCarthyist investigations launched to find dangerous radicals. "What happens is not that the state or city gets rid of a lot of subversives," he told the gathering of businesspeople. "Not at all. It rarely finds any." Instead, the government merely demoralizes the school systems and other institutions and sets them on a decline from which it is difficult for them to recover. "In the long run," he warned the audience at the Waldorf, "it will create a generation not only deprived of liberty but incapable of enjoying liberty."[13]

Commager eagerly signed public statements opposing the repression of individuals, even though it meant that sometimes he was subject to penalties himself. Along with A. J. Muste (who had thought of the proposal), Norman Thomas, Eleanor Roosevelt, Lewis Mumford, and over forty others, Commager signed an amnesty petition during the Christmas season of 1955 for the sixteen Communists who were imprisoned under the Smith Act. Although the appeal declared that the signatories were "in fundamental disagreement with the philosophy of the Communist party," this action was just the sort that earned Commager the distrust of many of his fellow citizens. A year later, for example, a Long Island high school canceled a forum at which he was to speak because he was too controversial for local residents. Complaints had been made about his support for the amnesty petition for the Communists.[14]

Cancellations and complaints had not silenced him before, however. In the spring of 1950 he received a letter from Row, Peterson and Company, the publishing house that handled his high school textbook.[15] G. M. Jones, the president of the firm, sent him an editorial from the *Detroit Free Press*, apparently criticizing Commager's statements against McCarthy, and told him "how difficult this makes it sometimes to sell your book." Jones assured him that "I know perfectly well you are not a Communist," but he reminded him that "a few editorials of this sort are probably as much of handicap to the sale of a high school history as anything that could happen." (The company's letterhead announced: "Publishers of Good Books.") Jones complained that editorials like this were occurring frequently, the book's sales were going to fall, and all of this without any real reason. "By that I mean I think you just get yourself in foolish places where you don't really belong or intend to be," he counseled, "and I am very frankly raising the question of whether or not it is worth the price that it will undoubtedly cost in decreased royalties." Commager would have to decide his future course for himself, but Jones reminded him that "the 'pressure of controversy' looms large in public school decisions."[16]

Henry Steele Commager as he was seen by thousands of Americans as he campaigned against McCarthyism. (Courtesy of Lisa Commager)

Throughout the 1950s, as McCarthyism reached a peak and then slowly began to decline into a quieter but still hostile rejection of dissent, Commager continued to give speeches, make appearances, and campaign publicly for intellectual freedom.[17] At the end of the decade he was still supporting groups that made controversial demands. Together with Leo Marx, Ray Billington, Harvey Wish, John Hope Franklin, and a few other scholars, Commager served on the screening committee for the Fulbright Scholarships in 1959. When the president's Board of Foreign Scholarships did not accept the committee's nomination of Sarah Lawrence College professor Bert Loewenberg that year, the committee threatened to resign unless the case was reviewed and, if Loewenberg's political affiliations were at issue, the evidence was presented to him.

Further, the committee demanded that the Board of Foreign Scholarships declare publicly any nonacademic criteria used in making its decisions. The committee members had heard through a "leak" from one of the board's members that Loewenberg's loyalty had been questioned. Commager wrote to Senator Fulbright that the best minds of the academic community would no longer participate in the program if the board overruled the committee's recommendations for political reasons. Not satisfied with a commotion of this magnitude, Commager was back in the *New York Times* the following week complaining that "the New York City Board of Higher Education does not know that the McCarthy era is over." The board, he complained, had continued to harass a professor already cleared by the Supreme Court.[18]

It was not a simple and unfounded paranoia that drove Commager's interest in maintaining intellectual freedom. At institutions such as the University of Washington, Reed College, Cornell, Tulane, the University of Colorado, Harvard, Yale, Columbia, Berkeley, Stanford, the University of Texas, and the University of Connecticut, to name only a few recognized battlegrounds, there were very serious threats to faculty members of being dismissed for their political beliefs or affiliations. Some lost their jobs and found it difficult to be hired elsewhere.[19] Even ignoring the suffering of the individuals who became targets of these political actions, Commager felt that great damage had been done to the possibility of real intellectual inquiry and discussion in the American university system.

Yet Commager claimed that during the McCarthy period no one came after him at Columbia and nobody really censored or threatened him. An incident at a faculty meeting illustrated his point about his relative freedom to dissent. At the session Columbia president Grayson Kirk suggested canceling a lecture to which the faculty had invited a radical. In response, Commager "rose and challenged the President on this." His colleagues, he implored, had to have the courage to override Kirk's suggestion. Faculty members followed Commager's lead, and by doing so they convinced him that in the midst of McCarthyism brave moves could still be made on some campuses. In the entire period, he maintained, the only repercussions he felt were that a woman's organization canceled one of his lectures, probably a talk at a Long Island high school, and a publisher took his name off a book of high school readings (likely not the Row, Peterson incident, because Commager's name continued on his textbook with Eugene C. Barker and Walter P. Webb at least until the early 1960s).[20]

But as Commager knew, friends and associates of his had been adversely affected by the anticommunist enthusiasm. F. O. Matthiessen, on the Harvard English faculty, committed suicide in April 1950, probably for several reasons, but the fact that he was heavily criticized for his leftist beliefs likely contributed to his decision. Matthiessen's support for Henry Wallace's presidential campaign in 1948 and his sympathy for some Soviet actions in his *From the Heart of Europe* in the same year earned him hostile remarks from most positions along the American political spectrum. In his suicide note Matthiessen cited "the state of the world" and "the present situation" as factors prompting him to leap from the twelfth floor of a Boston hotel room.[21] "I find myself much depressed by Matthiessen's death," Commager's friend Thomas Cochran at New York University penned at the bottom of a letter. "He stood for most of [the] things I approve of, but do nothing to further, and instead of cheering him up I spent most of the time arguing with him."[22]

Cochran hardly needed to apologize. Still, to prevent the need for this kind of cathartic confession, Commager, like many of his comrades in the profession, spoke out publicly against the repression. In the *New Republic* in 1949 he blasted the University of Washington for dismissing several faculty members for their political affiliations.[23] A national officer of the American Civil Liberties Union (ACLU), in the 1950s Commager let the organization use his name to raise funds from its countrywide membership. In addition he was part of the Executive Committee of the American Academic Freedom Project at Columbia University in the early 1950s, which helped produce *The Development of Academic Freedom in the United States* (1955) by Richard Hofstadter and Walter Metzger.[24] In short, Commager never stood still on this issue.

The articles and speeches Commager launched so often against McCarthyism were treated with great respect and gratitude by many of his readers and listeners and were attacked by others. When in 1954 Commager expanded several of his most important essays on McCarthyism into a short book titled *Freedom, Loyalty, Dissent*, it served as a concise expression of his campaign for intellectual freedom and won a Hillman Foundation Award for its contribution to civil liberties. The volume was praised by the Harvard historian Crane Brinton in the *Herald Tribune* book review and celebrated in the *Saturday Review* (hardly surprising given that Commager wrote regularly for that magazine), but it was criticized by many in the reading public.[25] Between 1947, when the articles that would make up the book began appearing in *Harper's, Saturday Review*, and the *New York Times Magazine*, and 1954, when they were collected and published as *Freedom, Loyalty, Dissent*, these writings provoked and crystallized the opposition to his ideas.

What did Commager say in *Freedom, Loyalty, Dissent* that so divided his audience? He began the book by reprinting a lecture titled "The Necessity of Freedom" that he had delivered at Swarthmore College. Following Jefferson, Commager suggested that if we outlaw dissent, we banish the criticism society needs to prevent it from making mistakes. Sounding like John Dewey, he warned that this would be a very impractical mistake, because the costs would far outweigh the benefits. The consequences would be prohibitive: "We do not encourage dissent for sentimental reasons," he instructed his fellow citizens; "we encourage dissent because we cannot live without it." We need to encourage dissent and rebellion, to expose our children to dangerous ideas so they know how to think and can distinguish true from false.[26]

Most of Commager's critics would have endorsed toleration as a positive trait, in principle. But he seemed to propose an infinite toleration, and that, of course, might actually encourage the destruction of freedom and the dissolution of society and culture. Others often became frustrated with him because he was so unwilling to suggest where the limits on toleration should be drawn and why.

His critics asked him why a group with loyalty to an outside force trying to undermine the democratic system ought to receive the same rights of dissent that nonconformists in America do. He was reprimanded for inquiring, in his book, how we are to decide on the limits of liberty and the rights of the community but then failing to answer that question except to say that there need be no contradiction between the two. The suggestion that he was inept at directly answering the complicated questions surrounding McCarthyism was a stinging insult aimed at Commager, who considered himself a pragmatist. He was told that to hold an opinion is a right (which his critics believed was not being damaged) but that to hold a job was a privilege and so was subject to certain conditions.[27]

Commager's piece criticizing the practice of guilt by association first appeared in the *New York Times Magazine* in November 1953, becoming the central chapter in *Freedom, Loyalty, Dissent* the following year. The heart of his argument was that guilt by association was a flawed method of estimating the danger of various individuals and groups, that it was harmful to establish one standard for what constituted loyalty, and that the repression of ideas and people characteristic of McCarthyism was damaging, from a pragmatic viewpoint, because the intellectual costs exceeded the benefits.

The doctrine of guilt by association was illogical, he complained, because "it assumes that a good cause becomes bad if supported by bad men." But two plus two equals four, even if subversives support that conclusion. If that were not the case, the U.S. Constitution could be invalidated simply by Communists' endorsing it. Legally, guilt should refer to acts, not ideas, and legal guilt should not be applied retroactively. Actually, Commager asked, "if the Republicans can associate with a McCarthy and Democrats with a McCarran without ostensible infection," then why do we assume that intellectual viruses pass so quickly and completely?[28]

Yes, a person could support so many political organizations that he or she might mistake some of their intentions. But that individual can be convinced by the court of public opinion that he or she has gone too far—and besides, it is better to "err on the side of generosity and faith than on the side of caution and fear." There exists the hazard of a divorce "between membership and responsibility," where individuals do not participate enough in the activities of an organization to know the reality of its methods and intentions. But why, he asked, should we require more of reformers than of the rest of the population? Most people who own shares in corporations have little idea what those organizations are really doing and are not held morally responsible for corporate actions. And he wondered why there was not instead a doctrine of innocence by association? Why were patriots so worried about the impact on student bodies of two or three communists within a faculty, rather than celebrating the great majority of democratic professors and assuming that gradually it would be the communists whose ideas would be changed?[29]

Commager's conclusions about guilt by association created a storm of discussion. His argument would be stronger, John Oakes suggested in the *New York Times Book Review*, if only he would propose concrete measures to protect society "against the few real subversives" while not forfeiting the Bill of Rights. Unfortunately, Oakes complained, "Mr. Commager does not quite meet the entire problem." After all, what about a person applying for a sensitive government job who denies he is a Communist but belongs to Communist organizations? Are his associations irrelevant?[30]

Although the letters received by the *New York Times Magazine* about "Guilt—and Innocence—by Association" were four to one in support of Commager, several contentious retorts were printed. Edward Heffron accused Commager of making bad distinctions as a pragmatist. An examination of a person's associations might not be the only test of loyalty, but it did have relevance. Further, a person would not be "prosecuted at law" because he associated with espionage agents, but he would be able to be barred from a sensitive job. Wouldn't a bank president be justified in asking prospective tellers if they had been an associate of Al Capone? Another respondent told Commager that "it is not wicked to consort with sinners for the purpose of helping them or doing good, but it is wicked to consort with them for the purpose of joining in their sins."[31]

Harper's originally published "Who Is Loyal to America?" in 1947, and seven years later it became the final chapter of *Freedom, Loyalty, Dissent*. In the article Commager insisted that dissent is not disloyalty. If loyalty is promoting the best interests of the community as a whole, then it "may require hostility to the particular policies which the government pursues, the particular practices which the economy undertakes, the particular institutions which society maintains." As the abolitionists knew, it might require opposition to part of the Constitution. Our national tradition has been one of "protest and revolt." The genuinely disloyal are those who are racists, or who persecute on the basis of religion or class, those who suppress the right to vote, deny equal education, or demand special favors or advantages that the rest of their fellow citizens are denied. "Will the House Committee on Un-American Activities," he inquired angrily, "interfere with the activities of these?"[32]

Over twenty thousand reprints of "Who Is Loyal to America?" were purchased from *Harper's* in less than two months. Still, not all the reaction was supportive. One correspondent accused Commager of "pinko bleatings," while a brigadier general sputtered that "America is in immediate need of an extraordinary dose of Divine help if such confused thinking is typical of what our adolescents are getting from their teachers of history."[33]

As might be expected, Commager's more conservative friends inhabited positions on McCarthyism rather distant from his. Although Nevins was an Adlai Stevenson liberal, for example, his assorted conservative convictions made him openly unsympathetic to Commager's anti-McCarthy operations.[34] The two had real differences only over the issues surrounding McCarthyism and later the Vietnam War, but Commager felt that "it never came to anything open." Still, Nevins was impatient with him at midcentury, as Commager saw it, "for spending so much time giving lectures, going around the country, writing books attacking McCarthyism." Nevins realized the danger in McCarthy's demagogic anticommunist approach but, more than his friend, also worried about the real threat of communism.

Nevins felt that it was the job of historians to write books and teach people, not to be activists, according to Commager. Historians should work indirectly at politics, not directly. A greater public service was done by training the right kind of scholars, who would see properly for themselves. "And from time to time he let me know his impatience," Commager recalled. "I should be getting on with the job, instead of spending my resources and energies lecturing on campuses and going to Washington and doing all these different things. He wasn't nearly as outraged by McCarthy as I was, put it that way, any more than he was [as] outraged by Standard Oil as Henry Demarest Lloyd was."[35]

Samuel Eliot Morison, Commager's partner on *The Growth of the American Republic*, was even more conservative and even further than Nevins from Commager's antagonism to McCarthyism. Morison testified against the anticommunist Whittaker Chambers by affidavit in the Alger Hiss case in 1949, and he was public in his belief that Communists similar to Hiss had "infiltrated" Washington. Morison told a Canadian audience that he was not "one of those who call the anticommunist crusade of the decade 1945–55 a 'witch hunt,' hysterical though much of it has been." Because Communists denied rights to others, they deserved none themselves, not even on college faculties. No teaching job should be given to any former Communist unless that person could prove a "reconversion." Because he believed that some of McCarthyism had gone too far and that universities should be left to themselves to police the campuses and drive out the communists, Morison satisfied himself that he was sufficiently liberal.[36]

Then there were those more extreme conservatives who flirted with the fringe political right. In the *American Mercury*, Louis Budenz, who made an energetic career out of being the Billy Sunday of the stridently anticommunist forces, attacked Commager for various liberal offenses. Commager had uttered words in defense of the National Lawyer's Guild, which Budenz took to be "the foremost legal bulwark of the Communist Party." Moreover, Commager had doubted the accusations of Senator McCarthy against Owen Lattimore and others, ignoring the "careful and extensive" hearings that were undertaken by the committee of Senator Pat McCarran. Instead, Commager depended on the work of fellow liberal Theodore White to help mislead the nation. Together, Budenz charged, Commager and his liberal friends were "always shouting for 'democracy' and helping to destroy it by aiding the immediate Communist objectives."[37] Thus despite the praise and awards received by Commager for *Freedom, Loyalty, Dissent*, it made him an identifiable target for those who thought liberalism was insufficiently anti-communist.

More interesting, however, than the reproach from conservatives, who might have been expected to disagree with him, was the notable amount of criticism Commager received in the 1940s and 1950s from fellow members of the liberal Left and other reformers who were unhappy with his conclusions. There is no reason to expect that all liberals would agree on the threat of communism, of course, and it reveals the shape and assumptions of midcentury liberalism to review those differences.

Lester Markel, Commager's liberal editor at the *New York Times Magazine*, scribbled a significant comment to him that characterized many of the complaints from other observers. "I think that the rightness of issues," Markel noted about Commager's writing, "must be kept distinct from the right to discuss issues."[38] Markel was perceptive about his author's tendencies. Commager often spoke about the sacred right to discuss problems but said little about the wisdom of various points of view in the debate. It left many of his most sympathetic liberal readers frustrated.

Commager, to the discomfort of even his supporters, was impatient with philosophical precision. It was part of his dash-about style of life, juggling a hundred different projects, sampling a dozen assorted opinions but hurrying on without steeping in them, writing at a breakneck pace because there was a briefcase full of other commitments to be fulfilled. His approach to life led to great productivity but also to some disappointment from those who demanded more powerful logical consistency.

Most surprising, considering Commager's strong civil libertarian focus, was that Roger Baldwin, a founder and director of the American Civil Liberties Union, took exception to his article "Who Is Loyal to America?" in *Harper's* in 1947. The real issue, Baldwin claimed, was whether Communists can make trustworthy federal employees. If the answer was no, then the government had the right to check its workers' affiliations. Given that logic, Baldwin felt that Commager's piece missed the issue.[39]

Observers must have raised their eyebrows at Baldwin's correction of Commager. After all, why would Baldwin, a founder of the central institution for the protection of civil liberties, reproach Commager, the person who was quickly becoming known as the most insistent voice for a Jeffersonian concern for democratic rights and freedoms? But Baldwin and the ACLU had decided in 1940 to bar from membership on their national board anyone who supported totalitarian regimes, because the ACLU thought that incompatible with democratic freedoms. By midcentury, Baldwin was probably more anticommunist than Commager.

In another apparent irony, Baldwin was pointing out to Commager— Commager, the disciple of Dewey and champion of pragmatism—that his approach was insufficiently pragmatic about pursuing solutions. Like Lester Markel, Baldwin thought that pieties about the right to discuss issues did not sufficiently address which opinions were most beneficial. Although a civil libertarian, Baldwin felt that Jeffersonian sermons were not enough to protect real liberties. But perhaps Commager was right. In an atmosphere of repression, the right to discuss issues is at least as important as which opinion is correct.

Markel and Baldwin were not the only liberals who corrected him on his response to energetic anticommunism. To Commager's political left stood those liberals at the *Nation* magazine. Although he was fond of the *Nation*, shared its hostility to McCarthyism, and respected its defense of civil liberties, he was never as sympathetic to the Soviet Union, with which he had neither imaginative nor ideological connection. The magazine's dissenting posture he found admirable, but its editorial voice was never sufficiently internationalist. If other magazines too strongly supported the United States, the *Nation* too firmly backed the Soviets.

To Commager's political right paced those liberals, known as the New York Intellectuals, who revolved around the orbit of journals such as *Partisan Review*, *Commentary*, and *Dissent*. Among that group were Daniel Bell, Lionel Trilling, Sidney Hook, Dwight Macdonald, Irving Howe, Irving Kristol, Mary McCarthy, Nathan Glazer, Diana Trilling, Seymour Martin Lipset, and other notable American thinkers. Allied to that crowd were Richard Hofstadter, Reinhold Niebuhr, and Arthur Schlesinger Jr.

Kristol, an editor of *Commentary*, featured Commager's shortcomings prominently in a 1951 article in the magazine. Like Baldwin, Kristol took aim at Henry's "Who Is Loyal to America." Of course it is true, Kristol admitted in his essay, that Commager "never was a Communist and never will be." Yet, because in his article Commager stood up for the right of schoolchildren to hear about Communism from Russian-born Shura Lewis, he supported "a tissue of lies" that could damage them. "For Professor Commager to defend the rights of Communists to free speech is one thing," Kristol warned, "for him to assert that there is nothing objectionable in mendacious pleading in support of Communism is quite another." Unfortunately, he reported, Commager thought Communism was just a little farther out on the spectrum than liberalism itself, only slightly less patient. Would the professor have defended a Nazi's right to speak to schoolchildren in 1938, Kristol wondered?[40]

Further, Kristol complained, Commager thought the attack on Owen Lattimore was really an assault on "independence and non-conformity." Kristol disagreed: Lattimore was a docile Communist sympathizer who never thought for himself. So Commager, the story went, was guilty of aiding the Communists despite his intentions. His "rhetoric, while not designedly pro-Communist," Kristol concluded, "is compelled by the logic of disingenuousness and special pleading to become so in effect." Commager refused "to see Communism for what it is: a movement guided by conspiracy and aiming at totalitarianism, rather than merely another form of 'dissent' or 'nonconformity.' "[41] Kristol charged that Commager could not tell the difference between conspiracy and nonconformist dissent. Yet it seemed to some observers, even those New York Intellectuals such as Irving Howe, that Kristol seemed to ponder this sensitive distinction very little himself. Others in the group agreed with Kristol. Dwight Macdonald, hardly the most anticommunist of the New York Intellectuals, referred to Commager as "a particularly naive and obtuse (simple-minded, clumsy) type of routine liberal," a liberal who was too soft on Communists, as both Baldwin and Kristol had charged.[42]

Arthur Schlesinger Jr., a fellow historian and friend of Commager, later noted that he seldom differed with him, but admitted that their politics diverged. "In the years immediately after the war, [when] I was much concerned with the damage Stalinism was doing to the liberal community and the labor movement," Schlesinger recalled, "Felix [Commager's nickname], with characteristic generosity of spirit, was more willing to give the Stalinists the benefit of the doubt; but he was never a fellow traveler himself, and our difference over this question was a matter of emphasis and timing, not of principle." But time clouded some of Schlesinger's memory on his relation with Commager. According to Schlesinger, his own book *The Vital Center* (on the threat to liberalism from communism) and Commager's *Freedom, Loyalty, Dissent* were not very different.[43] Schlesinger was wrong. Significantly, *The Vital Center* expressed worries over the dangers of communism, whereas *Freedom, Loyalty, Dissent* raised concerns over the dangers of *anti*-communism.

Although Commager, who was no friend of totalitarianism, agreed with much of what Schlesinger wrote in *The Vital Center*, it never would have occurred to him to adopt its apocalyptic tone or to write a book promoting cold war policies—partly because Commager never considered domestic communism a greater threat than the infringement of civil liberties. Schlesinger was one who, like Sidney Hook and other members of the New York Intellectuals, took ideological issues very seriously and realized that the future of freedom might hang in the outcome of intellectual battles. So when the fellow-traveling Waldorf Conference was staged in New York in 1949, for example, Schlesinger was drawn to oppose it publicly by addressing the anticommunist Americans for Intellectual Freedom conference at the Freedom House in New York.

Meanwhile, as the fierce debate surrounding the Waldorf Conference boiled across New York City, Commager, who taught a short subway ride away, was nowhere to be found. Not only did he avoid ideological polemics such as the Waldorf affair represented, but he also would probably have been on the other side of the issue from Schlesinger and the New York group. His political outlook was dangerously close to what in *The Vital Center* Schlesinger had contemptuously called "doughface" liberalism: liberalism that he considered too soft on communism. In his book Schlesinger was disdainful of the doughface Independent Citizens Committee for the Arts, Sciences, and Professions (ICC or ICCASP) and its outgrowth, the Progressive Citizens of America (PCA) (both of which were involved in staging the Waldorf Conference). Because Commager was chairman of the ICC's Westchester chapter, Schlesinger in 1947 warned him of its dangers. "In other words," he advised Henry, "I don't think you belong in the ICC, and I hope to hell you stay out of the PCA."[44]

When *The Vital Center* appeared in 1949 Commager reviewed it sympathetically but cautiously for the *New York Herald Tribune Weekly Book Review*. The book was useful in its criticism of totalitarianism, he found, and valuable in its promotion of moderation instead of extremism. But he also discovered that Schlesinger waged an uncomfortably narrow argument against the Left and was "pretty hard on the Progressives," to whom Commager had far closer ties than Schlesinger. Many of those criticized in the book as irresponsible leftists Commager considered merely well-intentioned dissenters. He reminded Schlesinger that "a complacent society has need of fanatics," and "a wholesome society has room for all shades of opinion."[45]

Their difference of opinion resulted from their slightly different vantages. So while Schlesinger warned that the United States was fatally slow to recognize the totalitarian threat, Commager responded that "fatal is a strong word, and we are still alive. The number of intellectuals who were ever taken in by Communism is certainly negligible." Commager felt that, because Schlesinger associated with those such as the New York Intellectuals who were acutely aware of the communist presence in the intellectual community, perhaps the author of *The Vital Center* had overreacted to the situation.

Arthur Schlesinger Jr. at the
National Teach-in on the Vietnam
War, May 15, 1965.
(Courtesy of Library of Congress)

"Mr. Schlesinger's investigations of Communism in New York and Washington," Commager suggested simply, "may have persuaded him of a danger which he might not have observed had he worked in Chicago or Minneapolis or Kansas City."[46]

Further, Commager would not have thought to disparage the *Nation*'s record on communism, as was done by Schlesinger and the New York group.[47] Being a civil libertarian and Jeffersonian, Commager wanted no element of speech or thought repressed, including unpopular Soviet ideas. In fact, as his writings reveal, he considered anticommunism to be a greater danger than domestic communism to the United States. Again, in the rhetoric of the period, Schlesinger and the New York Intellectuals were anticommunists, whereas Commager would have been considered by many to be an anti-anticommunist.

Another way to assess the ideological divide between Commager and Schlesinger is to study them through the lens of the New York Intellectuals. With the New York group of *Partisan Review* writers Commager shared few traits, but Schlesinger shared many. Sure, Schlesinger was raised in Cambridge rather than New York, amid affluence instead of poverty, and missed the socialist background and subsequent disillusionment of the New York group. Yet he shared their enthusiastic anticommunism in the 1940s and

1950s, joined them in fighting philosophical and political absolutism, wrote for their publications, was an active member of New York Intellectual organizations such as the American Committee for Cultural Freedom, and attended their conferences from New York to Milan. Perhaps most important, Schlesinger was keenly influenced by the work of Reinhold Niebuhr, so he held in common with members of the New York group such as Trilling, Hofstadter, and Bell their emphasis on tragedy, ambiguity, and irony. Like others of his generation who were sensitive to the passing winds of theory, in the wake of World War II Schlesinger felt the impact of the darker philosophical conceptions articulated by Niebuhr and others. It was a chastened postwar sensibility that many members of the New York group had learned either from Niebuhr or from their experience, during the cold war and the rise of mass society, of having to abandon their earlier socialist optimism and many of their former ideals.[48]

Although members of the New York group never phrased it this way, Commager was too optimistic for them, too much a product of the tradition of Jefferson and Emerson and the belief that everything would work out fine if left to the unimpeded competition between individual ideas. His antagonists looked at him as one might inspect an antique curiosity, thinking him unfit to live in the dark and threatening world following World War II. More like fallen Madisonians of the Constitutional generation (which followed Jefferson's and Paine's earlier Revolutionary generation), the Niebuhrian crowd felt compelled to guard against the evil tendencies of human nature.

Much of the difference between the liberalism of Schlesinger and Commager, that is, results from their dissimilar philosophical alignments. Commager was never a theoretical writer. On several occasions he acknowledged that he followed Trevelyan's advice that a theory was something that you should take from instead of bring to your work.[49] What theory he did employ was of a concrete sort: a Jeffersonianism, a Deweyan pragmatism, a vision of democratic process derived from his study of constitutional law and the works of figures such as Tocqueville. Like the New York Intellectuals, Schlesinger was quite different. As *The Vital Center* demonstrates, he was comfortable citing Marx or Leon Trotsky, Joseph Schumpeter or Rosa Luxemburg, John Maynard Keynes or Herbert Spencer, Søren Kierkegaard or Erich Fromm, Arthur Koestler or Niebuhr.

Schlesinger's *Vital Center*, for example, was a pragmatic book that belonged to the liberal literature of the cold war on the same shelf with volumes by Niebuhr and Sidney Hook. His book (although not the rest of his historical scholarship) revealed Schlesinger's tragic and ironic sense of history and his respect for ambiguity, complexity, and unpredictability. It was this estimation of the past that Schlesinger invoked when he repeated the now familiar progression of historiography from an initial heroic phase into one in which "later historians could at last see men as trapped in a structural predicament with right and wrong on both sides and the dominant tone one of tragedy."[50]

This Niebuhrian vision separated him from Commager, whose *Freedom, Loyalty, Dissent* was from a different lineage, a volume that echoed with the optimistic ring of unfallen Jeffersonianism, a philosophical statement and a stirring exhortation in defense of intellectual freedom. Yes, the world had been rocked by the ideological crises of the 1930s and 1940s, but Henry assumed that it was simply a legacy of Europe and that America would remain vaccinated and unthreatened domestically. "By contrast with the barbarism that so speedily overwhelmed many ancient nations," Commager wrote lightheartedly about European totalitarianism, "American failings came to seem superficial, her sins almost innocent. Theodore Dreiser could write of *Tragic America* . . . but Americans knew instinctively that it was Europe that was really tragic, and that—the depression notwithstanding—American promises had been as largely fulfilled as any others that had been held out to sanguine men."[51] Commager did not live in a tragic world.

In the midst of the argument over the threat of domestic communism, Commager was much more likely to rely on Jefferson's belief "that the opinions of men are not the object of civil government, nor under its jurisdiction . . . that truth is great and will prevail if left to herself; that she is the proper and sufficient antagonist to error, and has nothing to fear from the conflict unless by human interposition disarmed of her natural weapons, free argument and debate; errors ceasing to be dangerous when it is permitted freely to contradict them."[52] Consequently, in the decades after World War II Commager focused most of his activist energies on preserving civil liberties, a Jeffersonian concern, whereas Schlesinger aimed his initiatives at opposing totalitarianism, a darker task.

So even in the early 1970s, when Commager lamented signs of moral declension in America, his work had an optimistic scent: by contrast, Schlesinger had decided decades earlier that the threat of the Soviet Union had burst "the bubble of the false optimism of the nineteenth century." But while Schlesinger's detractors considered his fervent anticommunism a weakness, it reflected that Niebuhrian side of him that was tough enough to face the uncomfortable choices that Commager's critics accused him of avoiding. If not everyone embraced the solutions Schlesinger offered in *The Vital Center*, at least his readers found him addressing such problems as whether a citizen had a right to work for the government, what constituted the relevant details of political loyalty, and other related questions.[53] These were the kinds of dilemmas that Hook, Kristol, Baldwin, and others thought Commager left untouched. Still no one, least of all Schlesinger, thought that Commager was in any way sympathetic to the Soviets, only that he was insufficiently enthusiastic in his anticommunism.

Commager might have been more palatable to his liberal friends if he had simply read as deeply in the literature of communism and anticommunism as he did in constitutional history. He offered no evidence that he had wrestled with the issues raised by Arthur Koestler's *Darkness at Noon* (1941) or Richard Crossman's *The God That Failed* (1949). The seminal insights of Jefferson, some of his liberal friends believed, brought one no closer to understanding the brutality of Stalin's regime, which was not simply a Soviet counterpart to Shays' Rebellion.

The only theory to which Commager adhered was pragmatism. Even in his fight against McCarthyism his ammunition was drawn heavily from its armory. How could the nation determine if the enthusiastic search for domestic anticommunists was beneficial? Test the consequences. "What are the advantages," he asked, "what the costs of such investigations?" Will more or fewer good scholars be drawn to the universities under such a regime? What is the cost of the disruption of teaching? What is the effect on intellectual freedom on campus?[54] These, he warned, "are questions that the pragmatists require us to answer. They are questions that look not to abstract rights, but to actual consequences." Commager predicted that the consequence of McCarthyism would be that American culture would adopt "an official standard of conformity, orthodoxy, and loyalty," that good minds would no longer enter the university, that originality and criticism would wither, and that cultural disaster would result.[55]

In the passion of the moment, at a time when the nation seemed to be caught in the grip of an abstract preoccupation against all kinds of domestic radicalism and liberalism, Commager thought it best to bring policy considerations down to a practical level. While he admitted that principles were essential, when dealing with McCarthyism he urged that "it is in the application that we discover their meaning. It is the application that is the test. If we are to solve our problems, it must be by traveling the road of conduct and consequences. Theory may mislead us; experience must be our guide." The test Commager envisioned was a social test, meant to evaluate the impact of policy and ideas on the life of the community. "Look solely to the social interest, the community interest, in the matter," he advised a nation caught in an anticommunist fever, "and apply the test of consequences."[56]

While much of America worried, justifiably, about the Soviet threat to intellectual freedom, he fretted about a different kind of totalitarian threat. Pragmatist that he was, Commager, like William James and John Dewey, feared intellectual absolutism and a priori assumptions that would stifle the diversity of thought necessary to test ideas for their validity. At a luncheon arranged by the Freedom House in New York City early in 1952, Commager and Edgar Ansel Mowrer, a former foreign correspondent, presented a discussion titled "What Do We Mean by Freedom?" Commager suggested that "those who fear criticism or censor books and teaching subscribe to a policy of absolutism which makes no allowance for further truth to be discovered." So McCarthyism, like other kinds of absolutist approaches, was dangerous at least partly because it undermined the pragmatic method of proceeding with life and thought.[57]

In his fight against McCarthyism Commager came into conflict with the philosopher Sidney Hook, an even more recognized pragmatist. There are striking similarities between the careers of Commager and Hook. The two were born less than two months apart in 1902. In 1926 the young Commager began his teaching career at New York University, and the following year Hook joined the faculty. They taught under the same roof until 1939, when Commager took a job at Columbia. Both writers claimed to have been strongly influenced by Jefferson, and indeed the issues of free speech and intellectual freedom were central to their separate agendas. Both were self-proclaimed pragmatists who admired John Dewey. Hook studied under Dewey and became his friend and political ally. Commager paid a strong tribute to Dewey in *The American Mind*.[58] Both served as cultural critics and intellectual generalists who frequently wrote for the broad public on issues of political and cultural importance. Further, they were among the most prolific writers in America about the issues of repression and subversion during the McCarthy period.

Hook was a leading member of the New York Intellectuals. Raised in the Williamsburg section of Brooklyn, Hook attended City College and then did his graduate work at Columbia under Dewey. In the late 1920s and early 1930s Hook was an internationally recognized Marxist scholar who was attracted to communism and socialism, but in the wake of the Moscow Trials in the mid-1930s he joined the rest of the *Partisan Review* circle as a member of the anti-Stalinist independent Left. Throughout his career he constantly wrote articles warning of the dangers of totalitarian threats to freedom. Although after World War II he continued to call himself a socialist and associated himself formally with social democrats, Hook was actually a liberal who followed Jefferson and Dewey.

Although Commager and Hook shared many liberal and pragmatic axioms, the conclusions they reached on the issues of McCarthyism were sharply antagonistic to each other. Hook reviewed *Freedom, Loyalty, Dissent* for the *New Republic*. While he appreciated Commager's liberal concern for freedom, Hook thought it was weak broth and dismissed the essays as "heart-warming affirmations of the liberal faith." Commager had none of the toughness real liberals needed in a dangerous world in order to protect freedom, he felt. He complained that Commager avoided the question of whether national security was a justifiable concern and whether Communists threatened that security.[59]

Real pragmatic liberalism, according to Hook—the liberalism of Oliver Wendell Holmes and John Dewey—went beyond a passion for freedom and instead resolved dilemmas. That is what he felt Commager lacked. Liberals, Hook urged, needed to solve such problems as whether an allegiance to a foreign government disqualified a person from service to his own. Further, did the protections of the Bill of Rights guarantee the right to work for one's government? "Would Commager argue that to deny a fervent apostle of enforced euthanasia a post as director of a home for the aged and infirm is necessarily to deny him his civil rights?" he wondered. The problem, in effect, was not to catch offenders after they had committed espionage but to prevent it beforehand.[60]

To illustrate his point, Hook, like Kristol, brought the issue around to Nazism rather than Communism. "I am confident," he predicted, "that in 1939 if any State Department official had expressed the idea that Hitler's anti-Semitism was justified, Commager like the rest of us would have demanded his dismissal even as we defended his right as a *private* citizen to express his dangerous ideas." And it is true, Commager earlier had been in favor of similar censorship. In a *Senior Scholastic* column in 1946, Commager asked his adolescent readers whether organizations such as the Ku Klux Klan, "formed to destroy our institutions of liberty and to incite racial or class hatreds[,] should be tolerated on the plea of their right to those very freedoms they seek to destroy."[61] So Hook's belief that Communists should not be allowed to teach seemed not very different from Commager's own counsel to his high school audience about racists.

In addition, Hook thought that Commager was clumsy in his use of pragmatism because he misapplied the test of consequences. "He is like a man who ignores or denies there is a gas leak because consequences show that hunting for a gas leak with an open flame is dangerous. Meanwhile the smell of gas becomes stronger and stronger." The consequences of one proposal, Hook pointed out, are never decisive unless weighed against those of other proposals—including in this case the recommendation to do nothing.[62]

Not as polemical or contentious as Hook (the two never knew each other well), Commager never responded with the fire and passion characteristic of the *Partisan Review* crowd. He was not quick to anger. As he wrote to Nevins, he frequently met people who were "a bit aggressive, if you know what I mean. A kind of professional liberal, unlike your old friend Commager who takes his crusades with a jest on his lips and a hearty and affectionate embrace for his opponents."[63]

Commager was not particularly concerned with Hook's judgment of his pragmatism, for he considered Hook to be one who had never left the passion of his old communist ideas, one who never really became a pragmatist because his thought was deductive rather than inductive. He was a rigid thinker, according to Commager, and that fit well with his cold war anti-communism.[64] For, as Commager explained in the *Saturday Review* in the 1960s, cold warriors believe that "the struggle between democracy and communism is the struggle between Light and Darkness, Good and Evil, and that the moral distinction is an absolute one."[65] Commager felt that their disillusionment with Stalinism led them to the irony of becoming persecutors themselves.[66] Of course the New York Intellectuals, he acknowledged, had a right to change their views from socialism to liberalism and from persecuted to persecutors.

Hook, however, thought that if Commager were a pragmatist, then others were not—not Peirce, James, Dewey, or Hook himself—because the pragmatist tests a problem by its consequences, which he felt Commager ignored.[67] But, like Hook, Commager carried the credentials of a certified pragmatist. In the autumn of 1949, at the closing ceremony of John Dewey's ninetieth birthday, Commager was one of the few invited to address the crowd of one thousand at Teachers College at Columbia University.[68]

The conflict between Commager and Hook gives us two "liberal" and "pragmatic" approaches to preserving intellectual freedom during the McCarthy period. Each believed in testing a course of action by its consequences. But each was interested in testing and preserving a different feature of political society. Hook wanted to preserve the *system* of democratic freedom and was vigilant about any threat to it—such as totalitarianism. In Hook's case we test for a threat to the intellectual openness of the system, and finding it, we try to exclude the element that would subvert a system of continuing openness. Commager shared Hook's commitment to maintaining democratic freedom (to which he saw McCarthyism as a great threat), but Commager was more enthusiastic than Hook about preserving *dissent*. In Commager's approach we test not for dangers to the system but sample the tolerance for dissent itself. If we are damaging the freedom of dissent in our attempt to protect it, according to Commager, the solution is worse than the danger.

Part of their disagreement resulted from different concerns about freedom. Hook was most worried about remaining free of totalitarianism, which he felt could permanently close future options for political choice. So, according to Hook, there should be limitations on democratic decisions. Naturally, majority conclusions are acceptable only if reached freely and are illegitimate if forced. Further, democratic decisions are justifiable only if they keep future political choices and revisions open. That is, Hook would not support a democratic vote in Canada in which a majority chose a one-party, communist, totalitarian government, because that would preclude any future democratic choices. A pragmatist and democrat, Hook believed, could not support what was in effect an irreversible decision.

Commager, however, was far more vigilant about freedom in the marketplace of ideas and thought that Hook's anticommunism was a more likely threat than totalitarianism to that marketplace. If Hook's stridency would not be as devastating as totalitarianism to freedom of thought, it was still much more likely to interfere in the freedom of American debate.

Yet, contrary to the suspicions that most of the New York Intellectuals (including Schlesinger, Kristol, Macdonald, and Hook) cultivated toward Commager, the literary critic Alfred Kazin, another member of the New York group, put Commager's relationship to the circle in a different context. Henry and Alfred had been friends from their time teaching near each other in central Massachusetts, and the two had shared a politics of the democratic, liberal Left. Kazin, speaking of the *Partisan Review* crowd, scorned "what ex-Marxists like Hook & Howe think about [Commager's] 'softness' on Communism." Instead, Kazin considered Henry "an example of old-fashioned American freedom and integrity at a time when Hook and Kristol and that whole gang of sour ex-Stalinists and ex-Trotskyites were lending moral support and more to McCarthy."[69]

As Jacques Barzun, Commager's friend and colleague at Columbia, remembers it, Henry felt a "mingled annoyance and amusement" at reproaches he received occasionally from the glib but hornetlike conservative writers at the *National Review*.[70] As a prominent voice of liberal activism, he became a natural target for the antagonisms of the political Right.

Whatever mild amusement he might earlier have felt turned to undiluted annoyance—make that outrage—when he received a letter in September 1959 from William F. Buckley Jr., editor of the *National Review*. The magazine,

Buckley informed him, was going to do a series of profiles on activist pro-fessors and needed information on him for this purpose. "A Mr. Streeter writes us that he has reason to believe that you adopted your middle name at a time when you admired Joseph Stalin," Buckley noted to Commager. "Would you be good enough to let me know whether this is true?" Buckley later recalled that Streeter claimed to have gone to graduate school with Commager.[71] Since *stahl* is the Russian word for steel (and Stalin was thereby the man of steel), Buckley wondered whether Commager's Steele paid trib-ute to the Soviet leader.

Apparently Commager responded to Buckley with a hostile note, for Buckley, perhaps in mock surprise, claimed that he could not understand how a public figure, especially a historian, could be so dismayed over this sort of question. Buckley, following Commager's suggestion that he do the research himself, "learned that indeed your name was not always Henry Steele Commager but, stretching at least into the very early thirties, Henry Irving Commager. It appears then that the flowering of your name and the ascendancy of Stalin did[,] in fact, coincide, and the question has been raised whether there was causal relation between the two events."[72]

It is true that he had been born Henry Irving Commager and had used that name while in graduate school, signing his letters to his friend Hans Duus "H.I.C." in the mid-1920s.[73] Steele replaced Irving as a name sometime between early 1927, when he published his master's thesis in the *Oregon Historical Quarterly* without using a middle name, and 1928, when he filed his doctoral dissertation at the University of Chicago using Henry Steele Commager.[74]

But Buckley was wrong. In 1928, as throughout his career, Commager was under the spell of Monticello rather than Moscow. Later Mary Powlesland Commager, his second wife, said he had made the change to elevate his name after he began collaborating with the likes of the patrician Samuel Eliot Morison.[75] Yet it is not clear whether he knew Morison in 1928. Just as likely, Commager adopted the name of his great grandfather because his new wife, Evan Carroll, had such deep family roots in South Carolina that he felt prompted to establish his own workable family history.[76]

Offended by Buckley's intrusion, Commager felt he had been asked a leading and presumptuous question, such as whether he had taken advan-tage of a woman in college. "If you care to press the analogy between my question and one asking whether you seduced a girl while at college, please do so," Buckley encouraged him, "as I am interested that you should rank them together. I think I now understand more clearly the premises of your book, *Freedom, Loyalty, Dissent*, in which you do, come to think of it, appear to be saying that it is as much a man's personal business whether he had a flirtation with Communism, as it is whether he had one with a girl."[77]

Charging that Buckley was vulgar, Commager threatened that if the magazine published any of this information, "the consequences might be painful to you." Instead, Buckley should consult the dedication page to Commager's edited collection *The Blue and the Gray* for the source of his middle name. There he paid tribute to the name of his grandfather Henry Steel Commager, the lawyer, congressional candidate, and Civil War hero.[78] After trading letters about whether Commager's letters to Buckley could be reprinted, the correspondence came to an end with a final letter from Buckley. He reminded Commager that he was "not in the least shocked by men who flirted with Communism in the early thirties: indeed, at *National Review* I am surrounded by eminent men who did just that, and they are my friends and associates—but they would certainly not deny that their early experience was a formative intellectual influence, of authentic interest to anyone interested in the development of their thought."

True, Buckley fraternized at the conservative magazine with former leftists as Max Eastman, John Dos Passos, and James Burnham, among others. But Buckley, of course, was mistaken about Commager's past. There was nothing to the left of Parrington, Parker, and the New Deal in Commager's closet. He had been a liberal all his life, and socialism had never intruded into his plans as it had for so many intellectuals of his generation. Commager had always strolled the gardens of Wilson and Jefferson, Brandeis and Franklin Roosevelt, and at his most daring he wandered only so far as Bryan and Beard. So it must have surprised Commager to have Buckley tell him that "my interest in you is as a talkative spokesman for the strident Left. Your extremism, after all," Buckley continued, "is as well an object of concern to members of the responsible left (e.g., Sidney Hook) as to members of the responsible right (e.g., myself)."[79]

Lester Markel and others at the *New York Times Magazine* would have laughed at the idea that for two decades they had been featuring a member of the strident Left as one of their most prominent voices. The strident Left? The very trait that must have angered Buckley was that Commager was a principled liberal with none of the leftist ideological perspective that Hook and the New York Intellectuals (who, by this time, appreciated liberalism) still carried with them. Buckley liked Hook's crowd because they hated communism and perhaps even socialism with a passion that the *National Review* shared. The Communists and the rest of the Far Left, after all, had betrayed the New York group's youthful hopes. It was a disillusionment Commager missed, so he was never prompted to hate or fear the Far Left as much as either Hook or Buckley wanted him to. As the New York Intellectuals might have put it, Commager never underwent an appropriate vaccination against Communism.

At the end of his letter, Buckley tried to justify his Stalin-Steele inquiry. Clearly, "if by understanding your intellectual background better I could contribute to a better understanding of the peculiar views you take," he told Commager brashly, "I should be performing a service to our readers and the nation. It is not enough to say merely that you are a peculiar man—an adult who suddenly changes his name, a historian who turns ferociously on those who seek historical data from him, a gentleman of such wanton epistolary manners: there must be something else."[80]

Yet the real curiosity is not that an American changed his name in adulthood but that this act should raise the eyebrows of an editor of a magazine that claimed to understand the national culture. Buckley's surprise shows that, as a member of the upper-class elite, he had little understanding of the American experience—in which the changing of names and the shedding, adoption, and evolution of identities is common and absolutely central. Many of the New York Intellectuals, those members of the "responsible Left" who Buckley claimed to admire, no longer sported the names their families had when they first arrived in the United States. Daniel Bell, Irving Howe, and Philip Rahv—not to mention countless other immigrants and their families—had all undergone a process similar to the one Buckley found so abhorrent in Commager.

Unlike so many others in the forties and fifties who were the subject of investigations, the reticence—more, the outright anger—that Commager showed toward Buckley's inquiry had nothing to do with his political past, despite Buckley's suspicions. Rather, Commager's silence welled from a much deeper source: personal humiliation and grief about his family circumstances during his childhood. Farmed out to live with his grandfather after his mother died and his alcoholic father abandoned him, Commager shielded his childhood from public view and refused to allow biographical inquiries for the rest of his life.

In his late twenties, when he began publishing, he changed from Henry Irving Commager, or sometimes simply Henry Commager, to Henry Steele Commager. Especially around the social and intellectual elite he encountered in New York and New England, he felt sensitive about his beginnings. Around the well-bred, the literati, the old money, the well-connected, he never felt elegant. He did not change his middle name formally or legally— he just started writing under his new title.[81] It is sad that Commager's embarrassment about his childhood robbed him of a pride in that common and very American act: adopting a new name. This was a particularly ironic loss inflicted on one of the most enthusiastic interpreters of the American character. And it unfortunately left him open to be threatened by his conservative antagonists at the *National Review.*

Undeterred by his failure to make the Stalin-Steele connection, Buckley arranged a piece in the magazine in which Commager's allegedly leftist vision would be exposed as a collection of bankrupt yet dangerous ideas. The result was "The Spacious Ideas of Mr. Commager" (1960), written by William Frost Rickenbacker. The son of Captain Eddie Rickenbacker of World War I fame, he was an investment adviser who within two years would be a member of the Conservative Party of New York and a senior editor at Buckley's magazine. The occasion for launching Rickenbacker's assault was Commager's "Urgent Query: Why Do We Lack Statesmen?" in the *New York Times Magazine,* an uncontroversial and moderate article that, although his most recent outing, was hardly the best target for conservatives to use to illustrate his radical beliefs. Even the most ardent supporters of the *National Review*'s conservative agenda surely considered Rickenbacker's essay a vacuous and ineffective attack, a dull piece of boilerplate so lifeless and devoid of ideas that the magazine's staff must have been more distressed than Commager. Those who fought their way to the end of the article found a weak indictment of the target amid the cold and stilted prose.[82]

Consequently, those at the magazine decided to go on the offensive again, and two weeks later John Chamberlain produced another article concerning Commager's analysis of America's current shortage of statesmen. Chamberlain must have found the assignment frustrating, for the worst he could catapult at Commager were the accusations that he was "fast becoming America's Number One Worry Wart as he deplores the passing scene," that he "knows that something is the matter" but "can't quite put his finger on it," and that he did not see that statesmen lose their mystique "when people turn to government for everything from electric power to aspirin tablets."[83] This could not have been the indictment of a member of the "strident Left" that Buckley hoped for when he originally went fishing for a suspected admirer of Joseph Stalin.

It is easy to suspect that, unlike the severe and humorless members of the political Right, the witty and playfully conservative Buckley was merely tweaking Commager and trying to get a rise out of him. It worked. But the episode also provides an opportunity for some interesting observations. In his reaction to Buckley's letters, Commager revealed the mixture of shame and insecurity about his social past that he never let show in other situations. Perhaps more important, Buckley's characterization of him as a voice of the strident Left showed the extent to which Commager was frequently seen as a radical activist rather than as a Jeffersonian liberal dissenter.

As an activist whose earlier writing had explored the moral campaigns of Theodore Parker and the political wisdom of majority rule, it came as no surprise that Commager rose publicly against the threats of McCarthyism. His work as a public intellectual on this issue provoked an interesting reaction from across the political spectrum and provides a useful sketch of the political community at midcentury. Conservatives, of course, simply considered Commager a dupe whose cautions against excessive anticommunism only aided Stalin.

Significantly, liberals were much more varied in their response to Commager. Many of Commager's competitors considered his anti-McCarthyism talk to consist of only liberal clichés and utopian exhortations, complaining that he addressed none of the hard problems such as whether communists should be allowed to hold sensitive jobs.

But Commager forged an intelligent middle path between the two antagonistic wings of midcentury liberalism. Moderate in liberal principle, he remained fierce and courageous in the battle to defend intellectual freedom. Representing the best of liberal independence, Commager was unwilling to befriend Soviet or domestic Communism as did those in the *Nation* neighborhood of liberalism. Yet, unlike those liberals in the *Partisan Review* crowd, he worked strongly to protect the rights of communists to speak, meet, and promote an ideological debate in the United States.

CHAPTER 6

University, Family, and Race,
1945-1968

Residing in the top reaches of stately, brick Fayerweather Hall, only a short distance from the rotunda of Low Memorial Library, the Columbia University history department faculty in the 1950s contained an impressive collection of intellectuals and scholars. There, in quarters atop Morningside Heights, six flights above the honking and rumbling of Amsterdam Avenue, in offices whose rattling windows gazed out over West Harlem and then, in the distance, over the roofs and clutter of East Harlem to the jumbled skyline of Queens and the Bronx, were lodged Henry Steele Commager (at Columbia from 1939 to 1956), Allan Nevins (1928–58), Richard Morris (1946–73), Jacques Barzun (1929–75), William Leuchtenburg (1952–83), David Donald (1947–59), Dumas Malone (1945–59), and others. Richard Hofstadter (1946–70), among the most prominent of the Columbia historians, maintained his office in Hamilton Hall, a few buildings closer to the library.

By this time, Commager's reputation stood equal to that of any colleague in the department. Already he had served as the Pitt Professor of American History at Cambridge University and was recognized as a prolific scholarly figure in the field. Further, he was identified nationally outside the discipline of history as a cultural figure. In February 1952 he was elected to the National Institute of Arts and Letters, whose lifetime memberships were limited to 250. Others inducted with him into the institute's literary wing included Newton Arvin, Jacques Barzun, Louise Bogan, Waldo Frank, Carson McCullers, Eudora Welty, and Tennessee Williams.[1] So Commager's contributions to American letters were acknowledged nationally by midcentury. He claimed, probably with a mixture of humor, delight, and horror, that he was already being called "venerable" by 1950, two years before his fiftieth birthday.[2]

Around the Columbia campus Commager lugged with him a fat briefcase stuffed with books, "a smashed and ancient thing fit only for the ash can or an essay by Beerbohm." In his Fayerweather office, a "narrow, book-lined canyon" next to that of his friend Dick Morris, he worked on his scholarly writing and editing, kept his typewriter clacking turning out talks and articles for the general public, and met and advised his graduate students.[3] Teaching was, after all, one of the most important responsibilities for which Commager was being paid by Columbia, despite the many other goals on his scholarly and civic agenda. While Columbia has never been known for the amount of time history professors have been expected to give their students, teaching was still a requirement that had to be performed.

Commager's lecturing was typical of his personality: brilliant but sometimes disorganized and impromptu. Consider his performance in his course on American constitutional history, for example. Leonard Levy, who later would go on to teach at Brandeis and Claremont Graduate School, was a Commager Ph.D. student from 1947 to 1951. "When I was his assistant, in his office," Levy explained, "I saw him prepare for a class; he went to his file, opened a drawer, pulled out some illegible notes, scanned them, returned them, and went empty-handed into class, where he was brilliant and spoke magnificent English extemporaneously." Commager was animated. Unable to remain still behind a lectern, he paced the room, looking out the window, glancing at his students, speaking in "free association in perfect English without text," peppering his lectures with quotations he knew by heart, providing strong interpretations on such matters as judicial review and the formation of the Constitution.[4]

Historian John Thomas, who later taught at Brown University, as a graduate student also took Commager's constitutional history course and found that he had "a hard-driving lecture style closely tailored to hard-nosed law students." The energetic, stocky Commager "wandered back and forth across the stage, talking full blast with that lisp of his out of the corner of his mouth," explaining the historical context of important legal cases. "My own most vivid college memory," Linda Kerber noted about her time as an undergraduate at Barnard, "is of Henry Steele Commager, the great American historian at that point, very late in his life, short, a roly-poly man, pacing back and forth on a stage in a great big lecture hall, thundering that there are things a government, even a majority, may not do." As a lecturer, Commager

William Leuchtenburg
in November 1948, when
he was a Commager
graduate student.
(Courtesy of William Leuchtenburg)

was exercising his strengths. "Commager was a great teacher," Levy noted about Commager's love of speaking. "He lectured everywhere in the world. He would talk to kids in a grade school, to the faculty at Oxford, to a Senate committee, to the supporters of Brandeis U., to anyone, so long as he could talk."[5]

Most doctoral students who gravitated to Commager were interested in constitutional history. Those graduate students more engaged in intellectual history, such as Commager's future son-in-law Christopher Lasch, instead found themselves drawn to Richard Hofstadter or William Leuchtenburg.[6] At the time, Columbia offered doctoral seminars in which students would begin writing their dissertations. Commager's seminar met in his office, with him seated at the desk at the end of the room and his students propped stiffly in hard chairs that lined the walls. As a student delivered a report on his or her dissertation, Commager looked through papers on his desk, occasionally read the *New York Times*, and paid little direct attention to the orator who held the floor. Yet he would then suddenly interject a comment or question, "revealing the speaker to be an ignoramus." A week before a report, a student put on reserve in the library a chapter of his or her dissertation for others in the class to read. "Every student had to read the chapter and come to class prepared to savage it," Levy explained. "The more mistakes we could find, the more omissions, misjudgments, and conclusions that didn't follow, the better. He really taught us to be brutally critical. I loved it. Most couldn't take it." Levy remembered that Commager, in these sessions, "operated as if he believed in survival of the fittest. His seminar was like a jungle—a few of us were hunters, the rest the prey. . . . [H]e was a fierce seminar teacher: he scorched people who were weak or soft-hearted. He could be cruel in his comments."[7]

Commager left some of his students to themselves, as he did William Leuchtenburg, who wrote his dissertation in a year.[8] With other students he provided more direction. Levy, who had served in the military, said of Commager: "He gave orders; I followed them, literally. He said, next week you WILL choose your dissertation topic. . . . The week after one chose a topic he said, 'next week you will bring in your bibliographies. The week after you will bring in some written material. I expect a chapter to be completed the week after that.' " These orders showed how Commager approached his own writing: don't waste time, don't overresearch, and get right to it. "He used to say start writing immediately," Levy reported about Commager's advice, "never begin at the beginning, jump into the middle somewhere, write as fast as you can, compose at the typewriter, stop only to look up something you don't know. On the whole," Levy concluded, "he was right."[9] Yet if some of Commager's detractors felt his scholarship was too thin, his manner of writing, which was essentially that of a journalist, might provide them ammunition.

Harold Hyman, another Commager graduate student, arrived at Columbia after serving as a Marine and then attending the University of California at Los Angeles as an undergraduate and, like Commager's other students, found him rather overwhelming. As Hyman saw it, Commager knew every piece of writing being discussed and "could find exact pages and paragraphs relevant to any point one was making." Because Hyman and Commager "were both warm liberals," Hyman was drawn to Commager's anti-McCarthyism during the late 1940s and early 1950s. As a result, Hyman wrote a dissertation on loyalty testing that became *Era of the Oath: Northern Loyalty Tests during the Civil War and Reconstruction* (1954), his first book. "I am endlessly grateful to him," Hyman noted fondly of Commager's direction, "though my scarred back never healed from his emphatic criticisms."[10]

To some of Commager's students it seemed as though his mind was often somewhere other than on his students and their work. Some of his charges wondered whether he read their writing carefully and entirely, and their doubt conjures the image of him reading the *Times* during seminars. Even as close a student as Levy admitted that "it was hard talking *with* him. He was a compulsive nonstop one-way talker. He often did not listen (outside of class,

Harold Hyman and
his wife, Ferne, in 1952.
(Photograph by David Donald;
courtesy of Harold Hyman)

or in it)." Yet Commager, despite all of his distractions, worked to promote
the careers of the best of his students. He helped find Leuchtenburg a job at
Harvard and then called to bring him back to a permanent job at Columbia.
When Leuchtenburg was young and relatively unpublished, Henry asked
him to write a volume in the New American Nation Series, which ultimately
became the respected *Franklin D. Roosevelt and the New Deal* (1963), and
invited him to participate in the Morison and Commager textbook *The
Growth of the American Republic*. He recommended Levy to Swarthmore,
Harvard, Yale, and Brandeis, the latter of which hired the young constitutional historian and promoted him until the point he refused the university's
presidency. "I found him to be a booster of my career," Levy emphasized,
"even when he disagreed with me." Commager was worried that two of
Levy's books, *Legacy of Suppression* (1960) and *Jefferson and Civil Liberties:
The Darker Side* (1963), would give ammunition to the McCarthyites, but he
still gave *Legacy* a friendly review in the *New York Herald Tribune* book
section.[11]

Commager was elusive, but he provided his students a model of a prolific
writer, helped them find positions, and taught them the mechanics, assumptions, and conventions of historians. Despite his own partisan liberal political beliefs, Commager taught Hyman "the absolute priority we must give to
ascertainable facts," and he instructed Levy to "go where the evidence goes."

He was a formative influence on his students, as once Andrew McLaughlin and William Dodd had been on him. "He taught," Hyman said simply of Henry's influence on his students. "[W]hat more is there?"[12]

Commager's friend Allan Nevins was even more of a presence than he on the sixth floor of Fayerweather. Nevins's colleagues constantly heard the tapping of his typewriter through the glass in his office door. They saw him rushing through corridors, along the sidewalks between buildings, or to and from the subway, on his way to appointments or research or classes, "his short legs chopping the ground," oblivious to his immediate surroundings, often with both arms full of books, a briefcase, and manuscripts and hauling a portable typewriter that seemed a permanent appendage. Prompted by the work ethic of his farm background, Nevins raced through each moment of his life so as to defeat time, hurrying to finish his list of projects, with those who wished to speak to him often scampering alongside him, gasping out words between labored breaths.[13]

Although Nevins was already a legend in the profession, he had no arrogance about him. Consider his treatment of the young Civil War historian David Donald, who arrived at Columbia to teach as an instructor in 1947. One day Nevins wandered into the crowded office shared by Donald and some other instructors and was shocked at the lack of space. This will never do, he announced, and he pointed at Donald and said, you shall be my officemate. So Donald spent two years as a fellow faculty member in Nevins's quarters in Fayerweather. Still, while Nevins was concerned about students, Leuchtenburg "never found him a warm man. For some time after I joined the department, he referred to me as that 'young blond fellow down the hall with the German name.'"[14]

Lecturing in front of a class, Nevins was anything but electrifying. History, which inherently carried its own excitement, Nevins thought, did not need to be framed in neon. Lackadaisical students found him boring, and even some of the best students regretted that he "mumble-read his lectures, oblivious to his audience." He was not a quick and brilliant Commager onstage.[15] Nevins taught mostly nineteenth- and early-twentieth-century political history but also offered courses in biography, historiography, and historical methods. Because Columbia, in the late 1940s, began matriculating more mature and better-trained students who had returned from war and were looking toward careers in history, Nevins began to focus more on doctoral students. Reversing the normal pattern of teaching two lecture courses and a seminar, he instead taught two doctoral seminars and a lecture course. By the time Nevins retired from Columbia in 1958, he had guided 117 students to their Ph.D., and as he noted, that figure was "perhaps the more remarkable because I entered university teaching late, after a long series of years spent in journalism."[16]

While stories were told of Nevins reading book reviews during his students' reports in doctoral seminars, he was never accused of a lack of attention to his graduate students.[17] Commager noted his friend's "ceaseless benevolence" to his students, to whom Nevins acted "*in loco parentis.*" Other colleagues felt "mixed feelings about his role as stalwart champion of graduate students at subject orals and dissertation examinations," occasions at which "Allan became a lion at the side of the defendant, arguing his case so vehemently that the other inquisitors were cowed into silence." After his students left Columbia they continued to ask his help: would he read their most recent manuscript or write an introduction to their book? Nevins always obliged, and a waist-high pile of their manuscripts balanced uneasily in the corner of his office.[18]

Although Nevins had been rumored to employ a team of graduate students or postdocs to research and write his books for him, David Donald saw it differently. Instead it was more a charity operation for sad and useless academics who were not working on anything and had nothing else to do. Because he felt sorry for them, Nevins took them on and paid them out of his own pocket, although their contributions were next to useless for his work.[19] The rumors of Nevins running a "factory" arose, of course, because of his incredible productivity. Those who knew him understood that he simply had a talent for hard and efficient work. One observer remembered him working in the Illinois State Historical Library helping to sort a particular collection of papers, while at the same time, "typing rapidly with two fingers, Nevins was able to go through the papers as fast as six people could sort them."[20]

After his retirement from Columbia in 1958, Nevins took an office and became a senior research associate in the Huntington Library in Pasadena, where he could write his books. Nevins's life, particularly after World War II, had orbited around his impressive eight volumes addressing the Civil War. In slightly over a decade he published *Ordeal of the Union* in two volumes (1947), *The Emergence of Lincoln* in two volumes (1950), and *The War for the Union* in four volumes (1958).

Nothing was so representative of Nevins as his perpetual impatience to complete his work. On one occasion, Commager's two sisters-in-law, Lydia and Margaret Carroll, came to see the Nevins summer home in Vermont. In his wife's absence, Allan led them on a tour through the various rooms, ending in his study. "And this is my typewriter," he told his visitors distantly, beginning to forget they were there. At that point he sat down and began finishing the page in the machine. After standing uneasily for a short period, the two women let themselves out of the house.[21] Jacques Barzun remembered Nevins hurrying back to his office in the ten minutes between classes to add a few sentences to the book he was writing. Another story, probably apocryphal, finds Nevins and Commager straphanging on the subway together, with Allan telling Henry, "You should have brought your portable typewriter."[22]

At the Huntington, Nevins, in addition to his scholarship, had lunch with visiting scholars and led a regular legendary hike around the grounds at midday that left individuals half his seventy-five years of age soaked with sweat and begging for a rest. "No obstacle was too great to be surmounted," his Huntington colleague Ray Allen Billington remarked with amused resignation, "whether sprinkler to be braved, thicket to be bested, hill to be climbed, or ditch to be hurdled, whatever the effect on the scholars who straggled in his wake."[23]

Billington reported seeing him arrive at the office wearing two ties, one tied atop the other. On another occasion he forgot the name of his son-in-law. Dinner parties at the Nevins home featured Mary presiding over cocktail hour while Allan continued to work upstairs. When the main course was served and Mary called him, Allan would come hurrying downstairs still working his way into his jacket. Once, as Billington and Nevins drove to a friend's party, Allan suggested they synchronize their watches and meet back at the door after twenty-five minutes to return to work. "Few scholars could cut themselves off so completely from the world around them," Billington explained. "To extract Allan from his office at noontime required a patient wait in his doorway, a succession of increasingly notable coughs and throat clearings, moving closer in the hope of being noticed, and finally a touch on the shoulder. His jump, and often the 'Damn' that he shouted as his chain of thought was broken, attested to the distance that separated him from mundane affairs." Similarly, once, at the Huntington, Allan invited a friend to join him for lunch. When the friend arrived, he called Nevins's office from the reception room and was told to wait a few moments while Allan finished a thought on paper. After a considerable time the friend gave up and began eating alone in the lunchroom. When Nevins finally wandered in, he spotted his friend, went to the table, shook his hand, and exclaimed, "How nice to see you. You must come and have lunch with me some day."[24] Allan's friends understood and were patient with him.

In addition to juggling his scholarly and intellectual roles, in the 1950s Commager, like many other liberals of the period, struggled to find a workable balance between Jeffersonianism and Hamiltonianism. Despite his commitment to Jeffersonian principles of intellectual freedom and liberty and of relative equality, with most twentieth-century liberals he shared a belief in the beneficial qualities of a strong and active government.[25]

Rising out of the breakup of the feudal order in the European middle ages, the doctrine of individualism grew slowly in seventeenth-century Britain and eighteenth-century North America. In economics this individualist doctrine became capitalism, in the Christian religion it became Protestantism, and in politics it became classical liberalism. As classical liberalism passed from the seventeenth through the nineteenth centuries, it took as its task to guard the rights of the individual against the greatest threat to the individual: the state. So in these centuries liberalism was an antistatist outlook.[26]

But with the rise of the large corporation in industrial America at the beginning of the twentieth century, liberals, who continued to guard individual liberties, realized that the corporation was a far more dangerous threat to individual liberty than was the government. To maintain their consistent defense of individual rights, then, liberals had to switch enemies. So during the twentieth century liberals turned increasingly to their old adversary, the state, for protection from the new adversary, the corporation. Because they believed themselves consistent in their protection of the individual from harm, twentieth-century liberals still thought of themselves as Jeffersonians. Yet, as Herbert Croly had implied in 1909, increasingly those Jeffersonian goals were being achieved by the Hamiltonian ends of planning, strong government, and an organic rather than decentralized vision of society.[27]

Within these ironies of twentieth-century American liberalism Commager fit quite comfortably. Although he justifiably considered himself one of the leading and principled Jeffersonians of his age, he also realized the importance of coordinated and collective action to achieve a livable commonwealth. Action by the national government, especially before the New Deal, Commager acknowledged in 1943, had often been more harmful than good. Consider the example of labor. When the government intervened in disputes between labor and business, especially in the late nineteenth and early twentieth centuries, it usually was hostile to labor and would bring in militias or injunctions to aid the owners. But he pointed out that in the twentieth century the government had turned slowly toward legislative solutions and reluctantly saw the need for laws controlling hours, wages, and conditions.[28]

To those who were worried about increasing "red tape" with the growth of government, Commager suggested that bureaucracy was nothing new and not invented in the New Deal. "It is to be found," he assured them, "in any large organization—in corporations, labor unions, universities, churches, wherever administration is necessary." Patience and perspective is what were needed. Ever since the industrial revolution both political parties had asked more of government. After all, what was the alternative? Should we retreat to the days before administration was rationalized, regularized, and codified? Did we really want to go back to the days of favoritism and the spoils system instead of bearing some of the bureaucratic inconvenience of uniformity?[29]

In a review in 1946, Commager dismissed Friedrich Hayek's The Road to Serfdom, with its fear of big government, as an antiquarian Spencerian worry. Only those with simple minds such as Hayek's, he noted, would conflate the welfare state and dictatorship or planning and totalitarianism. He reminded Hayek that "Germany and Russia are not America and Britain, and that conclusions drawn from the former are not inevitably applicable to the latter."[30]

As one might expect, Commager's The American Mind in 1950 allowed him to articulate his beliefs about the proper role of government. "The pernicious notion that there was some inevitable conflict between man and the state had long embarrassed American politics," he reported, but Theodore Roosevelt and Woodrow Wilson had helped to dispel that conviction during the Progressive Era. Commager admitted that the distrust of government had been inherited from his hero Jefferson, and he was relieved that it had given way "to the realization that the government was man organized politically, and that vigilance—still the price of liberty—was not synonymous with paralysis. The 'necessary evil' of Thomas Paine had become so necessary that it was no longer an evil."[31]

The New Deal had taken the advances of the Progressives and created a new approach. The Tennessee Valley Authority (TVA), for example, "was planning, but planning not superimposed from above but worked out cooperatively by those who were involved. It was socialization, but socialization that prospered rather than impaired private industry. . . . It was centralization, but centralization that operated through local communities and that actually strengthened both the states and communities where it operated. . . . [A]nd its regionalism cut across artificial state lines to offer a new solution to the old problem of federalism." In a comment that was optimistic even for a liberal, Commager suggested that the TVA "was the justification of Lester Ward's thesis that public intelligence can operate most effectively through government and that government can be more efficient than business."[32]

In 1963 in response to the rise of the states' rights philosophy in the South to battle the civil rights movement, Commager replied that the fear of nationalism and the federal government was absurd. "What an extraordinary spectacle it is," he remarked, "this fear of the United States by its own citizens!" Citizens should not fear the national government, for most of the obstacles to liberty in the past had come from the states. Sure "bigness is dangerous; the welfare state can dry up initiative; power does tend to corrupt, and there is much to be said for fragmentation of political authority." But turning to state power was no solution.[33]

Yes, big government is hazardous, Commager admitted, especially in its interaction with art and ideas. But what is the alternative? "Of course governmental intervention is dangerous: government *is* dangerous; life *itself* is dangerous," he acknowledged. There were, however, risks in the alternative route. "Consider too," Commager reminded his readers, "the danger of *not* using all possible resources, those of government, at all levels, as well as individual resources. Some things we can do collectively better than individually, and for a good many collective things we use the instrument of government. It is certainly dangerous to let things go by default." It was not enough to identify the perils of government without weighing the hazards of the alternatives. "Our task," he counseled, "is not to bewail the dangers from government (which is us, of course) but to educate governments at all levels in their proper operation, and to perfect techniques which will frustrate dangerous or improper intervention."[34]

So Commager shared the same ambivalence about strong government with other liberals of his century. Woodrow Wilson, with whose papers Commager helped William Dodd as a graduate student at the University of Chicago, thought of himself as a Jeffersonian, but the legislation he supported in 1914 and 1915 prompted a more active national government. Herbert Hoover promoted voluntarism while also supporting some cooperative planning left over from his early Progressive days.[35] Name any president in the twentieth century, or nearly any liberal thinker except the most extreme, and one will recall a fundamental vacillation about centralized power. Commager was representative of this conflicted liberalism.

When Adlai Stevenson ran against Dwight D. Eisenhower for president in 1952, Nevins served as chairman of the Volunteers for Stevenson among the Columbia faculty. Although Nevins felt that Eisenhower was not qualified for the presidency, it was not easy for him to lead the Columbia contingent for Stevenson. His brother General Arthur S. Nevins was Ike's lifelong friend, their wives were even closer, and Arthur managed Ike's Gettysburg farm until the president's death. But Allan admired Stevenson enough to withstand the awkwardness in the family.[36]

Commager was one of twenty-three Columbia University faculty members, including Nevins, Morris, Hofstadter, Malone, and Trilling, who together issued an analysis of the campaign funds of Stevenson and Richard Nixon. Disturbed by newspaper accounts that equated the two funds, which in each case had been set up by private interests to defray extra political expenses, Nevins told the press that Nixon's television explanation of his finances "had been an essentially dishonest and emotional appeal confusing many people on the real issues involved." A significant difference, according to the Columbia group, was that Nixon knew who contributed to his fund, whereas donors to Stevenson's fund were anonymous. The signed statement admitted that Stevenson's fund was objectionable but argued that at least he had been contrite, he said it was unfortunate, and he believed in public funding. Nixon, however, had "set a vicious example."[37]

Later the same week a different group of thirty-one, this time including Commager, Nevins, Hofstadter, Niebuhr, novelist John Hersey, and editor Cass Canfield, signed a letter to the *New York Times*. The message began by calling the *Times* "our" paper and "the outstanding instance of a privately owned public utility" that recharged its readers' "intellectual batteries" daily. But the group complained about the paper's continuing support for Eisenhower, who they accused of giving in to Senator Robert Taft's demand for a greater hostility to active government.[38]

Like many intellectuals, the Commager and Nevins group was wary of Eisenhower, despite his presidency of Columbia University. Merle Curti, at a lecture in Tacoma, Washington, expressed a common complaint of university faculty members that Eisenhower was anti-intellectual. Curti protested to his audience that Eisenhower in 1954 had defined an intellectual as "a person who takes more words than are necessary to say more than he knows." But while Nevins was an active supporter of Stevenson, he was not contemptuous of Eisenhower. Eisenhower had an ability to get things done, like John D. Rockefeller, who could bring order out of chaos, and Nevins, a strong proponent of business history, always admired that about business-people and practically capable individuals.[39]

Nor did all Commager's friends line up behind Stevenson. The more conservative and patrician Samuel Eliot Morison, tired of hearing his fellow Harvard faculty members' enthusiasm for Stevenson, felt compelled to register his different views. "There has been so much talk about 'Professors for Stevenson,'" he reported in the *Boston Post* on October 27, 1952, "that I wish to place myself on record as a warm supporter of General Eisenhower." Morison admired Stevenson but thought the Democrats had been in power too long and that Eisenhower would bring "a fresh new breeze into our political life." Although Morison had voted Democratic for the previous forty years and had been affiliated with the Roosevelt and Truman administrations, he felt that a two-party system needed active representation by both parties. Further, he believed Eisenhower was the better candidate.[40]

Four years later, in 1956, when Stevenson again opposed Eisenhower, Commager was listed among 216 prominent Stevenson supporters who were charter members of the New York State committee to renominate him.[41] But in the election of 1960, Commager was one of the former Stevenson supporters to jump to the Kennedy camp. Nevins wrote him in October 1959 and said he had had tea with Adlai and had seen some of Kennedy. There was a "powerful underswell" for Stevenson, Nevins thought, and he felt that the best ticket would be "Adlai and Kennedy." Henry agreed with Allan, though neither were sure that any ticket could beat Nixon. By early 1960, Commager was convinced that only JFK could stop the Democratic nomination of either Texas senator Lyndon Johnson or Missouri senator Stuart Symington, both of whom Commager thought would be a calamity. Kennedy had not been "courageous on the McCarthy issue," Commager admitted, but he thought JFK was "showing real courage on many matters now."[42]

In a front-page story on June 8, 1960, the *New York Times* announced that a small but significant "group of so-called eggheads" who had been longstanding Stevenson supporters had now switched to Kennedy and were mailing a letter to that effect to a large list of liberals throughout the country. Commager, who along with Nevins, Arthur Schlesinger Jr., James M. Burns, John Kenneth Galbraith, Joseph L. Rauh Jr., and others, was a member of the group, reported that he was supporting Kennedy because Stevenson had not declared his candidacy and it was "now a little late in the day." Quickly another group of "eggheads" announced in support of Stevenson to counter the defection, and it included, among others, Niebuhr, Archibald MacLeish, Carl Sandburg, John Hersey, John Steinbeck, and Cass Canfield.[43]

In the aftermath of the "hornet's nest" they stirred up in the *New York Times* with their endorsement of Kennedy, Henry wrote Allan that Stevenson might have won if he had declared earlier. "But if Kennedy were to be maneuvered out of his top position now, the Catholic vote, or a substantial part of it, would swing to Nixon in indignation," he told his friend. "And perhaps it should. It is time we had a Catholic for President, and we should be grateful that we are getting a man like Kennedy instead of a [Joseph] McCarthy—or even a [Edmund "Pat"] Brown [governor of California]. I feel about this the way some Southerners feel about segregation and desegregation. We have to pay a penalty for our moral obtuseness and our prejudice in past years—we have to pay for our attitude to Al Smith, and so forth; we are lucky if a Kennedy is what History will exact from us."[44]

Despite his support for Kennedy during the election, Commager took his role as intellectual critic seriously enough to begin complaining about the new administration before it was even formed. On Thanksgiving Day 1960, he wrote Nevins that he was unhappy with the way Kennedy had started to assemble those around him. Although Abraham Ribicoff, governor of Connecticut, was a good person, he did not belong on the Supreme Court. Instead someone with great dignity and prestige should serve, such as Charles Edward Wyzanski or Adlai Stevenson. Henry suggested that Allan, who was closer to the president-elect, tell Kennedy that Stevenson would be a "more learned [Earl] Warren, a more impartial [Hugo] Black."[45]

And later when the administration's domestic policy transgressed what Commager considered proper in his own cherished sphere of civil liberties, he jumped to fight it. Why, he asked in the New York Times, did the Justice Department want to reopen a case against eight alleged Communists who were cited for contempt of Congress for refusing to answer questions, when meanwhile the executives of the big steel corporations "who openly defied a subcommittee of United States Senate and refused to put in an appearance are not even cited for contempt"? The administration, he pointed out, was operating a dual system of justice: one for the poor and weak, and another for the rich and powerful. Alfred E. Kahn, the professor of economics at Cornell who had been a senior staff member of the Council of Economic Advisors during Eisenhower's second term and who had studied under Commager at New York University before World War II, seconded his point and noted that "the very Congressmen who are so willing to invade the privacy of natural men are chary of doing so in the case of corporations."[46]

At least as early as 1925, when he was still twenty-two years old, Commager opposed American imperialism and the braying confidence of small-town, booster-club patriotism. "I wonder when, if ever, we are going to redeem our pledge of freeing the islands," he remarked disdainfully to Hans Duus about the Philippines. "It's rather amusing that that crowd of American Legionaries [sic] and business Babbitts which is always loudest in eulogizing our more or less unsavory American revolution and the radicals who led it, is always the first to denounce any attempt at revolution in the Philippines."[47] As the foreign conflict of World War II, which Commager had felt was justified, began to recede into the past, he resharpened his anti-imperialist attitude and became much more outspoken on matters of foreign policy.

Before any of the presidential candidates were even campaigning for the 1960 election, he predicted that the bipolar world of the United States against the Soviets was going into eclipse, and with a more equitable balance of power and lessening military tensions, he suggested that the United States should transfer some of its concerns from armaments to helping less fortunate nations.[48] Then, in the last months of the Eisenhower administration, Commager complained to the *New York Times* about U.S. use of foreign NATO bases for espionage activities that could lead to war and reprimanded the newspaper for calling opponents of that policy "breast-beaters," which he thought had a ring of McCarthyism.[49]

In the first months of the Kennedy administration Commager confessed to Nevins that he was distressed with part of the president's foreign policy. "He seems to have whipped public opinion up to a kind of frenzy," Commager noted, worrying that the tough guy attitude would get out of hand and lead the nation to trouble. Was the Berlin Wall really worth taking the world to the brink?[50]

Then a few weeks later he became even more disturbed and asked Nevins to go down to Washington "and try to beat a little sense into JFK." Here was the United States playing "brinksmanship about Berlin," backing Chiang Kai-shek over the inevitable dominance of mainland China, and spending $100 million to reach the moon for no good reason when we should be putting our own house in order. Here was the administration supporting the idea of bomb shelters, which were only a death trap or a vehicle to transport people to a nuclear-polluted world. "Still," Henry concluded grudgingly, "if the alternative is Nixon (who is a dead duck) or Goldwater—we must all rally to JFK." Nevins agreed that Kennedy had not handled foreign policy well. Out in California, Nevins reported from the Huntington, "people are madly erecting or excavating shelters, and some are talking about New Zealand."[51]

During the Cuban Missile Crisis, the day after Kennedy had announced the U.S. blockade of the island, Commager told Nevins that the United States was crazy to risk war in this way and that U.S. actions were based on a double standard. "It seems to me that Mao over in China could take Kennedy's speech word for word," Henry wrote with frustration, "and apply it to Taiwan and tell us that next time a plane flew from Taiwan they would hold us responsible and attack us! And what will Russia now say about our missile and other bases in Turkey, Greece, Pakistan and other countries that ring

Russia? I am beginning to wonder if we were not all wrong about Kennedy—Stevenson wouldn't have done it, Nixon would, of course." Nevins responded immediately that he felt the same and was "filled with the gravest doubts about Jack Kennedy's course." But even though Nevins thought there was too little evidence of hostile intentions from the Cubans, he admitted that "some elements in the situation are unknown to us."[52]

During the last year of Kennedy's life, both Commager and Nevins continued to have misgivings about the administration. Allan was closer to Kennedy and in 1963 was editing a volume of the president's speeches from his state papers and was a consultant for a television program based on *Profiles in Courage*. Still, he acknowledged that the president's papers were very uneven in quality. Further, Nevins was "a little out of temper" with the administration for its terrible fumbling of the tax bill, which had lost all the good reforms and kept all the inflationary measures.[53]

Commager, however, was adopting a more impatiently radical tone. In April 1963 he blasted New York governor Nelson Rockefeller for making "inflammatory speeches" suggesting that Cuban exiles should use American facilities for attacks on Cuba and maybe even Soviet shipping. Either Rockefeller was ignorant of the fact that this policy violated international law and treaty obligations, Commager charged, or the governor did not care.[54]

Part of the reason that Commager became so frustrated with U.S. foreign policy is that around 1960 it began to transgress his ideal of a unified and equitable world federation. Ever since he was "too young to know why," he had been a Wilsonian internationalist who was firmly committed to the old League of Nations.[55] After World War II that commitment was transferred, if not entirely to the United Nations, at least to a one-world vision. Nationalism was potentially dangerous, he thought, although this was an ironic realization from an American character historian whose work had focused on and celebrated American uniqueness.

So as the 1950s ended and the United States began to get more adventurous abroad with espionage and interference in foreign domestic matters, Commager began to emphasize world federalism, self-determination, and democracy. He told a group in Philadelphia in October 1959 that we needed to educate our children to work around the world, predicting that we would live in a multipolar world by the end of the century. Two weeks later, in the *New York Times Magazine*, Commager elaborated on his theme. "It is probable that we are even now entering a new era of international relations," he posited, "one in which nations may come to play on the world scene the role that states have played on the American scene, and that the insistence upon all the prerogatives of national sovereignty will come to seem as outmoded and irrational as insistence upon all the prerogatives of state sovereignty in the United States today."[56]

Again, as a public political critic in the 1950s and 1960s, Commager's example on matters of race is representative of the many ironies and contradictions of midcentury American liberalism. During World War II, he told an audience of high school readers that America could not fight a war for democracy if at the same time it ignored democracy at home. That meant that we could not fight German anti-Semitism if at home we discriminated against Jews, and "we cannot fight the wicked and unChristian doctrine of Aryan supremacy if we relegate Negroes to a position of inferiority." In 1943 Commager told those same high schoolers that although blacks had made progress in education, land ownership, and other factors over the course of the century, "we are impressed rather with the progress still to be made."[57]

But the racial problem did not call for a special solution, for its cause, Commager felt, was not so much racial prejudice as economic and social discrimination. African Americans were at the bottom of the economic ladder and were a threat to the jobs of whites. So the cure was "to raise the economic and social status of all concerned." In the end, he concluded, this approach would be far more useful "than will the more dramatic court decisions or commission plans." Similarly, the decision to intern Japanese Americans during World War II was "partly racial" and "partly economic," but its effect was to provide "a powerful impulse to that same racial discrimination which we are sworn to fight."[58]

Although Commager joined in the fight against racial discrimination in principle, he conducted that battle with no fury. In 1945 he subjected poll taxes to mild criticism but suggested that it was probably best to let states get rid of those laws themselves, given that several southern states had recently done so. Further, he pointed out, the Constitution from the beginning had given the states the authority to determine voting requirements. The exclusion of blacks or women from voting by law was unacceptable, but Commager believed that "there can be no objection to the literacy test if it is administered fairly by state and local officials."[59]

In response to Gunnar Myrdal's powerful *An American Dilemma* (1944), Commager maintained that on racial matters Americans were not hypocrites or insincere but merely inconsistent in their "inner conflict between profession and practice." Unwilling to make the necessary sacrifices, Americans instead chose to have guilty consciences. This hurt whites as much as blacks, and for their own good whites needed to eliminate the racial problem. But again Commager insisted that the problem was economic insecurity instead of racial hatred. And one of the problems with taking the approach of economic status is that status is a relative concept. If poor whites attained a secure economic status but many blacks were to do even better than that, racial anger would continue. "By abstract moral standards," he wrote, "it is perhaps less important that white men have jobs than that Negroes have justice. But it seems clear that unless white men have jobs, Negroes will not have justice."[60]

It is easy enough in retrospect to puncture Commager's opinions on race during World War II. What is more significant is that he was one of the few American writers at the time who found it important to address racial discrimination in a positive manner a decade before the Supreme Court's *Brown* decision. Further, he wrote articles on race during this period not only for intellectual publications but also in a high school publication intended to educate the next generation of Americans, a generation that would be pivotal in the history of American civil rights.

In 1950 the Morison and Commager textbook *Growth of the American Republic* was publicly criticized for its demeaning portrayal of African Americans, particularly in the first volume of the text, for which Morison was largely responsible. There, in a three-page discussion of slavery, Morison wrote that "Sambo" had probably "suffered less than any other class in the South" from slavery. The slave was "apparently happy," "incurably optimistic," and "devoted to his 'white folks.'" Many slaves were "childlike, improvident, humorous, prevaricating, and superstitious." And "there was much to be said for slavery as a transitional stage between barbarism and civilization," because the African American learned English, Christianity, and morals and in return contributed "rhythm and humor" to American culture. Morison did acknowledge, however inadequately, the evils of slavery. Slaves often were more intelligent and of higher moral quality than those southerners who owned them. Treatment of slaves was sometimes cruel, the separation of families was particularly haunting, and night patrols oppressed free blacks as well as slaves.[61]

As an undergraduate at Oberlin College August Meier had been assigned to read *The Growth of the American Republic*. Raised in a liberal household in Newark, New Jersey, by a Jewish mother who taught school and a non-Jewish father who worked as a chemist, Meier began his teaching career at Tougaloo College, a small black school near Jackson, Mississippi, where he taught from 1945 to 1949. A white scholar of African American history, Meier felt that the GAR, despite its faults, remained the best textbook at the time, so he assigned it to his students.[62]

Yet at the same time Meier wrote to Morison and complained of the authors' failure to capitalize "negro" and their use of the name Sambo for slaves. Morison responded that Meier should send him a list of all the places where "negro" should be changed to "Negro" and he would make sure the alteration was made. But he did not see what was wrong with Sambo, since that was his own nickname. Further, Morison doubted whether he could be thought prejudiced given that his daughter was married to Joel Spingarn, the Jewish president of the National Association for the Advancement of Colored People (NAACP). The second volume of the textbook, which was mostly Commager's work, Meier considered to be better on African Americans, since its treatment of Reconstruction was influenced by revisionism. Still, like other histories of the time, blacks were mentioned only in relation to slavery or Reconstruction.[63]

In the spring of 1950 students at the City College of New York (CCNY) in Harlem complained publicly about the racism in *The Growth of the American Republic*. At first, the City College history department defended the textbook because it alleged that there were Communist students denouncing it.[64] Morison wrote to Commager that he was sorry for the letters the controversy was generating but was unable to see their point. "Felix [Commager] the nigger-baiter is funny!" he wrote his coauthor. "I have a similar bushman squawk on my desk now." A month later, Morison wrote Commager that he was involved in a correspondence with a professor at a "dark college" in the South (presumably August Meier) and would make some changes but would not cut out words that gave the flavor of the antebellum period.[65]

In mid-June, Morison told Commager that Oxford University Press had made most of the changes in the text that he had requested and that he thought Meier was now satisfied. The press had missed a few words, unfortunately. Morison had discovered that there was still an instance of the word "pickaninnies" in the text, "and I endeavored to take out all *pickaninnies* and make them nice little seal-brown darlings." But there he drew the line. "Sambo, Uncle Daniel, etc. are left in, however," he reported to his coauthor, "and I'll be damned if I'll take them out for City College or anybody."[66]

Morison then wrote to Meier and asked him to provide a letter acknowledging that the changes in the textbook were satisfactory "and that you do not consider me or the history inimical to the Negro race." Morison's interpretation of the City College uprising showed how little he understood its intentions. "While the evidence indicates that the Negro issue was simply an excuse," he assured Meier, "and that the 'strike' was instigated by extreme left-wing students who regarded the *G.A.R.* as hopelessly 'capitalistic,' the incident has caused Commager and myself a good deal of embarrassment." Morison also asked John Hope Franklin, his former student at Harvard, for a similar letter exonerating the textbook, but Franklin declined on the ground that a person of Morison's standing did not need Franklin's approval for what he wrote.[67]

Despite his objections to the treatment of racial issues in the *Growth of the American Republic*, Meier became a doctoral student of Commager's at Columbia. During his last year at Tougaloo in 1948, he wrote his Columbia master's thesis on black American nationalism before Marcus Garvey. The following year Meier left Tougaloo, moved to Newark to live with his parents, and began work on his Ph.D. under Commager's direction.[68] One day Meier was present prior to a graduate seminar meeting in Commager's office when Henry received a phone call from one of the CCNY students involved in the protest. Commager told his caller that he considered the pressure against *The Growth of the American Republic* to be an infringement of academic freedom. On another occasion a group of angry black students "stormed into" Commager's office and complained about the use of "Sambo" in the textbook. But Commager said that he and Morison would not respond to the edicts of the students, because then every interest group would tyrannize them.[69]

As some of his students observed him in the late 1940s and early 1950s, Commager was often unintentionally clumsy about racial matters but willing to learn and change his mind. Leonard Levy from 1949 to 1951 worked as Henry's teaching and research assistant for forty hours a week. Working in Commager's office with him, he heard interesting comments. Once a six-foot, blond young man appeared in the office when Levy was there with his mentor. The visitor received a hearty welcome from Commager and talked with him for half an hour. It was William Leuchtenburg, but Commager never introduced him to Levy. When Leuchtenburg left, Commager remarked to Levy, "Isn't he the most perfect Aryan type?" Levy was Jewish. "It was the sort of expression that I would have terribly resented in anyone else," Levy later explained. "But I knew he was unthinking, not antiSemitic [*sic*]."[70]

On another occasion, Henry saw Levy struggling to replace a ribbon on a typewriter. "Let the old man try it," he told him. When Commager had it fixed, he told his assistant that he "thought all people of your race were good at this sort of thing. Look at Einstein, Oppenheimer, Teller, Rabi and all the rest." Then before Levy took his Ph.D. comprehensive oral exams, Commager counseled him not to talk with his hands, since it was allegedly a Jewish habit. "But he was not the least anti-Semitic," Levy concluded. "If he was, I would not have been his assistant."[71]

Further, Commager recommended Levy for the Harvard Society of Fellows. And after he sent Levy to Yale for a job interview, George Pierson wrote Commager that Levy would not fit with "the gentlemen" in Yale's department. As Commager's assistant, Levy opened his mail and saw the letter. But Levy drew a distinction between the outlooks of Commager and Yale. Henry, according to Levy, "was not anti-Semitic at a time when anti-Semitism was common in Ivy League schools. He made foolish remarks but he favored Jews. He was close to his colleague, Richard B. Morris; to Milton Cantor, Harold Hyman, and above all me, as students."[72]

In his constitutional history course in about 1950, according to Meier, Commager repeatedly referred to "the Anglo-Saxon genius for constitutional government." During the semester, Meier dropped by Commager's office to give him a copy of his first published article, "The Racial Ancestry of the Mississippi College Negro," derived in part from a questionnaire Meier had asked students in his class at Tougaloo to complete anonymously.[73] As they talked, Commager told Meier that it was the racial mixture of African Americans that made them intelligent. No, Meier replied, this early-twentieth-century belief had been discredited by social scientists. But, Commager asked with surprise, isn't the way Mediterranean people gesture when they speak genetically and racially determined?[74]

Then Meier told Commager that he objected to the use of the term "Anglo-Saxon genius." "I will say that Commager really listened," Meier remembered, "and I was impressed by the fact that I was actually able to have a full forty-minute personal and uninterrupted conversation with him. I guess what I said had an impact, because after referring to Anglo-Saxon genius in a few more of his lectures, one day he added 'and some people say there is no such thing as Anglo-Saxon genius,' and he never used the term again for the remainder of the course."[75]

In seminar class, Meier recalled, Commager told the group that he would not allow a black student to do a dissertation in the field of African American history because the student could not be objective about the subject. Meier has noted that "as Howard K. Beale said, historians like A. A. Taylor and John Hope Franklin displayed far more objectivity about whites than most white American historians did about blacks." Still, Commager offered, according to Meier, "to help two of us in the seminar working on black history topics, to arrange an introduction to Du Bois since he was going to some function where Du Bois was going to be. (And this was around 1950, in that period of anti-Communist hysteria in which Du Bois suffered.)"[76]

If his *Theodore Parker* was an indication, Commager was hardly a leader on race, Meier believed, because in the book abolitionism was not treated "with any particular empathy." The intellectual historian George M. Fredrickson had a similar doubt about Commager's racial commitment. Commager, Fredrickson reported, "once told me that he saw nothing objectionable in Theodore Parker's remarks about black inferiority!" Yet, despite what Meier saw as Commager's shortcomings, he was not willing to dismiss his case simplistically. In Meier's view, Commager did not have black friends, but he did operate in circles where blacks were appreciated. Meier found Commager "quite conventional in his views on race . . . but one who was open to learning and changing his mind."[77]

As indicated by Meier's comments about Commager's ambivalence on race, there was also a far more positive side to his actions and writings. As early as 1943, in his *Majority Rule and Minority Rights*, Henry complained that since its inception the Supreme Court had never yet "intervened on behalf of the underprivileged—the Negro, the alien, women, children, workers, tenant-farmers." Instead the Court had blocked congressional attempts to "free slaves, guarantee civil rights to Negroes," and protect workers. Although the thesis of his book was that democracies never threaten freedom, he admitted caustically that the determination of white southerners to oppress African Americans contradicted his point—and that the Jeffersonian solution of better education and economic security was needed.[78]

When John Hope Franklin was invited to read a paper at the Southern Historical Association convention in 1949, the first African American to be asked, there were objections to the invitation and questions about where he would sleep and who would participate with him. Henry asked if he could preside at the session, and Franklin considered his introduction very generous. Two years later, Commager and Franklin were the U.S. historians at the Salzburg Seminar in American Studies. During their two months in Austria, Commager and Franklin spent many hours together, occasionally with both of their families, and Commager was never offensive about race.[79]

In 1953 the NAACP solicited his advice on strategy for their argument before the Supreme Court on *Brown v. Board of Education*. During that summer, the Court asked the litigants to answer whether "the Congress which submitted and the state legislatures and conventions which ratified the Fourteenth Amendment contemplated or did not contemplate, understood or did not understand, that it would abolish segregation in public schools." Thurgood Marshall, head of the NAACP project, asked John A. Davis, professor of political science at Lincoln University, to lead the research on the Court's question. Davis, who had done graduate work under Commager at Columbia, asked him to help put together the answer, but Henry was in England.

Although Commager was sympathetic to the case, he shared the dominant but debatable belief that the Fourteenth Amendment had not been designed by its authors as a way to desegregate public schools. Commager's was a legal rather than a racial opinion. He wrote Davis that he "greatly feared" that the NAACP's approach would not produce "a valid point" and would be vulnerable. "The framers of the amendment," he reported, "did not, so far as we know, intend that it should be used to end segregation in schools." To support his position he told Davis of two law review articles on the subject. "I strongly urge that you consider dropping this particular argument," he concluded, "as I think it tends to weaken your case." One of Davis's associates at the NAACP, Robert Carter, confessed that Commager's "rejection of our position was a real blow—it put us right down on the ground." Davis merely dismissed Commager's advice with the thought that his former teacher did not really know that much about it. The NAACP asked other historians, many of whom agreed with Commager, but kept searching until they found scholars willing to make the case the organization envisioned. Commager was sympathetic to the NAACP's challenge of school segregation, and Davis never would have asked Commager for his opinion otherwise. But Commager did not want the organization to make a case that the courts could easily dismiss. His response was intended to prod the group into making the most defensible argument possible.[80]

Commager was thought to be a person interested in promoting equality for African Americans, which his list of invitations and activities suggests. He was invited to Fisk University in 1952 to address a conference on race relations. The National Council of Negro Women in 1957 asked him to be the keynote speaker for their Leaders Conference in Washington. Illinois senator Paul Douglas chose Commager as one of those he asked to help lobby public opinion for passage of the Civil Rights Bill of 1957. In the autumn of 1957 Commager invited John Hope Franklin to Amherst to lecture and entertained the Franklins at his home.[81]

Commager's concern prompted him to complain to Reinhold Niebuhr in 1958 that the Eisenhower administration was doing nothing about deteriorating race relations. More to the point was "the failure of the intellectual and moral leaders of our community north and south to provide leadership of any kind in this matter. Neither the churches nor the universities." Niebuhr should circulate "an appeal for a moral solution" and get leading intellectuals to sign it, he suggested, or call an intellectual conference to find moral and practical answers. For example, if southerners wanted segregated schools because they were afraid of mixing white girls and black young men, then let them segregate the schools by sex rather than race.[82]

Several prominent American historians participated in the final day of the civil rights march from Selma to Montgomery, Alabama, in 1965, including Richard Hofstadter, Harold Hyman, John Hope Franklin, John Higham, and William Leuchtenburg.[83] In response to the violence in Selma, Commager telegraphed U.S. Attorney General Nicholas Katzenbach informing him that federal law allowed the president to use force rather than merely injunctive power to suppress the violent obstruction of a vote. John Doar, an assistant attorney general in the Civil Rights Division, answered with a detailed list of the litigation the Justice Department was pursuing in the South. Commager responded that he had never questioned federal energy in the South but that Doar had missed the point of his telegram. The actions of some southern citizens to block the right of African Americans to vote was a conspiracy far worse than domestic communists had ever undertaken—although Eugene Dennis and his communist associates had been sentenced to twenty years in prison. "It does seem to me that we lay ourselves open to the charge of a double standard in the law," he informed Doar, "if we sent to jail for a long stretch of years a group of men whose misdeed was to teach some future possible action, and ignore beatings and jailings (mostly illegal) and intimidation in a matter so essential as the franchise."[84]

Commager's contribution to the debate on race in the United States provided a mixed legacy. In the 1940s and 1950s he held some ideas that today are embarrassingly out-of-date. But he also tried to address the problems of race in this country, beginning as early as World War II. In the 1950s and 1960s he turned up his moral intensity on these issues. His outlook depended on liberal equality and competition, Jeffersonian openness and free interchange, and a belief that through constitutional law these wrongs might be redressed. Perhaps August Meier is correct that Commager's significance was not in his actions or ideas about racial and ethnic ideas but instead "in his genuine commitment to civil liberties" and his willingness to be "open-minded and willing to learn" on racial and other concerns.[85]

Commager's midcentury generation of liberals was not as enlightened on race as the generation of baby boomers that followed. Yet this does not mean that Commager was less "liberal" in 1950 than a younger counterpart would be a half century later. Instead, the focus and commitments of liberalism changed during that period. The Old Left at midcentury adhered to a predominantly *political* and *economic* outlook concerned about income distribution, economic exploitation, and the organization of society into systems such as capitalism or socialism. The New Left, however, whose commitments influenced the focus of late-twentieth-century liberalism, adopted more *cultural* interests that orbited around gender and ethnic identities, alienation, semiotics, and cultural authority.

The liberalisms of 1948 and 1998, although they have shared much, have had different commitments and agendas. Each has its admirable qualities. The earlier would have benefited from the latter's greater respect for a multicultural society. Yet the latter would benefit by incorporating the midcentury scholarly commitment to public activism, an emphasis on free speech and democracy, and a respect for the rights of majorities.

In the autumn of 1956, after teaching for nearly twenty years at Columbia University, Commager left New York for a teaching position at Amherst College in the tranquil wooded hills of central Massachusetts.[86] After all, Nevins was preparing to retire, so Commager was less bound to the institution by friendships. His salary at Columbia hardly enticed him to stay, for the university paid notoriously low wages. He later complained that a full professor at Columbia received only what an assistant professor earned at Amherst, and at Berkeley, he maintained, faculty received half again as much as at Columbia. When David Donald left Columbia for Princeton in 1959, he too complained about the low salaries and poor benefits.[87]

Commager was ambivalent about New York anyway. It had the literary life that had excited him as a young man, but now he was fifty-four and middle-aged. When he had originally moved to New York thirty years earlier, he told his friend Hans Duus that he did not want to live in the big city. "I who want [the] peace and serenity of a small place," he protested, "am doomed to move from Chicago to the only place in the country that is worse, New York."[88] So now he was finally making his home in a charming, quiet, but intellectually alive New England town.

As he explained the move to Merle Curti, "I am buying time—I feel mortality these days. Charlie Cole [president of Amherst College] has given me a one term schedule, so I shall have 8 months to myself out of each year—for reading and thinking and maybe even writing." For his first semester he was to remain an adjunct faculty member at Columbia and go down each Friday to give lectures and meet with graduate students. Alfred Kazin, Daniel Aaron, and others were in the Amherst and Northampton area, and as he told Curti, "the very prospect of months and months of quiet, remote from the bustle and temptation of New York, has youthened me."[89]

In Amherst the Commagers occupied a large white house owned by the college, on a picturesque road about a half mile south of campus. The rooms were dusty and dark, scattered with books, and overcrowded and underorganized. One entire very large bookshelf among the others in the living room held the books that Henry had written, edited, or to which he had contributed. Although his study was a huge room above the garage, an office of sorts had been fashioned on the first floor from what appeared once to have been an L-shaped porch that ran along the side and back of the house. In the longer area of this *L*, along the back of the house, stood a Ping-Pong table scattered with books and work, and bookshelves lined the walls chest high. When he played Ping-Pong with his children or with intimidated guests, Henry simply put the books and papers beneath the table. In the shorter section of the room, a sunporch along the side of the house converted to work space, were some chairs, a short table, a door into the living room, more bookshelves, and more scattered work.

It is interesting to note that, for all Commager's interest in reaching a broad democratic public with his writing, he never attended or taught at a public university. Educated at the University of Chicago, he then taught at NYU and Columbia before finally moving to Amherst College. At most of these institutions he could expect to meet and teach only the children of the privileged. There were contradictory ambitions in his life. His intellectual ambitions, his writing and teaching, had been framed largely around the Jeffersonian ideals of broad democratic public debate. Yet with his social ambitions he hoped to leave behind an unstable childhood and rise into literary celebrity, estimable social contacts, and memberships in admired clubs. "Instead of lunching with people at the Century [Club] every week," Nevins asked about Commager's visits to New York from Amherst, "why not lunch with us at the Faculty Club?"[90]

If Commager expected his move to Amherst to quiet his life, he was wrong. He kept riding the circuit, lecturing and making appearances so often that he seemed like an itinerant secular preacher. With the inspiration in his youth from his preaching grandfather, Pastor Adam Dan, and the model of Theodore Parker about whom he had written, Commager certainly chose rather than stumbled into his lecturing lifestyle. William Leuchtenburg remarked to Henry at the time that his move to Amherst was a scheme to subsidize the New York, New Haven, and Hartford railroad because he would be forever riding trains to fulfill lecture engagements.[91]

Commager had written with admiration of Parker's speaking tours. Parker "had developed a talent for the popularization of learning, and he rationalized it into a duty," saying he would preach and lecture anywhere, city or field, eastward or westward, and would make the land ring. The New England minister considered lecturing "an original American contrivance for educating the people" and thought it combined some of the best of the church, college, and theater. "Parker," Commager reported with pride, "took to the platform like a sailor to the deck." Lecturing was exhilarating, and it educated the speaker as well as the listener, for the lecturer "came to know more of the country, came to know this America whose character he was always trying to penetrate." Traveling to speak was difficult, however. Parker lectured forty times from lyceum platforms around New England in the winter of 1844. Commager acknowledged that Parker "did not really approve of all this gallivanting about the country." It was a "hardship," a "nomadic, unchristian life," Commager admitted. Commager might later have written all this about himself, because he followed Parker's example so closely.[92]

Even his wistful comments about getting more scholarly work done by moving to Amherst contained echoes of Parker's own words. "To the end he hoped that he might find time for the fulfilment of his scholarly plans, and they were grandiose," he wrote about Parker. "There were a dozen books that he wanted to write: when he was fifty he would stop all this lecturing and get down to the business of scholarship, when he was sixty he would withdraw from public life and be a philosopher."[93] In his early fifties Commager moved to Amherst, but like Parker, he did not choose the library over the lecture circuit.

Lecturing was nothing new to Commager by the time he left New York for Massachusetts. Already during and after World War II he was stumping Britain for democracy, and the following decade it seemed as though he passed through each hamlet in the nation to speak against McCarthyism. His busy schedule was legendary among his colleagues, and close friends such as Nevins constantly chided him for skating through the life of ideas too quickly. "Quicksilver Commager, I call you," Allan wrote Henry with good-natured impatience; "brilliant, attractive, gleaming, and when the finger closes down on you, somewhere else!"[94]

Wherever a talk or a conference was to be given, Commager was invited. He addressed an international conference in London about the state of the American press; deliberated at the Pugwash Conference in Nova Scotia; gave a tribute to Louis Brandeis at Brandeis University; spoke at a farewell dinner at the United Nations for Israeli representative Abba Eban; gave the Gino Speranza Lectures at Columbia; flew to Aspen, Colorado, to a conference where seventy-five noted thinkers grappled with modern problems; traveled to New York to honor Thomas Paine in a ceremony before the City Council; and lectured at one of the seemingly countless colleges and universities at which he gave the commencement speech or where he was the recipient of an honorary degree or award.[95]

His schedule in the spring of 1967 might serve as an example. In April he was scheduled to speak in six locations from Denver to Pennsylvania, on five different topics. In May he had a dozen trips on his schedule that would force him to crisscross the country. His schedule called for him to speak on the May 2 at Wake Forest in North Carolina ("The Limits of Power"); May 5 at the University of Oklahoma ("The Limits of Power"); May 6 in Tucson at the Arizona Historical Society ("Was America a Mistake?"); May 11 in Newark ("The Nature and Limits of Foreign Power"); May 15 at Northern Illinois University (no topic); May 16 in Santa Barbara (no topic); May 17 at the Claremont Colleges outside Los Angeles ("Foreign Policy"); May 18 at Lake Forest College, Illinois ("Foreign Policy"); May 21 in Assilomar, California, to television executives ("What's Wrong with TV?"); May 24 in New York for luncheon ceremonies at the American Academy of Arts and Letters; and May 25 in Washington, D.C., for executive seminars. On May 30 he traveled to New York so that the next day he and Evan could set sail for England aboard the *Queen Mary*.[96] (Henry always preferred ships to planes when crossing the Atlantic, for the good food, Ping-Pong, and the chance to bring books. The Commager family traveled that way several times, as a kind of holiday.)[97]

During one of Leuchtenburg's early years at Columbia, Commager asked if he would take over his constitutional history class by reading to them a lecture that Henry had written on Joseph Story. He would miss only that one class, he told Leuchtenburg, because he was giving three lectures in Italy and one in Israel and would be back in less than seven days.[98]

His schedule indicates the life he led and priorities he pursued. The research archive of the scholar was not what lured him most. Instead, he chose to communicate his ideas directly to a live audience in a modern day lyceum circuit. It was that great democratic public, that secular and curious national congregation spread across the wide landscape of America, with which he wanted to communicate about issues of deep public importance. Part orator like William Jennings Bryan or Michael Harrington, part man of letters like Edmund Wilson or Malcolm Cowley, part lyceum philosopher like Ralph Waldo Emerson, he could not be satisfied to write works of scholarship alone. The auditoriums, magazines, and newspapers of the country caught and held his best thoughts.

"I'm not primarily a writer, but a teacher," Commager insisted wishfully. "That's what I like best, and it's what I do most." Although he claimed to love teaching, Henry was always more focused on other activities. Despite his occasional commendation of the teaching role, he belonged in a research university such as Columbia where other matters are more important instead of in a small liberal arts college such as Amherst, which promoted a close and nurturing contact with students. Speaking in front of a class, of course, he was still as riveting in lectures as he had been at Columbia, and he still needed few if any notes. On one occasion at Amherst, for example, Commager came into a team-taught American studies course in which he was to deliver the lecture. The course contained the entire sophomore class. He found that he was not to speak on the Bill of Rights, as he thought, but on Jefferson, at which point, according to a student, he promptly delivered "the most virtuoso lecture on Thomas Jefferson one could imagine." On another occasion he showed up late for lecture, asked the topic for the day, and then began speaking.[99]

But Commager's lecture courses, fostered in the classes he had taught to Columbia graduate students, did not have reading and paper assignments that were structured enough for the Amherst undergraduates, who felt adrift in them. Commager's courses were laissez-faire creations in which students were encouraged to make up their own reading and essay agendas.[100] His approach to lecture courses mirrored his view of the educational process. "At Amherst we used to joke about his annual speech about the way to solve curricular problems," Leo Marx explained. "We have lots of bright students, good books and good teachers, he would remind us, so why don't we get rid of all this stuff about requirements, and just let them get together to read and write? His model of course was Oxbridge tutorial education."[101]

So Commager preferred teaching in roundtable seminar situations with the undergraduates. Sometimes he held classes in the large seminar room that was part of the three-room suite of office space he inhabited in Morgan Hall. Frequently he taught his courses at his house on South Pleasant Street, where the class met once a week and discussed a book at each meeting.[102] In a representative seminar, two students gave presentations during each class. But, as a talker rather than a listener, Commager was too impatient to listen to the presentations completely, and at some point he interrupted and began asking questions or, more likely, simply started speaking himself.[103] Further, despite his affection for Oxbridge tutorial education, that model asked more of teachers than Commager had time to give. Many of his colleagues believed that Henry was too busy to learn students' names or read student papers thoroughly. Often Commager called students by the name of the author they were writing about. If the American studies program gave him a thesis student, he would riffle through a few pages of what he or she wrote and then utter his well-worn phrase that one needn't eat a whole apple to tell if it is rotten. He might make a few scattered notes on the draft and tell the student to read one or another book. Students did not like that treatment, so some other faculty member in the program would have to adopt the thesis student. Finally the program stopped giving Commager thesis students.[104]

From the start, when Commager arrived from Columbia in the late 1950s, the American studies department at Amherst enjoyed having him there but did not know how to relate to him. He never got to know the names of his colleagues, and he operated on his own wavelength in his own world. In the department he never threw his weight around or expected deference or special treatment; when asked to contribute money for common funds, he gave more than others. He had a quiet demeanor and simply followed his own star. While Commager never showed any interest in the American studies department, neither was he hostile to it. He attended few department meetings in either the American studies or the history department. In his first years he attended department meetings intermittently, but he was bored. During those occasions, sitting around the table with others in George Taylor's office, he would pull a book off the shelf and glance through it quickly, replace it, then pull down another.[105]

Although Commager never required deference, his shift from New York City to the quiet, stately Amherst surely made him feel as though he had lost the stage on which he had once starred so prominently. When he went unrecognized, especially in little Amherst, it irritated him. Once, when walking with a student in town, Commager stopped by a bank and wrote a check for eight thousand dollars. The teller politely asked for identification for the sizable transaction. "Don't you know who I am?" he asked her impatiently. She did not. "Well," Commager inquired, "can't you find someone who does?" If people in New York knew him, why couldn't everyone in Amherst recognize him? But, for his part, Commager failed to learn the names of those around him. He was a talker instead of a listener, one who expected to be known better than he knew others, expected to make the pronouncements instead of listening to the opinions of others. At Commager's house, for example, William Kennick, who taught philosophy at Amherst, once disagreed with him about the author of a line of Scottish poetry. The author was Robert Burns, Commager claimed, but Kennick knew otherwise. Commager dispatched a daughter upstairs to fetch the volume containing the complete works of Burns. When he was unable to locate the passage after flipping through the book, Commager announced that the volume was incomplete and hurled it out the window. That incident was representative of what some of his colleagues felt was his inability to work well with other people, shown also by the fact that "he was less and less interested as he grew older in other historians' work. At some point he seems simply to have ceased reading them."[106]

Instead, Commager's attention was trained on the lectures and articles he fashioned for the general public. The Amherst faculty did not resent his inattention to them, but they instituted the "Commager Rule," which mandated that a faculty member, after being hired, had to spend at least three years teaching before touring around the country pursuing a national agenda.[107] When in 1964 Commager asked Amherst president Plimpton to release him from "what has for some time been a purely nominal association with the Department of American Studies" and allow him to focus on his connection with the history department, his colleagues in American studies agreed that his request was only a formality because he had long ago allowed his attention to drift away.[108]

The ambivalence Commager felt toward teaching was more apparent in the monastic, tutorial, communal atmosphere of Amherst College than it had been in the professional, contractual, gesellschaft setting of graduate education at Columbia University. The bucolic yet civilized village of Amherst he embraced with the same affection he felt for the environs of his summerhouse an hour away in Williamsville, Vermont. If he did not know the names of all his students, he invited them to his house weekly for their seminar meeting. The depth of his commitment to a few of his young charges was apparent in 1972 when he changed his will to include a gift of ten thousand dollars each to two of his former students to finance their graduate educations.[109] Yet the conflicting signals that he directed to his colleagues and students at Amherst made it difficult to assess his assurance that "I enjoy what I'm doing. What a musician wants to do with his life is play music, a painter wants to paint, a teacher wants to teach."[110]

Like most men at midcentury, Commager pursued his career industriously and left much of the raising of the family to his wife, Evan. During the forties and early fifties, the family lived in Rye, New York, near Long Island Sound and the Connecticut border, in prosperous Westchester County north of the city. The house in Rye was outfitted as might have been expected: before the family moved to Amherst in 1957, Henry estimated that he owned fifteen thousand books, and David Donald remembered that Commager had three typewriters, at each of which he was in the process of typing a different manuscript.[111] As American involvement in World War II began, Henry Steele Jr. (Steele) was about to reach puberty, Nell was eight, and Elisabeth (Lisa) was two.

Although their father worked in New York City, the children lived a suburban life. They spent summers with their parents at the family house in Vermont and attended school beyond the urban clatter. When he was old enough, Steele went to school at Deerfield Academy in central Massachusetts. Later he attended Harvard, graduated summa cum laude in 1954, and

Evan Commager with children Nell, Lisa, and Steele. (Courtesy of Lisa Commager)

became a member of the prestigious Society of Fellows there from 1955 to 1958. After serving as an instructor in classics at Harvard for three years, Steele became a professor in the classics department at Columbia in 1961. While at Columbia he published *The Odes of Horace: A Critical Study* (1962) and edited *Virgil: A Collection of Critical Essays* (1966). Nell attended the Rye Country Day School and graduated from Barnard College. While at Barnard she met Christopher (Kit) Lasch, who at the time was a graduate student across the street in the Columbia history department where her father taught. Nell and Kit were married in 1956 at the house in Williamsville. Lisa attended the Northampton School for Girls and then Radcliffe College. Evan and the two girls went to England with Henry for the year he was Pitt Professor at Cambridge in 1947 and again when he went to Oxford in 1953. In 1954, they moved from Rye to a walk-up row house in New York City, on 114th Street across from the back of the university's Butler Library, where they spent Henry's last two years at Columbia. In 1960 the Commagers bought a vacation house in Linton, a few miles outside Cambridge, to which the family could return on occasion. So the children experienced a cosmopolitan, upper-middle-class lifestyle, but also the frenzied schedule of their father. For example, in June 1956, right after Henry, Evan, and Lisa returned from a semester in Copenhagen, Denmark, the family was staying in Vermont, Nell and Kit were to be married there within a week, and the family was trying to sell the house in New York City and move to Amherst.[112]

In Amherst, when the family finally settled there in 1956, Henry had little time for idle fun, but occasionally his "ferocious" will to win showed itself in Ping-Pong with Daniel Aaron, the literary critic and historian who taught nearby at Smith College.[113] The large, rambling, white Amherst house was always full of interesting people, but Henry left the social activities to the direction of Evan, "a person of considerable wit, charm, and conversational flair." Even when Nell and Kit Lasch visited, Henry's principal contribution to the evenings was usually to urge everyone to bed so he could finish whatever lecture or writing project was at hand. Always there was work to be done. Henry could not sit still very long, and he had little interest in idle chatter.[114]

The novelist and critic Storm Jameson portrayed a similar picture of the Commager household. "That house," she said of the earlier homestead in Rye, New York, "was a living spring of warmth, generosity, wit, gaiety, intelligence, all the active graces of living." There Evan, "a creature as purely good as salted country butter," spoke "in a slow warm voice" and "was the point from which the wit and gaiety rose and to which it returned." Henry, on the other hand, Jameson remembered as sleeping no more than four hours a night; the other twenty hours he spent "writing, reading, lecturing— at this time, when his children were young, he wrote through any disturbance, stopping only to take part in their violent games or to argue with friends."[115]

Two historians of the talent of Commager and Lasch might have been expected to get along well and talk incessantly. Neither was the case. As a student at Columbia, Lasch had been drawn to Leuchtenburg and Hofstadter instead of Commager. Lasch had been introduced to history as a youth by Morison and Commager's *Growth of the American Republic*, but as a graduate student, while he admired Commager's vigorous public writing, he found him too Parringtonian in his uncritical admiration of liberals and the liberal tradition. "As far as I could see," Lasch explained, "Commager had no interest in the reconsideration of liberalism that emerged after World War II, no interest even in replying to its critics (that is, to its critics on the left)—which didn't leave us much to talk about." Besides, around the Commager house Evan directed much of the conversation, and it was not about history. Even if they had talked more, Henry preferred anecdote to analysis, so Lasch did not feel as though many good ideas could be traded. Although Henry liked anecdote, he almost never talked about his early life, the years growing up with his grandfather Adam Dan or the early years before his mother died. Consequently, the family knew little about that period.[116]

So Lasch and Commager never were close, never exchanged ideas. Henry, according to his son-in-law, always had more work than could be finished, and it was work toward what was patently right. Of Commager's pantheon Lasch noted, "His heroes—Parker, say, or Jane Addams—were people who never had much difficulty distinguishing right from wrong," and, if they did, he was not interested in their complexities and self-doubts. Commager's beacons were figures "whose lives were a continuous bustle of activity on behalf of unimpeachably good causes. Much the same could be said of his own life—with the usual price such activity tends to exact."[117] Commager had a style of analysis and work and a commitment to certain values that asked a price Lasch did not care to pay. Lasch himself entered the public realm in his work, for he, like his father-in-law, often wrote essays at the intersection of history and contemporary ideological issues. But Lasch was committed to a greater complexity and scholarship than a civic Parringtonian such as Commager cared to muster.

Vision of a more literal nature became a problem for Commager in the early 1960s. When Henry was young, his uncle Bedstefar in Denmark experienced eye problems, and so did Henry's grandfather with whom he lived in Chicago.[118] Similarly, at the end of 1963, after a half-dozen years in Amherst, Commager suffered a detached retina. The night of John Kennedy's assassination, having undergone surgery the day before, Commager appeared on national television, his eye bandaged, and spoke of the dead president. Surgical procedures for retinas were not yet sophisticated, and Commager took at least six months to recuperate.[119] After that point, at age sixty-one, his eyes were a constant bother to him. A large-print typewriter became an instant necessity, and from that time forward, to read he needed to hold most writing inches from his face. The battle to maintain his vision slowed his work considerably for the rest of his life. Like both Francis Parkman and William Hickling Prescott before him, Commager fought the obstacle of poor eyesight as a historian.[120]

Soon after his eye surgery Henry received much worse news: Evan had cancer. Even distant friends by 1965 commiserated that eye problems and cancer had invaded the Amherst home.[121] Evan, Henry's frequent companion on trips abroad, his wife since their salad days at New York University in the 1920s, present at the tea where the two first met Allan and Mary Nevins, died in the spring of 1968, forty years after they were married. Together Henry and Evan had bought houses in New York, Massachusetts, Vermont, and England. They had worked together on such projects as the compilation of children's stories issued as *The St. Nicholas Anthology* in 1948. She also had written four children's books, including *Valentine, Tenth Birthday, Beaux,* and *Cousins*.[122] Evan had carefully proofread the galleys of all his books. Then, when Henry was sixty-five, she was gone.

The 1960s could not have been a particularly happy time for Commager. The difficulties in his life must have seemed oddly parallel to the turmoil in the soul of the nation at the time, when deaths, looting, marches, and assassinations punctuated the headlines, when battles spilled into the streets over civil rights, the Vietnam War, free speech, and changing values. In an undated reflection to himself, typed on his large-print machine, he acknowledged that the world of scholarship and public activism sometimes had to give way to the pressures of the spirit. On a simple blank page he typed to himself the words of a sonnet from George Santayana: "It is not wisdom to be only wise, / And on the inward vision close the eyes, / But it is wisdom to believe the heart." For a person whose life and values endorsed a Jeffersonian optimism and a belief in the final if gradual victory of knowledge, Commager's embrace of Santayana's sonnet showed the unhappy pressures, both personal and political, he felt around him. The extent to which Santayana's words contradicted Commager's normal Jeffersonian faith in the future is evident only a few lines further in the poem: "Our knowledge is a torch of smoky pine / That lights the pathway but one step ahead / Across a void of mystery and dread."[123]

Like the liberalism of the 1950s and early 1960s, then, during this decade Commager revealed a similar attempt to balance contradictions and live with ironies. The Hamilton avenue of large and energetic government, he decided, led most efficiently to the Jeffersonian ends of relative equality and personal liberty. This dilemma became especially pronounced for liberals like Commager in the 1960s and 1970s when the active foreign policy presidencies of Lyndon Johnson and Richard Nixon rose up to haunt them.

Another balancing act found Henry advising that the problem of racial discrimination, while harmful to society, should be solved without allowing special interest groups to silence the opinions of authors. Similarly, scholarship, teaching, and responsibility to one's department and university had to be balanced against the equally compelling need to take one's ideas to the general public by speaking on the global lyceum circuit. In life, juggling was necessary. Family involvement usually had to give way to career requirements. And in times of crisis, as at Evan's death, one had to search beyond a Jeffersonian optimism and confront the reality that life had a much darker and ominous side.

CHAPTER 7

The Call to Political Morality,
1964-1974

Commager became more insistently radical in his liberalism in the early 1960s with respect to those others in his political generation. While some in his age group began a political journey that took them from socialism in the 1930s to a neoconservatism in the 1970s, Commager, interestingly, moved the opposite way.[1] Although he was a liberal throughout his life, he defended his liberalism with such principle and boldness that his outlook seemed more pronounced by the 1960s. Some of his closest friends, such as Milton Cantor, labor historian at the University of Massachusetts and former student, noticed his increasing radicalism.[2]

Politics, even for the most principled, can be a confusing journey. For even if one holds tight to principle, inflexibly and rigidly, the background and surrounding context in which that principle must be applied is constantly changing. It is not only that the terms themselves change, that individualists are called classical liberals at one point and then libertarian conservatives at another. Even more uncomfortable is the spectacle of having to change principle to pursue a consistent goal over time. For example, in the pursuit of a humane, democratic domestic and foreign policy, many liberals fought for great power for Franklin Roosevelt against a conservative Congress and supported extra terms for him. Yet many of those same liberals denounced that similar power assumed by Lyndon Johnson and Richard Nixon when it was utilized against a liberal Congress and in execution of an unpopular war. Commager, like many other midcentury liberals, faced this contradiction.

Although he opposed the excesses of the cold war outlook, at midcentury Commager was not an unremitting critic of American foreign policy. He did believe that the United States was too militaristic and expected to treat other countries as we would not allow them to treat us. But he also endorsed at least some of the State Department view of foreign policy. In passing remarks in the *New York Times Magazine*, he defended the U.S. alliance with the "reactionary" Chiang Kai-shek during World War II for strategic purposes, and he justified U.S. support for the right-wing Peron regime in Argentina because we were pursuing Pan American unity. Sounding like a pragmatic diplomat, Commager reported that "great principles of foreign policy . . . are formulated in response to national needs—above all to the needs of collective security."[3] But he proclaimed quite a different international ethic a decade later when he objected to the abandonment of principle during America's Southeast Asia adventures of the 1960s.

Evidence of Commager's increasing dissatisfaction with U.S. policy is apparent in his question to Allan Nevins in October 1963, a month before Kennedy was assassinated. "Are we," he inquired, "being as stupid in Vietnam as it seems?"[4] In 1963, few others had yet thought to ask. But the Republicans offered no alternative. "What a spectacle, Allan," he remarked, "of this party of Lincoln and T. R. and Hughes and Taft and Stimson and Holmes, too, trying to select between Goldwater, Rockefeller, Romney and Nixon—four men who cannot even be described as intellectually bankrupt, because they were never intellectually solvent." When the election was finally over, Henry shuddered that the "wicked man Goldwater, in his conceit and his arrogance, dragged the whole party down with him in catastrophe."[5]

Lyndon Johnson's Great Society plans were a reason for optimism, and in early 1965 Commager condemned *New York Times* columnist Arthur Krock for suggesting that it was a "doctrinaire expansion of the welfare state." Were attempts to improve education, medical care, housing, and the environment doctrinaire? No, it was not Johnson's domestic agenda that upset Commager. "I am full of admiration for LBJ's domestic policy and achievements," he told Nevins, "but wholly out of sympathy with his foreign policy which seems to me as Goldwater's promised to be."[6]

Increasingly upset by American involvement in Vietnam, Commager launched an active campaign in 1964 to bring his opinions to government leaders and the public. Late in the year he wrote Senator William Fulbright, chairman of the Foreign Relations Committee, and told him of his opposition to the American escalation in Vietnam. Fulbright agreed and asked for advice. Commager answered that the United States should submit the problem to the Security Council of the United Nations. In addition, the United States should ask China to help with the solution, because the United States could not impose its solution unilaterally anymore than China or the Soviets could impose a solution on Cuba or Guatemala. If the United States tried to act alone, he told Fulbright, it would create a disaster.[7]

A few months later, Commager sent a telegram to Lyndon Johnson offering two solutions to the war: either invoke the sixteen-nation Southeast Asia Treaty Organization (SEATO) agreement of 1954, or turn the problem over to the United Nations Security Council. If U.S. troops retaliated every time the North Vietnamese attacked, the conflict would be escalated into a world war. "This," he told Johnson, "is the program Senator Goldwater advocated and the American people overwhelmingly rejected." Commager then sent telegrams to Secretary of Defense Robert McNamara, Under Secretary of State George Ball, and Senator Fulbright in which he suggested that the Vietcong attack in February 1965 on the American airfield at Pleiku was only the same kind of challenge as the Bay of Pigs operation was against Cuba. "Would we have tolerated retaliatory action from Russia or China," Commager asked them, "or even from Cuba?"[8]

Less than a week later, a Commager letter to the *New York Times* accused the United States of using double talk, a "two-level vocabulary" like that used by the Communists or characters in George Orwell's *1984*. McNamara, he charged, speaks of North Vietnamese sneak attacks of murder and terror. But are American attacks announced in advance, and do they avoid death and terror? Surely, he noted, U.S. bombing creates more terror to civilians than do guerrilla attacks on military installations.[9]

Continuing his spring 1965 campaign in the *Times*, he reproached Secretary of State Dean Rusk for distinguishing between the U.S. invasion of Cuba and the Vietcong invasion of South Vietnam because, as Rusk said, there had been no regular elections in Cuba. There had been no regular elections in South Vietnam either, Commager noted, and it was the Diem government and the United States that opposed them. Castro's government, he told Rusk, has more popular support than South Vietnam's. Besides, he asked the secretary of state, since there have been no popular elections in Taiwan, would that justify Chinese attacks?[10]

Switching two weeks later to the *Herald Tribune*, Commager asked why it was an outrage for the North Vietnamese to bomb the U.S. embassy when we were bombing public buildings in the North. Besides, the United States had a history of bombing indiscriminately in Tokyo, Dresden, and Hiroshima. The Vietnam War, he warned, was making Americans hypocrites as well as bullies. Several months later, Commager complained of a *Herald Tribune* editorial which alleged that the Chinese were the aggressors in Southeast Asia. Commager reminded the editors that it was the United States and not China that was bombing Vietnam. When the editorial suggested that if the U.S. allowed aggression in Southeast Asia, it would occur everywhere, he asked the paper whether the Soviets should take that same position and stop U.S. aggression in Vietnam or Santo Domingo. And at the end of the year Commager objected to the *Herald Tribune*'s headline announcement that two released American prisoners of war who said the war was a mistake had been brainwashed. Oregon senator Wayne Morse and others had also declared the war a mistake, he reminded the paper. Had those senators been brainwashed? Perhaps, Commager suggested, it was the *Herald Tribune*'s headlines that were brainwashing its readers.[11]

There was a pattern in his complaints about the war. The point Commager promoted in all his letters in his campaign of 1965 was that the United States could not operate by a double standard. In his view, the country wanted to act as the aggressor but be portrayed as the passive victim. But, like Theodore Parker, Commager was not willing merely to issue his angry denunciations from his study. Unable to resist mounting a platform, he crisscrossed the country, speaking about the war at graduations and before historical societies and other interested organizations. Enjoying his public notoriety, he debated Alvin Friedman, deputy assistant secretary of defense for international security affairs, before an audience at Commager's home institution, Amherst College, in December 1965.[12]

Commager also appeared with Dr. Martin Luther King Jr. and helped address an overflow crowd of over three thousand people at Riverside Church near Columbia in New York in April 1967. King asked the enthusiastic audience to boycott the Vietnam War by registering as conscientious objectors to the conflict, reporting that African Americans and the poor were "bearing the heaviest burden of this war." The use of new U.S. weapons on Vietnamese peasants, he told the crowd, was like the Germans testing "new medicines and new tortures in the concentration camps of Europe." While about thirty-five marching protesters picketed King outside the church, Commager rose to the platform inside and spoke to the gathering that had been put together by the Clergy and Laymen Concerned about Vietnam. Our involvement in the Vietnam War, Commager announced to them, "is the product of an obsession with Communism—we call it a conspiracy just as the Communists used to talk about capitalist conspiracies— something that is, therefore, not nearly a rival system, but an irradicable moral evil."[13]

A month later Commager was one of several principals who took part in a nationally broadcast peace teach-in that was formally called the National Day of Inquiry. From Harvard, John Kenneth Galbraith, John K. Fairbanks, Stanley Hoffman, and Jerome Cohen were heard. In the Midwest, Hans J. Morgenthau and Cassius Clay were the speakers, and from Amherst Commager broadcast his remarks.[14] Campaigning against the war so publicly was sure to make Commager the target of hostile fire. He became, for example, a favorite topic at the conservative *National Review*.[15]

Although he ignored most of the criticism of his war position, the disagreement on Vietnam that Commager found most painful was with Nevins. Allan had always been more conservative than Henry. When Nevins attended the University of Illinois, his mentor Professor Stuart Sherman remarked that Allan had the "temper to make a good Tory writer."[16] "He wasn't a crusader," Commager once noted of Nevins. "He wasn't passionate about wrongdoing. He was aware of it, and when the votes were counted, he was on the right side," as in his support of Adlai Stevenson.[17] But Nevins did not have the soul of a dissenter.

In 1964, after a disagreement about politics, Nevins chided Commager for his unswerving liberal commitments. Although Allan was happy that Henry's eye problems were getting better, he advised him to "try to improve the inward vision. It is not always March 4, 1933, in American history, and a lot of us are rather content with that fact," Nevins explained, suggesting that his friend remained frozen in time at Franklin Roosevelt's inauguration day. Allan suggested that the two of them should take the advice in Emerson's "Terminus" to slow down in their autumn years. Wistfully, Emerson had acknowledged that "it is time to be old / To take in sail. . . . Contract thy firmament / To compass of a tent." Yes, Allan told Henry, "I can think of ways in which we might both take in sail."[18]

But Commager was not the sort to take in sail and slow down. In 1965 Henry told Allan that "your infatuation with LBJ has blinded you to most of his failings." He warned Nevins that "we are making terrible mistakes in Vietnam and elsewhere; I think Rusk weak and McNamara and Bundy dangerous; they have the Acheson get tough philosophy. I am terribly disturbed at what it may all lead to." Johnson's domestic policy, Commager admitted, was quite admirable, but his foreign policy was dangerously reminiscent of Goldwater's.[19]

During this period, the two men were revising and updating their *Short History* for Knopf, and as usual Nevins was trying to organize, direct, and motivate his distractible coauthor. In August 1964 Allan instructed Henry to bring his part of the book up through the Kennedy administration and then

Henry Steele Commager and Allan Nevins in California in 1963.
(Courtesy of Library of Congress)

to include Johnson's successes in getting the Kennedy program passed, because Johnson's work with the 88th Congress was equal to Woodrow Wilson's and Franklin Roosevelt's legislative successes.[20]

But when Commager sent him the chapter eight months later, Nevins
became furious at what he had written, part of which was a criticism of some
of the early Johnson administration. Contradicting what he originally asked
Commager to do, Nevins asked him "who in Sam Hill said you should write
anything about Johnson? It is too early for anybody to do that." Allan wanted
the story of JFK's assassination, the Johnson success at passing the Kennedy
legislation, "the great knockout blow delivered to the Arizona lightweight,"
and then "STOP." Evidently it was not too early to celebrate Johnson's successes but far too early to judge his problems.[21]

Ignoring the professional requirement for Commager, as an ethically
responsible historian, to write what he felt was the truth about the period,
Nevins told him that Alfred Knopf, their publisher, wanted the book "to
cover the humiliation of Goldwater, whom he hated." Further, Allan wanted
Henry to write admiringly of Johnson's work on civil rights. "Why is it,"
Nevins asked him a few days later, "you hate Johnson as you once hated

Hoover, and later hated Eisenhower?—three good men, who wrought patriotically for the republic? I see no fault in Johnson's home policy, and on the whole support his foreign moves." Although Allan was obviously angry, he signed off both letters affectionately and reminded Henry that he still loved him despite his faults.[22]

Early in 1966, Nevins wrote his most direct and thoughtful response to Commager's unending letters and articles against the war. Nevins compared the Vietnam conflict to the Civil War, about which he was currently writing. "I do not see eye to eye with you on Vietnam," he acknowledged to Commager. "Of course everybody is unhappy about the mess, and I heartily wish we could get an agreement on a decent peace; but what alternative do we have for our present course? Peace at any price sounds attractive now as it did to Horace Greeley and Horatio Seymour and other high-minded men in 1864. But the price, and a steep one, would be paid at once by Siam and Laos and Malaysia; and a few years hence by India and Australia; and in time by ourselves." Nevins's friend Mort Lewis later recalled that "Allan would say he couldn't understand all the 'fuss' about our 'high' casualties in Vietnam. He was writing about a war [the Civil War] in which more that 600,000 Americans had died."[23]

Unconvinced, Commager informed Nevins that "I can think of nothing less useful or less relevant than to say, don't look at us, look at them. Look at how wicked they are. First it is not our business to go around the world punishing those who are wicked. . . . Second we are not responsible for their misdeeds, we are responsible for our own misdeeds. Let them take care of their own." Commager acknowledged that "this is the first time we have ever disagreed fundamentally about anything, and it makes me very sad," but he ended the letter on an optimistic note.[24]

Even the usually conservative Samuel Eliot Morison eventually opposed the war and was no comfort to Nevins. Although Morison had been the official historian of U.S. naval operations during World War II, he refused to support naval policy off the coast of Vietnam. By 1967 Morison had lost confidence in "the military-industrial complex," and he wrote to Lyndon Johnson that "I am not a peace demonstrator, signer of petitions, writer of angry letters to newspapers, but as a senior citizen who loves his country . . . I beg you freshly to ponder the situation."[25]

Unfortunately, Nevins became alienated from many of his friends during the last few years of his life because of their views on the war. He broke relations with his oldest friend, Walter Lippmann, because he thought Lippmann was too critical of Johnson on the war. "He thought that patriotism required that we win the war," Commager noted about Nevins. "He wrote the famous letter to Johnson, saying, don't listen to all these critics. Lincoln, too, had his critics." Commager was sorry to see his friend plagued by these issues in old age. "It's very sad at the end of his life that the Vietnam War should have come between himself and so many of his friends," he said of Nevins. But he "never allowed it to come between us, except perhaps in a kind of aura, when I saw him from time to time, of reluctance and aloofness, but his letters remained as ebullient as ever."[26]

Despite his early complaints about the war, perhaps Commager's brand of liberalism contributed to America's involvement in Vietnam. In the liberal community of the 1940s and 1950s broadly defined, it was mainly those around the *Nation*, *PM*, and related publications who opposed the cold war assumptions that led to Vietnam.[27] Although Commager contested strident anticommunism, was a leader in the fight against McCarthyism, and was a friend of the *Nation*, he was during these years a more enthusiastic supporter of U.S. internationalism than others in the *Nation* orbit. Commager had been a Wilsonian since the 1920s.

It was Woodrow Wilson who Commager quoted in 1942 and 1943 about the need to win the peace as well as the war. Sounding much like Henry Luce in his *Life* editorial "The American Century," Commager counseled that the United States must abandon not only political isolationism but also "economic and social, cultural and moral isolation." If we were to adopt the leadership role in the world community for which nature had cast us, we had to "prepare for it psychologically as well as politically." The United States could never again allow itself to be weak. "War came," he reported, "because we were inadequately prepared for it." Never again should the United States follow the lead of such isolationists as Senator Borah, who had a misguided fear of "foreign entanglements." A decade later in the *New York Times Magazine* Commager was still warning against isolationism, and two years later, in 1954, he was holding up the example of Winston Churchill as a fellow critic of "isolationist pressures."[28]

Perhaps we would expect Commager to have been an interventionist during World War II and so we find it unsurprising that he also maintained that position during the dark years of the cold war in the 1950s. But what are we to make of his criticism, as late as 1964, that the Republican Party should be ashamed that it was isolationist and had abandoned its earlier internationalism of Theodore Roosevelt and Elihu Root?[29] How can we reconcile that with his complaints to Nevins and the *Times*, from 1960 onward, about American intervention in Cuba and Vietnam and his disgust at Kennedy's enthusiasm for meddling?[30]

Indeed, how can we harmonize Commager's criticism of isolationism with his rise, during the mid-1960s, to a position as one of the most articulate public critics of American intervention? On Monday, February 20, 1967, Commager appeared before the Senate Foreign Relations Committee to discuss foreign policy. The headline on the front page of the *New York Times* the next day reported "Commager Declares U.S. Overextends World Role" and was followed by a lengthy article wrapped around his photo. The *Times* described him as "a dean of American historians" who, when he appeared before the Fulbright hearings, "spent most of the three hours in what often sounded like a graduate seminar."[31]

The assembled senators heard from Commager that great powers have to use their power lightly. Because nationalism effectively had countered the powerful nations, which were not able to employ their force absolutely, the strong nations had to exercise their might sparingly. Wasn't our complaint against Britain in 1776 that they used more power than they needed? America is a nation, he told them, whose Constitution and traditions were founded on a limitation of strength. It must continue to be so.

Did the committee believe that the United States had the resources and will to be an Asian power, as our excursion in Vietnam seemed to forecast? Trained initially as a Europeanist, Commager insisted that we had none of the same responsibility for Asia that we did for Europe. The United States, he regretted, was driven by a fear of communism, which he saw as a replay of our long-standing fear of a corrupt European Old World. That fear of the Old World was the flip side of what Commager viewed as the unique American sense of mission in the global community. But in that community, he complained, the United States had a double standard. We needed to admit that we mounted our own aggressions against other countries and that the Communists did not invent aggression. After all, the eighteenth-century American ideology of democracy was as subversive to Europe as communism is to America in the twentieth century. So, he told the senators, we need to take the long view and cultivate patience with the revolutions and ideologies of other nations.[32]

Walter Lippmann and C. Vann Woodward complimented Commager on his performance; another friend told him that his talk was covered for about an hour on television and that "John Stuart Mill couldn't have defended intellectual freedom any better." After Commager's remarks appeared in the *New York Times Magazine*, an American studies scholar declared that "the published version of Henry Steele Commager's testimony before the Fulbright Committee is one example of what sense American Studies can make about our own times." And at a conference a week later, Martin Luther King

Jr. told the audience that he endorsed Commager's talk.[33] Alfred Kazin sent a letter assuring Henry that he "was very happy to see your noble mug so prominently displayed in a part of the Times usually reserved for the Mafia and Arthur M. Schlesinger."[34]

Yet some liberals, as well as most conservatives, surely blanched at Commager's suggestion that Americans had to be patient with other ideologies. Much of the liberal intellectual community thought that the very function of the intellectual was to struggle against rival ideologies to produce the best result. After all, didn't even Commager's Jefferson believe in the active competition and struggle of contending ideas?

And again, how can we explain his earlier hostility to isolationism in light of his strong opposition to Vietnam? Did Commager change from interventionist to isolationist? No. Despite the appearance, he never was an *interventionist*. Instead he was an *internationalist*. Nurtured on Wilsonianism, Commager saw a sharp distinction between the two terms. The United States needed to maintain an international role by joining an organization such as the League of Nations or the United Nations, he thought, because nationalism was a great danger. But he felt that a one-world outlook, in which only an international body should settle problems, was not interventionist. So his criticisms of American isolationism were quite consistent with his opposition to American intervention in Vietnam.

This concurrent internationalism and hostility to interventionism was apparent in his writing throughout his career. In 1946, for example, while advising the United States against starting an arms race, Commager warned that our very reliance on atomic warfare "means that though we have abandoned isolationism intellectually, we have not yet abandoned it emotionally, or adjusted ourselves to the reality of One World." At the dawn of the cold war, that is, Commager cautioned that "though we have formally committed ourselves to the United Nations Organization and are active in its deliberations, we prefer to conduct our security policy as if that organization did not exist or were condemned in advance to impotence. It means that we are using our position as the leading nation in the world to inspire fear rather than confidence."[35] That is, the United States was acting as an interventionist instead of an internationalist power. Twenty years later Commager used that same argument against the Johnson administration's Vietnam policy. Late in 1964 he wrote Senator Fulbright and told him that the United States should submit the Vietnam problem to the Security Council of the United Nations.[36]

Some of Commager's professional friends, such as Arthur Schlesinger Jr., were content to be known as interventionists. In his *The Vital Center* (1949)

Schlesinger pondered the most "effective means of overthrowing an established government," wondered how to stop "the loss of Asia and Africa to the Soviet Union," and concluded that while one-world government was a noble ambition for the future, in the present it would only "serve to distract men of good will from the urgent tasks of the moment."[37]

Because many liberals such as Schlesinger were committed interventionists, they had a more difficult time than Commager extricating themselves from the outlook that produced American involvement in Vietnam. Consequently, their opposition to the war was more ambivalent and muted, and it developed later. Commager's internationalism is part of what accounted for his greater foreign policy radicalism in the 1960s than was evinced by many others in the liberal community.

If Commager had been discouraged with Lyndon Johnson's America, he had only to wait until the administration of Richard Nixon to know real despondency. Nixon, in his view, became a more underhanded operator of Johnson's foreign policy without the saving virtue of LBJ's admirable domestic vision. Nixon's New Federalism, after all, was an attack on the strong national government that Commager had spent his career defending. The national government and not the states, Commager maintained, freed the slaves, gave blacks and women the vote and some increased rights, provided workers' protective legislation, instituted social security and Medicare, kept local police authorities in line, tried to cure inequalities in education, and worked to improve the environment. Nixon's domestic program threatened these advances.[38]

But Commager was not unalterably opposed to Nixon's presidency from the start. Actually he had some optimism about it early on. "I am greatly pleased by the way this administration has taken hold," Commager wrote Nevins from Vienna. "I suppose because Nixon has no principles, he can do the right thing, or at least the popular thing." The president was standing up to the Pentagon, he thought, and might even end the antiballistic missile system. As he confided to Nevins: "Above all—and I am not at all sure we agree on this—he seems to be making the right decision on the greatest of all issues, whether we are part of Asia or part of Europe. You and I know we are part of Europe . . . and that we cannot be an Asian power because we do not and never will understand Asia. If Nixon can swing us back into Europe, where we belong, he will have justified his administration by that one thing."[39]

His honeymoon with Nixon was brief. By late 1969 Commager had already conceded that Nixon was the enemy. When at the end of September the president admitted that the Vietnam War was unpopular, acknowledged the opposition, but promised that he would not be influenced by the protest, Commager wondered in the *New York Times* "if any American President since Jefferson Davis has so explicitly proclaimed his contempt for the democratic principle."[40]

Nor did he forget Nixon's past ties to the McCarthyist contingent in the late 1940s and early 1950s that, Commager felt, had ruined the careers of State Department Asianists such as Owen Lattimore and scientists such as Robert Oppenheimer. After Nixon had been "statesmanlike" in his reversal of the U.S. hostility to China, Commager asked in the *Times* whether the president might now offer an apology and help clear the record of Lattimore, who, "though completely cleared of the frivolous and vindictive charges leveled against him, never recovered from the effects of official harassment and eventually removed to England, where he could carry on his China studies without interference."[41]

A surprised Lattimore answered from England. Commager's letter was another "in his long career of courageous defense of civil liberties' and academic freedom," he noted, but it was "misleading" to suggest that Lattimore had never recovered from his persecution. During the years that he had been under investigation he remained on leave with full pay from his American university, while at the same time his notoriety brought him worldwide opportunities. He lectured at the Sorbonne, in Britain, and throughout Europe. "The outrageous Department of Justice indictment," Lattimore reported to the *Times*, "became an international passport." To have Nixon set his record straight would be inappropriate, because Lattimore had done nothing wrong. Nixon's time would be better spent renovating his own ragged record from the period.[42]

Commager's complaints about the Vietnam War underwent only slight modification from the Johnson to the Nixon era. During the over ten years that he publicly commented on the conflict, he portrayed it as an essentially ethical and moral crisis in the spirit and values of America, a malady that could be traced to unfortunate myths Americans had constructed about themselves. Before either Daniel Bell or Godfrey Hodgson used the concept to explain the 1950s and 1960s, for example, Commager saw his fellow Americans' belief during the 1940s in this nation's exceptionalism as the cause of Johnson's war. American exceptionalism was the faith that America was specially chosen and blessed by God, who had therefore exempted the nation from the same cruel laws of history that other nations had to face. While other countries had to contend with laws of economics, scarcity, military prudence, and other pressures toward sacrifice, America would prosper naturally because of its location, work ethic, morality, subscription to capitalism, and providential protection.

"Because in 1945 we were the most powerful nation on the globe," Commager pointed out, "we assumed that our power was and would continue to be limitless."[43] That is, American economic and military strength was not assumed to be a product of unique circumstances (our being the only nation left standing intact after the war) that would end. Instead it was believed that America, blessed by God, was an exception to the normal rules of history by which other nations had to play (American exceptionalism) and that there would be no decline in our ability to accomplish what we wished, unimpeded.

This produced, by the 1960s, an overextended military and economy—most visible in the Vietnam War—by which time much of the world was beginning to catch up with American power. It also brought about in the 1960s a deep disillusionment with the promise of America, a promise Americans felt had been guaranteed to them by their experience in the 1940s. That sense of disillusionment and moral crisis pervaded the Vietnam War, and it also saturated its critics—such as Commager himself. So his commentary on the war became not only an indication of the nation's political and military crisis but also a reflection of the moral crisis felt within much of the intellectual community itself.

So in 1966 Commager was worried about "a double standard in political and moral conduct, one for the United States and one for the rest of the world," and troubled over "the ethical implications" of the war. The United States, he charged, was "guilty of violating international law. . . . guilty of violating the Charter of the United Nations. . . . guilty of trying to overthrow unilaterally the Geneva Agreement, in trying to create unilaterally two nations where the law, and history, know but one. . . . guilty of self-deception in pleading that we are in Vietnam in accordance with formal requests from the South Vietnamese government." If the United States was to claim that South Vietnam's request for military aid justified our intervention, then we would also have to agree that Cuba's request for military aid from the Soviet Union in 1962 justified its intervention.[44]

The war in Vietnam caused a war in America. "We engage in the deception of our own people," Commager warned. The corruption of our language, as Orwell knew, was "a sign of corruption of mind and spirit." America could not escape its sentence. It was, he counseled, "no use saying that the other side is equally guilty: it is our morals we must take care of."[45] This immoral war had brought a pestilence to feed on the spirit and character of the nation.

The double standard Commager saw in our foreign policy infected our sense of economic and racial justice at home. "Perhaps the most odious violation of justice," he protested during the Nixon administration, "is the maintenance of a double standard: one justice for blacks and another for whites, one for the rich and another for the poor, one for those who hold 'radical' ideas, and another for those who are conservative and respectable." While Black Panthers were on trial for murder, those police officers who murdered Black Panthers were punished with demotion. "Here," Commager counseled his fellow citizens, "is our greatest failure: that we destroyed slavery but not racism, promised legal equality but retained a dual citizenship, did away with legal exploitation of a whole race but substituted for it an economic exploitation almost as cruel. And this political and legal failure reflects a deeper psychological and moral failure."[46]

As Commager made evident in his celebrated article "The Defeat of America" in the *New York Review of Books* in October 1972, Nixon aggressively brought the immorality of the war back to the home front and practiced deception abroad. Our moral capital was being frittered away for a principle we were unable to articulate to our own satisfaction. We were performing acts in Vietnam—indiscriminate bombing of villages, dropping napalm—that we worked to outlaw at Nuremberg as crimes against humanity. Jefferson cared about moral power, but today Americans cared only about military power. "Not material power but moral power," Commager remarked about Jefferson's vision, "was to spread American influence about the globe."[47]

Now our very moral existence was at stake. "This is not only a war we cannot win," he told his fellow citizens, "it is a war we must lose if we are to survive morally. . . . We honor now those Southerners who stood by the Union when it was attacked by the Confederacy, just as we honor those Germans who rejected Hitler and his monstrous wars and were martyrs to the cause of freedom and humanity. Why do we find it so hard to accept this elementary lesson of history, that some wars are so deeply immoral that they must be lost, that the war in Vietnam is one of these wars, and that those who resist it are the truest patriots?"[48] In a note to Commager after "The Defeat of America" appeared, his old friend Henry Nash Smith called the article "a state paper worthy of the great tradition—a paper that McGovern ought to have written but doesn't (alas!) seem capable of," telling him that it was an "expression of the almost intolerable frustration thousands of us feel."[49]

Yet with Commager's increasingly critical tone in comparison with many liberals of his generation came the burden of having to live with some of the contradictions of his outlook. For example, certainly his was not the only position a Jeffersonian liberal could take about the war in Vietnam, as surely he must have known. With equal validity a Jeffersonian could support American involvement in the war—the United States represented a liberal, market-oriented society characterized by civil liberties and free expression (Jeffersonian virtues) fighting against a totalitarian worldview that represented its greatest threat. Nor did Commager's pragmatism provide him an easy rationale against the war, for pragmatists argued that communism was an absolutism that threatened pragmatic views and thus had to be opposed vigorously.[50]

Sidney Hook, for example, was a self-described Jeffersonian liberal and pragmatist who felt differently from Commager about the war.[51] The U.S. military involvement in Southeast Asia, Hook admitted, was not necessary for our own security. But once we became involved, he believed, "we incurred obligations that we could not honorably disregard, if only to make credible our reliability as an ally in a common cause elsewhere." So Hook supported the gradual withdrawal of American troops and the Vietnamization of the war that constituted the core of Nixon's program.[52]

Commager was too impatient to support a withdrawal in small increments and felt that we should simply get out because we did not belong there. But, while morally admirable, his position on Vietnam also left him open to charges that echoed from his past: that he failed to weigh the consequences of his proposals sufficiently. When in the early 1950s Commager and Hook had disagreed about McCarthyism, each claiming to be the true pragmatist, Commager's suggestion that the nation should simply stop fretting about domestic Communism was one that Hook found to be weak. As a fellow pragmatist, Hook had reminded him that "the consequences of one proposal are never decisive unless we weigh them against the consequences of other proposals including the proposal to do nothing."[53]

Similarly, critics of Commager's stand on Vietnam could ask him if he had weighed the consequences of immediate withdrawal and doing nothing for the South Vietnamese or the cause of freedom. When, in the pages of *Saturday Review* in 1965, an article of Commager's appeared next to a piece by Leo Cherne, chairman of the executive committee of Freedom House in New York, the distinction was highlighted. Cherne pointed out that an individual could make a moral and conscientious plea for a simple American withdrawal. "But there should be no illusion about the consequences," Cherne warned. "There will be a bloody purge of the non-Communist leaders and intellectuals, such as has occurred in every other Communist takeover."[54] In the article following Cherne's in the magazine, Commager spoke of the principles and ethics that were violated by fighting in Vietnam, but he never seriously addressed Cherne's (and Hook's) problem of consequences—the consequences of doing nothing.

A similar disagreement arose between Mary McCarthy and Diana Trilling in the *New York Review of Books* in January 1968. McCarthy recommended that intellectuals not sully themselves with the details of an incremental pullout from Vietnam but instead appeal to morality and demand an immediate withdrawal. Intellectuals deal with principles, not consequences, she suggested. But Trilling asked her what would happen to those left behind? McCarthy responded that, like all those on the wrong side of a revolution, they would likely "be left to face the music; that is the tough luck of being a camp follower."

Yet is morality so easy, Trilling wondered? "If South Vietnam falls to the Communists, who stifle opposition and kill their enemies," she asked, "is this not of moral concern to intellectuals?" McCarthy replied that all of us condemn thousands to death daily by not responding to charities, but we live with it. "When Mrs. Trilling reproaches me as an intellectual for my lack of moral concern," McCarthy retorted, "she makes me think of the Polish proverb about the wolf who eats lamb while choking with sobs and the wolf who just eats lamb."[55]

Perhaps Sidney Hook and Leo Cherne were wolves who sobbed when they ate lamb, whereas Commager simply ate lamb. But some thought the issue more serious than that and subscribed to Max Weber's contrast between the "ethic of ultimate ends" and the "ethic of responsibility." Those involved in politics, Weber advised, need to be strong enough to make difficult choices in light of the consequences of their actions.[56]

Like Mary McCarthy's proposals, Commager's opposition to Vietnam stressed the moral necessities at the expense of the practical consequences of withdrawal. It was a courageous and principled posture, but it was strongly resented by those who felt that intellectuals did not have the luxury of ignoring the consequences of their proposals. Again, Commager's position on Vietnam was reminiscent of his stand on McCarthyism twenty years earlier that had earned him such disapproval from Hook, Roger Baldwin, and others.[57]

Yet Commager's was an early public commitment against American involvement in Vietnam. Because he had always been less actively anticommunist than were some other liberals, he was able to function as a more vigorous and more useful critic of the Vietnam War—a war that was, after all, the result of decades of anticommunist ideology and policy produced by the intellectual community.

Another contradiction, shared by many liberals of his generation, confronted Commager with respect to the power of the presidency. Not surprising for the Hamiltonian ethic interlaced with his Jeffersonianism, so characteristic of early-twentieth-century Progressivism, he admired a strong presidency. As a New Dealer he had promoted Roosevelt's active leadership style. In 1941 Commager, then under the spell of war, declared enthusiastically that "all the 'strong' Presidents were 'great' Presidents, and all the 'great' Presidents were 'strong' Presidents." No weak president had ever been permanently cherished by the nation.

Further, when the power of the presidency declined and Congress transgressed the Constitution during Reconstruction, it showed that a strong legislature and not a strong executive was the greatest danger. So "the only dictatorship in our history that seriously threatened the foundations of our constitutional system and of our liberties was Congressional dictatorship." Conversely, "without exception periods of democratic advance have coincided with periods of Executive power."[58]

Then in early 1951, when there was a national debate about whether President Truman or Congress had the right to decide if and how many U.S. troops would be committed to Korea and to North Atlantic Treaty Organization (NATO) forces bound for Western Europe, Commager supported the presidential prerogative. Sending troops to Korea without congressional authorization was not a usurpation of power, he announced, and he ridiculed a resolution to require congressional approval before military forces could be sent out of the country in the future. The Constitution declared that the president was to make sure the laws were faithfully executed, and Commager maintained that "laws" meant treaties as well as statutes.

The U.S. Constitution, he reported, was not only a document but also a tradition of precedents, and presidents had ordered troops to a variety of places. These acts had "involved the danger of war" abroad, so in effect presidents were able to encourage wars if they so wished. Congress or the courts had never repudiated those presidential powers or failed to fund them. When Congress approved U.S. involvement in NATO and the UN, it fit the president with the defense and security obligations membership entailed. If the Congress now denied the president "the right to use troops or arms abroad," then the charters of those organizations to which we belonged would be meaningless.[59]

Angered, conservative senator Robert A. Taft, Republican of Ohio, accused Commager of believing that the president "has the right to start a war whenever he sees fit to do so." Taft pointed out that Commager confused the president's valid right to direct a war that was already being waged with an alleged right to make whatever peacetime troop maneuvers he wished. Until war is declared, Taft asserted, the right of Congress "to restrain warlike actions is fully justified." In response, Commager admitted that he supported "the Presidential system of government" but denied that he defended a president's right to start a war whenever he chose. Standing with Commager on this issue, Arthur Schlesinger called Taft's opinions "demonstrably irresponsible."[60]

When the Bricker Amendment was proposed in 1953 to limit the president's power to make agreements with foreign governments, Commager denounced it. The Founders, after all, had given the president the "amplest authority" in foreign relations. It was conservative conspiracy theorists and McCarthy's isolationist paranoiacs who supported the amendment at just that time "when our international responsibilities imperatively demand the strengthening, not the weakening, of the executive branch." Unfortunately, Commager noted, the Bricker Amendment was "inspired by an unwillingness to assume the great role which the United States is now required to play in world affairs."[61]

During the thirty years following Franklin Roosevelt's assumption of power, Commager was an enthusiastic proponent of strong presidential power. In the pursuit of an appropriate domestic and foreign policy, he and many liberals fought for great power for FDR against a conservative Congress and supported extra terms for him. Even Truman, except for an occasional loyalty oath, had been considered by liberals to be fighting popular struggles abroad and was not at war with citizens at home. Congress during the 1930s and 1940s was more conservative than the executive branch and so in Commager's view less trustworthy. But by the mid-1960s this had changed. Commager and other liberals now began to denounce the enlarged presidential power assumed by Lyndon Johnson and Richard Nixon when it was employed to stage unpopular military excursions abroad, assault a liberal Congress at home, and combat citizens on issues of civil rights, war protest, dissent, and drugs. In Commager's perception it was now Congress instead of the executive branch that housed figures who questioned the established orthodoxies.

In this reversal of opinion, Commager was in good company. While Senators Fulbright and Wayne Morse in 1951 had, like Commager, supported Truman's presidential power with respect to military commitments, by the

1960s those senators were among the most notable opponents of presidential prerogative in the Vietnam War. Schlesinger was another who had changed his mind. Initially standing with Commager against Taft's support of Congress, by the time Nixon was in office Schlesinger wanted limits on the presidency and admitted that "Senator Taft had a much more substantial point than [I] supposed twenty years ago." Commager, meanwhile, never acknowledged that he had altered his position. But liberals did not have to worry about monopolizing the backflips. Nixon and other conservatives who had supported the increased power of the conservative Congress at midcentury magically had come to realize, by the time he assumed the executive office, the national importance of increasing the strength of the presidency.[62]

During the Johnson administration in 1968, when the Senate was considering a resolution to limit the presidential use of armed force outside the United States, Commager turned from his earlier position and supported the resolution vigorously. Now he found in the history of past administrations, from Monroe to the present, a tradition that would caution us against trusting the president's war powers instead of encouraging executive leadership as he formerly suggested.

Why should we restrict presidents when we had not in the past? Because now they were motivated by ideological instead of practical concerns, an interesting distinction that would be so impossible to demonstrate that Commager did not even try. Further, now we were part of an international body that was responsible for keeping the peace. Yet he did not mention that the United States had already been a member of the United Nations several years prior to his arguing the opposite side of the issue in his debate with Taft and his criticism of the Bricker Amendment.

The misuse of presidential power, Commager determined, was driven by our obsession with communism and would not end until we had regained our sobriety. The abuse of executive power was a reflection "of abuse of power by the American people and nation" that had characterized the preceding two decades. We were destroying not only our moral authority in the world but also our political institutions at home.[63]

Then on March 8, 1971, Commager was the first person to give testimony before the Senate Foreign Relations Committee when it began considering whether to create a War Powers Act that would limit the president's authority. The *New York Times* reported that he gave "a 45-minute history lecture followed by a 90-minute seminar" before "his new senatorial students." As he had suggested in earlier decades, Commager told the senators that a judgment of the war powers had to be rooted in history instead of theory, precedents rather than the written constitutional document. But now Commager believed that the unambiguous intention of the constitutional framers was "to make it impossible for a 'ruler' to plunge the nation into war."

Further, the committee heard that presidential war powers were now being used for a new kind of intervention. Recent military excursions were global instead of domestic or hemispheric, and they were motivated by the new doctrine that the United States had vital interests in distant locations. Interventions were no longer justified as emergency moves but instead were assumed to be a routine use of presidential power. All this was part of the cold war disease, a psychology obsessed with power, and the American belief that the United States could solve uncomfortable problems quickly with force.[64]

Over the course of a generation, Commager and Schlesinger had changed their minds on the appropriate level of presidential power. Perhaps contradictions may be forgiven. A political life, at least for the principled, can be pursued, as in sailing, only with occasional tacking and jibing, because a person's strongly held commitments must be applied in a constantly shifting context. As time passes, that is, a person must change policy to maintain a consistent principle and goal.[65] Liberals were not alone in their inconsistency, for conservatives changed their commitments when it suited their needs.

Who would suggest that historians such as Commager or Schlesinger should never change their minds on an issue of such importance or that they were wrong to do so in this case? Arguing against a position they formerly supported took courage and could not have been comfortable. To produce what they considered to be a more liberal, humane, and democratic political culture, they changed their opinions on the balance of power between Congress and the president. If, by fear of contradiction, they had failed to pursue their vision of the proper democratic process, it would only have suggested arid and inflexible minds.

More than most of his friends, Nevins and Sam Morison for example, Commager was outspoken in his support of the student protesters in the sixties. He welcomed the dissent of those young radicals who had not committed themselves to intellectual repression or terrorist tactics. As an ACLU member, much of his defense of the New Left derived from a Jeffersonian respect for open debate and free dissent.

In the spring of 1964 Commager published an article in the *Saturday Review* in which he emphasized that universities needed to remain intellectually open and refrain from hounding leftist faculty members.[66] But a simple Jeffersonian exhortation about the need for intellectual freedom bothered some of his editors. Initially he had sent the piece to the *New York Times*, but they suggested changes he chose not to address. The *Times* editors, Harvey Shapiro explained, thought that the article was more an "emotive statement" than a real analysis of the problems. "For example, would you define academic freedom as the freedom to teach anything?" Shapiro asked, sounding like Commager's critics during the McCarthy period. "Should a teacher of anthropology be allowed to teach that Negroes are subhuman? Should Nazis in uniform be allowed to drill on campus if there are a sufficient number of students interested in that kind of organization? . . . After all, most of us are in favor of academic freedom; but we disagree about how we would define that freedom and who is to define that freedom."[67]

At the end of 1965, Commager stood up for the right of the young to protest government policy without being harassed. We were not legally at war with Vietnam, Johnson himself had protested the war in his 1964 campaign for president, so why couldn't students now agitate against the war? Dissent was not only a right but also a necessity. "The point," Commager emphasized, "is that when a nation silences criticism and dissent, it deprives itself of the power to correct its errors." Students did not need to be shot to repress their opinions, as it was "enough that an atmosphere be created where men prefer silence to protest."[68]

Instead, during the 1960s Commager believed that we were fortunate to have students who were interested enough in politics to protest and independent enough in spirit to criticize their own universities. Independent thinking, of course, could result in bad manners when practiced by either adults or students. The older generation, therefore, should not be so critical of the student protesters. The *Herald Tribune*, for example, used the term "draft dodger" instead of "draft protester." That, Commager noted with disgust, was "like calling Chauncey Depew a tax evader because he opposed the income tax back in 1894!"[69]

When students began to object to the Central Intelligence Agency (CIA) and Dow Chemical Company recruiting on campuses, Commager defended the young activists. The students, he said, were merely taking into their own hands what earlier the administration should have taken into theirs, so the officials had no one to blame but themselves. Administrators were told that "an excess of imagination and of moral passion in the young is to be preferred to the absence of either in their elders." Let those students who wanted to talk to the CIA or Dow visit them off the campus—like they would visit the International Workers of the World or the Jehovah's Witnesses. The CIA was particularly unsuited to recruit on campus because "it has, by its own admission, subverted universities, scholars, student organizations, research, publications, and even churches and philanthropic institutions. Its whole character is at war with what the university stands for. It loves secrecy, but the university flourishes only in the light."

Yes, the students occasionally behaved very badly, and he disapproved of their "discourtesy" and violence. But Commager reminded his generation in the words of William Ellery Channing that "the great interests of humanity do not lose their claims on us because [they are] sometimes injudiciously maintained." Unfortunately officials in the government and the universities "are avoiding moral issues and taking refuge in questions of conduct or manners." And if they were not willing to protect the responsibility of the university to address difficult problems, they should be grateful to the students who have picked up that burden.[70] So, with other noted individuals in an advertisement in the *New York Times*, Commager supported the right of young activists to march in Washington against the war in November 1969.[71]

Then, to a commencement audience at Kent State University in April 1971, he spoke about the indictments "not against those who shot students but—as in fascist and communist countries—against the victims." Part of that reaction, he felt, was because of an anti-intellectualism against the students. Afterward some invited officials in the audience complained to the administration about his speech. Brooks Maccracken wrote both Commager and Kent president Robert White that the talk was "ill-timed, ill-placed and ill-phrased." Since commencement was on the day between Good Friday and Easter it was an opportunity for reconciliation. Commager replied that Maccracken's note was "not only ill-natured, which is pardonable, but ill-considered, which is not." The speech, Commager claimed, had actually asked for reconciliation between the older generation and the ideals of the Founding Fathers as the price of national survival. Maccracken agreed that some had heard Commager that way, but others had not.[72]

When he addressed the Senate Subcommittee on Administrative Practice and Procedure on March 1, 1972, about the issue of amnesty for Vietnam draft resisters, Commager stirred up mixed feelings again. Important policies, he told the senators, should not be adopted "out of petulance or vindictiveness" but "rather on the interests of the commonwealth" in the long run. It was not so important whether the draft resisters were right or wrong but that they acted on principle, "a position that the American people have always respected." And there were historical parallels. "In many ways the deserters and draft avoiders of today are like the 'premature antifascists' of the 1930s" who had been persecuted in the McCarthy era because the rest of the nation had not caught up with them. Similarly, "most of those who have deserted or gone underground merely took 'prematurely' the position that most Americans now take; more, that they took prematurely the position that the government itself now takes." Finally, amnesty now might make it more difficult to recruit an army in the future, he acknowledged, but it would be useful to have the nation know that another conflict like Vietnam will mean trouble.[73]

After reading his testimony, Nicholas Violante, a citizen from nearby Holyoke, Massachusetts, told Commager that if he were representative of professors then it was a good thing most young people did not go to college or take professors seriously. Violante respected peoples' right to express their opinions but resented professors getting more media attention than those "who have worked with their hands and heart for this fine Country of ours." Mimi Gallo, a citizen of Saddle River, New Jersey, could understand the "vote getting posture" of a politician like subcommittee chairman Edward Kennedy, but not a scholar like Commager. Didn't his antifascist background, she asked, prompt him to want a victory over the Communists in Vietnam? And Joseph Ellis, an assistant professor of history at Trenton State College, explained, in his "not-so-humble opinion," that the "gutless draft-dodgers" should be heavily penalized. The "crybabies in Canada" had not shown enough fortitude to deserve forgiveness.[74]

But Commager was not unremittingly soft on the students. Like other liberals, he was particularly angered by the young activists when they transgressed Jeffersonian standards of dissent. He admitted that some student protest was "not only deplorable but absurd," especially when radicals objected to violence violently, used force instead of reason to oppose force, denied freedom of speech in the name of freedom, and employed "brutal intolerance" in the name of tolerance.[75]

At the end of the 1960s Commager noted his discouragement with the young in a letter to Nevins at the Huntington. "As I remember," Henry reminisced to his friend, "our generation didn't wholly approve of the world of the twenties or thirties, but we attacked it with humor and high spirits; this crowd has no humor whatsoever. . . . I am convinced that our own liberalism was far nearer the real thing than that of the present crowd." The young were interested in destruction rather than reform, ignored the value of academic freedom, and, because they had no interest in history, were "making the mistakes Nazis and Fascists made of insisting on having what they want taught regardless of whether it is true or not." He told Nevins that the student radicals were "rather an oddity in the history of reform."[76]

Some of the young radicals answered his charges. Commager, for example, suggested that if students at Columbia and other urban universities did not want them to expand into surrounding poor communities, then they should go to rural schools where that was not a problem. Ann Chandley replied in the *New York Times* that this amounted to saying, if you don't like it here, go back where you came from. Because he did not comment on the real underlying issue, she countered, he "provided no inspiration to a student generation" that desperately needed it.[77]

When Commager remarked in the *Times* that the Revolution of 1776 was creative and constructive, whereas the current student protesters were destructive, he angered Louis Lomax, professor of humanities at Hofstra University. Lomax accused Commager of "nothing short of sheer arrogance." To begin, the American Revolution, Lomax noted, had disenfranchised American Indians, women, and blacks. "Professor Commager is of the breed of historians who have a compulsion about romanticizing the American past," a historian who "has adopted the theology of Americanism," so Lomax hardly expected a different interpretation of 1776. But the student revolt was neither negative nor destructive, and he found it "amazing how long Professor Commager managed to remain on campus without discovering this truth."[78]

Similarly, some fellow historians did not find Commager's liberal creed radical enough. Leo Marx, Henry's literary colleague in American studies at Amherst, saw him as one who opposed the Vietnam War but stood "aloof" from the protest movement. William Taylor, at the University of Wisconsin, noted that Commager during the 1950s and 1960s was trying to update a liberal faith that was "in trouble." Even though Commager was discouraged with American policies, he was hopeful and patriotic, Taylor reported, and also a little naïve. Commager was someone who would proclaim that people everywhere should be free but would not ask the harder questions of why they were not and what we should do about it. Instead of emphasizing economic and political developments, Taylor complained, Commager thought that "much of what has gone wrong can be corrected by the power of the word, that an apathetic public can be awakened by hortatory means." This, he said without hostility, was the vulnerability of both Commager and liberalism itself.[79]

During the difficult year of 1968, the period when his wife Evan died of cancer, Henry worked hard against Nixon in the presidential campaign. He and his friend the historian Barbara Tuchman were active in the National Committee for an Effective Congress (NCEC; Commager was vice chairman at one time), an independent and nonpartisan group supported by public contributions that worked to elect liberal candidates. Through the NCEC he and others worked to raise money for liberal senators such as Wayne Morse of Oregon, Frank Church of Idaho, and George McGovern of South Dakota, and the organization's large fund-raising appeal in the summer of 1967 was sent out over the signature of both Tuchman and Commager. Then the two historians joined the Citizens for Eugene McCarthy organization in the spring of 1968. Later that summer Commager was reported in the *New York Times* to have joined Rod Steiger to raise five thousand dollars for McCarthy at the London Playboy Club, an appearance that the conservative *National Review* reported acerbically.[80]

Having lost what little hope he had for Nixon soon after his presidency began, Commager worked on behalf of George McGovern in 1972. For years he had admired the senator from South Dakota. In August 1968 Henry told Nevins that he would not mind McGovern at the top of the Democratic ticket that year. By the spring of 1972 he was giving speeches for McGovern and writing in his defense. Bothered by the way the Democratic nominee had been treated on the CBS program *Meet the Press*, Commager wrote and accused one of the panelists of posing deceptive and "belligerent" questions to McGovern—particularly about whether the South Vietnamese would be left helpless in an American pullout from the war. Commager, who thought the South Vietnamese would be safe, was proved wrong by later events.[81]

As the campaign heated up in September, he told readers of the *Times* that "a curious sense of *deja vu* hovers over Mr. Nixon's attack on Senator Mc-Govern and the Democratic party. This, we feel, is where we came in, in 1946, in 1950, in 1954." In the Republican campaign against McGovern the nation had been thrust back to Nixon's attack "on the amiable Jerry Voorhis of California," to "the 'Pink Lady' campaign against Helen Gahagan Douglas in 1950," to the "Twenty Years of Treason" campaign against the Democrats in 1954 for "losing China." Now, instead of charging his opponents with being soft on communism, Nixon accused McGovern of being a socialist. Commager thought it was "nonsense" and denied, not altogether correctly, that Democratic leftists wanted to socialize the economy. McGovern, he emphasized, simply wanted to "carry the Roosevelt revolution to its logical conclusion." Was it really so radical, Commager asked, to stop wasting money on an immoral war? Was it radical to simplify tax laws so they served social justice instead of special interests? Is reducing an army of occupation radical? Is stopping educational discrimination based on race or wealth radical? Wasn't the most radical suggestion actually the Republican's own proposal to fund private schools? He concluded that Nixon's acceptance speech at the Republican Convention was "the most dishonest speech ever made by an American President."[82]

Commager had worried about civil liberties in America at least since the 1940s when he published *Majority Rule and Minority Rights* (1943) and began to fight McCarthyism. The anticommunist reaction to the cold war had kept him vigilant about the Bill of Rights in the 1950s. The increasing secrecy and guerrilla mind-set of the Kennedy and Johnson administrations, both at home and abroad, continued to fuel his fears about liberties in the 1960s. In 1967 he warned about the U.S. Information Agency and the CIA prompting the nation toward Orwell's vision of 1984. Both agencies produced propaganda promoting the Vietnam War for schoolchildren in this country. "When Communists sponsor such propaganda," Commager warned, "we call it brainwashing."[83]

But his realization in the early 1970s that the deceptive and underhanded Nixon was emblematic of the worst aspects of the cold war spurred him to an even greater worry about government threats to individual liberties. Already by 1970 he cautioned that "if repression is not yet as blatant or as flamboyant as it was during the McCarthy years, it is in many respects more pervasive and more formidable." A year later Commager accused Nixon of distrusting free speech and the press more than any other president since John Adams. Nixon was trying to ride "roughshod" over constitutional liberties by wiretapping, using police force, and trying to silence journalists. The Nixon administration was eager to use censorship and coercion instead of reason and persuasion.[84]

The handling of the Pentagon Papers case by Nixon's lieutenants was typical. Not only had they tried to intimidate the television networks and then filed suit against the *New York Times*, but now at the end of 1971 they had subpoenaed a legislative assistant to Senator Gravel, who had read some of the papers into the *Congressional Record*. Nixon's officials at the Justice Department, claiming that Gravel's action threatened national security, were, according to Commager, threatening "the constitutional privileges of a co-ordinate branch of the Government." Nixon's executive branch was trying to subordinate the other branches under its dominance, in violation of constitutional principles.[85]

Because of his outspoken public criticism of the Nixon administration, Commager was asked to join the Committee for Public Justice (CPJ), a liberal group that was formed to battle the erosion of constitutional liberties. The group began in the spring of 1970 with a handful of individuals associated with the *Nation* and the *New York Review of Books* and then broadened out to take in a mix of Hollywood stars and various academic notables—

including historians such as Commager, Schlesinger, and C. Vann Wood-ward.[86] "Now we are to have, God help us, four more years of what is surely the most constitutionally insensitive administration of this century," Schlesinger lamented to Commager when Nixon was reelected in November 1972. "And what a ghastly irony that Nixon should be President at the time of the Bicentennial of the Declaration."[87]

His writing, activity, and associations did not earn Commager friends in the executive branch, and it was reported that he was on a Federal Bureau of Investigation (FBI) "no-contact list" of individuals who agents should avoid unless given special permission. This meant that he and others on the list were considered to be antagonistic enough to the bureau that unfavorable contact by the FBI could result in bad publicity.[88] And indeed Commager was critical of the FBI. Secrecy and deceit, he warned, were "now fundamental not only to the conduct of the war but to the conduct of foreign and even domestic affairs." While totalitarian countries lived by deceit, the Nixon presidency was hardly better, since it operated by "lies so innumerable that no one can keep up with them, so insolent that they confound refutation, and so shameless that in time they benumb the moral sensibilities of the American people."[89]

His friend Schlesinger appeared on a different enemies list. Late in June, 1973, Schlesinger and several hundred others found that they were included in a White House file, several inches thick, entitled "Opponents List and Political Enemies Project." Apparently Schlesinger was considered to be one of Nixon's antagonists who the administration, as John Dean so thoughtfully phrased it, would attempt to "screw" with "the available Federal machinery" such as the Internal Revenue Service. Among those sharing space on the list with Schlesinger were such dangerous enemies of the republic as Barbra Streisand, Paul Newman, Joe Namath, and *Baltimore Sun* writer Thomas O'Neill, who had died three months before the list was constructed. "I suppose Hitler and Stalin may have had such lists," Schlesinger remarked, "but no American President. Nixon saw himself as being above the law, and those under him acted accordingly."[90]

Commager was recognized as a leading voice about a presidency out of control. In a front-page article in the *New York Times* in the spring of 1973, he was prominently quoted as saying that Nixon had used powers for which there were no precedents. In what the *Times* called "an extreme but not uncommon view," he explained that Nixon had "usurped or aggrandized authority in almost every field" and, by his attacks on Congress and the Court, had assaulted the constitutional system as no earlier president had done even in wartime—Lincoln not excepted. Others clearly thought that Commager was wrong and that Nixon merely had expanded the power of the presidency in degree but not in kind. The real expansion of presidential power, many observers thought, had occurred under Kennedy and Johnson.[91]

Later in the week, at a nationally reported conference on the constitutional conflict between the president and Congress, Commager and others urged representatives to stand up to Nixon, for Congress had all the powers to do so if it could only invoke the will. It should begin by rejecting presidential nominees, investigating the executive branch, and punishing officials who intimidate others for testifying before committees.[92]

How could we explain the travesty of Watergate? The great paranoia about communism during the cold war era—evident in the American people as well as the government—had helped produce the mind-set that led to Watergate. The American people could not avoid responsibility for the declension in the nation, for they had elected Nixon after knowing his record since 1946. Yet Nixon had played the central role in promoting the moral decline, because he perverted the Jeffersonian vision of a moral mission and substituted an ethic of forcing the weak in society to acquiesce to the wishes of the strong.[93]

In October 1973 the *New York Times* ran the headline "Commager Urges Nixon Impeachment," under which it reported a speech in which Commager claimed that Nixon had violated the law thirteen times and should be dismissed from office for his "long, unparalleled record of corruption and illegal actions." Although Commager's friend Barbara Tuchman had earlier called only for Nixon's voluntary resignation, less than a week after Commager's challenge she supported his position and declared that it was now up to Congress not to set "a precedent of acquiescence" that could destroy our political system near its two hundredth birthday.[94]

As the problems of impeachment began to be discussed by national leaders, Commager took to the newspapers on two occasions to outline Nixon's five specific crimes that justified the action. First, by lying to Congress and the American people about the conflict in Cambodia, he circumvented the constitutional right of Congress to declare war. Second, that action also prevented Congress from exercising its right to appropriate funds for war. Third, Nixon's impoundment of funds for domestic programs denied Congress its constitutional independence. Fourth, he transgressed the Bill of Rights by applying prior censorship over the press. Finally, he undermined the democratic political process by resorting to dirty tricks.[95]

Yet, as Melvin Grayson pointed out in the *New York Times*, "each of the five putative grounds for the impeachment of President Nixon" in Commager's articles "could have been applied with equal validity to John F.

Kennedy." JFK, after all, usurped war powers in the Bay of Pigs invasion, used electronic surveillance against the Reverend Dr. Martin Luther King Jr., and performed what the press referred to as "pranks" against opponents. These five charges could have been leveled against many other presidents as well. "Mr. Commager's failure to point this out," Grayson concluded, "leads me to suspect that, despite his credentials, he is not so much a historian as he is a pamphleteer."[96]

That was not the only problem with Commager's position, of course. Equally uncomfortable was the contradiction, as in the case of the War Powers testimony, that he had been for much of his early career a supporter of a strong presidency. If Commager's earlier endorsement of presidential power had not envisioned a Nixonian misuse of the office, it promoted the changes that led to it. Still, despite the dramatic evolution on this issue by Commager and other liberals, he was one of the principled voices attempting to re-create a tolerant democratic ethic during the sixties and their immediate aftermath by reining in arbitrary and unconstitutional actions. Although some might have thought Commager's liberalism weak and naïve, others found it a useful antidote to the arrogance and misuse of power poisoning America in this period.

Some of those of Commager's generation called themselves leftists, but they agreed very strongly with the conservatives on cold war foreign policy. As Commager aged, however, he appeared to cut across the political grain of his generation. Elbowing his way through those who were moving to the right, he seemed, in his insistently moral liberalism, to be moving to the left.

III

The Meaning of the
American Past

CHAPTER 8

The Character and Myth of

Historians at Midcentury,

1937-1997

Because of the way he wrote history, Henry Steele Commager serves as a convenient representative of one side in the cultural wars that were rooted in the 1960s and waged most heavily in the 1980s and 1990s. He has been a lightning rod for the antagonisms that have thundered across the American cultural skies, storms that have swept both the popular and the academic landscapes.

In the cultural revolution of the 1960s, which to its credit searched for greater equality and visibility for the voiceless in society, many younger baby boomer historians rejected those figures of Commager's generation as conservative and elitist, too preoccupied with concepts of national character and too out of step with the late-century multicultural ethic.[1] So those intellectual historians in the aftermath of World War II who constructed studies of the American myths and mind—and became known, fairly or not, as American studies figures—have been the subject of unsympathetic articles at least since the early 1970s.[2]

But it is impossible to understand Commager's role in this cultural change unless we also discuss the colleagues who were linked with him at midcentury. It seems particularly important now at the end of the century, when culture and curricula are prominent battlegrounds, to arrive at an intelligent relationship with our immediate cultural past.[3] And Commager's example cannot help us unless we situate him within his relevant surroundings. We can then determine whether midcentury American studies scholars, figures such as Commager, Daniel Aaron, Henry Nash Smith, and Leo Marx, really led us to the late-twentieth-century cultural battleground.[4]

Let's begin by recalling briefly how preoccupations with American identity became central to midcentury historians such as Commager. In the course of American history there have been two primary waves of cultural nationalism (cultural patriotism) that encouraged a greater sense of American identity and cultural independence. The first began early in the nineteenth century, after the War of 1812, with the end of the last serious vestiges of direct European involvement in the United States. At this point, the United States first began to feel unified, more just than a collection of localities. Emerson's "American Scholar" address in 1837, in which he asked his fellow citizens to focus on their own culture instead of looking to Europe, is a fitting representative of this first impulse.

The second wave of cultural nationalism coincided with the arrival of the Industrial Revolution in the United States at the beginning of the twentieth century, when the nation became prominent enough internationally that its intellectuals felt they needed to account for themselves with a respectable and independent culture. The early work of Van Wyck Brooks is representative of this second impulse. Out of this latter burst of cultural assertion the field of American intellectual history grew very slowly.[5]

During the first decades of the century Americans were still accustomed to ignoring their culture, a condition that Brooks, Harold Stearns, and others worked to reverse.[6] As the intellectual historian Ralph Henry Gabriel reminded us, "In 1913 an ambitious young literary scholar normally looked across the Atlantic for material with which to test and display his talents. . . . When put beside this gallery, American writers seemed diminutive." Malcolm Cowley and other Lost Generation figures showed that conviction: Cowley was taught European rather than American literature at Harvard before World War I and consequently went to Europe to find culture. Or one thinks of the talented American critic F. O. Matthiessen who claimed that when he graduated from college in the early 1920s "I knew very little of our own literature except some contemporary poetry that I had read with my friends," because colleges were not in the habit of teaching American culture.[7]

In this atmosphere few people wrote on American ideas before the 1930s. One was Brooks, whose *America's Coming-of-Age* was published in 1915. Another was Vernon Parrington, who taught American literature at the University of Washington, despite the derision from his colleagues who complained about including it in the English curriculum. American subjects were scorned in English departments across the country, even at the graduate level and even in Boston. There, at Harvard, which was near the heart of the American literary experience, only three doctoral dissertations in the English Department before 1926 analyzed American literature. Before the founding of *American Literature* in 1929 there was no scholarly journal devoted entirely to the subject. At its convention that same year, the Modern Language Association sponsored its first panel session on American literature.[8]

So when Parrington began his ambitious three-volume *Main Currents of American Thought* in 1913, he was indeed a pioneer as an analyst of American intellectual history. Arthur Lovejoy was teaching ideas at Johns Hopkins, but he was not involved in American topics. Themes from the country's own culture were thought to be so irrelevant, and intellectual history was still so unknown in the profession, that *Main Currents*, published in 1927, was not even considered to be history by most historians, even though it won the Pulitzer Prize in the field. If the establishment of an academic field can be marked by the founding of a publication as its forum, then intellectual history did not exist in any formal way before the *Journal of the History of Ideas* was published in 1940. And much of the credit for the new interest in intellectual history was due to Parrington's landmark work, in addition to the efforts of Lovejoy at Johns Hopkins and James Harvey Robinson at Columbia.[9] This was the condition of the history of American ideas early in Commager's career.

Thus in the 1930s, American topics had a more difficult time being accepted than did the history of ideas generally. The study of *American* intellectual history faced obstacles as this discipline began to establish itself in the 1930s, and its eventual success was in question. So it prompted a few scholars during that decade, most of them from the field of American literature, to create a new interdisciplinary field of American studies in which American subjects would be taken seriously. Initially, then, both disciplines—American intellectual history and American studies—were established around the same time and promoted similar agendas and inquiries.

If the underemphasis of American topics was a key motivation for the establishment of American studies, so was the cultural nationalism that had contributed to the growth of intellectual history. As Robert Spiller, one of the seminal figures in American studies, remembered it, "A good deal of our feeling during this formative period from 1920 to 1950 was negative: a revolt against the way things were rather than a positive movement for reform. Why, we asked, should we be the exception to all other peoples who boast national cultures?"[10]

But there were additional factors that also spurred the growth of American studies, and they help us better understand the character of the field. One important impetus was the cultural disorientation that accompanied the Great Depression in the 1930s. The economic collapse produced a corresponding cultural vertigo in which people no longer felt sure of their surroundings. The rise of European ideologies of the Right and the Left further unsettled stunned Americans. After a decade in which the Lost Generation and others had fled or withdrawn from American culture, in the 1930s there was a renaissance and perhaps even a rediscovery of American culture. The therapeutic value of this renaissance was easy to see. If depression era American culture seemed to wobble dangerously out of control, a search through the cultural attic might find ways that former generations had held America stable. Americans, who in their confusion no longer knew who they were or how to proceed, might, by sifting through past histories, biographies, myths, traditions, and ideas, regain their identities and relocate a path to the future.[11]

Yet another catalyst for the creation of American studies was that the major academic disciplines had become professionalized by early in the century. The humanities and social science organizations that were formed within two decades include the Modern Language Association (1883), the American Historical Association (1884), the American Economic Association (1885), the American Academy of Political and Social Science (1889), the American Philosophical Association (1901), the American Anthropological Association (1902), and the American Sociological Society (1905).[12]

During this period, Henry Adams had suggested a more scientific approach to history than the earlier romantic approach of Parkman and others. By the 1920s and 1930s James Harvey Robinson's and Charles Beard's New History, based less on the romance of past royalty, began to merge with a nascent growth of social scientific history. The gradual move from a humanities narrative to scientific analysis produced a more pronounced specialization among historians and, consequently, a fragmentation.

To combat the problems that accompanied specialization, in 1906 Harvard College established an undergraduate concentration in history and literature, chaired by George Santayana. At first it excluded an American emphasis, but by the end of the 1920s it provided a blend of American history and literature. Similarly, at Columbia College in 1919 the "war issues" course, which had trained student military personnel, was adapted to an interdisciplinary course entitled Contemporary Civilization. These interdisciplinary concentrations caught on elsewhere as well.[13] Those such as Commager who were antagonistic toward academic specialization began to murmur the phrase "intellectual synthesis" instead, and this sympathy for synthetic approaches was a strong contributor to the American studies movement.

In the late 1930s Harvard and Yale began their graduate departments in American studies, and by 1947, when Commager was writing *The American Mind*, there were more than sixty undergraduate and fifteen graduate programs across the nation. The early days of the movement were not always easy. As historian Linda Kerber reminds us, "We no longer appreciate the innovativeness of American studies in its early days." Theodore Greene recalled that in the early 1940s Amherst College students, despite having an American studies program, considered the study of American culture beneath them. Students in the field were held in "low esteem" by their peers. At the beginning of World War II, he later reported, American studies "was looked upon with much the same intellectual suspicion which in more recent times has greeted the advent of Black Studies or Women's Studies."[14]

Finally, establishment of the American studies movement was fueled by greater international interest in America as well. As Henry Luce suggested in his famous *Life* editorial "The American Century" of February 1941, Americans had already exported their culture to the rest of the world; the rhetoric of Coke, jazz, and American slang was the only recognizable international language. Marcus Cunliffe, the prominent British analyst of American culture, pointed out that his generation became interested in America because the United States had saved Britain in the 1940s with its military and the Marshall Plan. "We naturally turned to America," he acknowledged, "to find out how this was done and how we could do it in the future."[15]

So American intellectual history and American studies each expanded simultaneously during the 1930s and 1940s. Peter Novick has suggested that before World War I, American culture was focused on its English origins; between the two wars it fixed its sights on its own American distinctiveness; and after World War II it interpreted itself as part of an Atlantic community.[16] If so, Commager and the other initial American studies figures belonged squarely to the interwar period.

The structure of the American studies movement began in the 1930s with people such as Kenneth Murdock and Howard Mumford Jones at Harvard, both of whom helped found in 1937 one of the first graduate programs in what they called American civilization—a program that included involvement by Perry Miller and F. O. Matthiessen. Before the end of World War II, the program had awarded Ph.D.'s to Henry Nash Smith, Edmund Morgan, Daniel Aaron, and Richard Dorson.[17] In 1949 Tremaine McDowell founded the *American Quarterly* at the University of Minnesota as a journal for the movement, and soon after that Robert Spiller moved it to the University of Pennsylvania, where its financial prospects were better. In 1950 and 1951 Carl Bode helped found the American Studies Association, assisted in that effort by Carl Bridenbaugh, Arthur Bestor, Merle Curti, David Donald, Ralph Henry Gabriel, Richard Hofstadter, Oliver Larkin, Tremaine McDowell, Roy Nichols, Robert Spiller, Dorothy Thomas, and Louis Wright.[18]

In the first stage of the movement, until the early 1960s, contributors were roughly split into two overlapping categories: a myth-symbol school and an American character school, both of which were strategies to help strengthen the liberal democratic identity, a value system that would prevent the growth of fascist or authoritarian sympathies.[19] Inheritors of this tradition, with some significant changes, continued writing into recent decades.[20]

Let's review the course of Commager's own involvement with the intellectual history of American identity. From his early years, Commager's traits foreshadowed his interest in national character. His influential and prominent Danish Lutheran grandfather was a strong cultural nationalist (although for Danish rather than American culture). Commager also brought to adulthood a love of literature and a desire to produce it. The novels and poetry of his grandfather stood before him as a reminder of his own obligation to public culture, as did the journalistic writing of professor William Dodd at the University of Chicago. Already by the early 1930s Commager was reviewing regularly for the *Herald Tribune*, practicing the kind of interdisciplinary connection between history and literature that the American studies movement professed a few years later.

Further, Commager was a contextualist in literature and an environmentalist in history, which connected him to others who helped form the American studies outlook. As Robert Spiller wrote later: "The surveys of Morison, Commager, Nevins, and others were only a few of the many reinterpretations of old facts in terms of immediate environmental causation. To these men, literature was one of the many sources of documentation for movements which embraced the entire human experience in any given time and place. They were drawn to the literary historians at about the same time that the literary historians were turning to them and for much the same reason, a desire to broaden their field of inquiry, their methods, and their range of usable data."[21]

Yet it was not until the late 1930s, at the dawn of the American studies movement, that Commager began writing self-consciously about the American character. On the fiftieth anniversary of Lord James Bryce's *American Commonwealth* of 1888, a book that discussed the American character from the vantage of a British observer, Commager reassessed the work for the *New York Times Magazine*. Here he began his own musings on the subject. Bryce had painted a flattering portrait of Americans, Commager admitted, and saw optimism, democracy, order, unity, flexibility, and practicality instead of more troublesome traits. But Bryce had also worried about the unequal distribution of wealth, which Commager seconded. And Commager was willing to be more critical yet, pointing out changes that were producing problems: a waning democratic spirit, and a growing intolerance, repression, militarism, and lawlessness.[22] From this point in time the idea of assessing the American identity caught Commager's imagination. For the rest of his career he regularly punctuated his writing with contemplations about the mind and attributes of the American population.

In 1939 he realized that conservative Chief Justice John Marshall represented that cultural nationalism which was so important to Commager and other American studies writers during the crisis of the Great Depression.[23] Amid the apparent cultural breakdown, those across the political spectrum, including liberals such as Commager, felt they needed to emphasize cultural unity, community, and republican commonwealth to preserve the fragile democratic culture that existed. Cultural cohesion and a national coordination was thought to be necessary for any reformist agenda to be successful in the midst of the crisis.

By 1940 he had become more effusive about the American identity. What had made us a unified culture? Like other nationalities, Americans shared "language, literature, folklore, history, law, education, heroes and symbols." Echoing Frederick Jackson Turner, he also reported that physical expansion westward was unifying instead of disintegrating. It was the West that was the best example of the melting pot and therefore "always the most American part of America and the most nationalistic." Like other nations, we had already sanctified our heroic figures and interwoven them into a fabric of myth and symbol. The Roman George Washington, Father Abraham Lincoln, and our hallowed Constitution all served this function.[24]

Writing for a high school audience in *Senior Scholastic*, Commager reminded his young readers that while other nations also drew from varied ethnicities, the process was still taking place in the United States. But now that immigration was being more restricted, he predicted, "the process of creating the American type is now finally under way," because "we now have, for all practical purposes, the various racial ingredients that are going to make up the final American type." Neither celebrating nor endorsing this transition, as a historian Commager was trying to project a social trend that seemed (incorrectly, in retrospect) to be occurring. Although the United

States was one of the most ethnically tolerant cultures, he reported to his young readers, if it became more ethnically stable it would run the risk of becoming less tolerant than when it was a diverse "frontier society."[25]

Because by the mid-1940s Commager was already associated with the inquiry into American identity, Robert Spiller asked him to contribute to the *Literary History of the United States* (1948). A midcentury assessment of the American literary and cultural mind, the volume was framed in the contextualist approach of intellectual historians and American studies figures.

In fact, during World War II Commager became interested enough in the concept of American studies that he thought of creating the appropriate institutional structure around him at Columbia University. He asked the history department at Johns Hopkins for a report that Charles Beard had written on interdisciplinary study, and he obtained an account of the first years of the American studies program at Barnard that its director, Elspeth Davies, wrote in 1941.[26]

To infuse the history department with his convictions, Commager put together a proposal for an American studies program at Columbia. The department had ignored him, he complained, when five years earlier he had made a similar suggestion, so now he was resubmitting his plan for a program, a formal institute, and a Ph.D. degree. Why was it necessary? Well, there was a demand for broad Americanists not only in the universities but also in museums, foundations, and the State Department. Besides, it was better intellectually to approach American culture as an integrated subject. Overspecialization was damaging scholarship. When American civilization was compartmentalized, the students could neither understand it well nor utilize the resources of other departments appropriately.

Columbia was losing out to other universities (Harvard, Yale, Pennsylvania, and Minnesota) that had developed programs to meet this demand. This was a shame, Commager told his colleagues, because Columbia was the natural place for such a program, given New York's libraries, museums, magazines, book publishers, musical offerings, and even the United Nations.[27] Despite his efforts, his proposal was never adopted.

Although he was unsuccessful on the institutional front at Columbia, Commager pursued his American studies ideas in his scholarship. Most prominent, he wrote *The American Mind* (1950), one of the books that most clearly represented the American character school of the American studies movement. The book, widely admired in some circles, had a rocky reception in others. Although *The American Mind* remained admired by some historians for its broad inquiry and was popular with the public for its evocative title, the book had a firm core of detractors within the discipline.

Typical was the judgment by David Hackett Fischer, two decades after the book was published, who wondered whether the "behavior patterns of individuals can be transferred to groups." *The American Mind* began, Fischer maintained, with Commager admitting that his title was fictional, that there is no "American mind," but then in the first chapter proceeding to describe the national identity in precisely the manner he had admitted could not be done. While some of characteristics might have been "statistically descriptive of most Americans," Commager had bound them into "a single autonomous superbeing called 'The American,' a creature who appears to possess . . . a mind and will of its own." Both Commager and his readers became unable to "distinguish a rhetorical device from a conceptual structure." Further, "character," undefined by Commager although it was the focus of his inquiry, was one of those terms—such as democracy, capitalism, culture, or romanticism—that always required a specific meaning.[28]

If Commager was hurt by its critical reception, it did not deter him from continuing to employ the concept of American character. Although he occasionally acknowledged the limitations of pursuing a national mind, he continued to write about it throughout his career.[29] And although he did not like the way Amherst College taught American studies (as one problem after another) and transferred from the American studies to the history department in 1964, he remained interested in the concept of American studies.[30] In the summer of 1951 Commager served as a faculty member of the Salzburg Seminar in American Studies, a summer program for Europeans interested in the subject, taught by the most prominent names in American studies (R. W. B. Lewis, John Hope Franklin, Alfred Kazin, and others joined him that summer). On at least two other occasions in the late 1950s and the 1970s, he also made an appearance at the seminar. In 1978 he remained interested enough to ask to be included in a conference on the state of American studies in Europe.[31]

As the reviews of *The American Mind* illustrated, Commager was not universally acclaimed for his work on American character. In addition to those critics who felt his book was not analytically precise enough, there were many who had already started to question the validity of intellectual historians pursuing an American identity.

As early as 1941, while Texas Democrat Martin Dies led the House Committee on Un-American Activities on a national tour to determine who and what was sufficiently American, Lee Coleman, who worked in the economics section of the U.S. Department of Agriculture, published an analysis of what magazines and books declared to be American traits. Observers had not agreed on what constituted national characteristics, Coleman found. Although many described the United States as a country founded on democratic ideals, others noted that the Founders had aristocratic goals. Coleman decided that while a few traits were mentioned more than others, the evidence suggested that American identity was strikingly diverse and that "it may be that this very diversity can be shown to be the most fundamental of all American characteristics." David Riesman, who in his landmark *The Lonely Crowd* (1950) offered a more ambitious analysis of the American character than had any of the character historians, admitted that investigators "have inadequate indexes for the things we would like to find out" about character and confessed that "inevitably, our own character, our own geography, our own illusions, limit our view."[32]

By midcentury the works of Turner, Parrington, and Van Wyck Brooks and other influences on the American studies movement were already under attack. Brooks was now thought to be passé, partly because he had evolved from a critical spirit into an anecdotal chronicler of culture and partly because he celebrated the culture that preceded modernism. The sins of Turner and Parrington were that they were Progressive historians who simplified the past into dichotomies: in Turner's case, the Old World versus the New World, or the American East against the West; in Parrington's work, the democratic, agrarian common person against the elite and wealthy plutocracy.

In the view of some of his critics, Commager was tainted by his relationship to all these tendencies. Like Brooks, Commager had moral requirements for literature, and he was likely to celebrate Edward Arlington Robinson or Hamlin Garland instead of F. Scott Fitzgerald or e. e. cummings.[33] Lionel Trilling, a few buildings away in the English department at Columbia when *The American Mind* was published, must have shivered when Commager pledged his gratitude to Parrington. Trilling, whose *The Liberal Imagination* was published the same year as Commager's volume, had started his own book by attacking Parrington's liberal Left simplicity that had made Parrington so attractive to the Far Left in the 1930s and 1940s. Although Trilling was cordial to Commager about *The American Mind*, he told his colleague that his disagreement with the book was "deep and sometimes violent."[34]

Richard Hofstadter, like Trilling a member of the New York Intellectuals, made it clear that he did not share Commager's admiration for Parrington. Still, Hofstadter was not willing to reject altogether Commager's fondness for American character topics. When one day in the 1950s William Leuchtenburg objected to American character study, Hofstadter agreed with some of his points but stressed that it was an important area of inquiry anyway.[35] C. Vann Woodward admitted that with respect to Commager's book, "I shared the opinion of Hofstadter and may have been influenced by his lack of regard for it."[36]

So, with some ambivalence, historians at midcentury were already having some doubts about American studies. In the early 1950s even David Potter, an American character historian himself and chairman of the Yale American studies department for several years, felt it necessary to reassess identity studies. His *People of Plenty* (1954), which proposed that economic abundance had been the greatest factor influencing American identity, suggested that character inquiries were important but had been performed sloppily.[37]

At midcentury national identity studies were starting to be shunned, Potter admitted, at least partly because they seemed to endorse a belief in inherent racial characteristics. But this racial element was explicitly rejected by those such as Commager and Potter who used the concept at midcentury. The problem was that observers, while justifiably discrediting the race theory of character, attacked and dismissed the entire idea of national character. "But to deny that the inhabitants of one country may, as a group, evince a given trait in higher degree than the inhabitants of some other country," Potter emphasized, "amounts almost to a denial that the culture of one people can be different from the culture of another people. To escape the pitfalls of racism in this way is to fly from one error into the embrace of another."[38] To avoid the suspicion that national character theories were racist, a pluralistic view of character formation was proposed by many behavioral scientists.[39]

The skepticism about the American character school in the 1950s, however, was only the first rumbling of an avalanche of reevaluation and disapproval that swept over the American studies movement beginning in the 1960s, casting it into a crisis whose disorientation is still detectable. As Cecil Tate acknowledged in the early 1970s, "it is a commonplace among many scholars that American Studies is in a state of crisis," brought about partly because, having destroyed what was once the heart of the movement, it now "has no discernible method."[40]

Further, by the early 1970s younger scholars associated with the insurgent American studies journal *Connections 2* began to suspect that American character historians such as Commager had conservative overtones. Even many of those established scholars who worked in the field of intellectual history accused it of the same shortcomings that others found in American studies. At the Wingspread Conference in Racine, Wisconsin, in December

1977, Laurence Veysey told his fellow intellectual historians that their field in the 1950s "was uncontroversially nationalist; it contributed to, rather than challenged, the basic ideological mood of the decade. It reenforced the sense of a distinctive American national culture and of the power and dignity of leading ideas or 'myths' that were attributed to it. And it did this despite the germ it contained of a conservative or aristocratic critique of America, along lines laid down by Tocqueville and Henry James."[41]

Bruce Kuklick rebuked the myth-symbol school for its use of hazy concepts and for attributing a single American mythic structure to all the population. It was arrogance and folly to suppose one could describe the various imaginations of the population with a few general images. Supporting what some others in the movement had already pointed out, Kuklick thought it elitist to assume that the ideas of intellectuals represented common people and diverse subcultures. And although he predicted that American studies practitioners would deny it, he claimed that the "critiques of 'conservative' 'consensus' history" were "applicable to the American Studies school" as well.[42] Midcentury American studies, that is, had been allied to conservative ideas.

Similarly, Robert Sklar suggested that midcentury American studies adopted an elitist, modernist approach that focused on individual values and minds and was tied to the conservative "ideological context of the cold war years." The American studies method might have been different if it had not been so reluctant to employ Marxist theory. But "this reluctance," Sklar concluded, "may be a legacy of the cold war and the links between American Studies and United States foreign policy objectives."[43]

Yes, there had been, in the American studies movement, an "intellectual history consensus" that was tied to the conservative Cold War liberalism of the consensus historians, Gene Wise agreed. Wise reported that younger scholars, repelled by the styles of the older American studies figures and intellectual historians such as Commager, mounted "a massive retreat from the consensus of the previous decade" because it was "elitist," conformist, "irrelevant," "distorted," and it "masked the real motive forces in human behavior." The conservative intentions of American studies and midcentury intellectual history were not difficult for the younger generation to detect, because "those studies tacitly acquiesced in the ideological premises of cold-war liberalism."[44]

Christopher Lasch, Commager's son-in-law, was another who suggested that an anticommunist impulse underlay American studies. He detected "the infatuation with consensus; the vogue of a disembodied 'history of ideas' divorced from considerations of class or other determinants of social organization; the obsession with 'American studies' which perpetuates a nationalistic myth of American uniqueness," and he reported that "these things reflect the degree to which historians have become apologists, in effect, for American national power in the holy war against communism."[45]

This tie between midcentury American studies and the conservative intentions of the consensus historians and the cold war seemed clear to many young critics. "During the social and political ferment of the 1960s," Luther Luedtke reported about the uprising against American studies, "critics attacked the ideas of a strong national character and democratic faith that had been articulated in American literary and historical studies, finding there the germs of chauvinist ideologies which, if they were not directly culpable for the nation's invasions of Asia and Latin America and the repression of ethnic minorities at home, at least had helped to rationalize acts of cultural imperialism." Allen Davis, former president of the American Studies Association, noted the tendency among some scholars to assume that the movement was influenced by a "cold war mentality," a "cold war climate," and an "uncritical patriotism and nationalism."[46]

Nor was this unflattering characterization of midcentury scholars such as Commager confined to the 1960s and 1970s. More recently Sacvan Bercovitch edited *Reconstructing American Literary History* (1986), a volume which broadcast the voice of the younger group in American culture that unseated the generation responsible for Robert Spiller's *Literary History of the United States* (1948). Bercovitch reported that the contributors to *Reconstructing American Literary History* were "trained in the sixties and early seventies" and that "the burden of the essays in this volume" resulted from "the political-academic upheavals of the late 1960s." The wisdom that separated these younger scholars from their 1940s and 1950s counterparts such as Commager, according to Bercovitch, was their perception of cultural discontinuity instead of consensus, their awareness that language undermines power structures, their realization that "narrative devices may be said to use historians" rather than be used by them "to enforce certain views of the past," and their recognition of race, class, and gender as cultural categories.[47]

As the cultural agenda of Bercovitch and others makes clear, midcentury writers such as Commager were guilty of more than a rather conservative support of liberal anticommunism and consensus. "In short," as Giles Gunn remarked a few years ago about the criticism of American studies writers, "they have been held accountable variously for the sins of elitism, modernism, exceptionalism, Cartesianism, and presentism."[48]

The term "conservative," as it was used by this diverse group of scholars to criticize midcentury American studies and intellectual history, had little relationship to what historians typically mean by conservatism. While conservatism is at best a vague label, it usually describes a collection of often unrelated political groups in the United States that support one or more of such values as antistatism, libertarianism, radical fundamentalist populism, community support for private business and corporations, or commitment to traditional, hierarchical, and inherited norms.[49] Instead, what most of the critics of American studies meant by "conservative" was a retrograde cold war liberalism, a belief that American society was homogeneous and bound by consensus, and an elitist sympathy for high culture.

The solution for those younger scholars, mostly baby boomers, who rejected midcentury American studies values such as Commager's, was to embrace social instead of intellectual history. They attempted to solve the problems created by midcentury scholars by investigating the common person instead of the elites, actions instead of ideas, the mass instead of the individual, numbers instead of vague abstractions, the disfranchised instead of the powerful, rituals and habits instead of prose, effects instead of intentions, and daily routines instead of special occurrences. Consequently, anthropology, the social science most able to empower social historians to mount these new ethnographic investigations, became increasingly influential in the field of history.[50] Yet, since social historians in history departments were already investigating race, class, and gender, this focus provided the American studies movement with no unique reason to exist as a field. Nor could the discipline find an anchor studying popular culture, because that material was being investigated throughout the university in departments from literature to sociology to communications. This wandering among the like-minded only added to the identity crisis in American studies.

What were the political commitments of the leading midcentury American studies writers? Were they cold war liberals who advanced a political agenda based around consensus and conservatism? While one might think it unnecessary to demonstrate the liberal Left credentials of the leading figures of a half century ago, the complaints against them, as the preceding discussion shows, range from accusations that they were politically conservative to those deeming them to be culturally retrograde. It is true that the intellectual worth of such midcentury writers as Commager does not rest on their political affiliations. Yet neither should their work be assigned to oblivion, as it sometimes is, because they are considered insufficiently critical, insufficiently able to avoid the ideological preoccupations of their time.

Although Vernon Parrington and his three-volume *Main Currents in*

American Thought (1927–30) preceded the American studies movement by a decade, he, more than anyone but Van Wyck Brooks and Constance Rourke, laid its foundation. Are we to consider Parrington an example of consensus thought, that lonely rebel who, as Hofstadter said, held an ecumenical radicalism? Parrington, after all, was thought an embarrassment by Hofstadter, Trilling, and others after World War II because of his allegedly simplistic leftism.[51] None of his contemporaneous critics believed his radicalism lacking. And who among his late-twentieth-century poststructuralist assailants has been shunned as Parrington was? Which of his boomer detractors has fought with the same determination against the loss of democratic power by the common majority?

F. O. Matthiessen, a decade after Parrington, also appears unemployable as a cold war consensus figure within American studies. Matthiessen was a socialist at Harvard in the 1930s and 1940s who led the Harvard Teacher's Union and was a trustee of the Sam Adams Labor School.[52] Criticism of his leftist politics was commonplace among the New York Intellectuals and others who found him insufficiently opposed to the Soviet Union. Yet it was Matthiessen's leftism and not his political activism that was a matter of criticism, because political activism was expected of radical intellectuals in this period. Nearly all the figures in the classic cohort of American studies believed that political activism was an important part of their intellectual role.

Nor did Commager fit the image of a conservative or consensus-thinking, cold war liberal any better than Matthiessen. Commager was a disciple of Parker and Parrington, a campaigner for economic justice during the New Deal, an assailer of the cold war mentality, a figure who legions of readers of his political journalism thought soft on Communism. An often lonely defender of intellectual freedom during the McCarthy era, a board member of the ACLU, Commager was a participant in countless reform groups after midcentury, a crusader for a dozen unpopular causes.

Like all political outlooks, the liberalism that Commager shared with many of his American studies colleagues had its contradictions. Although he was a strong supporter of intellectual dissent, he, like many in his generation, looked for the sort of consensus that could bind the culture together in support of democratic values. While he spent his energies vigorously opposing McCarthyism, he also opposed totalitarianism and thought that American democracy, with all its limitations, was superior to the Soviet system. Although he was an early supporter of the environmental movement, population control, and the idea of a one-world government and frequently criticized the excesses of capitalism, Commager never voted for a candidate to the left of the New Deal agenda.[53] Still, those who read his essays collected in *Freedom and Order* and *The Defeat of America* can barely judge him a moderate, not to mention a conservative.

Similarly, the political sympathies of Commager's friend Daniel Aaron disqualify him as a conservative or a cold war proponent of consensus. While at Harvard in the 1930s as one of the first graduate students in the History of American Civilization program, Aaron considered himself "considerably to the left of the New Deal." At his apartment on Sumner Road he hosted the weekly meetings of the Marxist study group led by Granville Hicks. Many of the members were Communists, but Aaron considered that "scarcely more exotic than being a Republican or an Elk." When Hicks suggested he join the Party, Aaron politely declined because he saw it as a form of church.[54] Aaron became an admired figure after the 1960s among those such as the Trotskyist Alan Wald who wanted to keep alive the hope of a leftist political alternative. Aaron's *Writers on the Left*, according to Wald, "was *the* pivotal text establishing U.S. 'literary radicalism' as a distinctive field," and Aaron himself, "in some important ways, transgressed the bounds of the conventional scholarship of his day."[55]

Henry Nash Smith was even less likely as a cold war conservative. Smith and Aaron knew each other well as early members of the graduate program in American civilization at Harvard in the 1930s. By 1940 Aaron was teaching at Smith College, Henry Nash Smith had joined the literature department at Southern Methodist University, and the two were corresponding about politics and other matters frequently. During most of his adulthood, Smith told his friend, he had gravitated around either a League of Nations utopianism of the 1920s or a "Marxist hope for peace at last after world revolution and the establishment of a classless society." Texas was too conservative for him, and he was sickened by the 1940 Constitution Day parade and celebration in Dallas that featured as a speaker Texas congressman Martin Dies, the first chair of the House Committee on Un-American Activities. As a firm friend of labor, Smith complained to Aaron in 1941 that the Congress of Industrial Organizations (CIO) was being dismantled and that Roosevelt was allowing strikebreaking measures. The Wagner Act, he predicted angrily, would soon be swept away.[56]

A leftist such as Smith was quite visible among the conservatives in Texas. Soon after Smith took a job at the University of Texas, the state government began to suspect many of the faculty members of communist sympathies, and he was among those who felt eyes on him. He was thankful that the president of the university "stood up & let the boys have it with both barrels when they were about to snap the handcuffs on the faculty." Smith and others were attacked for using John Dos Passos's *The Big Money* in a sophomore literature course. Although he worried that leaving the university might be seen as "running away," he did not see how matters could improve without replacing Governor Coke Stevenson. So Smith left for a year's fellowship at the Huntington Library in Pasadena and asked Aaron to keep watch for another job for him.[57]

It was just as well that he left Texas; later in the decade he confided to Aaron that he was supporting the presidential candidacy of Henry Wallace and had attended rallies, which would have made him even more vulnerable in the Lone Star State. Although he was not entirely sold on Wallace and proclaimed himself "a middle-of-the-road liberal," he backed Wallace because "there is nobody farther to the left with any prominence." When Smith joined the American studies program at the University of Minnesota in the late 1940s, he reported that he liked the state, especially "since our Communist Purge bill got neatly shunted into a dead-end committee two days ago."[58]

In the summer of 1949 Smith publicly criticized the University of Washington for its dismissal of two communist professors. That kind of anticommunist activity, particularly in an educational institution, Smith warned, "legislates the idea of a closed society" and prevents "that constant play of mind over all the possibilities of human existence which is the life of culture." The anticommunist purge was not likely to satisfy its thirst with political radicals only, because "the fear to which these efforts give expression is much broader and vaguer than a simple fear of Russia. It is fear of any sort of vital disagreement—in short, of heresy."[59]

In 1986 Smith noted without enthusiasm that his *Virgin Land* (1950) had been identified as "an example of 'consensus history'" and that he had been lumped with Daniel Boorstin and others as a consensus historian.[60] Does it make sense to call Smith a consensus historian considering his political history or his work? And, if so, does that designation properly suggest Smith lacked a critical or dissenting quality? The label "consensus historian," with its conformist connotations, now seems unsuited to describe the complex mix of liberal Left attitudes held by such figures as Commager, Smith, and Hofstadter. As a result, for more than two decades historians such as Arthur Schlesinger Jr., Christopher Lasch, Bernard Sternsher, and Daniel Singal have been challenging its simplistic use to characterize 1950s writers as moderately conservative.[61]

Leo Marx, Smith's faculty colleague at Minnesota and fellow graduate of Harvard's American civilization program, an American studies figure who later taught with Commager at Amherst College, was even more tenaciously radical than Smith. While an undergraduate at Harvard from 1937 to 1941, Marx was a member of the Harvard Student Union, which put on radical plays, published a magazine, and helped local labor unions with their strikes. An important influence on the young Leo Marx was the radical economist Paul Sweezy, a teacher at Harvard and later an editor and founder of the Marxist *Monthly Review*. Marx told an audience in 1976 that when Sweezy had taught him as an undergraduate he "persuaded me to adopt a radical view of American society, to recognize that the great contradictions of American society are deeply systemic or structural and probably cannot be resolved by piecemeal reform. It's a view of the world which I've since modified in many ways, but I also think I have held onto it ever since."[62]

Marx felt that there was a radical element in the American studies movement and that many faculty members were drawn to American studies because they were first "inspired by the movement for cultural democracy of the New Deal era." Further, one of the unplanned results of the American studies movement was to bring minority faculty members into the university, which he predicted would not have occurred without a radical orientation in the field. Marx believed it "not inaccurate to think of American studies at the outset as having been subversive of the established academic order," because it challenged the hegemony of the traditional British literary culture that was the heart of the liberal arts curriculum.[63]

Further, Marx thought of many of his American studies colleagues as liberals or leftists. Matthiessen and Richard Slotkin, he believed, were, like himself, "sympathetic to the anti-capitalist left." Others, such as Commager, Perry Miller, Robert Spiller, George Rogers Taylor, Tremaine McDowell, John William Ward, and Richard W. B. Lewis, he viewed as New Deal liberals.[64]

Those who suspect that the leading American studies figures at midcentury were voices of the conformity and unity of the Eisenhower era should consider the department at Amherst College, in which Commager, Marx, John William Ward, and Allen Guttmann later taught. While throughout his life Ward remained drawn to the individualism he wrote about in *Andrew Jackson: Symbol for an Age* (1955), his politics and style are represented by an incident that occurred while he was president of Amherst. In May 1972 students asked him to write a letter protesting Nixon's escalation of the Vietnam War. "Write a letter! To whom?" he asked in a speech before the student body. "One feels like a child throwing paper planes against a blank wall. I might write such a letter and you might cheer and, if the world goes on, you might think me a pleasant and sympathetic fellow." Instead he led an illegal sit-in by several hundred students and faculty outside the gates of Westover Air Force Base in Massachusetts, for which he was arrested. For that action, and for his leadership in turning the college coed, many Amherst alumni opposed his presidency.[65]

Another member of the Amherst American studies faculty was the econo-mist Colston Warne, one of the most noted consumer leaders in the country. Early in his career he taught in the Bryn Mawr Summer School for Industrial Workers. During the New Deal Warne became president of the Consumer Union of the United States, and at various points in his life he served as chair of a branch of the ACLU and chair of the Academic Freedom Committee of the American Federation of Teachers. For his social activism Elizabeth Dill-ing included him in the "Who Is Who in Radicalism" in her *Red Network*.[66]

Or consider the sophomore American studies course at Amherst de-signed by the economic historian George Rogers Taylor, philosophy pro-fessor Gail Kennedy, and others and started in 1948. In 1938 Taylor had been a New Deal agricultural economist for the United States Department of Agriculture, and in the mid-1950s he became president of the American Studies Association. The materials for the course were reprinted by D. C. Heath as a series of books under the general heading of Problems in Ameri-can Civilization and included a debate between the Left and the Right on such topics as *Hamilton and the National Debt* (1950) and *Democracy and the Gospel of Wealth* (1949).[67]

"This course *did not* grow out of any complacent consensus of the 1950s," Theodore Greene of the Amherst department later reminded his colleagues. "Its very structure assumed conflict and significant differences in viewpoint. It grew out of George Taylor's Populist predilections, out of Colston Warne's militant labor unionism, above all out of Gail Kennedy's hope derived from his mentor John Dewey that it would be possible to educate citizens toward a 'socialized intelligence' by seriously examining the consequences of various intellectual options."[68] The development and orientation of the Amherst sophomore course might serve as a fitting representative for the ideological outlook of many of the American studies curricula and programs in the country at midcentury.

When Allen Guttmann, another mainstay of the Amherst program, was a graduate student in American studies at Minnesota, it hardly appeared to him to be a conservative field. Aside from Boorstin, Guttmann considered the central figures of the discipline to be liberals or leftist critics of liberal-ism. Yes, there was an inattention to questions of race and gender (although not class), and those in the movement were for a Jeffersonian elitism of talent and standards. But Guttmann knew Smith to be a radical, and as he recalled, Marx "has always been unrelenting in his angry criticisms of Amer-ican capitalism." Mulford Sibley, who directed Guttmann's work at Min-nesota, "was a philosophical anarchist who criticized [Karl] Marx as too far to the right." Sibley, a political scientist, was a pacifist Quaker who listed himself as a Socialist. Not only did he attend several Socialist Party conventions as a delegate, but he was also chair of the Twin Cities chapter of the Socialist Party from 1948 to 1954—which was not an easy time to be a party official. His scholarly work on conscientious objectors during World War II was representative of his sympathies.[69]

That was only the faculty at Minnesota. "In fact," Guttmann noted, "I remember my classmates at Minnesota as a band of (sometimes naive) radicals." It was not so different later when Guttmann taught in the American studies program at Amherst with Commager. It was important, Guttmann thought, "to scotch the myth that American Studies was somehow an unwitting accomplice of Eisenhower, Dulles," and the CIA.[70] Guttmann's own politics were similar to those of his mentors. In *The Conservative Tradition in America* (1967), Guttmann told his readers, "Socialism with a sense of the past is the name of my desire."[71]

Alan Trachtenberg was a fellow student at Minnesota and hardly a conservative. Later, responding sharply in the 1980s to the detractors of myth-symbol work, Trachtenberg complained that critics regularly ignored "the radical cultural criticism embodied in the formative works of the school." The movement began in the radicalism of the 1930s, and by the 1950s its members were "significantly united by a shared politics, a critical vision of Cold War America, and by a critical view of American historical experience." American studies, Trachtenberg reported, had a commitment to "critical and adversarial dialogue with the dominant and dominating culture: the commitment to contribute somehow to the reshaping of the collective culture in the act of studying and criticizing it."[72]

Even some of those critics who wished that American studies had been more radical acknowledged that it had pursued a reformist agenda. In the heat of the cultural conflict in the 1980s, for example, Michael Denning agreed that the movement had been forged in the leftist political and social upheavals of depression America. Although Denning was sorry that the growth of American studies prevented Americans from turning to Marxism during the 1930s by offering an alternative to it, he admitted that it mounted a radical cultural critique of America by opposing commercialism, capitalist dominance of America, American imperialism, and cold war postures.[73]

Although most American studies figures supported the West and the democratic ideal in the cold war, the examples of Commager, Matthiessen, Smith, and others show that the endorsement was qualified. Many of them were liberal anticommunists, but their anticommunism took the form of a principled, moderate opposition to Soviet totalitarianism. There were conservatives such as Boorstin within the American studies ranks, although even he had briefly been a Communist at Harvard in the 1930s.[74] But from our present vantage some mistakenly assume that the American studies founders were cut in the image of Boorstin instead of Commager. The leading midcentury writers, however, were at least as activist in their liberal Left politics as their later boomer critics. The point here is neither to celebrate nor to condemn the political outlook of the early American studies writers, left or right, but merely to end the misunderstanding and misrepresentation of them.

The most important consideration, of course, is whether the classic American studies texts remain useful in furthering the ethics and convictions we still support and whether they provide analyses that, although possibly outdated, continue to offer worthwhile perspectives. While the myth-symbol and character books are written with a different set of inquiries than would be employed today and have the inevitable weaknesses of old age like cracks in weathered wood, the classic works promote liberal, humane values, a respect for civil liberties and intellectual freedom, a concern for economic justice and relative equality, a recognition of the importance of popular culture, and a sympathy for pluralism and diversity.

In his *American Renaissance*, for example, Matthiessen produced a volume on authors wrestling with ideas on the individual and community as the nation expanded. He admitted that he could have written a more radical book instead: a book on the economic and social views of American writers, in the style of Granville Hicks's *The Great Tradition*, or perhaps a book on all the radical movements during the age of Fourier, including Orestes Brownson's anticipation of Marxist class analysis. But instead Matthiessen decided to write on several authors who, like himself, believed "that there should be no split between art and the other functions of the community, that there should be an organic union between labor and culture." *American Renaissance* was intended to produce the "clash and struggle" of the period. In his account, Matthiessen admired those like Theodore Parker who thought that a historian "must tell us of the social state of the people, the relation of the cultivator to the soil, the relation of class to class."[75] But the clash and struggle of the book was not simply between classes but also between individual and community, technology and spirit, soul and nature. Perhaps, with the increased "greening" of the humanities in the late twentieth century, Matthiessen's values need less defense than they have during the past several decades when he has frequently been dismissed as merely the architect of an oppressive canon.

Henry Steele Commager in 1954, when he was already recognized as a writer on the American character. (Photograph by John H. Hill; courtesy of Lisa Commager)

Commager's *The American Mind*, another classic, shared the liberal democratic motivations of American studies scholars in the thirties who were part of the rediscovery of the nation's culture. As Commager acknowledged, it was "economic convulsions at home and political, social, and moral convulsions abroad" that prompted him and others into "a reconsideration of the significance of America, a search for what was valid in the American past, sound in the American present, encouraging in the American future." He and his associates on the liberal Left were worried about "a world where familiar ideas such as democracy, liberty, equality, the dignity of man, and the rule of law, were callously repudiated." Liberals such as Commager who were involved in a "search for the meaning of American civilization," were, like Franklin Roosevelt and his New Deal, more "concerned to save the spiritual than the material heritage of the nation."[76] That liberal attempt to preserve the nation's spiritual democratic heritage, in both politics and the humanities, makes it important for the university not to dismiss Commager's volume.

As a supporter of the liberal Left, Daniel Aaron, in the midst of an atmosphere of crew-cut cold war rigidity, in 1961 wrote critically but sympathetically about 1930s literary radicalism in his classic *Writers on the Left*. Although some depression-decade writers had bowed to Communist pressure to subordinate their craft and critical spirit to party dogma, Aaron believed that most had been drawn to Communism by admirable motives: "because they thought the economic system had gone kaput, because they saw too many hungry and desperate people, and because men and ideas they detested seemed in the ascendant." Those literary radicals "were disgusted with capitalism" and "damned social iniquity." The books these literary left-wingers published with obscure companies were "unjustly ignored by the bourgeois press."[77] Aaron's work was a balanced yet critical analysis during the cold war, in which he was unwilling to bow to conformist political pressures.

Henry Nash Smith's *Virgin Land* was a cultural text carrying a political message critical of the capitalist development of the West. The book's central image of the myth of the garden stemmed from what he described acerbically as "the iridescent eighteenth-century vision of a continental American empire," and he complained that the myth "interpreted the whole vast West as an essentially homogeneous society in which class stratification was of minor importance." Like his contemporary Richard Hofstadter, Smith suspected that the reality of the West was shaped more by capitalism than by a "yeoman" myth. Clearly disappointed with his own conclusion, Smith acknowledged sadly that the growth of cities and transportation networks even in the early nineteenth century eclipsed agricultural life to the point that "the virtuous yeoman could no more stand his ground against the developing capitalism of merchant and banker and manufacturer in the Northwest than he could against the plantation system in the Southwest." Unfortunately, Smith told his readers, the Populist dream could not be salvaged because in capitalist America the railroads sold more land than the Homestead Act conveyed, and the introduction of steam-driven machinery prompted the development of large farming at the expense of yeomanry.[78] If there was a moral to be drawn from his book, Smith wrote to Aaron, it was "that you will be powerless in an industrial society if you imagine that the society is essentially agrarian and Utopian and homogeneous."[79] With the muted echo of Parrington in his account, Smith, like Commager, was probably closer to the Progressive than the consensus historians. The turn-of-the-century academic community cannot afford to drop Smith's volume, a petition for greater economic and political democracy, from the list of its valued influences.

Leo Marx's celebrated American studies classic *The Machine in the Garden* used "the political and the psychic dissonance associated with the onset of industrialism" to probe an uncomfortable chapter of American culture. Employing the tension in American thought between nature and industrialism, Marx complained that even Jefferson did not realize that the machine in America would produce the same sort of repressions it did in Europe. The pastoral ideal hoped to offset the inequalities that accompanied industrialism, but according to Marx, that ideology was effective only in the South. American writers began books such as *Walden*, *Moby Dick*, or *Huckleberry Finn* "with the hero's urge to withdraw from a repressive civilization," but Marx reported with frustration that most were unable or unwilling to end with a radical conclusion. "The machine's sudden entrance into the garden," Marx concluded, hoping for more widespread dissent, "presents a problem that ultimately belongs not to art but to politics."[80] Marx's account, exposing the ideological dissonance in technological society, remains useful.

Allen Guttmann's seminal *The Wound in the Heart* (1962), a democratic leftist's account of the American response to the Spanish Civil War, was a repudiation of the "liberal consensus in the United States, the consensus that Daniel Boorstin applauds," a consensus that "has led, in a sense, to the ideological equivalent of the one-party system and to the emotional and intellectual stagnation of a [liberal] tradition that does not constantly define itself against an opposing tradition."[81] Like Aaron's work, Guttmann's book was a dissenting voice celebrating radicalism at the height of the cold war, and it continues to be a useful model of nonconformity and intellectual opposition.

Despite the rich and frequent examples in the work of the midcentury writers of cultural criticism, political nonconformity, intellectual dissent, and support for greater democratic participation and economic equality, in recent decades these authors have been interpreted quite differently. Myra Jehlen's opinion of the midcentury works is representative. Smith's *Virgin Land* demonstrated to her that, by the early fifties, "ideological analysis and literary criticism appeared inherently contradictory" to American studies writers. The myth-symbol writers thought criticism "could take place entirely in the realm of language" and be "independent of social and political factors." The separation between literature and history "was what identified them as literary critics." This "sidelining of history" at midcentury, "combined with the period's general ideological conformity," produced a criticism that was "hardly even aware of its ideology or of its representation of social issues," hardly aware of "larger contradictions."[82]

Studies published in recent decades contradict Jehlen's picture of the fifties as a period of simple ideological consensus.[83] Similarly, her portrayal of American studies writers as oblivious of ideology and history only sanctions misunderstandings of them that have circulated for thirty years. Classic American studies figures, as literary critics should know, were far closer to the contextualism of New York Intellectuals such as Lionel Trilling than to the formalism of the New Critics. The *Literary History of the United States*, to which Commager contributed, actually was his generation's monument to contextualism. As Steven Watts has pointed out about the lineage of poststructuralism, however, its "sterile and isolated analysis mirrors the worst features of the New Criticism—highly refined and formalist, but totally disembodied, textual analysis—that American Studies itself arose to challenge back in the early 1950s."[84] American studies figures such as Smith or Aaron no more ignored history and ideology than did members of the New York Intellectuals such as Alfred Kazin or Irving Howe. Smith and Aaron were in the initial class of Harvard's graduate program in the history of American civilization, a framework with a strong emphasis on history and contextualism. Their scholarship is suffused with that influence. How will we define the concept of history if poststructuralists are thought to grapple with it more directly than Smith, Aaron, Commager, and their counterparts?

The reader of classic American studies works is presented with the ambiguities and conflicts of American social thought. In Commager's portrayal of American ideas between 1880 and 1940, we are shown the friction between a visionary reformism and a conservative business culture, a pragmatic and utilitarian temper torn between hoping for practical results in social justice and wanting to increase material affluence. In Smith's inquiry we find the conflict between the myth and the reality of the West as it was fought out by entrepreneurial speculators and populist settlers. In Aaron's investigation we recover the dilemma radical writers faced in the 1930s between joining a Communist Party with vigorous plans for ending social misery and keeping their intellectual independence. In Leo Marx's probe into the mechanization of America we uncover the contest between Jeffersonian rural culture and the encroachment of industrial capitalism.

The reason that the work of many of the classic generation remains useful is not that the authors represent any particular political persuasion but that their volumes endure as models of important political and cultural analysis, examples of critical nonconformity and intellectual dissent. So, similarly, the writing of Daniel Boorstin, a conservative, and one of the best minds that American studies can claim, remains equally useful no matter what his political commitments.

The midcentury American studies texts have many of the weaknesses of which they have been accused in the previous several decades. Marx, in his *Machine in the Garden*, for example, fails to convey his point clearly, concretely, and systematically enough, and his book is an example of Bruce Kuklick's complaint that many of the classic American studies texts were caught in a conceptual and methodological fog.[85] But it is a mistake to view these classic authors and works as disengaged from history, unaware of social and political contradictions, disconnected from nonconformist criticism and intellectual dissent, or oblivious to the ideology that they both analyze and represent.

If we can dismiss the misperception that most American studies figures were political conservatives or represented the cold war consensus in their scholarship or public lives, the charge of cultural elitism (a focus on high culture and white males to the exclusion of women, minorities, and subcultures) is a more fitting accusation. Even that case has been overstated, however.

If Parrington was a political predecessor of American studies, Constance Rourke was a cultural forerunner. Yet consider whether she was an elitist. Her *American Humor: A Study of the National Character*, did not assume a collective mind without subcultures. Humor, she thought, allowed and even promoted diversity and distance from the dominant culture. "Each in a fashion of his own had broken bonds," Rourke maintained, "the Yankee in the initial revolt against the parent civilization, the backwoodsman in revolt against all civilization, the Negro in a revolt which was cryptic and submerged but which none the less made a perceptible outline. As figures they embodied a deep-lying mood of disseverance, carrying the popular fancy further and further from any fixed or traditional heritage." In her work as national editor of the Federal Art Project's Index of American Design, she hoped that she could help to shed "fresh light . . . upon ways of living which developed within the highly diversified communities of our many frontiers," in addition to "new knowledge of the American mind and temperament."[86]

Commager did tilt toward high culture. As a Jeffersonian he believed that education and discussion were public ventures that raised the abilities of citizens and that public discourse should aim high—although so did most socialist intellectuals, for that matter.[87] Yet while Commager's *American Mind* was loaded with philosophers, jurists, scholars, and other high thinkers, it was also crowded with popular and unacclaimed minor novelists, poets, and books.[88]

Typical of Commager was a draft he wrote for an article for *Senior Scholastic* in 1943, which demonstrated his belief that, despite the importance of the melting pot, to which he was always committed, diversity was an essential value. Culture in the United States was made up of a mix of different nationalities and ethnicities, and he believed that "what makes Americans American is precisely this heterogeneity—just as we might assert, without being too paradoxical, that New York City is really the most American of cities, really is America." All standards and backgrounds were necessary and beneficial: the offspring of a marriage between a Norwegian and an Irishman were welcome, and "so too, for that matter, is the Alabama Negro." Although these opinions sound more mainstream today, they were less typical in 1943.[89]

Nor did Daniel Aaron or Henry Nash Smith represent the elitism of the movement. Aaron wrote considerably on ethnicity and the literature of outsiders before it was fashionable to do so. In the decades surrounding midcentury, well before the current vogue for gender studies, Aaron tried to get his students at Smith College interested in women writers and women's history and was involved from the beginning in the formation of the Sophia Smith collection there.[90] And in *Virgin Land* Henry Nash Smith wrote mostly of popular Western heroes and dime-store novels. His embrace of popular culture was as enthusiastic as that of most of his later critics. It is revealing that when he was writing *Virgin Land*, he told Richard Dorson he was trying to do sociology instead of literature.[91]

The University of Minnesota, where the myth-symbol school was represented by Smith, Leo Marx, and others, was hardly suffocating in a worship of high culture. "Tremaine McDowell was so in love with popular culture," Allan Guttmann remembers from his student days, "that he wanted parties to end with a rendition of 'Joe Hill,' and he arranged for his memorial service—which took place on campus—to conclude with a rousing version of 'The Saints Go Marching In.' "[92]

Even Linda Kerber remembers that, when she entered the field of American studies in the 1950s, although it was not perfect, it was "hospitable to diversity, particularly diversity of ethnicity or race and of gender." The early issues of *American Quarterly* carried many articles on African Americans, folk art, and women, "which compared quite well to what other academic journals were doing at the time." She found the movement "quicker than literature and quicker than history as an academic field to welcome feminists." It led other disciplines in its embrace of popular culture and interdisciplinary emphasis.[93]

But the midcentury generation held a higher regard for high, white male culture than we do today. By several measures the classic American studies crowd was more culturally elitist than the academy is at present. But often what seems to be meant by the charge of elitism is that these earlier writers depended on a more unified conception of American identity and that this holism promoted the interests of the intellectual community with a self-serving, imperious, and "elitist" vision of what constituted American culture.

So we need to consider the debate about the benefits of cultural unity and fragmentation that has torn the intellectual community since the 1950s civil rights movement. To talk about fragmentation is to cast the issue in pejorative terms, of course, for that impulse might rightly be called diversity or pluralism. And no matter what we call it, is fragmentation necessarily harmful? "Belief in the virtue of synthesis and in the badness of fragmentation," Allan Megill has reminded us, "seems deeply ingrained within our academic culture and within the culture of professional historians in particular. . . . Let us be warned, however: all calls for synthesis are attempts to impose an interpretation."[94] While interpretations are not necessarily structures to avoid, Megill has properly warned us to consider whether a general call for holism or unity is actually only an ideological agenda being promoted under other pretenses.

Yet in response to the increased formalism in literary circles, the expansion of monographical social history, and a gradual move toward tribalistic ethnocentrism in the culture, many observers indeed have been worried about cultural fragmentation, and assurances such as Megill's have not convinced them. Already by the 1970s even those who were committed to an expansion of American identity saw hazards to negotiate. Doris Friedensohn, director of Women's Studies at Jersey City State College and an active member of the Radical Caucus of the American Studies Association in the early 1970s, warned in 1979 that pluralism had to be handled carefully "as one would a rose with thorns." She thought it important to avoid "spiritual fragmentation," complaining that "the politics of pluralism has mercilessly carved up our landscape—into sometimes separate, sometimes interlocking spheres of class, race, ethnicity, language, religion, region, sex, and sexual orientation. Let us not do justice to diversity," she advised, "by proclaiming pluribus si, unum no."[95]

While postwar American studies and intellectual history were more culturally elitist than late-century fashions, much of their embrace of diversity has been ignored. Particularly overlooked in this regard is their promotion of the concept of liberal pluralism, in which each person is thought to have overlapping and offsetting allegiances to a mix of ethnic, religious, political, economic, and interest groups. The idea of pluralism, as it was constructed by midcentury social scientists such as Edward Shils, Robert Dahl, Seymour Martin Lipset, and Daniel Bell after World War II, proposed that each individual belonged to *many* groups (such as a Southern Baptist Association, the National Rifle Association, an environmental group, an African American group, the Democratic Party, or a local gardening organization). This kept us from being separatists who were willing to see only one side of our identity. It prevented us from being fanatical proponents of any one political or social solution. This pluralist vision of overlapping attachments, a vision that Commager shared, promoted the virtue of keeping and nurturing our own ethnic (and other) group identities, while it encouraged us to value what we shared together as a culture through our different group commitments.

Further, even those historians who are most committed to promoting diversity in American culture often find it impossible to avoid generalizing about large cultural units. After all, what is the alternative to generalization? "What distinguishes the historian from the collector of facts," E. H. Carr once remarked, "is generalization."[96] It has been thought since the 1960s that social historians might be able to avoid unfair generalizations by focusing monographic studies on appropriately small groups of people. But how small? Social historians might choose a town, but towns have many different ethnicities and classes. Then perhaps a single ethnic group would be a better focus than a town? But the experience of all members of an ethnic group might not be the same on the West Coast as in the East; they might have significantly different experiences in Philadelphia and Boston. Even within a single city, say Boston, the Irish might have an experience in the neighborhood of Charlestown different from one they would have in Brookline. So should ethnic histories be written block by block instead? But even there we can detect differences of class and education. So perhaps we should focus our studies around a family? Yet even within families there exist wild variations of religion, ambition, education, and culture. Is the answer then to write 250 million separate histories of the individuals who constitute American society? In addition to being impractical, it transgresses the very project of historians: to make sense, by generalization, of the main currents of a culture.[97]

Besides, all cultures are more diverse than we admit. Robert Spiller has proposed that "there was never such a thing as an ethnically, geographically and temporally pure culture" without variations and subcultures, yet we feel comfortable speaking about Greek, Roman, Chinese, French, or Mexican culture.[98] When we will not allow that same latitude to the concept of American cultural identity, are we holding America to a standard from which other nations are exempt?

And frankly, most historians, even social historians, generalize about identity anyway, whether or not they formally oppose that practice. Ironically, even though baby boomers repudiated the concept of character studies they never stopped employing it in their own work. For the past thirty years historians, despite rejecting character at the theoretical level, have continued to use it in practice—often packaging these volumes as "studies in" or the "voices of" a particular group.[99] The end of the century witnesses the rather uncomfortable situation of a generation of historians who frame much of their writing around a concept that they do not endorse philosophically. Younger historians continue to generalize, as Commager did before them, because of the needs of history as a medium. And perhaps, although it is uncomfortable to say, we cannot shake the idea of identity because it is so necessary to the notion of culture. The concept of national identity might be as important (or unimportant) as ethnic identity; perhaps the idea of national identity has the same significance for the world community as ethnicity does for pluralistic American society.[100]

While at one time Americans believed that ethnicity was good and ethnocentrism was bad, by the 1980s it had been resolved that ethnocentrism was a beneficial necessity. Whereas, in the twenty years after World War II, adherents of liberalism believed in a universalism that embraced equality of opportunity and fought racism and discrimination, a later generation found that this midcentury universalism was really only a cover for the interests of the powerful. But, as David Hollinger has suggested, instead of trying to create a more perfect universalism, increasingly after the 1960s the American intellectual community decided to abandon universalism completely for ethnocentric localism, "to live within the confines of the unique civic, moral, and epistemic communities into which we are born, to devote ourselves to our ethnos." In this multicultural age, the image of the "melting pot" became the "salad bowl," and the "ideological and constitutional tradition protecting the rights of individuals was asked to reform itself in order to protect instead the rights of groups."[101]

So the criticism of the old American studies movement and midcentury intellectual history is entangled with the cultural debate over diversity. Its critics are right to worry about generalizations, myths, and identity studies, especially if they are used for racist or other dangerous ends. But generalizations and identity characterizations will not be eliminated completely, and they continue to be used even by those who denounce them most loudly. Midcentury American studies and intellectual history of the kind Commager wrote were not perfect, but neither were they as uniquely flawed as we sometimes believe.

There are several reasons why the two generations of academic Americans have employed such different scholarly assumptions about American life. One explanation is that resentments over the cold war, and what constituted an appropriate level of anticommunism and defense of democracy sparked the two groups into an explosive animosity toward each other, animosity that has still not abated. The young who criticized the midcentury writers thought them insufficiently neutral in the cold war, too partisan and celebratory toward America and its exceptionalism. The older generation, many of whom were suffused with the anti-Stalinism of the Old Left, shuddered at the New Left's unwillingness to take a strong anticommunist stand in the cold war.[102]

A much more important reason for the generational division in American scholarship is that it reflects a separation between the Old and New Left convictions about the importance of culture. The Old Left (which included many of the leading figures of the myth-symbol and character school of American studies) had roots in the soil of Marxism and the depression, and for them radicalism was political and economic. Radicalism, for this midcentury generation, had more to do with ending economic exploitation than with addressing race, ethnicity, gender, the authority of institutions, or the sexual revolution. Politics and culture are intertwined, of course, and they cannot be neatly divided. Jewish members of the Old Left, for example, were concerned about ethnic discrimination. Some older members of the Old Left such as Malcolm Cowley had inhabited Greenwich Village in their youth and taken part in the assault on bourgeois values.

But as difficult as these distinctions are to draw exactly, they possess a great gravity. The Old Left's economic and political enthusiasm prompted it to brandish concrete legislative and policy concerns. The essays that constitute Daniel Bell's *The End of Ideology*, Irving Howe's compilation *Twenty-Five Years of "Dissent"*, or any of the work of Michael Harrington, Sidney Hook, or Seymour Martin Lipset, make it apparent that these Old Left writers, related by generation and contextualist outlook to the midcentury American studies figures, were pragmatic, concrete, and political. The Old Left was satisfied to leave cultural relationships as they were—including questions about sexual identity, the challenge to parental authority, dress codes, and other related matters. More pressing to the Old Left was the redistribution of political and economic power. Its adherents were not trying to unseat the value system of the bourgeoisie so much as they were trying to spread the material and political benefits of middle-class life to a broader public.[103]

In contrast, the New Left (which included many critics of the myth-symbol and character writers) grew out of an antagonism toward postwar mass society, suburban middle-class values and lifestyles, and racial intolerance. Radicalism for the New Left was cultural. Countless political activities serve as exceptions: the work for Eugene McCarthy, Bobby Kennedy, and George McGovern, or the voter registration drive in the South. But the first principles of the New Left radicalism, especially as it matured in the later 1960s, were essentially cultural in nature. The emphasis was to change the cultural landscape so it would alter the political surroundings.

The French New Left expressed well the cultural foundation of the 1960s. "The consumer's society must perish of a violent death," it explained. "The society of alienation must disappear from history. We are inventing a new and original world. Imagination is seizing power." The transformation was to be partly a matter of consciousness, and so the task was as much psychological as political. Most revolutions had failed because political uprisings had focused on overthrowing governments, economic systems, or ruling classes. Those revolutions made only minor redesigns at the top of the political structure. Instead, what was needed was to change the foundation of life's structure: the visionary imagination, values, and sense of human community from which everything else is produced.[104]

Before the mid-1960s, most elements of the protest community subscribed to a political radicalism. The civil rights movement, the early New Left, and the women's movement, for example, all depended on either the federal government or some legislative or political process to deliver constitutional rights. But increasingly after 1965 these movements turned from politics toward black power and separatism, individual or gender liberation, and the exploration of personal consciousness.[105] Instead of lobbying, registering voters, designing boycotts, and teaching political skills door-to-door, as had been done earlier, now in the late 1960s cultural and symbolic acts became the weapons of change. The cultural radicalism of black liberation, dashikis, draft card burnings, bra burnings, Woodstock, and style as countercultural statement replaced the earlier pragmatic politics.

The early New Left was born out of the essentially political orientation of the Old Left. C. Wright Mills, Paul Goodman, Dwight Macdonald, Michael Harrington, and the Student League for Industrial Democracy had all influenced the disciples of the Port Huron Statement.[106] But the later New Left, especially but not solely in the late 1960s, divorced themselves sharply from the Old Left's political agenda and pursued questions of alienation and liberation. While the Old Left fashioned its analysis from the older Karl Marx's concern with exploitation, the New Left subscribed to the young Marx's preoccupation with alienation.[107]

Many ideas of the early and late New Left ended up in the academic Left of the past quarter of a century.[108] This impulse, a post–New Left that we could simply call the Cultural Left, brought to its scholarly work the cultural radicalism of the late 1960s. Consequently, its inquiries have revolved around such cultural issues as subcultural and ethnic identities, matters of gender power, race, the influence of popular culture, the hidden motives behind language and texts, and the desirability of a multicultural ethic (a post–New Left conception arising from the liberationist and separatist commitments of the late-1960s New Left) instead of a liberal pluralist society (an Old Left design).

Because the Old Left and the Cultural Left had different ideas about what constituted appropriate radicalism, since the early 1970s proponents of a multicultural democratic ethic mistook those midcentury Old Leftist and American studies figures for conservatives. In the past quarter century the Cultural Left, largely represented by an academic Left, has placed such a central importance on the role of culture in the reformation of society that earlier American studies writers such as Commager, who could not anticipate the current multicultural turn, have simply been dismissed as illiberal and retrograde—regardless of their actual political commitments.

Because of their widely different political visions, it is hardly surprising that the two generations would clash in a scholarly field that attempts to construct a usable past. And the animosity of this generational struggle is increased by the threat, envisioned by the Cultural Left, that the midcentury liberal pluralist ethic of shared cultural values, of a shared cultural identity in which all subgroups could partake, might undermine the present multicultural project. Little wonder that the older and younger generations split apart so decisively. How could two so dissimilar sets of goals hope to meld into a shared reformist academic approach?

The Old Left and its liberal inheritors such as Commager, after all, believed in political and economic equality, equality before the law, the rights of labor and minority opinions, and the importance of dissent. But they also believed in a commonwealth of sharing where the rich had responsibilities toward the poor; where races, ethnicities, and nationalities combined in an interwoven, harmonious sharing; where there were recognized standards of culture, merit, and intelligence toward which all were encouraged to climb and from which none were barred; where ethnic identities were not erased but shared in an overlapping set of allegiances with others and were no more important (and no more disqualifying) than any other aspect of one's mix of interests; where the democratic majority would cast off the age-old tyranny of the powerful minority; where the community of humankind would join together for the benefit of all. In the opinion of the Old Left in the decades after the 1930s, radicals, as it turned out, shared many commitments and values with liberalism.

The later New Left and Cultural Left, however, had a quite different vision of the most beneficial political agenda. Here an appropriate radical was one who was willing to play a vanguard function, one who had closer ties to cultural than to political change. The Cultural Left worked for a new society where the oppressed and embattled minority would throw off the yoke of the omnipotent majority; where the expressions of the few and powerless could be heard as clearly as those of the hegemonic many; where the rich not only had an economic responsibility for the poor but also were obliged to value the cultural insights of the poor equally with their own; where the opinions of the ethnic and political majorities were to be limited, but the rights and ideas of the economic majorities were to prevail; where the prerogatives of political and ethnic minorities would serve as a wedge into the power that their numbers, in a democracy, prevented them from attaining; where the formerly disfranchised would be elevated to the position of a vanguard able to enlighten the majority and rescue them from their false consciousness; where the ideas of harmonious community and majority rule would acquiesce before the commitment to subcultural identification. Liberalism, rediscovered as revolutionary by the younger generation in Eastern Europe and Asia in the 1980s, remained passé and unworkable for those Americans in the orbit of the Cultural Left.

The issue regarding midcentury intellectual historians and American studies figures such as Commager is not so much that they were conservative, illiberal, or oppressive. Rather, many of these writers derived their principles from the Old Left, which was a more politically and less culturally oriented form of radicalism, and those Old Left values conflicted sharply with the basic commitments of the young academic and multicultural forces influenced by the New Left following the 1960s. The rejection of Commager's style of 1950s intellectual history and American studies by a younger cohort was part of a generational disagreement between acutely different visions of American culture and society. Should America be built on the midcentury values of a color-blind liberal pluralism, integration, majority rule, shared identity, and a prevention of economic and political exploitation as Commager hoped? Or should it be constructed on the Cultural Left values of multiculturalism, ethnic and subcultural identification, minority rights, personal liberation, and a prevention of cultural alienation?

Commager and the older American studies figures were at least as politically radical and activist as their younger counterparts have turned out to be. It is only in the cultural realm, because they could not anticipate our current multicultural ethic, that Commager's generation now seems less "liberal." We need to understand the political intentions behind their cultural vision so we stop thinking of them as an illiberal force. Commager and our past intellectual historians and American studies leaders, through their allegedly retrograde beliefs, did not cause or bequeath us our current sense of cultural warfare. In many ways they hoped for a far more harmonious and open liberal society than we now propose.

In our current period of cultural acrimony there is much to be gained by remembering the example of the former generation of intellectual historians and American studies scholars and reviving at least part of what they offered us: a civically activist dedication to political and economic equality; a commitment to the rights of democratic majorities combined with a protection of minority safeguards; a framework of analysis with a strong emphasis on history, contextualism, and narrative; that liberal attempt to encourage greater democratic participation in economic, political, and cultural life; and a belief in a liberal pluralism whereby citizens are connected by a common, shared culture while not losing their subcultural identities. If we decide to reject their example and advice, let us do it knowledgeably and fairly with a clear understanding of their political intentions and vision.

CHAPTER 9

Liberals and the Historical Past,
1948-1997

Although Henry Steele Commager was a civic activist in political culture, he dedicated himself from his early years to working as a professional historian. Naturally, his liberal ideas and civic commitment to shared culture manifested themselves in his historical scholarship. While he shared many of the beliefs of others in the field of history at midcentury, he emphasized the need for intellectual dissent more than did some of his colleagues. Further, his public life forced him to decide whether scholarship and intellectual activism were compatible and, if not, which one was more important. As the discipline of history changed after midcentury, and especially after the 1960s, Commager had to determine the importance of theory versus traditional narrative in the field of intellectual history. Where was a liberal and civic historian to stand on these matters?

Through the example of Commager, who held a key vantage in his generation, we can see the nature of historical thought at midcentury, during which period it gained a reputation for celebrating consensus and conformity. American studies scholars were not the only ones who speculated about a national character and identity in the years immediately following World War II. They were joined in their investigation of the American character by many members of the history profession at midcentury. As the historian John Higham recognized, the pursuit of an American mind was not undertaken solely by those in American studies but was also "an analytical tool of the consensus history of the 1950's and the basis for its major achievements."[1]

The American studies scholars and what for decades we have followed Higham in calling "the consensus school" of American historians were intertwined at midcentury. The parallels are hard to miss. American studies figures such as Henry Nash Smith, for example, were of the same generation as consensus historians such as Louis Hartz. American studies writers such as Daniel Aaron were close personal friends with such consensus historians as Richard Hofstadter. And the American studies preoccupation with American identity and myth addressed many of the same issues as did the consensus school, with its fascination for the common values of the national population. So intermixed were these two groups, in fact, that in the person of some scholars, such as Daniel Boorstin, the schools seemed to be condensed indistinguishably.

Much has been written about the consensus historians in the past several decades, most of it unflattering. In that respect consensus history has experienced the same unfriendly reception from the baby boomer generation as have both midcentury American studies and Henry Steele Commager himself. And in fact Commager turns out to be a useful lens through which to view consensus history, the diversity of views it contained, and the liberal intentions under which it was written.

Most simply, consensus history was a reaction against the historical perspective of the previous generation of historians. Those called the "Progressive historians," including most prominently Frederick Jackson Turner, Charles Beard, Vernon Parrington, and Carl Becker, had in their work in the first three decades of the century dualized American history into good, common, mostly agrarian democrats against bad, wealthy, mostly merchant or landowning elitists. The perpetual conflict between these two "main currents of American thought," as the Progressive historians portrayed them, had characterized the nation's history from the Puritans to the present.

Increasingly at midcentury, the dualized world of good and bad, liberal and conservative, seemed too simplistic to a younger generation that had witnessed a world shaped by the confusion of wars, mass society, and technological sophistication. The consensus historians, impatient with the certainties of the Progressive view, turned instead to the values of irony, complexity, ambiguity, nuance, capriciousness, chance, tragedy, and multiple causation. Further, the consensus view became suffused with the perceptions of an increasingly affluent society. The widespread belief in the essentially prosperous and middle-class nature of most of American existence, that the great mass prospered under the fat middle section of the economic bell curve, prompted the consensus historians to emphasize the continuity instead of the conflict in the nation's past.

It is typically thought that the first signs of consensus interpretations arrived with the publication of Richard Hofstadter's *The American Political Tradition* in 1948.[2] Yet Perry Miller, whose two-volume *New England Mind* was completed in 1953, had been employing consensus themes (such as battling Progressive historians in the name of complexity) since his essay on Thomas Hooker appeared in *New England Quarterly* in 1931.[3] But consensus history found its greatest widespread expression in the 1950s in Daniel Boorstin's *The Genius of American Politics* (1953), Edmund and Helen Morgan's *The Stamp Act Crisis* (1953), Clinton Rossiter's *Seedtime of the Republic* (1953), David Potter's *People of Plenty* (1954), Louis Hartz's *The Liberal Tradition in America* (1955), Robert E. Brown's *Middle-Class Democracy and the Revolution in Massachusetts, 1691–1780* (1955), John Morton Blum's *The Republican Roosevelt* (1955), and Benjamin F. Wright's *Consensus and Continuity* (1958), among others. Higham, always keen about historiographical shifts, was the scout who warned of the consensus uprising. First in an article in *Commentary* in 1959 and then in a talk at the American Historical Association conference in 1960 that was reprinted two years later, Higham announced and described the consensus approach.[4]

Although Commager was only partly in agreement with consensus values, he began expressing them early, as Perry Miller had done. In 1938, three years before the country fell startled into the crucible of World War II, ten years before Hofstadter's *American Political Tradition* was published, and fifteen years before the rush of consensus books began to crowd the bookstores, Commager was already articulating some of the themes that consensus historians later employed.[5] Many of the liberal observations Commager pronounced before World War II were later adopted at midcentury and repackaged as consensus history.

Only two years into Franklin Roosevelt's second term of office and in the midst of the depression, Commager admonished the president for complaining that the two parties in the United States were so alike. Roosevelt worried that the nation lacked a clear liberal and conservative party. A national "election cannot give a country a firm sense of direction," the president warned, "if it has two or more national parties which merely have different names but are as alike in their principles and aims as peas in the same pod."

Yet, as Commager explained to the president and the American people in

1938, while there should be conflicting ideas in political discourse, they should be scattered through both parties. It was more confusing for voters, given that heterogenous parties do not act as automatic ideological beacons, but it was more beneficial for the stability of the nation. In contrast to FDR's opinion, it was reassuring to Commager that American political parties were not explicitly based around narrow principles. "We have escaped, in this country," he noted with relief, "the strife which seems to result from parties which represent particular sections, particular classes, particular interests."[6] The divisiveness, factionalism, ideological antagonism, and political fanaticism produced by the European multiparty system was an example to be avoided. History showed that when the parties in the United States became committed to particular sectional interests, for example in the decades before 1860, the Union broke apart.

Yet an absence of ideas, a shortage of principle, is not what Commager recommended in politics. Although the interests of each party reflected the diversity of the population as a whole, he saw "no reason why the major parties cannot represent cross-sections of American life and still stand for distinct aims and principles." But the parties should not be built on contrary principles, since it was best to have "parties that differ on means rather than ends." That same phrasing, of course, was to be repeated frequently by those historians who promoted consensus interpretations. Throughout the nation's history, according to the consensus viewpoint, Americans, no matter how far apart their politics seemed, really differed only on the means by which to reach a shared end. "This country is fortunate beyond any other great country," Commager explained, "in that its people present a united front on almost all basic questions of the nature and purpose of government. . . . Republicans and Democrats may differ upon the power issue, but the difference is one of means, not ends." As he neatly arranged the two sides, "the chasm which appears to separate them is in reality but a gently sloping valley."[7]

His friend Nevins, a more pro-business liberal, fit even more comfortably than did Commager within the consensus beliefs. When Nevins described the most beneficial features of the American political system, he agreed with Commager that the two-party system had prospered in the United States because it fit the genius of the citizens. The heterogeneity of each party allowed broad democracy to exist within the two-party structure. Like Commager, Nevins felt confident that it was a great benefit that neither party stood for firm ideological or political principles. It was an asset that our system was not constructed from a liberal and a conservative party. The parties' "fundamental value in the United States," Nevins reported, "is in pulling together an immensely varied mass of social groups, economic constituencies, racial stocks, and local and sectional interests for the purpose of governing by consent."[8] A division of our parties, our political institutions, along economic and class lines would be a disaster that would infect the country with further European maladies.

Nevins insisted that proportional representation and third parties were loaded political guns. "The spectacle of irresponsibility, confusion and intolerance presented by some Continental European nations of multitudinous parties may be exciting," Nevins admitted, "and some of their parties may suggest an intellectual rigor unknown in our politics; but the practical results do not commend themselves to us." What our system lacked in intellectual spectacle was offset by our calming stability. Nevins found it encouraging that "the two great parties are ponderous cross-sections of our varied society, representing every element," because that would delay "the day when the losers in an election would begin throwing up barricades in the streets."[9] Nevins and Commager agreed on the beneficial role the two-party system played in American political stability, although Allan never experienced Henry's occasional conviction that the system dampens intellectual dissent.

In the autumn of 1940, as the discouragement of the depression began to be replaced by the fear of war, Commager, in a series of articles for the *New York Times Magazine*, began to ponder the bonds that linked parts of American society. The culture was not glued by a formal political philosophy, he reported. Instead, as a pragmatist, Commager proposed that "nationalism is to be found not in the teachings of the schools but in the hearts and habits of the American people." His insight echoed the perception of Frederick Jackson Turner fifty years earlier that it was the conditions of life that gave people their values and ideas.[10]

Further, during World War II Commager foreshadowed Daniel Boorstin's consensus assertion more than a decade later that "no nation has ever been less interested in political philosophy," because Americans believe that their values emanate from experience. Well before Boorstin was to make similar claims in his celebrated *Genius of American Politics* (1953), Commager was already maintaining that experience rather than theory guided American political and social thought. Legal doctrine in the United States, for example, was not to be piloted by the theories of philosophers but by fact and experience. As Alexander Hamilton told his fellow citizens in the Federalist Papers, Charles Montesquieu had suggested that a benefit of a union of states is that they can watch one another. Not only can they protect one another from the excesses of their respective citizens, but they also can learn from the results of unique actions in other states. That is, states become laboratories from which other states learn—and the teaching is by experience rather than theory.[11] Commager agreed. "We are most fortunate," he announced during World War II, "in having here, in the United States, the most elaborate political laboratory in all history. . . . We have, for our edification, the history of the experience of the thirteen colonies, of the national government, and of thirteen to forty-eight states, for varying periods of time." History was the record of the experience that pragmatists needed to judge the consequences of the actions and ideas they wanted to evaluate. History and pragmatism, therefore, were intertwined in any intelligent analysis of policy or thought. When questions arise, "the history of the American nation is after all the most effective answer" to be found.[12]

Commager also spoke of the Civil War in terms used later by consensus historians. The Civil War "dramatized profound economic and social cleavages," he explained, but "North and South, men asserted that they were the true representatives of the American tradition" and the Constitution. The healing after the conflict was made easier because "there were no deep-seated differences in political philosophy to be overcome" and no fundamental disagreements concerning constitutionalism, democracy, or "established social institutions." North and South, that is, despite the spectacle of bitter antagonism, actually shared more than they disputed. According to Commager's account, within two generations the Civil War itself "was, curiously, a shared heritage and a bond of union."[13] Boorstin and other consensus historians later wrote similarly of the Civil War.

Ideas employed by Commager were echoed by consensus historians when they began articulating their views after World War II. Commager and Hofstadter, while intellectually and politically quite different, knew each other well in the forties. Older and more established than Hofstadter, Commager served as an occasional adviser and mentor for him. That relationship made the connection between their consensus ideas more expected.

Consider, for example, the opening of Hofstadter's *American Political Tradition*, the 1948 volume in which he debunked the heroic images of America's most famous political leaders and portrayed them as opportunists who mostly tried to help the middle class achieve greater profits. In his introduction Hofstadter admitted that he had become convinced "of the need for a reinterpretation of our political traditions which emphasizes the common climate of American opinion. The existence of such a climate of opinion has been much obscured by the tendency to place political conflict in the foreground of history." Hofstadter was beginning to suspect that leaders as different as Jefferson, Jackson, Lincoln, Cleveland, Bryan, Wilson, and Hoover had supported property rights, economic individualism, competition, capitalist culture, and individual opportunity.[14]

Richard Hofstadter in the 1960s, when the idea that there is a beneficial role for consensus in society began to draw criticism.
(Photograph by Dwight W. Webb; courtesy of Alfred A. Knopf, Inc.)

Societies that work well have a kind of "organic consistency," Hofstadter reported, and they do not "foster ideas that are hostile to their fundamental working arrangements. Such ideas may appear, but they are slowly and persistently insulated. . . . They are confined to small groups of dissenters and alienated intellectuals, and except in revolutionary times they do not circulate among practical politicians." Consequently, Hofstadter concluded that "above and beyond temporary and local conflicts there has been a common ground, a unity of cultural and political tradition, upon which American civilization has stood."[15]

Five years later Boorstin endorsed Hofstadter's assertions by arguing, in *The Genius of American Politics*, that such ostensible conflicts as the American Revolution produced little real conflict at all; Americans simply wanted to conserve British rights. Further, according to Boorstin, who had been trained in law, the Revolution produced no ideological theory, because the uprising was essentially legalistic, practical, and pragmatic. After all, Jefferson was a lawyer, and the Declaration of Independence, a lawyer's brief. Even the *Federalist*, Boorstin claimed, was a practical document arguing in favor of a particular, practical, written constitutional system. Similarly, in his concise book, Boorstin discounted the ideological conflict involved in other American struggles such as the Civil War, as Commager had done.[16]

Louis Hartz, professor of government at Harvard, advanced an analogous point. In his *Liberal Tradition in America*, Hartz claimed that America had always lacked the feudal attributes of Europe. Therefore its radicals never saw wealth as an unmediated enemy but aspired for a widespread prosperity for themselves and others. Even American radicals were "petit bourgeois" in nature, capitalist people of the land, and its artisans and laborers "showed a liberal, non-proletarian orientation." Basically middle-class in outlook, society was not divided strongly by class interest. The U.S. Constitution had lasted so long "because fundamental value struggles have not been characteristic" of the country.[17]

When conflict erupted it was often produced by the mistaken belief on the part of political party leaders that significant disagreement was present between opponents. As Hartz explained, the Federalists and Whigs, for example, did not comprehend that the democrats they denounced as enemies were simply liberals like themselves. Political contention, usually unwarranted, occurred mostly because people failed to realize that, as New York's General Root announced, "We are all of the same estate—all commoners."[18]

Acute observers almost immediately detected a common theme in Hofstadter, Boorstin, and Hartz. "Not conflict, therefore, but consensus," Higham remarked of these historians shortly after their works appeared, "was now taken as the normative reality of American life."[19] From the moment it surfaced, consensus history was characterized as a conservative set of convictions. Higham, in 1960, described consensus assumptions as "moral complacency, parading often in the guise of neutrality."[20] Peter Novick's account, more than a quarter of a century later, echoes Higham's tone. Beginning with Hofstadter's *American Political Tradition* in 1948, Novick noted, there has been in the field "an accelerating abandonment of dissidence, a rapid accommodation to the new postwar political culture." The consensus historians, Novick explained disapprovingly, began "a veritable cult of complexity, with its inevitable strong suggestion that any but the most piecemeal and modest tinkering with the social mechanism was ill-fated." Complexity might have been the altar at which they worshiped, but it did not hide the fact that a strongly conservative liberalism was the faith they exalted. "The deeply conservative implications of all of this are clear enough," Novick reported about their historical convictions, "and were reflected in countless ways in postwar scholarship." And there was some truth to these charges. In the early 1950s Hofstadter admitted as much when he wrote Merle Curti that he had "grown a great deal more conservative in the past few years."[21]

Yet, considered differently, it might be argued that consensus history was not very conservative at all. Louis Hartz first arrived in public view interested in labor history. Near the end of 1940, before the depression had yet broken, Hartz published an article sympathetic to Seth Luther, an ante-bellum labor radical. Luther, before becoming a labor leader, according to Hartz, worked in the New England mills and was subjected to the "rigorous factory discipline" of "merchant capitalism." The "militant tone" of Luther's work impressed Hartz, because the labor leader's slogan of "peaceably if we can, forcibly if we must" led to "radical action." True, Hartz reported, Luther did not consider "junking the capitalist dream of wealth for an attack upon the property principle," yet he challenged the American inequality of wealth.[22] While Hartz had lost interest in labor history by the time his *Liberal Tradition in America* appeared in 1955, that volume described the American political and economic landscape in a tone of critical impatience.[23]

Before World War II, Hofstadter flirted with the Communist Party at Columbia (he was active and attended some meetings, but it is not clear whether he joined formally), and though he dropped those sympathies after the war, he did not entirely abandon his Marxism.[24] When Progressive history failed in the 1940s to explain America's continuing capitalist ethic and its ongoing tie with the "Old World," Hofstadter turned for answers to the more international Marxism of his youth. After that time he no longer subscribed to the Progressive historians' division, in the words of David Noble, "between productive, democratic property and parasitical, capitalist property." Hofstadter saw no conflict between the "interests" and the people; in Europe and America all classes had long been committed to private property and capitalism. There was no evidence for Hofstadter to believe, as the Progressive historians did, that a unique American tradition of reform could tame an international capitalism. The historical record, as Hofstadter read it from his Marxist background, showed that American reform had taken part in furthering capitalism rather than opposing it. "In effect," Noble points out about Hofstadter's continuing internationalist Marxism, "Hofstadter was replacing the conflict theory of American history with a new consensus approach. As he recalled, 'My own assertion of consensus history in 1948 had its sources in the Marxism of the 1930s.'"[25]

When the book appeared in 1948, Hofstadter did not see it as a conserva-tive tract. At the time he told Merle Curti that it was "slightly—tho not very much—to the left" and had a "disgruntled, critical, alienated tone."[26] Nor did Hofstadter see himself as more conservative than the Progressive historians he criticized. While he thought their dualistic history was too simplistic, he sometimes found them insufficiently critical. In his *Progressive Historians*, written at the end of his career, Hofstadter repeatedly criticized Frederick Jackson Turner for being too easy on the frontier process, for promoting its "smiling aspects of life" as William Dean Howells might have. Turner was not only too optimistic but also "too conservative" in some respects for Hofstadter's taste.[27]

By 1969 Hofstadter seemed to be uncomfortable with his tie to consensus history, as with a family member he knows is related but does not like very much. At that point, shortly before his death, he confessed "an essentially ambivalent attitude" and reported that "while I still find use for insights derived from consensus history, it no longer seems as satisfactory to me as it did ten or twenty years ago."[28]

Hofstadter pointed out that there was nothing inherently conservative about the consensus conclusions. There was, after all, a large difference between a *prescriptive* recommendation that consensus assumptions are desirable and a merely *descriptive* historical observation that consensus values exist within a given society. If the concept was viewed this way, he explained, "I believe it will be understood that the idea of consensus is not intrinsically linked to ideological conservatism. In its origins I believe it owed almost as much to Marx as to Tocqueville, and I find it hard to believe that any realistic Marxist historian could fail to be struck at many points by the pervasively liberal-bourgeois character of American society in the past."[29] Arthur Schlesinger Jr. made the same case. "It is a fallacy to regard consensus history as only a right-wing phenomenon," Schlesinger insisted, since Gabriel Kolko's *The Triumph of Conservatism* (1963) "is a good example of consensus history from the viewpoint of the New Left."[30]

Similarly, William Leuchtenburg, Commager's former graduate student, told his Columbia University colleague John Garraty at the end of the 1960s that New Left historians, ironically, targeted "the 'consensus' historians, who, they say, homogenized American history, yet their own commentary homogenizes American history to a far greater degree by making it appear that nothing really ever happened. Since socialism was not attained, they seem to suggest, no other development mattered. In short, they are interested less in what happened in the 1930s than in what did not happen—the triumph of socialism."[31]

Representative of his hesitation about elevating consensus onto a pedestal, Hofstadter observed in the 1960s that consensus ideas worked better to suggest historical questions rather than answers, and he recommended that "in one form or another conflict finally does remain, and ought to remain, somewhere near the center of our focus of attention."[32] Further, he was angry when he was accused of denying the distinction between liberal and conservative political thought in America and making them both seem reactionary. That was "a view which I not only do not hold but consider utterly untenable," he answered sharply. His *American Political Tradition*, Hofstadter explained, had merely demonstrated that "our politicians, liberal and conservative, have had more in common with each other than the agitated rhetoric of political controversy usually suggests."[33]

Commager felt a similar but even more profound ambivalence about consensus history. When in 1950 he assessed the American mind, Commager decided that the "greater uniformity of character and habit than had been common in the nineteenth century" was actually the result of nothing more sinister than the growing technology of recent decades. Those who thought that this increased homogeneity had been thrust consciously on the culture had a misplaced paranoia. "Regimentation was not, as political critics would have it," he counseled, "a product of government regulation or of a Communist conspiracy but of a technological economy, and it was, perhaps, inevitable."[34]

Commager judged the more level playing field created by technology a benefit for society. But this equality also had its drawbacks; like Tocqueville, Commager believed that greater uniformity meant that in many cases democracy "seemed a matter of leveling down rather than up." And unfortunately this greater homogeneity also featured a diminished patience for dissent and skepticism. "With the growing emphasis on conformity," Commager sighed, "eccentricity was no longer so amiably indulged. . . . and with interdependence went some impatience with independence."[35]

So by the time the roots of McCarthyism became apparent in the late 1940s, Commager was already becoming uncomfortable with the conformist assumptions of consensus liberalism. Although he had articulated some of the values of the liberal consensus before World War II, in the face of the cold war he became doubtful about their benefits. Consider, for example, the ambivalence in his 1956 explanation of why so few Americans vote. Nonvoting was the expression of a contented and indifferent instead of an alienated apathy. Commager reported that America was "not wracked by dissension, by deep political cleavages, by class warfare, by religious controversies, by social fears and jealousies, or even by deep political differences." Except in the South, there were few divisions and antagonisms, and those that existed were inconsequential or "not ordinarily identified with one political party or permitted to assume political form."[36] Clearly, Commager felt that the lack of social and political combat was healthy, stable, and promoted cordial self-government among the citizenry. In these convictions he agreed substantially with the consensus historians.

But in the 1950s, bruised and angry from his battles against McCarthyism, he was not willing to rest at ease with these conclusions. Instead, he claimed it was important to stimulate active political behavior such as voting and essential to encourage dissenting voices. So he suggested, in a fleeting and uncharacteristic recommendation, that despite the calm amicability produced by the two-party system, the country should adopt a multiparty system with real choices. To create greater citizen participation and hear new voices, the United States should support minority political power and be "encouraging minor parties, and even giving them proportional representation in some fashion."[37]

The potential consequences of Commager's proposal were clear to his readers. "Proportional representation," an individual from Massachusetts wrote with alarm, "opens the floodgates to multi-party systems which inhibit efficient majority rule, perhaps essential to democratic government when coupled with adequate safeguards for civil rights."[38] Here Commager's critic was advancing the same argument about the benefits of the two-party system that Henry had been proposing for years. Having argued for nearly two decades about the dangers of a multiparty system and the benefits of diverse and nonideological major parties, Commager had now in 1956 briefly switched horses and was kicking the steed at the same speed in precisely the opposite direction. No statement was more uncharacteristic of the consensus values that he had nurtured since the New Deal than his proposal about multiple parties.

Under the pressure of the McCarthyist repression of intellectual and political liberties in the United States since the late 1940s, Commager was becoming ever more defiant and radical with respect to his demand for greater freedom of opinion. Dissent was much more important to him than it had been decades earlier when it was merely an abstract proposition. In 1938 Commager had been among the first wave to articulate the consensus historians' conviction that American society was tied more than it was divided by values. By the mid-1950s, at that point when consensus history had completed its first great rush onto the intellectual stage, Commager was one of the first to have genuine misgivings about it. It showed his frustration with the dangers of consensus and unity as those values were being employed to harden American society into conformity during the cold war.

So while Commager shared the limited optimism of the consensus school about American conditions, he exercised active doubts as well. Affluence, education, and the welfare state might at some point "bring about a truly classless society in the United States." If so, this would be accomplished "by a general leveling up of the poorer classes and a taxing down of the richer." But at present we were far from perfect. Looking about him, he admitted that "our progress toward true equality has been slower than anticipated."[39]

Unlike many in his generation, Commager became more instead of less radical as the 1950s and 1960s progressed. With the distasteful spectacle of strident anticommunism growing around him in the late 1940s as he wrote *The American Mind* and then with McCarthyism spreading its destruction shortly after that, by 1956, when Commager wrote his *New York Times Magazine* article suggesting multiple parties, he was clearly skeptical about the influence of consensus values on intellectual freedom, nonconformity, diversity of opinion, and dissent. Increasingly after midcentury, he put his scholarly emphasis on the conflict in American society.

Thus Commager, like many of his colleagues, does not fit very well in our popular conception of the rather conservative consensus historian. Whether in his chapters for *The Growth of the American Republic* or *The American Mind*, Commager always noted the conflict in American society at the same time he acknowledged the shared culture and the muted ideological nature of the country's two-party political structure. He held a combination of the old Progressive historians' respect for conflict and Populist dissent and the popular picture of the consensus historians that America's population was bound together by common perceptions and beliefs. After all, Commager wrote about the "American mind," a term that inferred a national consensus on beliefs and culture, but he also noted in that volume that one of his greatest influences was the Progressive historian Vernon Parrington.[40]

In retrospect, consensus history was not a militant movement organized in advance to storm the left-wing establishment of Progressive history. Rather, it was the individual, piecemeal, and cumulative work of a few historians, not that of a generation of historians all of whom agreed on consensus values.[41] If we classify these writers as consensus historians, then it constitutes such a broad category that it means little. If liberal reformers such as C. Vann Woodward and Commager, along with such conservatives as Daniel Boorstin, were all part of this group, it represents such a broad ideological sweep that it undermines itself. Most of the figures labeled consensus historians had very different agendas. Remember, the term "consensus" was used most often as an epithet instead of a descriptive statement, and those assigned to that school would rarely have been happy with that designation.

John Higham, the originator of the term "consensus history" and the school's first critic, believed by the end of the 1980s that most of its members had been mischaracterized. "Although its authors shared a dissatisfaction with Progressive history and certain attitudes about how it should be revised," he explained, "they felt little programmatic affinity with one another. They never became a school." The consensus historians never envisioned an American past devoid of conflict or contrast. "Theirs was a picture of social diversity, not of solid uniformity," Higham reminded his colleagues. "One of their objectives was to encompass within American history a greater variety of groups and impulses than could find a place in the simple social dualisms of the Progressive school. They proposed, therefore, that Americans were a variegated people held together by a unifying ideology or a common way of life."[42]

Christopher Lasch, a member of the liberal Left who might have been expected to be hostile to consensus ideas, remarked that "the controversy about 'consensus' has always struck me as artificial and unimportant—one of those nondebates that academic historians invent for their own amusement, for the making and breaking of academic reputations. Some sort of consensus sustains every society that is not held together by sheer force; the real question is how societies deal with ideas that fall outside that consensus."[43] Further, Lasch distinguished Commager from many of the rest of those in the consensus circle. Commager was too Parringtonian for Lasch to conceive of him being in the consensus category.[44]

For all Commager's affinities to the consensus historians, he was more skeptical than his friend Nevins about many of that school's convictions. Nevins represented a side of liberal consensus history which was more conservative and which was inhabited by Boorstin and others who admired many of the tenets of conservatism. Commager occupied that side of consensus history in which liberalism flirted more with the Left than with the Right, and he found that figures such as Hofstadter and Hartz populated his vicinity of the consensus spectrum.

And Commager still was not on even the same political page as Hofstadter and the other more liberal consensus historians. Commager, for all his emphasis on the benefits of a two-party system and the shared culture uniting the American mind, demonstrated an allegiance to Progressive history. He was a kind of bridge between the two camps, and even Hofstadter realized that Commager did not belong with him. Shortly before he died, Hofstadter expressed his disapproval that Commager had registered his intellectual debt to Parrington in *The American Mind*. Commager's respect for Parrington's *Main Currents of American Thought*, Hofstadter wrote with a discouraged sigh, "was widely shared among his colleagues in the historical profession" at midcentury.[45] Commager, that is, was too closely related to Parrington and the Progressive historians ever to be included on the membership roll of the consensus historians.

Both midcentury American studies and the consensus history of the same period have been miscast as retrograde, conservative scholarly schools. The myth-symbol and American character schools of American studies had in common with consensus history an interest in shared values and visions that held together a diverse nation. Neither the American studies nor the consensus outlook recommended destroying diversity in the name of unity; neither did they endorse ignoring the shared convictions and goals of an essentially middle-class and pragmatic society. Both schools were liberal, reformist, critical of mainstream society, and impatient with much of the conformity they saw. Commager, who was related to both schools, shows their strengths and weaknesses: strengths that reflect his liberal emphasis on equality, shared cultural values, and critical dissent; weaknesses resulting from too much optimism about American life and too vague a method of constructing his analyses.

The point is not that the consensus writers, to be judged important or beneficial, have to be exonerated of the charge of conservatism. It is not a sin to be a conservative, nor does it make one less perceptive, analytic, or beneficial to society. Instead the task is to set the historical record straight so that we can understand the present by understanding the past. The animosities aimed at midcentury scholars must match the positions they held or the mistakes they made. Otherwise we confuse the lineage of conservatism, liberalism, and radicalism, and we know ourselves no better than we know our forebears.

If Commager was at least tangentially connected to the consensus historians, where else did his midcentury liberalism fit in the broader landscape of American historiography? What other issues and figures were important to him in his professional life? To the baby boomer academics of the 1970s and 1980s, Commager's historical preoccupations might have seemed passé, but increasingly, as the field of history turns toward the beginning of the twenty-first century, his vision and values seem more current and useful.

Although in the thirties and forties, when intellectual history and American character studies rode high, Commager wrote history in a respected style, after midcentury he was seen as a historian far from the cutting edge. He was, after all, one of those who believed that history was a branch of literature and the humanities, not the social sciences, a conviction that placed him at odds with most new work in the discipline. In the final decades of the nineteenth century the battle had started between those who wrote history as an avocation and those who saw it as a job for certified professionals. Commager, his friend Nevins, and a few others had a foot in each camp, whereas increasingly in the twentieth century most historians kept both feet on the professional side.

Professional specialization in history, at first justified by the claim that it would set the stage for better and wider syntheses, was by midcentury justified for its own sake. The narratives and broad syntheses were simply banished from the discipline to the realm of the "amateur." The freelance historian was treated with suspicion within the field and was a stranger at historical conferences. The wider readership attracted by the freelance historians served as evidence of their lack of seriousness. Degreed and institutionalized historians, who wrote for tenure rather than the market, could always find a university publisher willing to do its duty and publish abstruse material. Insulated from the pressures of the publishing market, professionals could ignore the craft of writing and, in a logical reversal, assume that good writing did not reflect serious history. Freelancers, however, disciplined by the market, had to appeal to the public with engaging prose and historical matters of genuine public interest. The public no longer read history on the subway because narrow and monographical scholarly material swamped the better-written freelance history. If the public ignored history, the profession had itself to blame.[46]

Although he conceived of himself as a professional scholar, Commager believed that "history is a branch of literature" and bore literary responsibilities. Consequently, he warned that if history failed to be written well and tell a story it would lose its authority and its public. Writing history, he explained, is more like painting a picture than taking a photograph. "It is not enough to compile statistics; if it were, the *Statistical Abstract of the United States* would be, each year, our best historical volume," Commager counseled. "It is not enough to pile up mountains of historical and social details; if it were, the raw materials of newspapers would suffice for historical literature. It is not enough to put together strings of episodes and anecdotes, no matter how dramatic; picture magazines which do this dull rather than excite the mind." Instead history had to rest on all these features, blended artistically and bound by a strong interpretation. Further, part of the recipe of history as a literary art included a strong dash of drama and imagination. The inclusion of imagination was a "dangerous thing," he admitted, because "once we introduce the element of imagination we imperil the integrity of the historical record." Yet, he asked, how could history function without it?[47]

Social historians, since Turner in the 1890s, had already begun to abandon the narrative. But the use of a plot was attacked in a far more concerted and principled fashion by the poststructuralists and linguistic radicals after the 1960s. Commager, like Nevins and others of his generation and outlook, committed himself to telling a story, yet interpreting that narrative within the intellectual, political, social, and economic context of the period. He denied that he was a narrative historian and that he had done narrative scholarship as had Nevins.[48] But Commager's fondness for biographical sketch and his affection for framing a plot for the history of ideas to fit within show the extent to which he was devoted to the precepts of the storyteller.

In the 1980s the intellectual historian Dominick LaCapra, for example, thought that contextual narrative of the sort that Commager wrote "has often encouraged narrow documentary readings in which the text becomes little more than a sign of the times or a straightforward expression of one larger phenomenon or another." LaCapra complained that this "becomes a detour around texts and an excuse for not really seeing them at all." Nurtured by the theoretical influences of French linguist philosopher Jacques Derrida and the German philosopher Martin Heidegger, LaCapra concluded that ideas come from language. Words are not an expression of our ideas but the other way around: our ideas are an expression of our language. To pursue a study of ideas, then, we need an "understanding of intellectual history as a history of texts."[49]

So our daily task as intellectual historians, LaCapra recommended, is to look at the opposition between what is inside and outside texts. Of course the historian, who after all lives in the world, is always implicated in problems of language when trying to analyze these problems critically, "and it raises the question of both the possibilities and limits of meaning." As historians their knowledge is limited, and as humans they interact with and thereby alter the ongoing history they are writing. Further, LaCapra explained, it is implausible for contextualists "to believe that a relatively simple understanding of 'real life' problems provides the causal or interpretative key to the meaning of the texts or to the interaction between life and texts." Moreover, the intellectual historian's focus on language, recommended by LaCapra, "questions historians' rights to the position of omniscient narrators."[50] So meaning itself, in both historical analysis and narrative, is unstable, shifting, and perhaps meaningless.

Similarly, Hayden White in the 1980s doubted the effectiveness of Commager's kind of literary and narrative intellectual history. There has been, White remarked, "a reluctance to consider historical narratives as what they mostly are: verbal fictions, the contents of which are as much invented as found and the forms of which have more in common with their counterparts in literature than they have with those in the sciences." Plots, in a work like Commager's, are not objective structures found in the historical record. Instead, historians situate unfamiliar events out of the past into culturally familiar mythic or symbolic plots in order to domesticate the event and to provide a culturally understandable message. "We do not live stories," White insisted, "even if we give our lives meaning by retrospectively casting them in the form of stories. And so too with nations or whole cultures."[51]

But Commager's active scholarship was finished by the time the post-structuralists and linguistic radicals made narrativity such a battleground in the last quarter of the twentieth century. Although occasionally, in passing, he grumbled about it in print, he never answered the challenge to narrative history directly. Even if he had been more active, Commager was unlikely to have gone to war with the poststructuralists. To become involved in a theoretical debate, as that would have entailed, was not his style. He rarely read theory and never wrote based on its prescriptions. In the same way that Randall Jarrell pronounced midcentury "the age of criticism," the humanities, after 1970, wandered in "the age of theory."[52] Commager, in what late-century historians considered a rather old-fashioned recipe, was interested in history instead of theory.

"To suggest that we cannot profitably study or write history until we have answered all of our questions about the nature and the function of history," Commager explained to the theoreticians, "flies in the face of common sense. It is as if we should say that we cannot paint pictures until we know the meaning of art and of beauty . . . or that we should hold up the machinery of law and the courts until we have answered ultimate questions about the nature of law and of justice."[53] But what Commager seemed unwilling to acknowledge is that we must commit ourselves to seeking the ultimate meaning of beauty and justice, even while we continue to paint pictures and empanel juries. His critics would have liked to hear him call occasionally for greater study of the meaning of history.

By nature, as well as by intellectual conviction, Commager was a pragmatist, and pragmatism was the key he felt freed him from being imprisoned by theory. Experience and philosophy, he reported, show that both the rewards and "the understanding of any great subject come pretty much out of study and practice." Experience and practice, central to pragmatism, demonstrated the way to pursue historical perception. Therefore Commager announced that "I subscribe to G. M. Trevelyan's observation that philosophy is not something you take to history, it is, or should be, something you carry away from history." An understanding of history resulted from an interaction with the historical record. Commager's advice was to look to the immediate, and the ultimate would be answered in due time. "Because we cannot answer ultimate questions," he advised, "it does not follow that we cannot answer immediate questions."[54]

Further, experience revealed that "most of the great historians have been innocent of formal training." Yes, he admitted, it was useful to have instruction in history, just as one would want to be trained to drive a car or cook. But because history had only recently undergone professionalization, most of the best historians of the past had been amateurs by today's standards. Instead of beginning with theory, the Commager method was to get right to the heart of the writing as quickly as possible. Do not "waste time and energy in what is amiably called 'reading around' a subject," he advised others. Reading for background usually was "an excuse for not getting on with the job." Instead, plunge into the subject, "get your problem by the throat and grapple with it." It is not necessary "to read everything, take notes on everything, track down every reference, look at every piece of manuscript before you begin to write." Again, "start with the particular, not with the general," he insisted; "read deeply in the history of the particular, and you will find that the general takes care of itself." History was a task for the modest, not the arrogant. "Who are we, after all," he asked the theorists, "to impose our will on history? Who are we to require that it embrace our theories, dance to our tunes, march to our commands?"[55]

Without theory to organize his inquiries, Commager, like Nevins, frequently employed individual or group biography or, as in his *American Mind*, used short, comparative biographical sections in a volume as a tool to analyze ideas. Yet when he initially took his antitheoretical bias to biography, he found trouble. "I have no theory of biography," he proclaimed in *Theodore Parker*. Precisely, answered his reviewers, and it had led to a lack of interpretation that weakened his study.[56] Commager learned from this early experience and thereafter made sure to weave a strong interpretation into all his biographical accounts.

As a contextualist, a historian who believed in putting events and concepts within the greater context of their period, Commager supposed that people and their ideas were influenced by their surroundings. Yet as his devotion to biography illustrates, he was not a strict determinist who thought there was an inescapable influence of forces that sealed the fate of each individual. Biographies would have little drama or function if individuals were only the vehicles for larger forces. As Commager stood somewhere midway between the Progressive and consensus historians, so also he located himself in the gray area between determinism and free will. Francis Parkman's celebration of the hero appealed to Commager too much for him completely to endorse Henry Adams's remark to Samuel Tilden that Jefferson, Madison, and Monroe "appear like mere grasshoppers kicking and gesticulating on the middle of the Mississippi River. . . . They were carried along on a stream which floated them, after a fashion, without much regard to themselves. . . . My own conclusion is that history is simply social develop-ment along the lines of weakest resistance, and that in most cases the line of weakest resistance is found as unconsciously by society as by water."[57]

What Bernard Bailyn said of members of the historical profession, in his presidential address to the American Historical Association, could be said comfortably about Commager. "We are all Marxists," Bailyn pointed out, "in the sense of assuming that history is profoundly shaped by underlying eco-nomic or 'material' configurations and by people's responses to them; few of us are Marxists in the doctrinal sense of believing that these forces and these responses alone are sufficient to explain the course of human affairs."[58]

Still, like most contextualist historians, Commager was convinced that the conditions of life influenced the shape of thought. As a reporter on the shape of the American national character, his work suggested that national conditions (geographic, economic, social) helped form a common shared collection of characteristics. But these convictions were tempered by the biographer's belief that the individual can make a difference in the world, can influence the world as well as represent it. Part of Commager's enthusi-asm for biography was a reaction against the impersonal quality of some of Progressive history, particularly that of Turner and Beard. Commager's use of biography was partly an attempt to counter the economic determinism of the Progressives, an attempt to humanize history, an attempt that had liberal Left political roots as deep as Parrington's.

Commager's relation to Turner is instructive. As a midwesterner he felt an instinctive identification with many of Turner's insights. In the early pages of *Majority Rule and Minority Rights*, he cited Turner's account of the growth of government in America "from the time of the Mayflower Compact" to the nation's arrival at Oregon's Willamette farmland. Commager, not Tur-ner, wrote that it "was the West that first showed itself receptive to new political ideas . . . and it was the Populists who most nearly anticipated the course that American politics was to follow in the twentieth century."[59] In addition, Commager's emphasis on the American studies tenet that the New World was unique and a polar opposite of Europe owed a debt to Turner's rather deterministic belief that the conditions of the North American conti-nent had created an American value system without precedent.

Yet Commager preferred the anecdote, biographical sketch, and narrative panorama over the sociological analysis and study of patterns that Turner employed. Further, Turner was too simplistic for him. It is said that Nevins considered Turner "a one-theory historian," and Commager probably agreed with his colleague in that judgment.[60] Despite the strong American character emphasis of much of Commager's work, he was not parochial. He was, after all, an Anglophile with a summerhouse in Linton, England. He had taught at both Oxford and Cambridge and was a fellow of the latter. During World War II Commager had lectured throughout Britain. In his graduate school days he had traveled through Europe, living and researching in Germany and Denmark, and his doctoral dissertation in European history earned him the Herbert Baxter Adams Prize of the American Historical Association. So Commager was unlikely to accept Turner's idea that democracy in America was simply the result of the conditions settlers faced and had no connection to the deep intellectual heritage that immigrants brought with them across the Atlantic.

The assumptions of Vernon Parrington fit Commager's convictions much better than did those of Turner.[61] Parrington was an economic determinist who believed that only a few of the rich and well-born ever took the side of democracy against their class interests. Parrington employed a contextual determinism that was related to Turner's belief in the environmental creation of ideas. About the Puritan leader John Cotton's undemocratic tendencies, Parrington noted that "the age was more to blame than the man. It was no fault of John Cotton's that he was the child of a generation reared under the shadow of absolutism, fearful of underling aggression, unable to comprehend the excellence inhering in the democratic faith." Similarly, John Winthrop and Thomas Hooker were the products of their background. Although this economic and intellectual determinism did not absolve them of their political sins, it accounted for their behavior. "With his abundant offices and honors," Parrington said with pity of Massachusetts colonial governor Thomas Hutchinson, "there was every temptation to conservatism." The economic determinism of Progressives such as Parrington and Charles Beard was more Madisonian than Marxian, but they were not very good Madisonians, either. Unlike Commager, Parrington was simply too clumsy to search for the multiplicity of economic interests, classes, and ideologies that Madison had.[62]

More important, Parrington, like Commager, emphasized the European antecedents to American thought. Figures in Parrington's *Main Currents* were products of the rich intellectual heritage of the Atlantic world. Roger Williams's fondness for democracy, in Parrington's account, was the product not only of his immediate physical and cultural environment but also of his English intellectual ancestry. Williams "brought with him the fine wheat of long years of English tillage to sow in the American wilderness," as Parrington told it, and "he transported to America the democratic aspirations of English Independency."[63] Parrington's mix of environmental determinism (a contextualism) and recognition of the contributions of the nation's intellectual antecedents fit Commager's own interpretation better than did Turner's. Although conditions shaped ideas, ideas also shaped conditions.

Yet, while Commager had genealogical connections to Parrington, he still took a significant step away from Progressive assumptions. Commager disagreed with Beard, for example, who assumed that ideas had social origins (for example, that the Constitution had its roots in ideas from a particular economic class) and could be discredited on those grounds. In the words of Robert Skotheim, Commager "dissociated the origin of ideas from the validity of ideas." Unlike Beard, Commager, while he acknowledged the social origin of ideas, made a separate evaluation of the worth (as a pragmatist, the consequences) of those ideas. Thus, contrary to Beard, Commager believed that although the ideas undergirding the Constitution indeed had some economic derivation, those ideas resulted in a worthwhile doctrine. "Commager, a generation younger than Beard, Becker, and Parrington, and at the height of his powers during the period of totalitarianism," Skotheim reported, "was more concerned with whether ideas were moral or immoral, humane or inhumane, than he was with relating ideas to their environmental origins."[64]

Although Commager felt that even the ideas of historians were strongly influenced by their environment, he did not see this as an obstacle to writing useful history. During his graduate work, he endorsed the advice of the nineteenth-century German historian Leopold von Ranke to be a value-free historical investigator who renders history *wie es eigentlich gewesen*, or "as it really was." William Dodd, Commager's major professor at the University of Chicago, said of his American students in Germany (one of whom was Commager) that they had "with much objectivity and little partisan or patriotic pleading . . . idolized" Ranke.[65]

Consequently, in his first writing Commager tried to fulfill Ranke's dictum. "It is not, indeed, the task of the historian to make out a case for Struensee as a typical child of the Enlightenment, though he may discover that he was such a one," Commager cautioned at the end of the first chapter of his doctoral dissertation. "We shall attempt, rather, to trace, critically and methodically, 'wie es eigentlich gewesen.' This approach to the problem is not along the primrose path of generalization, but on the straight and narrow way of inductive criticism, and synthesis, but only so can we arrive at any understanding of the significance of Struensee and of his reforms in the history of Denmark and in the history of the Enlightenment in eighteenth century Europe."[66]

Commager's Rankean ambitions were also reflected in *Theodore Parker*, his 1936 volume that declared that he had no theory of biography other than to tell Parker's life as it happened. Reviewers of the book issued a chorus of complaints about Commager's unwillingness to provide a strong interpretation in the book. The criticism of *Theodore Parker* jolted Commager out of his Rankean aspirations and spurred him toward more interpretive and partisan writing. Later in his career, he had changed his mind about the value of Rankean objectivity. "Ranke and his successors taught us to rely on documents for our history; the documents, they were confident, would speak for themselves. Alas, they do not speak for themselves," Commager admitted. "They speak, rather, for us, and with a hundred different voices, usually raucous and clashing. They tell us not what actually happened but, more often than not, what we want to hear."[67]

As he aged, Commager increasingly became a relativist, as perhaps all pragmatists must—for, as Dewey knew, judging the meaning of a concept by its consequences means that as our experiences and judgments change, so does the meaning of the world around us. The mirage of objectivity was left behind in Commager's youthful years. "Let us admit at once that history is neither scientific nor mechanical," Commager later decided, "and that the ideal of history, completely objective and dispassionate, is an illusion. . . . Consciously, or unconsciously, all historians are biased: they are creatures of their time, their race, their faith, their class, their country—creatures, and even prisoners."[68] Besides, as a pragmatist, one of the most compelling reasons to acknowledge and live with our own contextual biases is that it is impossible in practice to rid ourselves of them. We might as well have our theoretical world match our real world. "There are many things to be said for accepting our limitations and looking at the past through the eyes of the present," he remarked, "but this is the most persuasive: no matter how hard we try, that is what we do anyway."[69]

Commager might have been expected, then, to celebrate the ideas of such noted relativists as Charles Beard. But, like Nevins, Commager thought the relativism Beard promoted was unnecessarily radical.[70] The problem with Beard's relativism, Commager complained, "was not that it repudiated certainty but that it was sterile and, in a literal sense, inconsequential. The doctrine of subjectivity and uncertainty, like the doctrine of economic motivation, was not a conclusion but a point of departure, and everything depended on the route and the destination." As a working historian, intent on participating with the public in a dialogue about historical issues, Commager needed to know how to overcome the apparent obstacle that Beard identified. "That history was subjective, fragmentary, and inconclusive—like almost everything in life—would be readily acknowledged," Commager explained impatiently, "but if history were to be written at all it was necessary to go on from there."[71] Beard, Commager felt, did not take that essential next step.

As a pragmatist, Commager was willing to recognize the relativism of history, but as a pragmatist he also demanded that a tentative result was better than no result. So he counseled that, while "we admit the limitations and difficulties of history, item by item, if we take them too hard, we will find ourselves out of a job." And the culture would be without a public dialogue on matters of history. "If we are to get on with the job," he concluded, "we must agree upon some kind of factual foundation or framework for our histories."[72] Tentative structures and conclusions were more useful than waiting fruitlessly for unattainable and absolute truths.

But if history was so impermanent that we needed to accept only tentative accounts and conclusions, was the discipline worth very much? How useful was it to work in a field like history, an area that offered more speculation than certainty? Commager was one of those who felt almost a missionary zeal about the benefits of history, and the impermanence of the shifting sands of history failed to undermine his confidence in the mission of his profession. Part of the reason for his sense of calling was rooted in his conviction that history was part of that essential civic dialogue that intellectuals needed to promote between citizens at all levels. More than simply a conversation in classrooms, history, as Nevins reminded his peers, was part of that vital discussion among all who inhabited that "one democratic public—the public to which Emerson and Lincoln spoke."[73] That civic mission of history is what enlivened Commager.

But that goal suggested a distinction between the role of the historian as a scholar and as an activist intellectual. In the last half of the twentieth century, that differentiation began to be made more frequently. The scholar works researching in libraries and archives, deals with the past, teaches in the academy, and maintains an Olympian, objective, nonpartisan, professional attitude. Addressing his or her professional peers, the scholar is a specialist who writes books for the initiated. Intellectuals, however, are partisan activists who are involved in contemporary political and social issues. As generalists and popularizers of their specialties to the larger public, their work is often interdisciplinary in substance. Because they are involved in current debates and therefore need to trade ideas more quickly than writing books allows, intellectuals utilize essays, reviews, or cultural criticism in magazines, newspapers, or journals. The roles of scholars and intellectuals are not mutually exclusive, and a person can operate as a scholar on Monday and Wednesday and as an intellectual on Tuesday and Thursday. But because there are different standards for the two functions, it is best that the two roles not be performed simultaneously on the same project.[74]

The distinction between these two roles in the world of ideas was sketched by Commager, in his work on the Enlightenment, as the difference between the philosopher and the philosophe. "The philosopher," he explained, "was a scholar, a savant, one who devoted himself single-mindedly to the search for Truth which was both universal and permanent. The Philosophe was interested chiefly in those truths which might be useful, here and now." The philosopher was concerned with the moral and theological questions of the individual soul, and the philosophe, with society and its institutions. The philosopher studied systems, whereas the philosophe constructed programs. The philosopher was reclusive, but the philosophe was "a man of the world, eager to enlighten, to change, to reform, even to subvert, and ready to take an active part in each of these enterprises."[75] Commager chose to see himself as both philosopher and philosophe, both scholar and intellectual.

Commager's scholarly work was primarily as an intellectual historian, although he collaborated on surveys of American history for extra revenue. His definition of intellectual history was clear in the areas he asked Merle Curti to cover in a book that he wanted Curti to write in the mid-1950s for the New American Nation Series that Commager edited. In the book, he told Curti, should be "not only literature and philosophy but art, education, science and technology all embraced in the broad category of cultural history."[76] Even as early as the 1950s, Commager knew that he was not on the cutting edge of scholarship in intellectual history, but he felt too old to refashion himself. Perhaps that was a lazy decision. To Curti, Commager confessed his admiration for the younger historians such as Hofstadter who were "disciples of [David] Riesman" and who gained new insights from the social sciences. That, Commager could see, was one of the new directions intellectual history was taking. "But it may be," he wrote with resignation, "that we are too old to start over on psychology and sociology and all the rest of it. There seems so little time left for all the things we want to do."[77]

A decade later Commager complained that Perry Miller did not know whether intellectual history should simply include the old recipe of philosophy, religion, literature, science, politics, law, and economics—the old stew that was the "history of thought"—or whether it should be popular culture and cultural anthropology, investigating "the daily life of ordinary folks, courtship, marriage, child-rearing, food, drink," and recreation.[78] Of course, Commager was no closer than Miller to solving that mystery. Throughout his life, Commager served up intellectual history from the old recipe. He offered, in his books, a history of thought, frequently spiced with short biographical sketches and occasional re-creations of historical events—as R. G. Collingwood suggested.[79]

Commager wrote his scholarship in the approachable style the French sympathetically call *haute vulgarisation*, by which they mean "sophisticated readability."[80] As opposed to specialized and technical historians, these more accessible writers such as Commager, according to Nevins, promote democracy in three different ways: "by giving occasional guidance to leaders, by affording instruction to the general leadership, and by helping create a climate of opinion." Nevins, of course, supported Commager's combination of scholarship and journalism, for he himself also worked at the intersection of these fields. "Many a newspaperman, like Frederick Jackson Turner, has gone to the academic world with a sense of relief," Nevins said about the borderland in which he and Commager toiled; "many a university man, like Carl Van Doren, has moved into the world of journalism with elation."[81]

Consequently, Commager as a popularizer was not a major influence on the direction taken by intellectual historians. Yet he was an important figure in the field. Merle Curti, for example, whose own impact on his peers was limited to the forties and fifties, respected Commager's work. *The American Mind*, Curti has said, was an affirmation of the democratic culture in the United States that overthrew fascism, yet with a criticism of the lack of justice at home. Curti thought Commager's *American Mind*, like his own books, echoed too much of Parrington's environmentalist approach to ideas without a sufficient balance toward Perry Miller's emphasis on the "interior" focus on ideas—a balance Curti felt Stow Persons's *American Minds* (1958) achieved far better. The contribution of Commager's volume, Curti said, "was less in any interpretation or new finding than in the achievement as a whole." Curti's judgment, that Commager's book lacked a reorienting quality to it but still stood as a kind of landmark, is a conclusion many intellectual historians would endorse. Yet Curti did not dismiss Commager. "Did any of his predecessors, including [Ralph Henry] Gabriel," he asked in Henry's defense, "do anything equal to what Commager did in bringing into convergence constitutional and intellectual history?" Even "if it were the only thing that Commager had written," Curti concluded about his scholarship in *The American Mind*, "he would still be a major historian."[82]

Commager's background made him sharply aware of the distinction between the scholarly and the intellectual functions. After all, his grandfather Adam Dan had been both a scholar and an intellectual in the Danish Lutheran Church. Andrew McLaughlin and William Dodd, the two professors who influenced him the most at the University of Chicago, were also intellectuals and scholars. Consequently, Commager thought that at some important moments scholars were almost obliged to become intellectuals, too. At midcentury he acknowledged that a decade earlier, in 1940, when the trials of the depression were blending together with the threat of war with the fascists, "it was no longer convenient to draw a sharp line between scholarship and pamphleteering." In the midst of such an important period, Commager explained, and "to a people whose most notable contribution to the literature of politics was *The Federalist*[,] the distinction could not be thought important." Scholars could not take part in the vital public dialogue as well as could intellectuals. "Academic insularity," he concluded, "was no longer tolerable" in such a time of crisis.[83] That critical period of fifteen years, from the Stock Market crash until the end of World War II, was the time when he grew into his identity as a figure who wrote both as a scholar and as an intellectual.

Some of Commager's close associates, however, believed his activist reputation was not warranted. William Leuchtenburg said that he never thought of Henry "marching with the oppressed." When Leuchtenburg was preparing his presidential address for the American Historical Association on the historian and the public realm, he explained, "I thought of a lot of people, but, despite all of my association with HSC, I do not believe I ever once thought of him in this particular connection." Leuchtenburg was even more specific about Commager's disconnection from the real world of politics. "I don't see him in the same category as Arthur Schlesinger, or, still less, Dick Wade, who managed Bob Kennedy's campaign in Illinois," Leuchtenburg reported. Instead, he thought of Commager "as someone who lent his name to organizations occasionally and wrote articles and letters to the editor, but, to put it bluntly, did not have a great deal of feel for how politics actually functioned." Similarly, Leo Marx, who taught at Amherst with Commager, had trouble envisioning him as a certified activist. "If he was an 'activist' it was only in a very special, pre-Sixties sense of the word—a from-the-top-down liberal defender of constitutional rights, especially first amendment rights," Marx felt. "What moved him most was the defense of the Bill of Rights. His activism was that of a speaker, letter-writer, testifier, but not that of a theorist, joiner, or demonstrator."[84]

Even those who considered Commager an intellectual activist hardly thought that he stood alone in that identity among his fellow historians. Nevins was a journalist and Democratic Party activist, Schlesinger was an activist allied to the causes of the anticommunist Americans for Democratic Action, Hofstadter marched at Selma, and Woodward and others were similarly active in public causes.[85] Still, Commager's intellectual activism on matters such as McCarthyism and civil liberties was notable. In addition to battling in the civic arena, he also constantly wrote popular articles on politics for the general public, and in a manner that could be understood by the average educated reader. Many of his essays, later republished as *Free-*

dom, Loyalty, Dissent, Freedom and Order, and *The Defeat of America,* used history and historical analogy to argue on behalf of liberal and democratic public policy. Commager's activism endorsed Nevins's remark that "sometimes we university men, I fear, think too much of our note-padded cells, too little of the breastworks to be manned and armed."[86]

It is difficult to perform the two different roles of intellectual and scholar successfully at the same time. Since professionalization began to dominate the field of history at the end of the nineteenth century, the fear has been that intellectual work would compromise a historian's scholarship. That is why so few historians in the past century have become intellectual activists, as opposed to the far greater percentage of literary critics or sociologists (who have not operated under the same requirements of "objective scholarship") who have performed that function. The fear among historians has been that activists would allow their intellectual partisanship to invade their scholarly work and turn those books into political tracts. Commager, however, had little trouble keeping his political views in check in his scholarship. Although he admitted a respect for Parrington's political prose, he also paid tribute to Trevelyan's dictum that a theory is something you take from rather than to a work of history. Consequently, Commager's work was more often criticized for lacking an interpretation, as in the case of *Theodore Parker.*

An equally serious danger of mixing the intellectual and scholarly roles is that a historian will not have enough time for both functions and will perform one of them badly. Activism, that is, might compromise the intellectual's time. Many observers, even close friends, thought that Henry stumbled into this hazard, and Commager himself complained of his condition. "Writing plans! I haven't any," he wrote Curti in the early 1940s. "I don't even get time to read books, much less write them. I have a lot of things I want to do . . . but I doubt that I'll ever get any of them done. If I were to write a book it would be on Story, but that means lots of work and travel and concentration and I'm getting increasingly unable to do any of those things." A decade later he reaffirmed the same opinion. "I scatter my energies," he confessed to Curti, "and fear that I may never have time to get down to the really big works that I keep thinking of."[87]

Those of his colleagues who knew him well had similar estimations of the effect of his intellectual activism on his scholarship. Woodward thought Commager was a good journalistic writer but not on the frontier of scholarship. Unlike a Miller or Samuel Eliot Morison, Commager was not deeply into archival research, according to Woodward, but instead reported recent historical findings in his textbooks or essays. Leuchtenburg thought that the unfriendly reception of *The American Mind* was "an end of things for him" and that "he no longer did serious work after that." John Garraty, who knew Commager from Columbia, believed "he spent much too much time being an activist and polymath and therefore (unlike his close friend Nevins) did not produce much serious scholarly history. Whether that was a mistake or a loss to society is hard to determine."[88]

Leonard Levy, the constitutional historian who worked for Commager while he did his graduate studies under him, observed Henry's scholarly frustrations as closely as anyone. "He was a great disappointment to himself as a scholar," Levy later explained. "He wanted to be the kind of scholar Nevins and Morison were. He couldn't do it." Commager tried. "But he was not a research scholar. Soon after I began working for him, Nevins came into the office one day with someone named Paolo Coletta, and they wheeled out a filing cabinet of notes that Commager had compiled over the years for a book on Wm. J. Bryan, which he abandoned. Coletta wrote the books on Bryan." Yet Henry did not give up his scholarly ambition. "Commager turned to Justice Joseph Story," Levy continued. "For two years I worked forty hours a week on Story for him. [Harold] Hyman did it for a year. Commager wrote the Gaspar Bacon Lectures at Boston U. on Story—three lectures, brilliant. But he wanted to write a detailed 'life and time of.' One day he said to me, 'I'll show them; I'll write a scholarly book, with footnotes.' Never did. He abandoned the Story, too."[89]

Yet with all of this said, Commager was more of a national treasure than a failure. Peer reactions to one's scholarship are not everything. Where would we begin if we were to name those on the long list of important American figures who were not held in the highest professional esteem by their peers?

Look at Commager's success from a different angle. Winston Churchill was one of his favorite historians, as Commager told Nevins before a national television audience on a CBS program in July 1963, and he admired the British leader for his participation in the history he wrote.[90] While Commager was not a Churchill, he admired Churchill's ability to function as a recognizable participant in the culture he wrote about, and Commager's ambition to become a figure in the political and cultural drama of midcentury America was at least partly realized. The example of yet another historian can make the same point differently. Turner, who wrote about the end of the American frontier, was so associated with the concept of the frontier that he became part of the mythic structure that he was addressing. Whether Turner was right or wrong about the effect of the frontier on American culture, he could not be dismissed, because, like the frontier, he was planted in the American imagination and became a participating character. The opinions of other professional historians were not enough to remove Turner from the pantheon. More than simply a historian, Turner became an important figure in his own right.[91] Commager was not a Turner, but like Turner, he became a recognized figure who participated in the culture and society he wrote about. Like Turner, Commager's importance outlives the criticism of his scholarship.

Or consider a tie between Commager and a different set of figures. The rejection in recent decades of the tradition of Parrington, Constance Rourke, and Commager by the baby boomer generation is reminiscent of the dismissal of painters such as Grant Wood and Thomas Hart Benton by the dominant New York School in art in the 1940s.[92] The reputations of Wood, Benton, and other representational artists, however, experienced a revival in the 1980s, prompted by a search for cultural roots in the midst of poststructuralist uncertainty. The reputation of Commager, as well as those of Parrington, Rourke, Van Wyck Brooks, and others in that lineage, might be similarly rekindled in the future. Commager performed a function similar to Wood's: to look into the common soul of America and interpret it in a serious, accessible, and evocative form.

Finally, Commager's public vision connects him in spirit with the consensus historians, despite his greater emphasis on dissent and conflict. His enthusiasm for civic activism and a historical dialogue with the general public demonstrated his commitment to a kind of participatory democracy in the world of ideas, a dedication to forging a shared culture in which all citizens could take part. That goal required a basic consensus in society, and at the same time it encouraged diversity and dissent. History, for Commager, was a way of opening instead of closing dialogue, for remaining active rather than passive in society, for being intellectual as well as scholarly, and for bringing citizens together to realize what they shared as well as where they differed.

CHAPTER 10

Legacies,

1971-1997

Late in the summer of 1974, in the heat of August in Washington, Richard Nixon appeared on television and with furrowed brows somberly told the nation that he was resigning the presidency. Watergate was over. Nixon climbed the stairs of an official helicopter, turned one last time to face the cameras, and was gone. A few months later, in April 1975, North Vietnamese soldiers overran Saigon, and South Vietnam collapsed at last. The Vietnam War was over. With a fascinated horror, Americans at home watched television news footage of U.S. helicopters leaving the American Embassy, rising slowly and uneasily into the sky with panicked South Vietnamese officials clinging to the landing skids below. Thus in two helicopter scenes, a few months apart, two of the most monumental episodes connected with conflicts of the 1960s—the Vietnam War and Watergate—came to a close.

Several decades elapsed between the end of World War II and the Vietnam War, during which Commager wrote about the American character and offered insights into the tensions between consensus, dissent, and diversity in American society—after which the cultural wars of the late twentieth century began to be fought. First they arose as isolated skirmishes and then gradually appeared as a more sustained conflict waged in the university, academic journals, government agencies, and national newspapers. Although the substance and approach of work like his became one of the prominent battlefields on which blood was spilled, Commager never personally took an active part in the cultural struggle.

In his associated role as a public activist, Commager had fought against American involvement in the Vietnam War and for a more open democratic government at home. With the end of the Vietnam War and Watergate, about which he had been a vocal and prominent critic of official Washington, Commager, now in his early seventies, began to face that final period of his life. His wife, Evan, had died of cancer in 1968. A year later, Allan Nevins, a senior research associate in the Huntington Library in Pasadena since 1958, suffered a stroke and then began to write at home. Two years later, in the spring of 1971, Nevins died.[1] "Death plucks at my ear and whispers, make haste, I am coming," Commager wrote to a friend of his, quoting the jurist Oliver Wendell Holmes. "Indeed he does," Commager acknowledged, "and indeed we must make haste for indeed he is."[2]

"No one, I suppose, outside my own family," Henry wrote to Nevins's wife, Mary, "has meant so much to me as Allan, over these long years." The first meeting between the Commagers and Nevinses, back in the early years of the depression, he recalled, had been over tea, "in those innocent days, before we all took to cocktails." Since that time he and Allan had been best friends, especially close at Columbia in Fayerweather Hall, "where Allan and I formed a kind of alliance, each at one end of that long corridor." Henry's reverence for his friend was genuine and immense. Characteristically, in the first part of Commager's oral history interview for the Columbia Oral History project, he talked more about Nevins than about himself.

If a Nevins biography ever were written, Commager claimed, it would be evident that "he was in all likelihood our greatest historian, more productive than Bancroft or Parkman or Henry Adams, as original as any of them, more concerned with digging up the facts from every conceivable source," with the strengths "of McMaster with his passion for newspapers and Rhodes with his study of official documents, and Parkman with his narrative skill, and on top of it broader interests and knowledge." He encouraged Mary Nevins to consider the accomplishments of her husband. "Imagine Parkman turning out a hundred Ph.D.'s—Allan's are everywhere," he noted with pride. "Imagine Prescott dreaming up Oral History and carrying it through all over the country. Imagine Henry Adams getting the [American] Heritage started, and endlessly popularizing history while he advanced scholarly history."[3]

Further, Allan led a public life that he maintained without sacrificing his scholarship. Nevins served in professorships abroad, helped the U.S. Embassy in London, acted as chair of the Civil War Centennial, edited books and series of books, worked to improve Columbia University, and corresponded with many of the major public figures of his time. "Allan was in fact an institution as well as an individual," Henry said with an elegiac respect; "we mourn his loss as we mourn the passing of an institution." Because Nevins always lived at a fast pace because of his pressing work ethic, Commager calculated that he had lived 160 rather than 80 years. Allan "left few aspects of his society untouched," Henry concluded. "There is no one who can take his place, for his kind of scholar is pretty well a thing of the past; modern scholars are technicians who are afraid of big projects, or public enthusiasms; what is really at stake here is the attitude towards history, and modern historians have lost faith in history—as Allan never did."[4]

Henry's letter to Mary Nevins revealed as much about Commager's own values and his hopes for the field of history as it did about the life of Allan Nevins. The values that Commager highlighted in this letter became the ones he tried to promote in his own work in his last years. That is, Commager, like Nevins, worked in the final decades of his career to promote a dialogue between historians and the public, to speak to issues of contemporary politics such as the conservatism of the Reagan revolution, and to write on periods such as the Enlightenment or on figures such as Tocqueville, thus addressing the need for democratic political process, majority rule, and cultural cohesion.

Yet there was a clear distinction between the work of Commager and that of Nevins. Allan, a more determined historian, more enthusiastic about primary research, more the scholar, wrote better history than Henry. But Henry had the quicker and more facile mind. He was, as Allan said, "Quicksilver Commager." Vernon Parrington remarked that "we may begin as critics but we end up as historians."[5] That comment characterized Nevins, who moved from newspaper work to the history department at Columbia. But Commager moved the other way, beginning as a historian and moving toward journalism. Still, when asked late in life whether, under other circumstances, he could have been happy as a journalist, Commager said no. If he were a journalist, he replied, he could not have written about the eighteenth century that he so loved. Further, he insisted, he would not have wanted to be tied to contemporary events and the journalist's perspective.[6] Commager considered himself a historian.

In 1971, the same year Nevins died, Commager announced that he was "theoretically retiring," which, as it turned out, meant switching to a half-time position. Commager gave up the Smith Professorship of History, which he had held since 1956 when he arrived at Amherst College. Now, at the age of sixty-nine, he became the John Woodruff Simpson Lecturer, a chair reserved to honor someone past retirement age or not a member of the regular faculty, a chair held previously by Robert Frost and Archibald MacLeish. In his half-time, "theoretically retired" post, Commager continued to teach a seminar in American intellectual history that met once a week. Despite his continuing interest in public intellectual dialogue, he was not prepared to stop teaching, and he promised that if Amherst prevented him from teaching in his old age he would join a faculty elsewhere. Teaching was important because ideas had to be passed to the young as well as to the national body of citizens. "What every college must do is hold up before the young the spectacle of greatness, not necessarily in the teachers but in history or in life or in literature," he explained about the transference of culture. "You become a historian, for example, not so much because you're interested in history, but because you admire people who are interested in history."[7] Commager stayed on teaching at the college to provide a model to the young of one who engaged ideas seriously both in the academy and in public conversation.

Teaching half-time gave him time for work, but it failed to support him adequately. By the end of the 1970s Commager gave lectures and wrote essays for money and began actively searching for a fellowship year somewhere to help him make ends meet. Amherst provided him with the stately white house south of campus he had occupied since 1956, but money was still tight. To George Kennan at Princeton's Institute for Advanced Study and others at various institutes, Commager inquired in 1978 about funding and affiliation. Living off of a small retirement pension that he said would end the following year, supported by dwindling royalties and a salary of six thousand dollars a year, Commager had to write essays and deliver lectures to keep afloat. "The Simpson Chair is one of distinction," he sighed in frustration, "but not of material reward." He was not hungry, but he was unable to focus sufficient attention on a book on the foundations of American nationalism. "I could 'sustain' myself by lecturing and popular writing," he admitted, "but at a high price in scholarly concentration."[8]

To earn money and because it was the rhythm and lifestyle he had always pursued, he continued to lecture. On one such expedition to Lincoln, Nebraska, to lecture at the university, Commager was ferried around by Mary Powlesland, a graduate student. Soon she became his research assistant, and in 1979 they married. Mary moved into the white house on Pleasant Avenue in Amherst with Henry, helped organize his life, and commuted to teach Latin American history at Salem State College.

As he reached seventy-five, Commager grew his white hair longer than before and combed it straight back so that it obscured his ears and fell slightly below his collar. Often he wore a blue suit with a tie and a pair of slippers while at home, and he employed his black-framed reading glasses only occasionally. He shuffled around the house in a rather sprightly state of health, looking about ten years younger than his age, drinking coffee, and quipping with a quick sense of humor. If a visitor arrived, Commager might be scurrying around his study trying to accommodate a call from the British Broadcasting Company about the date of the first presidential primary or writing on an active manuscript. With strangers he was not excessively private or reticent; about his accomplishments he was forthright but very modest. Asked in his later years about intellectual disagreements from previous decades, he showed no anger. He took little offense when people disagreed with his positions, and some disputes he simply shrugged off with a genial explanation.[9]

When Commager reduced his teaching load at the beginning of the 1970s, what would come to be known as the multicultural perspective was just beginning to take root in earnest. As a liberal, he was suspicious of the multicultural program in the 1960s. Then after another decade he warmed to the agenda of diversity, but he never fully embraced the multicultural ethic in the same way that the baby boomer Cultural Left did. After all, he was a midcentury liberal. Although they endorsed a limited affirmative action, such liberals as Commager believed in a color-blind meritocracy and equal opportunity society, blind to race, toward which they had worked for decades. As a result, in the 1960s Commager opposed the creation of black studies departments on campuses and in 1968 considered the attempt to bring minority faculty representation immediately to the proper proportion nationally both wrong and impatient.[10]

By the early 1970s Commager was beginning to worry about the balkanization of American society, although his concern was set in a much broader frame than ethnic multiculturalism. In an essay on Lincoln, who opposed secession, he cautioned about separatism between blacks and whites, young and old, skinheads and eggheads. Fifteen years later, in the early 1980s, he was still worried that ethnocentric history would dissolve the social glue that bound diverse people together. Even the idea of American studies, he feared, had the potential to divide the cohesion of traditional American history. Properly taught, history should include "subordinate disciplines such as black history, women's history, and immigration history." But "I don't know," he warned, "that giving them different titles and teaching them as separate courses really enlarges the subject."[11]

As Lincoln had worried about southern nationalism leading to secession, so Commager and other liberals worried about ethnic nationalism leading to subcultural secession. And once initiated, how much cultural fragmentation and dissolution would this nationalism produce? "If a minority, in such case, will secede rather than acquiesce," Lincoln suggested in his First Inaugural Address, "they make a precedent which, in turn, will divide and ruin them; for a minority of their own will secede from them. . . . For instance, why may not any portion of a new confederacy, a year or two hence, arbitrarily secede again?"[12] Liberals such as Commager had similar worries about multiculturalism. If portions of the American population could proclaim a separatist nationalism, then where might the division, the rending of the social fabric in such a diverse nation, naturally end?

Commager's liberal convictions did not mean he thought that ethnic and gender discrimination had been solved in the United States. He denounced the racism, dual citizenship, and economic exploitation that continued to shackle black Americans and reflected the "deeper psychological and moral failure" of the nation. At about the same time he reminded the readers of the *New York Times* that Theodore Parker's position on women was to be admired. Parker, who presided over the largest antebellum congregation in Boston, made all his prayers to "Our Father and Our Mother God" and was "the first clergyman to invite women to preach from his pulpit."[13]

Further, in the autumn of 1974, Commager, then in his early seventies, stood and proposed at a meeting of the exclusive Century Club in New York that women be admitted to membership; he was hooted by colleagues. "I was with Henry that night at the Century. It was truly a disgraceful affair," William Leuchtenburg later recalled. "He was jeered at mercilessly." Leuchtenburg, infuriated, tried but failed to organize a mass resignation from the club. "I cannot be sure what Henry's attitude was," he explained. "In one sense, he was in his element, a leader of the Opposition jabbing at the leadership of the party in power—precisely the role that Henry was destined for—and perhaps enjoying the joust. His willingness to speak out for what he must have known was an unpopular cause was Henry at his finest. I can't believe that the coarse reception he received did not hurt."[14]

If he was stung, Commager did not admit it. "Don't be disturbed by the Century affair," he reassured Leuchtenburg. "Some of the old gentlemen there are really like college fraternity boys; we must indulge them in their childishness. I certainly didn't take the matter personally." Commager encouraged Leuchtenburg to take the long view. "Russell Lynes sought me out later and said that my proposal had had a good effect; that things were moving towards a liberalization of admission of women, and that he was sure it would come in the next year or so. I am not sure it will come that rapidly but sure that it will come in your time."[15]

Commager's position on multiculturalism derived from the midcentury liberalism shared by other liberal reformers in the historical profession such as Arthur Schlesinger Jr. and C. Vann Woodward. In the early 1990s, Schlesinger made a splash and many enemies by articulating a tough and principled liberal stand on multiculturalism, as forty years earlier he had helped forge an unyielding liberal position on the cold war. Commager agreed with Schlesinger's conviction that "when multicultural education means telling our children about other races, other cultures, other continents, it is a salutary development." Black history, women's history, and the history of America's mistakes should be taught, although Schlesinger did not convince his opponents that this was how American history actually had been presented since World War II. What Schlesinger found most offensive in the Cultural Left's program was that history and literature should be taught "as emotional therapies" instead of as intellectual disciplines. History, according to Schlesinger, should not be employed to teach children to feel good about their ancestors or to celebrate separate ethnic and racial communities at the expense of common culture.[16]

Woodward, a liberal reformer whose scholarship was a stimulus to greater racial harmony and an elevated perception of blacks, expressed fears similar to those of Commager and Schlesinger. Discussing the contemporary use of myths, in 1981 Woodward complained that baby boomer academics had turned the national myth of innocence on its head. These younger multicultural academics had found that most sins had occurred in the past, and now "ancestral atrocities and injustices" had revealed that "bargains in guilt are to be found mainly in the past." With this "inversion of myths," a "new image of the past sometimes replaces the ethnocentrism of the mythmakers with that of its victims." Under the reconstruction performed by the new mythmakers of the Cultural Left, Woodward pointed out scornfully, "American history becomes primarily a history of oppression, and the focus is upon the oppressed." This younger multicultural generation, ostensibly eradicating myth and symbol, creates a new mythology of their own. "Inverting myths," Woodward sighed, "may be a way of preserving them."[17] Commager, Schlesinger, and Woodward shared hesitations about the multicultural ethic, but they considered themselves defenders of the color-blind, equal opportunity society for which liberalism had worked so hard during their generation.

At about the time Commager reduced his teaching load to half-time in 1971, Samuel Eliot Morison wrote him a note from the Bahamas. "For me American history ended with J.F.K.," Morison confided. "Nothing since to be proud of. What's landing on the moon to discovering America?"[18] One shudders to think what those in other cultures might think of Morison's monumentally ethnocentric pronouncement. As with many other of Morison's opinions over the years since they had initiated their collaboration on *The Growth of the American Republic*, Henry surely dismissed his friend's comment. Commager never ranked the European colonization of the Americas as the most significant occurrence of the previous five centuries. Even further, he would never had thought that history ended with John Kennedy or, for that matter, that it would ever end.

But, like Morison, he worried about the decline of narrative history. A central reason for the decrease in the general public's interest in history, Commager explained in 1982, was the decline in the literary character of the field. "What we need is a revival in narrative history," he warned, "which is something that has gone out of style." One way to encourage more narrative would be to revive the tradition of amateur historians. Before Henry Adams in the late nineteenth century, "all great historians were amateurs," including Thucydides, Voltaire, and others. "We enormously exaggerate the importance of professional and technical training," he warned, "at the expense of the literary, philosophical value of history." The narrow, monographical history of professional historians was useful and necessary, but it would not engage the public. "You're not going to find much interest in a book on, let us say, the changing class prosperity in Scranton, Pennsylvania, 1840–1860," Commager told an inquirer. "That's a good doctoral dissertation subject, but it's not ever going to create a run on the bookstore." History did not have to be popular to be good and worthwhile. But if history was going to engage the broad educated citizenry, it would need to ask the large human questions, because "a vast majority of people who watch television and read novels want narratives about human beings, not just institutions, trends, or something of that kind."[19]

Commager's own answer for appropriate sorts of subjects for historians to address were, for example, the interaction between Enlightenment figures on each side of the Atlantic and the observations of Alexis de Tocqueville

Henry Steele Commager in 1977.
(Photograph by Mary Cross; courtesy of Lisa Commager)

about the nature of politics, society, and culture in the United States. On both these subjects Commager studied and wrote at the end of his career. Many historians felt his work lacked appropriate sophistication, not because of the subjects he tackled but because of the breezy manner in which his histories were framed. Yet, while those in his own field sometimes dismissed his work, figures in the letters tradition found it admirable. Alfred Kazin, for example, that acute interpreter of American literature and culture, considered Commager "a remarkable savant and one of the few historians left who is a true man of letters."[20] Late-twentieth-century historians, with a shrinking connection to the life of broad letters and culture, did not share Kazin's estimation of Commager.

The reason for Commager's interest in the Enlightenment went beyond its value as a broad and important topic for a discourse with the general public. It also took him back to his youth. "I myself have returned, in the end," he wrote to a friend, to that eighteenth century on which "I began over 50 years ago with my thesis on Struensee in Denmark; my recent books have been returns to Jefferson and his age—the *Empire of Reason* should really have been dedicated to him—he used the phrase, in one form or another, again and again." In addition to Jefferson, the other figure to whom Commager owed his "deepest intellectual debt" was Vernon Parrington, as he acknowledged in the preface to *The American Mind*. Fittingly, what Richard Hofstadter said of Parrington might equally have been said of Commager: "With his love of balance and proportion, his taste for elegance, his awakened secularism, and his affection for the ideals of humanitarianism and progress, [he] belonged intellectually, as he fully realized, to the eighteenth century. For him the American Enlightenment remained the high point in national thought."[21]

When Commager published *The Empire of Reason* in 1977, its theme was announced in its subtitle: *How Europe Imagined and America Realized the Enlightenment*. The reviews were respectful but underwhelming. Many of the criticisms were reminiscent of the weaknesses reviewers had detected in *The American Mind* more than twenty-five years earlier. J. H. Plumb, a British historian who knew Commager from Cambridge University, told readers of the *New York Times* that it was a bold book, but he warned that moments of doubt were obliterated by Commager's self-assured and dramatic rhetoric that "seizes the imagination and holds it." The Enlightenment volume passed "lightly—too lightly for some scholars"—over some of the blemishes in the American record of the time. "At times so galloping is the prose and so poetic that the book is almost in danger of being a prose hymn to the Republic." As had been noted by critics of *The American Mind*, Plumb believed that Commager's case in *Empire* would have been stronger had he been more critical of America and in less of a rush for his narrative to skate lightly across the surface of the dilemmas and paradoxes. As it stood, the book was "weakened by overstatement on the one hand, and elision on the other." What Alfred Kazin admired in Commager, colleagues in his own field did not. "Had Commager qualified his dramatic and forceful prose," Plumb concluded, "the pace would have been less vigorous, the rhetoric less vivid," but "it would, I think, have gained in substance and conviction."[22]

Historian Jack Thompson emphasized other problems. In "his characteristically conversational narrative style," Commager, by asserting that the American Enlightenment was founded in Philadelphia, avoided the necessity of dealing with the Puritans and their New England Calvinism. So religion was not part of Commager's Enlightenment. Nor, complained Thompson, were any ideas. Instead, like Daniel Boorstin and Frederick Jackson Turner, Commager, believed that "special conditions in the New World situation were more prominent and more creative than ideas" in forming the Enlightenment. Why, Thompson asked with exasperation, did Commager "bother to study the two eras of the age of philosophy in the empire of reason? Why not study the *Empire of Conditions and Instinct*?"[23] Yet would we choose to believe, with Thompson, that good intellectual history was impossible to write in the tradition of Turner, Merle Curti, Boorstin, and Commager?

What neither reviewer mentioned was that *The Empire of Reason* was far stronger in some sections than in others. As in *The American Mind*, in his volume on the Enlightenment Commager's work was the least satisfying when he ranged freely over wide topics—as he did in the first eight chapters of *The Empire of Reason*. By contrast, the final two chapters and appendix were quite good, combining narrative clarity with analytic strength and sophistication. Ironically, the first chapters had the most specific titles (on the spirit of the laws or new governments as compared with old governments), but it was there that Commager allowed himself to catalogue and skip quickly and broadly. In all his books, as in the final chapters of this one, he did best when he focused on a problem or a narrowly definable issue. The last chapters of *Empire*, such as one on "the blessings of liberty," were more penetrating because Commager was not so consumed by the amorphous question of American national character. The real objection to studies of national character should not be that they are oppressive (at least when they are done intelligently) but that they are often analytically weak and wandering.

In a similar volume which was published at about the same time and which drew far less attention, he packaged a number of his essays or lectures from the previous decade under the title *Jefferson, Nationalism, and the Enlightenment* (1975). It was not the sort of work that would increase Commager's estimation among scholars, because the pieces were not based on primary research or challenging scholarly reinterpretation. Identical to *The Empire of Reason*, his explanation of the Enlightenment in *Jefferson* was that "the Old World imagined the Enlightenment and the New World realized it. The Old World invented it, formulated it, and agitated it; America absorbed it, reflected it, and institutionalized it" politically, constitutionally, intellectually, and socially.[24]

Unsurprisingly, some of the most frustrating Commager tendencies from the past persisted in the *Jefferson* book. At the end of a wide-ranging introduction, he noted that in an introduction a writer could ask questions about the relationship of history to the present that might not be warranted in the main text. "Here, then," he confided to the reader, "I can ask more explicitly questions the essays themselves merely suggest." Then followed a full page and a half of interesting questions that went unanswered throughout the book. How, he asked, "did we get from Independence Hall to Watergate, from Yorktown to Vietnam, from Washington to Nixon?" This and a string of equally provocative inquiries Commager let die on the vine rather than risk answering them himself. Unfortunately, this trait was characteristic of much of his professional scholarship. He unearthed many of the fascinating questions but had neither the time nor the patience to dig in the proper primary and secondary sources to settle them. "When we have answered these questions we may perhaps set about restoring the intellectual and moral world which the Enlightenment created, and which we have lost or betrayed," he proclaimed at the end of his introduction.[25] In the remainder of the volume Commager never bothered the reader with these questions again.

Because of his fascination with questions of national character, evident even in his Enlightenment books, Commager also had a lifelong interest in the work of Alexis de Tocqueville, the nineteenth-century French observer of American values. Yet it was not until his retirement years that he began to write about Tocqueville in earnest. On Commager's seventy-sixth birthday he was visited by Bill Moyers, the former aide to Lyndon Johnson, who in the 1970s produced the regular television series *Bill Moyers' Journal* for public television. Moyers joined him as he taught one of his Amherst seminars and spoke with him afterward in his study. The program revolved around Commager's study of Tocqueville and the French thinker's relevance to contemporary American society.[26] Although Moyers mentioned during the show that Commager's study of Tocqueville would be published that same year (1979), *Commager on Tocqueville* did not actually appear until 1993.

As Commager pointed out, Tocqueville realized the paradox inherent in American values: people's desire for individualism at the same time that they wanted political and social equality. Individualism and equality, of course, work at cross-purposes (if one defines equality, as Tocqueville did, as "equality of condition" rather than as "equality of opportunity"). Both Tocqueville and Commager acknowledged the reality that, when Americans are given the choice between the conflicting values, they overwhelmingly choose individualism over equality.

Further, Tocqueville believed that centralization and bureaucratization were the greatest threats to American liberty. And, Commager told Moyers, while those dangers had not yet materialized, they were currently on the rise. Centralization had been a peril in Nazi Germany, the Soviet Union, and other nations, and Commager worried that the United States increasingly would be "a national security state, which means a military state; it will be more and more a government that has to resort to secrecy and that cannot therefore tolerate the full degree of freedom permitted, and indeed demanded by the Bill of Rights. What I fear," he said, "is that centralization will continue and bureaucratization will continue" as a response to the nature of modern society. What Commager wanted, however, was "a turn from a militarized society and government," an abandonment of the cold war, and "a return to the great traditions of an open government." He dreamed, he told Moyers, of "a return to the great doctrine of the subordination of the military to the civilian power, and not merely in law but in fact and in the allocation of resources." In addition, he hoped for a greater economic equality in the nation, as the Scandinavian countries experienced. Fittingly, Commager concluded that all these changes would be accomplished best through a one-world government, a solution he had proposed thirty years earlier.[27]

Five years after the Bill Moyers show aired, Commager wrote in the *Atlantic* that Tocqueville's biggest mistake was his fear of strong central government, a worry that had been adopted by the neoconservatives of the Reagan era. Commager challenged Tocqueville's assumption that liberty was more closely connected to local than to national government. To the contrary, Commager pointed out that most of the significant liberties protected in the twentieth-century United States were achieved by the federal government. Such measures as racial integration, women's rights, labor protections, and the conservation of natural resources were won despite rather than because of the states.[28]

Commager's book on Tocqueville, published in 1993, was a revision of lectures he delivered in 1978, in which he used Tocqueville's insights to underline America's infractions of its own values. Americans had feared a tyranny of the majority but had imposed a majority tyranny on blacks through slavery and, later, white supremacy. Whereas the Founders had worked to benefit posterity, in the intervening centuries Americans had ravaged resources, polluted the land, incurred debts for the future, and created a military stockpile that threatened future generations. Americans talked of justice at home but encouraged injustice abroad. The welfare state was denounced by Americans, but they promoted corporate welfare. While the majority had not created a tyranny, neither had it lived up to the potential of democratic justice.[29]

Despite his scholarly work late in life, if observers expected, in the wake of Watergate, the Vietnam War, and his retirement, that Commager would bury himself in a library, forsake intellectual activism, and settle into the comforts of conservatism, he proved them wrong. While his contemporaries embraced conservatism, especially in the aftermath of the student uprisings and the criticism of Lyndon Johnson's Great Society programs, Commager in the 1970s and 1980s became even more energetic in his outspoken liberalism.

With a handful of other prominent figures, in 1975 Commager urged President Ford to review U.S. policy toward Spain to make sure that a transference of power from Generalissimo Francisco Franco to Prince Juan Carlos would not perpetuate totalitarianism in that country. A year later Commager publicly defended CBS News correspondent Daniel Schorr against charges from the House Ethics Committee that he was endangering national security. Schorr was accused of receiving a draft report of the House Special Committee on Intelligence from an unidentified source and then passing it on to the *Village Voice*. Commager claimed that, like Benjamin Franklin in the eighteenth century and Daniel Ellsberg in 1971, Schorr was adhering to a practice of putting "loyalty to his countrymen and to the cause of liberty ahead of loyalty to a private official" and was following "the principle that the American people have a right to know what their Government is about." Within half a year, Commager became chair of the Citizen's Committee Concerned with Freedom of the Press, an ad hoc organization formed in defense of Schorr.[30]

Not above using his command of American history to argue for the benefit of the Democratic Party and his own preferred candidates, Commager maintained that history showed Jimmy Carter's lack of political experience would be a benefit instead of a drawback. After all, hadn't inexperienced presidents such as Lincoln, Teddy Roosevelt, Woodrow Wilson, and Franklin Roosevelt proved superior to those with more seasoning such as Andrew Johnson, William McKinley, William Taft, Richard Nixon, and, in this case, Gerald Ford—against whom Carter was running for office at the moment? Then four years later, when Commager switched his allegiance and supported the more liberal Senator Ted Kennedy against Carter for the Democratic nomination for president in 1980, he denounced the Carter administration for threatening to punish Chicago because the city's mayor supported Kennedy.[31]

During this period of his retirement, Commager was still as eager as he had been in the 1960s to identify the hypocrisy and double standards at work in American foreign and domestic policies. The Carter administration, he charged, had "irreparably compromised its moral position" by supporting the South Korean government, an ally with human rights abuses, while the United States cut off aid to those of our enemies like Argentina because of their human rights offenses. Later the Reagan administration, which mounted a public relations campaign against terrorist countries, needed to admit the United States's "own history of terrorism against those they feared or hated or regarded as 'lesser breeds,'" such as the Pequot Indians or the Vietnamese nationalists. Similarly, the Reagan White House objected to other nations breaching international law but expected the United States to be able to launch military strikes in other countries such as Grenada with impunity. Nor did Reagan and his followers appreciate dissent. "The Reagan Administration believes nothing is complex, that it has easy solutions for everything," Commager told his seminar at Amherst just before his eightieth birthday. "I prefer what Justice Holmes said, 'We should be ever receptive to loathsome ideas.' That is a noble way of putting it."[32]

In his last decades, as throughout his career, Commager promoted a liberalism critical of official policy, but a liberalism that also shunned ideology. Consider his criticism of Reagan's ideological maneuverings. In 1980 Reagan had announced that Congressman John Anderson of Illinois was not a true Republican. Commager countered that Reagan obviously knew little of the history of inclusiveness in the Republican Party since its nineteenth-century beginnings. The entire two-party system in the United States, moreover, had been flexible and inclusive throughout its history. Jefferson, in his Inaugural Address, correctly noted that "we are all republicans, we are all democrats." Extending Jefferson's logic further, Commager suggested that because of America's diversity it was important that "we are all liberals, we are all conservatives, we are all nationalists, we are all localists, we are all in favor of private enterprise, all in favor of public enterprise." This inclusiveness did not mean that ideology and criticism should be absent from the political arena but that they should not be inflexible and absolutist. "The political relativism and catholicity," he explained about the American approach, "is not so much a preference as a necessity."[33]

Again, because such liberals as Commager opposed inflexible ideology did not mean they opposed moral passion or ideological partisanship. In 1986 Commager complained publicly that the University of Massachusetts at Amherst, near his home, had welcomed CIA recruiting on campus and enforced it with police dogs. Student protesters, who "substitute force for reason" were "misguided," but the university was worse. If the CIA needed to recruit in a public spot it should use federal facilities such as the Post Office. Universities need not follow the dictates of the federal government, as was the case in totalitarian countries such as Nazi Germany or the Soviet Union.[34] Ideology was important to exercise, but it should be independent instead of an official state ideology. Moral passion, such as the students displayed, was beneficial so long as it did not turn to violence. Dissent, criticism, and flexible and inclusive ideology strengthened political culture.

Yet Commager's own ideological lenses often caused him to misread the landscape and produce his own inconsistencies. When the Moral Majority led Christian fundamentalists into political activity in the Reagan era, for example, Commager accused them of connecting "morality with a particular brand of religious faith and this, in turn, with political policies." Serving as a spokesperson for the Christian right, Reagan had made a terrible mistake, because "by identifying religion with morality, and morality with politics, he has challenged the spirit, if not the letter, of constitutional restrictions on the alliance of church and state, and almost recklessly invited renewal of enmities that Americans had been the first to foreswear. It is the freedom from these that has been the most conspicuous feature of the American experience in union and democracy."[35] Yet the limitations of his own ideological vision led Commager to an intellectual hypocrisy. Never would he have criticized the Reverend Martin Luther King Jr. for bringing together religion, public morality, and politics. The civil rights movement, centered in the black church, never seemed a threat to Commager. Nor, for that matter, had he opposed the involvement of churches in the politics of the 1960s peace movement or the 1980s refugee sanctuary movement. Commager tried to have it both ways, criticizing Reagan and the conservatives for the same traits he admired in liberals.[36]

On March 2, 1998, at the age of ninety-five, Henry Steele Commager died of pneumonia at his home in Amherst. Newspapers and periodicals across the country described him as one of the leading American historians and acknowledged his role in the civic life of the nation. Yet these respectful, elegiac obituaries struggled unsuccessfully to identify the significance of his death to the intellectual community. They might have said that with his passing a breed of midcentury cultural figures, grounded in the ideas of literature and history, neared extinction.

A decade earlier, while in his mid-eighties, Commager had sat with a visitor in the sunporch office beside the living room of his rambling white house in Amherst, a house that maintained its dignity though it showed signs of wear. Sorting through the magazines in front of him, he explained that the *Nation* was the best weekly and the *Progressive* the best monthly and that the *New Republic* had declined into conservative rubbish. That opinion put Commager significantly to the left of center and to the left of most of the American population. Similarly, Alfred Kazin remembered that the last time he saw Commager "he told me that his Op-Ed articles for the LA Times were too staunch to be always accepted." Commager was asked how he became increasingly more insistent in his critical liberalism as he grew older, when many in his generation had moved from being socialist youths to centrist or neoconservative adults. The question obviously baffled him. In his opinion, he had never drifted from his initial liberal position, had never been under the influence of Marx on the left or conservative thinkers on the right, had never had a period of romance with ideology as had many in his generation. Where was the change?[37]

Perhaps Commager was right that he remained simply a consistent liberal. Maybe he appears to have become even more aggressively critical of American politics and society after World War II because many in his generation drifted gradually toward conservatism. True, he was mainly a Jeffersonian, which hardly makes him part of a radical breed. Perhaps the example of his liberalism is so salient and stands out so clearly, making him seem more radical than he was, because many liberals were afraid as the century wore on to admit they were liberals. Liberalism was under attack by conservatives who characterized it as unpatriotic, fiscally wasteful, and godless. From the left, liberalism was denounced as weak soup, as insufficiently multicultural, as ambivalent. And let's face it: who in the intellectual world celebrates the principles of the center? The intellectually brave are thought to be those who press the envelope, flirt with the margin, whether or not their principles are beneficial and honorable. By being an unashamed and principled liberal, Commager seemed to stand out as a particularly visible and critical liberal. What Richard Hofstadter said about other opinions, Commager believed about liberalism: that if the "idea is worth anything at all it is worth a forceful overstatement."[38]

Part of the problem with assessing the legacy of Commager and the midcentury generation of liberal historians and writers is that they were swept aside by a flood of cultural change in the 1960s. This flow deposited midcentury liberals in a landscape very different from what they had inhabited, and it obscured their real political identities. Many midcentury liberals were to the left of center politically but did not conceive of themselves as cultural radicals—outside the normal anticommercialism of American writers such as Thoreau or the antiphilistinism of such critics as Edmund Wilson or Malcolm Cowley. So when the cultural tide of ethnic and gender liberation hit in the 1960s, at the same time as an anthropological and linguistic radicalism invigorated the baby boomer generation of academics, the midcentury liberals seemed culturally conservative by contrast. It was natural, although mistaken, for the younger poststructuralist generation to confuse culture and politics by assuming that the older liberals were *politically* conservative, despite their liberal and in some cases leftist pedigrees.

"The fact is that men and women do not live in compartments labeled 'politics' or 'law' or 'religion' or 'economics,' " Commager once noted; "they live in all of these simultaneously." Nor can their entire outlook be judged, he might have added, on the basis of only one of those compartments. That the midcentury liberals had not partaken of the cultural transformation of the 1960s did not mean that their political identities were retrograde. As the sociologist Daniel Bell argued in the 1970s, an individual's different ideological realms had to be evaluated separately. Thus, Bell claimed without any intellectual contradiction that he was "a socialist in economics, a liberal in politics, and a conservative in culture."[39] Yet if midcentury liberals are not extended this same room for ideological flexibility, then their work and legacy will continue to be misunderstood. If we resist reevaluating the midcentury generation of scholars, we will have fulfilled John Dewey's prophecy that "problems are often not solved . . . they merely give way to others."[40]

In his passion for intellectual activism and public dialogue, Commager was reminiscent of Progressive historians such as Charles Beard and Vernon Parrington. In his optimism about America and enthusiastic commitment to descriptive rhetoric and literary style, he also demonstrated traits suggestive of George Bancroft, a historian who was thought by the 1960s to be hopelessly passé, no more than a historical curiosity, which was one of the reasons the New Left had little use for Commager's scholarship. Yet in his function as a kind of Bancroft, he bore a folk wisdom and served as a scholar of broad learning. In this role, Commager was to the field of American history what a painter like Grant Wood was to American painting. Can the profession of history afford to ignore and bury its intellectual heritage in a way that painting and literature have not? If so, what a painful irony from a field— history!—that is the least grateful to its own intellectual past, an occupation in which a book a decade old or an interpretation a generation old are not only thought to be out-of-date but also considered an embarrassment.

Although Commager's scholarship was never as challenging as was that of Charles Beard, what Hofstadter noted about Beard could also be said of Commager, who, like Beard, went east to New York from the Midwest. He was, Hofstadter remarked of Beard, "a man so clearly bred out of the native grain, and yet [at] once so cosmopolitan in his interests and experiences; a bearer of something like folk wisdom, and yet a scholar of broad learning; a radical who was also a patriot in the classical and untarnished sense of the word. One prefers to think of him in this way—as a productive scholar who was also an intrepid public spirit, as the patron and guide of younger colleagues, the distinguished and embattled defender of civil and academic liberties, the scourger of Hearst, the spokesman of the native decencies—and one remembers that the life of a man does not end as a series of propositions that can simply be assessed and found true or false, but as a set of lingering resonances that for our own sake we must be attuned to hear." As Hofstadter concluded about Beard, we might also decide about Commager: "Some scholars choose to live their lives, usefully enough, amid the clutter of professional detail. [He] aimed to achieve a wisdom commensurate with his passion, and to put them both in the public service. No doubt he would rather have failed in this than succeeded in anything else."[41]

Notes

ABBREVIATIONS USED IN THE NOTES

AMP   Alexander Meiklejohn Papers, State Historical Society of Wisconsin, Madison

ANP   Allan Nevins Papers, Butler Library, Columbia University

Commager reminiscences   Henry Steele Commager, "The Reminiscences of Henry Steele Commager," 1983, oral history interview of Henry Steele Commager by John Niven, Amherst, Mass., August 1979, Oral History Research Office, Columbia University

DAP   Personal correspondence between Daniel Aaron and Henry Nash Smith, Daniel Aaron Papers, provided to author by Daniel Aaron

HSCP   Henry Steele Commager Papers, Amherst College Archives and Special Collections

MCP   Merle Curti Papers, State Historical Society of Wisconsin, Madison

Nevins reminiscences   Allan Nevins, "The Reminiscences of Allan Nevins," 1976, oral history interview of Allan Nevins by Frank Ernest Hill, Bermuda, June 1963, Oral History Research Office, Columbia University

All interview quotations come from interview notes taken by the author.

PREFACE

1. For recent accounts of the intellectual activities of historians, see Michael Wreszin, "Arthur Schlesinger, Jr., Scholar-Activist in Cold War America: 1946–1956," *Salmagundi* 63–64 (Spring–Summer 1984): 255–85; Roy Rosenzweig, "Marketing the Past: *American Heritage* and Popular History in the United States, 1954–1984," *Radical History Review* 32 (March 1985): 7–29; Peter Novick, *That Noble Dream* (New York: Cambridge University Press, 1988); Jonathan Wiener, "Radical Historians and the Crisis in American History, 1959–1980," *Journal of American History* 76, no. 2 (September 1989): 399–434; and Michael D. Bess, "E. P. Thompson: The Historian as Activist," *American Historical Review* 98, no. 1 (February 1993): 18–38.

CHAPTER 1

1. Norm Kramer (Taft High School, Woodland Hills, California) to Commager, April 15, 1964, in Biographical file, HSCP.

2. Henry Steele Commager to Norm Kramer, April 25, 1964, Biographical file, HSCP.

3. Harvey Breit, "Talk with Mr. Commager," *New York Times Book Review*, March 12, 1950, 27.

4. James Reston, "Where Are We Going?" *New York Times*, Sunday, August 3, 1980, sec. 4, p. 19; Herbert Mitgang, "A Bouncing, Zestful Commager Turns 80 Today," *New York Times*, Monday, October 25, 1982, sec. C, p. 15.

5. Malcolm Cowley, *Exile's Return* (1951; reprint, New York: Penguin, 1976), 15–16.

6. Henry Steele Commager, ed., *The St. Nicholas Anthology* (New York: Random House, 1948), xix. Christine Nasso, ed., *Contemporary Authors*, First Revision, vols. 21–24 (Detroit: Gale Research, 1977), 186.

7. Robert F. Commagere, Genealogy of the Commagere Family (unpublished), Los Angeles, 1997; copy in possession of the author.

8. Nevin O. Winter, *A History of Northwest Ohio* (Chicago: Lewis Publishing, 1917), 3: 1468–71.

9. Winter, *History of Northwest Ohio*, 1468–71. Commagere, Genealogy.

10. Winter, *History of Northwest Ohio*, 1468–71. Commagere, Genealogy.

11. Commager to Hans Duus, August 8, 1925, Hans Duus file, HSCP.

12. Mary Powlesland Commager, interviews by author, Amherst, Mass., June 4, 1991, June 18, 1992, and February 26, 1993. Nardi Reeder Campion, "Commager's Enormous Energy Is Undiminished," *Valley News* (West Lebanon, N.H.), October 28, 1987, 21. For mention of his aunt and uncle in Syracuse, see Commager to Hans Duus, January 25, 1925, and June 8, 1925, Hans Duus file, HSCP. There were also aunts and uncles in Minneapolis and Toledo with whom the brothers might have lived. On Adam Dan's knighthood, see Paul Nyholm, *The Americanization of the Danish Lutheran Churches in America* (Minneapolis: Augsburg, 1963), 235, 27.

13. Stig Pilgaard Olsen, "Danish-American Literature," in *Danish Emigration to the U.S.A.*, ed. Birgit Flemming Larsen and Henning Bender (Aalborg, Denmark: Danes Worldwide Archives, 1992), 52–54. Nyholm, *Americanization*, 235, 103 n. 25, 70, 72.

14. Quoted in Nyholm, *Americanization*, 235–36.

15. Ibid., 62–63.

16. Enok Mortensen, *The Danish Lutheran Church in America* (Philadelphia: Board of Publication of the Lutheran Church in America, 1967), 13, 51–54.

17. Nyholm, *Americanization*, 235. Commager reminiscences, 250. For the house location, see Commager to Hans Duus, September 17, 1925, Hans Duus file, HSCP.

18. Esther Lindegaard Sorensen to Commager, March 10, 1965, Biographical file, HSCP.

19. Mary Powlesland Commager, interview, June 18, 1992. Henry Steele Commager, interview by author, Amherst, Mass., August 22, 1988.

20. Commager reminiscences, 248–49. Later, Commager remembered that as he had grown up his family had been ardent Republicans and that the Commagers had believed that all Democrats were either Irish or saloon-keepers and therefore weren't "proper people" (ibid.). Yet in 1854 his great-grandfather Henry Steel Commagere had been a Democratic candidate in Ohio for Congress.

21. Ibid., 139. Milton Cantor to the author, June 7, 1996.

22. Commager reminiscences, 139, 149, 152–53. Commager to unidentified correspondent, January 15, 1971, Biographical file, HSCP.

23. Commager reminiscences, 140. Stanley Kunitz and Howard Haycraft, eds., *Twentieth Century Authors* (New York: Wilson, 1942), 886. Obituary for Andrew McLaughlin, *American Historical Review* 53, no. 2 (January 1948): 432.

24. Obituary for Andrew McLaughlin, 433–34.

25. Andrew McLaughlin, "American History and American Democracy," *American Historical Review* 20, no. 2 (January 1915): 257, 263–65.

26. Ibid., 257–58.

27. Ibid., 276.

28. Obituary for Andrew McLaughlin, 433–34.

29. Avery Craven, "William Edward Dodd," in *Dictionary of American Biography*, ed. Robert L. Schuyler and Edward T. James (New York: Scribner, 1958), 152.

30. Ibid., 153. David Potter, "C. Vann Woodward," in *Pastmasters*, ed. Marcus Cunliffe and Robin Winks (New York: Harper and Row, 1969), 393, 379.

31. Robert Dallek, *Democrat and Diplomat: The Life of William E. Dodd* (New York: Oxford University Press, 1968), 57. Craven, "Dodd," 153. Forrest McDonald, "Charles Beard," in *Pastmasters*, ed. Cunliffe and Winks, 136–37.

32. Dallek, *Democrat and Diplomat*, 62–63.

33. Franklin L. Ford, "Three Observers in Berlin: Rumbold, Dodd, and François-Poncet," in *The Diplomats, 1919–1939*, ed. Gordon A. Craig and Felix Gilbert (Princeton: Princeton University Press, 1953), 447–48.

34. Ibid., 452, 455.

35. Commager reminiscences, 159. Henry Commager, "Some Factors in the Acquisition of Oregon by the United States" (master's thesis, University of Chicago, 1924).

36. Eric Darmstadter, interview by author, by telephone, March 2, 1993. Commager to Hans Duus, January 13, 1925, and January 1925, Hans Duus file, HSCP.

37. Commager to Hans Duus, January 1925, Hans Duus file, HSCP.

38. Commager to Hans Duus, January 25, 1925, Hans Duus file, HSCP.

39. Commager to Hans Duus, March 18, 1925, Hans Duus file, HSCP.

40. Commager to Hans Duus, January 13, 1925, Hans Duus file, HSCP.

41. Ibid.

42. Commager to Hans Duus, January 13, June 4, and May 1925, Hans Duus file, HSCP.

43. Cowley, *Exile's Return*, 93–97.

44. As a "lawyer manqué," see Commager to unidentified correspondent, January 15, 1971, Biographical file, HSCP.

45. Commager to Hans Duus, June 4, 1925, Hans Duus file, HSCP.

46. Commager to Hans Duus, June 8, 1925, Hans Duus file, HSCP.

47. Ibid.

48. Commager to Hans Duus, August 8, 1925, Hans Duus file, HSCP.

49. Commager to Hans Duus, August 8, 1925, and December 14, 1925, Hans Duus file, HSCP.

50. Commager to Hans Duus, April 10, 1926, Hans Duus file, HSCP.

51. Henry Commager, "England and the Oregon Treaty of 1846," *Oregon Historical Quarterly* 28, no. 1 (March 1927); no middle name was used in this article.

52. Commager to Hans Duus, July 6, 1926, Hans Duus file, HSCP.

53. Henry Steele Commager, "Struensee and the Reform Movement in Denmark" (Ph.D. diss., University of Chicago, 1928), 103–16.

54. Ibid., 211.

55. Commager reminiscences, 156–61.

56. Ibid., 1.

57. Nevins reminiscences, 1–4. Allan Nevins, *Allan Nevins on History*, compiled and introduced by Ray Allen Billington (New York: Charles Scribner's Sons, 1975), 204.

58. Nevins reminiscences, 4–6, 9.

59. Ibid., 10–11.

60. Ibid., 27–30.

61. Ibid., 34–40. Ray Allen Billington, "Allan Nevins, Historian: A Personal Reminiscence," in Nevins, *Nevins on History*, x.

62. Nevins reminiscences, 42–43.

63. Ibid., 51.

64. Ibid., 54–55, 58–59; "Henry Seidel Canby: SRL Founder and Editor," *Saturday Review*, April 22, 1961, 14–15.

65. Nevins reminiscences, 109. "Saturday Reviewers," *Saturday Review of Literature*, July 22, 1939, 24.

66. Nevins reminiscences, 99–100. Wilbur Jacobs, "In Memory of Allan Nevins," *Pacific Historical Review* 40 (May 1971): 255.

67. Nevins reminiscences, 101–3.

68. Ibid., 105–10.

69. Allan Nevins, "The Life and Death of the *World*," *Saturday Review of Literature*, March 14, 1931, 662.

70. Nevins reminiscences, 113.

71. Ibid.

72. Ibid., 134–37. Jacobs, "In Memory of Allan Nevins," 253.

73. "Saturday Reviewers," 24; Jacobs, "In Memory of Allan Nevins," 253–54; Nevins, "Life and Death of the *World*," 662–63.

74. Commager to Hans Duus, April 10, 1926, Hans Duus file, HSCP.

75. Ibid. Commager reminiscences, 209–10.

76. For representative discussion of the distinction between intellectuals and scholars, see Russell Jacoby, *The Last Intellectuals* (New York: Basic Books, 1987); Neil Jumonville, *Critical Crossings: The New York Intellectuals in Postwar America* (Berkeley: University of California Press, 1991); Theodore Hamerow, *Reflections on History and Historians* (Madison: University of Wisconsin Press, 1987); and Christopher Jencks and David Riesman, quoted in Peter Novick, *That Noble Dream* (New York: Cambridge University Press, 1988), 52–53.

77. Commager reminiscences, 204–5.

78. Ibid., 1–3. Nevins reminiscences, 164.

79. Commager reminiscences, 202–3, 210.

80. Lewis Gannett, "A Quarter Century of a Weekly Book Review . . . and of the World," *New York Herald Tribune Book Review*, September 25, 1949, 4–5.

81. Allan Nevins, "Henry S. Commager as Historian: An Appreciation," in *Freedom and Reform: Essays in Honor of Henry Steele Commager*, ed. Harold M. Hyman and Leonard W. Levy (New York: Harper and Row, 1967), 7.

CHAPTER 2

1. Samuel Eliot Morison, "Albion, Nova, and New England," *Oregon Historical Quarterly* 28, no. 1 (March 1927): 1–17; Henry Commager, "England and the Oregon Treaty of 1846," *Oregon Historical Quarterly* 28, no. 1 (March 1927): 18–38.

2. Gregory M. Pfitzer, *Samuel Eliot Morison's Historical World* (Boston: Northeastern University Press, 1991), 57.

3. Ibid., 72–73.

4. Ibid., 82.

5. Samuel Eliot Morison to Henry Steele Commager, September 13, 1944, and April 30, [1953?], Samuel Eliot Morison file, HSCP.

6. Henry Steele Commager, interview with author, Amherst, Mass., August 22, 1988. Emily Morison Beck, letter to author, February 23, 1998.

7. Pfitzer, *Morison's Historical World*, 255.

8. Ibid., 256–57. Samuel Eliot Morison to Henry Steele Commager, April 30, [1953?], Samuel Eliot Morison file, HSCP.

9. Pfitzer, *Morison's Historical World*, 114.

10. Samuel Eliot Morison and Henry Steele Commager, *The Growth of the American Republic* (New York: Oxford University Press, 1930), iii.

11. Alden Whitman, "Growth of 'Morison and Commager,' " *New York Times*, November 4, 1969, 56.

12. Morison and Commager, *Growth of the American Republic*, 655–56, 659–60, 662.

13. Ibid., 653.

14. Frances FitzGerald has complained that "the nineteen-thirties textbook that bears Commager's name contains no intellectual history at all." Not only is she wrong, but she forgets that intellectual history didn't really exist in the late 1920s when Commager wrote his chapters. Even if it had, why would one expect much of it in a general survey textbook? Frances FitzGerald, *America Revised: History Schoolbooks in the Twentieth Century* (Boston: Little, Brown, 1979), 21.

15. Richard Hofstadter, *The Progressive Historians* (New York: Knopf, 1968), 375–76. See Edward Eggleston, *The Transit of Civilization from England to America in the Seventeenth Century* (New York: Appleton, 1901); Moses Coit Tyler, *A History of American Literature during the Colonial Time* (New York: Putnam's Sons, 1878); and Barrett Wendell, *A Literary History of America* (New York: Scribner's Sons, 1900).

16. Commager to Hans Duus, August 8, 1925, Hans Duus file, HSCP.

17. Commager to Hans Duus, September 7, 1925, Hans Duus file, HSCP.

18. Commager to Hans Duus, May 10, 1926, and July 6, 1926, Hans Duus file, HSCP.

19. Commager, interview. Commager to Hans Duus, January 25, 1925, Hans Duus file, HSCP.

20. Commager to Hans Duus, July 6, 1926, Hans Duus file, HSCP.

21. Henry Steele Commager, "Farewell to Laissez-Faire," *Current History* 38 (August 1933): 513.

22. Ibid., 515–19.

23. Henry Steele Commager, " 'Regimentation': A New Bogy," *Current History* 40 (July 1934): 386–87.

24. Ibid., 388–90.

25. Ibid., 390–91.

26. Allan Nevins, "The Battle of 1936 Begins," *Saturday Review of Literature*, October 6, 1934, 170; Nevins, "Is the Roosevelt New Deal Proving Successful?" *Congressional Digest* 13 (June 1934): 182.

27. Nevins, "The Battle of 1936 Begins," 155; Nevins reminiscences, 165.

28. Commager, interview.

29. Herbert Croly, *The Promise of American Life* (1909; reprint, Cambridge: Harvard University Press, 1965), esp. chaps. 2, 8, and 13. See also Charles Forcey, *The Crossroads of Liberalism* (New York: Oxford University Press, 1961), 29–30.

30. Commager, interview. August 22, 1988.

31. Henry Steele Commager, "Nation or the States: Which Shall Dominate?" *New York Times Magazine*, November 28, 1937.

32. Ibid.

33. Allan Nevins, "What Jefferson Thought," *Saturday Review*, July 1, 1939, 15.

34. Commager reminiscences, 251–52.

35. Ibid., 217, 263–64.

36. Commager to Merle Curti, July 8, 1933, MCP.

37. Henry Steele Commager, *Theodore Parker* (Boston: Little, Brown, 1936), 30, 118.

38. Ibid., 139.

39. Ibid., 140, 144.

40. Ibid., 143.

41. Ibid., 88.

42. Ibid., 234–36.

43. Ibid., 239.

44. Ibid., 188, 211, 203–4.

45. C. Hartley Grattan, "Theodore Parker, Who Was the Conscience of America," *New York Times Book Review*, April 12, 1936, 3; Merle Curti, review of *Theodore Parker*, by Commager, *New England Quarterly* 9, no. 3 (September 1936): 540; Newton Arvin, "A Yankee Savonarola," *New Republic*, April 15, 1936, 284.

46. Commager, *Theodore Parker*, vii–viii.

47. Merle Curti, letter to author, December 18, 1991.

48. Curti, review, 540–41.

49. Grattan, "Theodore Parker," 3; Arvin, "Yankee Savonarola," 284.

50. John Chamberlain, "Portrait without an Attitude," *Nation*, July 25, 1936, 108.

51. Ibid.

52. Commager, *Theodore Parker*, 45, 240.

53. Ibid., 121.

54. William Leuchtenburg, letter to author, June 10, 1996.

55. Commager reminiscences, 216.

56. Henry Steele Commager, *The American Mind* (New Haven: Yale University Press, 1950), ix.

57. Vernon Louis Parrington, *Main Currents in American Thought*, vol. 1, *The Colonial Mind* (1927; reprint, Norman: University of Oklahoma Press, 1987), xv. Hofstadter, *Progressive Historians*, 349.

58. Parrington, *Main Currents*, 37, 42, 179. On the influence of Taine, see Ralph Henry Gabriel, "Vernon Louis Parrington," in *Pastmasters*, ed. Marcus Cunliffe and Robin Winks (New York: Harper and Row, 1969), 151.

59. Parrington, *Main Currents*, 52.

60. Ibid., 62.

61. Ibid., 196–97, 233–36, 243.

62. Ibid., 28–31, 34.

63. Robert Skotheim, *American Intellectual Histories and Historians* (Princeton: Princeton University Press, 1966), 148–49.

64. Peter Novick, *That Noble Dream* (New York: Cambridge University Press, 1988), 245–46, 346.

65. Commager reminiscences, 65–67.

66. Ibid., 66–67.

67. Quoted in Hofstadter, *Progressive Historians*, 360.

68. Commager to Hans Duus, December 19, 1926, Hans Duus file, HSCP.

69. Quoted in Hofstadter, *Progressive Historians*, 389.

70. Ibid., 429–30.

71. Henry Steele Commager, *The Search for a Usable Past* (New York: Knopf, 1967), ix.

72. On the relation of these themes, see Novick, *That Noble Dream*, 272.

73. Henry Steele Commager, *The Study of History* (Columbus, Ohio: Charles Merrill, 1966), 68–69.

74. Ibid., 70.

75. Ibid., 71.

CHAPTER 3

1. Merle Curti, letter to author, December 18, 1991.

2. Letters from Merle Curti to Commager, June 17, [1942?], and May 17, [1944?], Merle Curti file, HSCP.

3. Henry Steele Commager to Merle Curti, February 13, [1944 or 1945?], and February 19, [same year], MCP.

4. Richard Hofstadter to Henry Steele Commager, December 30, 1942, November 24, 1943, May 5, 1944, and April 15, 1945, Richard Hofstadter file, HSCP.

5. Henry Steele Commager, interview by author, Amherst, Mass., May 27, 1991. For Hofstadter's shared outlook with the New York Intellectuals, see Neil Jumonville, *Critical Crossings: The New York Intellectuals in Postwar America* (Berkeley: University of California Press, 1991), esp. 124–26, 214, 221–26.

6. Commager, interview, May 27, 1991.

7. Harold Hyman, "Requiem for a Constitutional-Legal History Heavyweight: Richard Brandon Morris, 1904–1989," *Georgia Journal of Southern Legal History* 1, no. 1 (Spring/Summer 1991): 2.

8. Richard Morris, "The View from the Top of Fayerweather," in *Freedom and Reform*, ed. Harold Hyman and Leonard Levy (New York: Harper and Row, 1967), 1.

9. *New York Times*, October 8, 1942, 17.

10. Conversations with Theodore Greene, Hugh Hawkins, and Gordon Levin, Amherst, Mass., June 1991.

11. Handout for History 235–236, Studies in Recent American History, no syllabus date, in American Studies file, HSCP.

12. Morris, "View from the Top of Fayerweather," 1–3.

13. Ibid.

14. Richard Hofstadter, *The Progressive Historians* (New York: Knopf, 1968), 290.

15. Commager reminiscences 40–41.

16. Ibid., 44.

17. Israel Shenker, "A 'Theoretically Retired' Commager Teaches On," *New York Times*, September 27, 1971, 70.

18. Denis Brogan to Henry Steele Commager, September 19, 1944, Denis Brogan file, HSCP.

19. August Meier, letters to author, May 14, 1992, and June 5, 1992.

20. Irita Van Doren to Henry Steele Commager, October 24, 1957, *New York Herald Tribune* file, HSCP.

21. The historian Milton Cantor, a close friend of his who lived with him for several years in the 1960s, concurs with this interpretation. Milton Cantor, interview by author, Amherst, Mass., June 13, 1991.

22. Henry Steele Commager, interview by author, Amherst, Mass., August 22, 1988.

23. For Markel as Stalin, see ibid. For Markel's comment about never having too much Commager, see Lester Markel to Henry Steele Commager, November 2, 1948. For Markel on ideas dying by the wayside, Markel to Commager, May 8, 1945. For examples of Markel's frustration with Commager's work habits, see Markel to Commager, February 8, 1944, February 21, 1944, April 18, 1944, and September 15, 1944. All Markel correspondence is in the *New York Times* file, HSCP.

24. Kenneth Gould to Henry Steele Commager, July 26, 1943, *Scholastic Magazine* file, HSCP.

25. Meredith Mayer (Nevins's daughter), letter to author, June 13, 1996.

26. Allan Nevins to Henry Steele Commager, no date but probably in the mid-1940s, Allan Nevins file, HSCP.

27. Allan Nevins to Henry Steele Commager, July 30, 1941, Allan Nevins file, HSCP.

28. Henry Steele Commager, Obituary for Allan Nevins, *American Historical Review* 77, no. 3 (June 1972): 871.

29. Roy Rosenzweig, "Marketing the Past: *American Heritage* and Popular History in the United States, 1954–1984," *Radical History Review* 3 (March 1985). Peter Novick, *That Noble Dream* (New York: Cambridge University Press, 1988), 194–97. Allan Nevins, "What's the Matter with History?" in *Allan Nevins on History*, compiled and introduced by Ray Allen Billington (New York: Charles Scribner's Sons, 1975), 3–12; first published in *Saturday Review of Literature*, February 4, 1939.

30. Nevins, "What's the Matter with History?," 8–10.

31. Donald F. Tingley, "Allan Nevins: A Reminiscence," *Journal of the Illinois State Historical Society* 66, no. 2 (Summer 1973): 178.

32. Commager, Obituary for Allan Nevins, 871. Henry Steele Commager to Mary Nevins, March 16, 1971, Allan Nevins file, HSCP.

33. Meredith Mayer, letter to author, May 28, 1996.

34. Allan Nevins, "Recent Progress of American Social History," in *Allan Nevins on History*, ed. Billington, 112; first published in the *Journal of Economic and Business History* 1 (May 1929).

35. Allan Nevins, "Business and the Historian," in *Allan Nevins on History*, ed. Billington, 70–73, 81; first published in the *American Petroleum Institute Proceedings* 33, no. 1 (1953): 85–89.

36. Harvey Wish, *The American Historian* (New York: Oxford University Press, 1960), 326.

37. William Leuchtenburg, letter to author, June 10, 1996.

38. Commager, Obituary for Allan Nevins, 871. "Allan Nevins," *Political Science Quarterly* 86 (September 1971): 559.

39. Bruce Catton, "In Memoriam: Allan Nevins, 1890–1971," *American Heritage* 22 (June 1971): 3.

40. Allan Nevins, "Henry S. Commager as Historian: An Appreciation," in *Freedom and Reform*, ed. Hyman and Levy, 13.

41. Henry Steele Commager, *Majority Rule and Minority Rights* (New York: Oxford University Press, 1943; reprint, Gloucester, Mass.: Peter Smith, 1958), 4.

42. Ibid., 9–14.

43. Ibid., 14–24, 9.

44. Ibid., 32–33.

45. Ibid., 40–43.

46. Ibid., 44, 56, 39.

47. Ibid., 57–60.

48. Ibid., 62.

49. Ibid., 64–66.

50. Ibid., 71–72.

51. Ibid., 77–78.

52. Henry Steele Commager, "Echoes of John Marshall," *New York Times Magazine*, June 11, 1939, 17.

53. Ibid., 17.

54. Quoted in Herman Belz, "Andrew C. McLaughlin and Liberal Democracy: Scientific History in Support of the Best Regime," *Reviews in American History* 19, no. 3 (September 1991): 454.

55. Henry Steele Commager, "Civil Liberties and Democracy," *Senior Scholastic*, March 22–27, 1943, 13.

56. Richard Hofstadter to Henry Steele Commager, November 24, 1943, Richard Hofstadter file, HSCP.

57. Sidney Hook, "The Perpetual Debate," *Nation*, December 11, 1943, 709–10.

58. Henry Steele Commager, letter to the editor, *New York Times Book Review*, February 23, 1958, 44.

59. Henry Steele Commager, *Freedom and Order* (Cleveland: World, 1966), vii.

60. "*Literary History of the United States*, Information for Contributors," March 27, 1943, and Commager's contract with the editors, March 27, 1943, in Spiller and Johnson: *Literary History of the United States* file, HSCP.

61. Robert Spiller to Henry Steele Commager, September 26, 1944, in Spiller and Johnson: *Literary History of the United States* file, HSCP.

62. Henry Steele Commager, "The Hope of Reform," in *Literary History of the United States*, ed. Robert Spiller et al. (1946; rev. ed., New York: Macmillan, 1953), 1111.

63. Ibid., 1108.

64. Ibid., 1110–11.

65. Nevins reminiscences, 278–79.

66. Allan Nevins to Commager, July 15, 1947, Allan Nevins file, HSCP.

67. Allan Nevins to Commager, June 25, 1948, Allan Nevins file, HSCP.

68. Ibid. Fifteen years later, in his oral history for Columbia University, Nevins remembered the episode quite differently and put all the blame on Arthur Brook. Nevins claimed that Brook "dealt me a treacherous stroke with relation to the Commager volumes. Henry Commager wrote what I deemed an admirable account of the cultural and intellectual history of the years from 1912 to 1950. Arthur Brook took fright,

however, at some of Henry Commager's expressed views, which seemed to him excessively liberal: he feared that they would deprive him of a sale in the colleges and high schools in the more conservative parts of the United States. Behind my back, and without my knowledge, he arranged for the transfer of Commager's book to the New Haven office of the Yale University Press, removing them from the series of eight volumes which I had planned, and enabling New Haven to bring them out as an entirely separate, independent work which, under the title *The American Mind*, won an instantaneous success." Nevins reminiscences, 279–80. For Commager's discussion of sexuality, see *The American Mind* (New Haven: Yale University Press, 1950), 120–25.

69. Commager, *The American Mind*, 281.

70. Richard Hofstadter, *Social Darwinism in American Thought, 1860–1915* (Philadelphia: University of Pennsylvania Press, 1944); Morton White, *Social Thought in America: The Revolt against Formalism* (New York: Viking, 1949); Perry Miller, ed., *American Thought: Civil War to World War I* (New York: Rinehart, 1954).

71. Jumonville, *Critical Crossings*.

72. Commager, *The American Mind*, 320.

73. Ibid., 326, 374–390.

74. Ibid., 102.

75. Ibid., vii.

76. For example, ibid., 407, 409, 413, 420.

77. Dixon Wecter, "How We Tick," *Saturday Review*, March 11, 1950, 11–12; Morton White, "The American Soul and the Brave Historian," *New Republic*, April 24, 1950, 19–20.

78. Arthur Schlesinger Jr., "America: Inventory and Appraisal," *Nation*, April 22, 1950, 376–78; Richard M. Weaver, "Books," *Commonweal*, May 5, 1950, 101–3.

79. William Leuchtenburg, letter to author, June 12, 1992.

80. *New Yorker*, April 8, 1950, 106.

81. *Time*, March 27, 1950, 110–12.

82. Commager, *The American Mind*, 262.

CHAPTER 4

1. Henry Steele Commager, "Our Entrance into the World War," *Yale Review* 27, no. 4 (June 1938): 855–57.

2. Henry Steele Commager, "The New Year Puts a Challenge to Us," *New York Times Magazine*, January 1, 1939, 1–2, 12. See also Henry Steele Commager, "Conduct of the War," *Senior Scholastic*, April 20–25, 1942, 6, 35.

3. CDAAA letter, over Commager's signature, June 5, 1940, WWII-CDAAA file, HSCP.

4. For Kirchwey, Schuman, and Hook, see Neil Jumonville, *Critical Crossings: The New York Intellectuals in Postwar America* (Berkeley: University of California Press, 1991), chap. 1.

5. Henry Steele Commager, "Far-Reaching 'Distortions of History,'" *New York Times Magazine*, October 27, 1940, 5.

6. Ibid., 18. See also Henry Steele Commager, "Why the War Came," *Senior Scholastic*, February 2, 1942, 8, 32. Here Commager told his high school readers that "war came because we were inadequately prepared for it," for if we had been "completely prepared," then "no power would have dared to attack us." This is a far more military argument than the philosophical and moral case he made to his *New York Times Magazine* audience.

7. Henry Steele Commager, "Are We Creating a Dictator?" *New York Times Magazine*, March 2, 1941, 3, 23–24.

8. Peter Novick, *That Noble Dream* (New York: Cambridge University Press, 1988), 247–48.

9. Ibid., 248.

10. Merle Curti, letter to author, December 18, 1991.

11. Novick, *That Noble Dream*, 282–83.

12. Herman Belz, "Andrew C. McLaughlin and Liberal Democracy: Scientific History in Support of the Best Regime," *Reviews in American History* 19 (September 1991): 446.

13. Gregory M. Pfitzer, *Samuel Eliot Morison's Historical World* (Boston: Northeastern University Press, 1991), 64–67, 172.

14. Barbara Tuchman, *Practicing History* (New York: Ballantine, 1982), 6–7.

15. "Historians Forecast Fate of Nazi Empire," *New York Times*, June 8, 1946, 22.

16. Major Frank Monaghan to Henry Steele Commager, October 23, 1943, in WWII: Work for Military during the War file, HSCP.

17. Memorandum from Lt. Colonel John M. Kemper to the Assistant Secretary of War, June 26, 1943, in WWII: Work for Military during the War file, HSCP.

18. Memorandum from Oliver L. Spaulding, Brig. Gen., U.S.A., Ret., to the President of the Committee on Historical Work in the War Department, June 24, 1943, in WWII: Work for Military during the War file, HSCP.

19. Memorandum from J. A. Ulio, Major General, The Adjutant General, August 3, 1943, in WWII: Work for Military during the War file, HSCP.

20. A series of three memos, two in rough draft form, and one slightly more polished on Columbia University letterhead, written by Commager probably in 1943, but with no date, WWII: Work for Military during the War file, HSCP.

21. Stanley Silverman, OWI Special Events Section, to Henry Steele Commager, February 22, 1944, and Mabel Travis Wood, managing editor, *USA*, to Henry Steele Commager, April 17, 1944, WWII: Work for Military during the War file, HSCP.

22. Dorothea Beckman, OWI Special Events Section, to Henry Steele Commager, August 1, 1944, and Marion Lowndes, OWI Features Division, to Henry Steele Commager, January 22 and May 2, 1945, WWII: Work for Military during the War file, HSCP.

23. Lt. Colonel Alpheus Smith to Henry Steele Commager, November 5, 1945, WWII: Work for Military during the War file. Colonel T. V. Smith to Commager, January 4, 1946; Perry Jester, Division of Training Services, Department of State, to Commager, January 24, 1946; William Nelson, editor of *Amerika Illustrated*, to Commager, May 9 and October 29, 1946; and Rear Admiral Thomas Binford to Commager, December 10, 1951; all in Military and Government Work after WWII file, HSCP. *Amerika Illustrated* was a publication produced by the Office of International Information and Cultural Affairs (OIC), part of the Department of State, and intended for distribution in the Soviet Union. The OIC wsa created in January 1946 to replace the Office of War Information and was predecessor to the United States Information Agency (USIA), created by Congress in 1948. Paul Claussen, Office of the Historian, U.S. Department of State, interview by author by telephone, May 7, 1998.

24. Marion Sanders, Magazine Branch OIC, to Henry Steele Commager, November 20, 1946, and Royce Moch, Magazine Liaison Section, Department of State, to Commager, December 27, 1946, Military and Government Work after WWII file, HSCP.

25. Dixon Wecter, "How We Tick," *Saturday Review*, March 11, 1950, 11.

26. Henry Steele Commager, interview by author, Amherst, Mass., August 22, 1988. Allan Nevins and Henry Steele Commager, *The Pocket History of the United States* (New York: Pocket Books, 1942), ii, iv; Nevins and Commager, *The Pocket History of the United States*, 5th ed. (New York: Washington Square Press, 1967); and Nevins and Commager, *A Short History of the United States* (New York: Random House, 1945).

27. Nevins and Commager, *A Short History*, ix–xi.

28. Ibid., v, 3–4.

29. Ibid., 99, 110, 115.

30. Ibid., 126.

31. Ibid., 295, 301, 304.

32. Theodore Hamerow, *Reflections on History and Historians* (Madison: University of Wisconsin Press, 1987), 46–47.

33. For discussion of the movement toward specialization and away from narrative history, see David Levin, *History as Romantic Art* (Stanford: Stanford University Press, 1959), chaps. 1–2, and ibid., chaps. 1–2.

34. Commager reminiscences, 61–62.

35. Allan Nevins, "Henry S. Commager as Historian: An Appreciation," in *Freedom and Reform: Essays in Honor of Henry Steele Commager*, ed. Harold M. Hyman and Leonard W. Levy (New York: Harper and Row, 1967), 7.

36. Allan Nevins, "Popularizer Plus," *Saturday Review of Literature*, January 4, 1941, 6.

37. Walter Lippmann to Allan Nevins, December 5, 1940, Professional Correspondence boxes, ANP.

38. Allan Nevins to Henry Steele Commager, no date but probably 1941, Allan Nevins file, HSCP.

39. Nevins reminiscences, 178–90.

40. Ibid., 190.

41. Ibid., 198, 208–9.

42. Ibid., 216–23. Allan Nevins to Henry Steele Commager, August 5, 1946, Allan Nevins file, HSCP.

43. Henry Steele Commager to Hans Duus, May 1925, Hans Duus file, HSCP.

44. "Will Lecture in England at Cambridge University," *New York Times* October 8, 1942, 17.

45. Denis Brogan to Henry Steele Commager, September 19, 1944, December 2, 1946, and November 2, 1949, Denis Brogan file, HSCP.

46. Leo Marx, letter to author, May 15, 1992; William Leuchtenburg, letter to author, June 12, 1992.

47. Curti, letter to author.

48. Ibid.

49. Henry Steele Commager, *The Study of History* (Columbus, Ohio: Charles Merrill, 1966), 54–55.

50. Henry Steele Commager, "Propaganda in American History," *Senior Scholastic*, November 2, 1942, 12.

51. Allan Nevins to Henry Steele Commager, February 17, 1945, Allan Nevins file, HSCP.

52. Henry Steele Commager, "Where Are We Headed?" *Atlantic*, February 1946, 54.

53. Ibid., 55, 57.

54. Ibid., 58.

55. Ibid., 59.
56. Ibid.

CHAPTER 5

1. Henry Steele Commager, "Struensee and the Reform Movement in Denmark" (Ph.D. diss., University of Chicago, 1928), 252–53.

2. Henry Steele Commager, *Theodore Parker* (Boston: Little, Brown, 1936), 169–70; Thomas Jefferson, "Notes on the State of Virginia," in *The Portable Thomas Jefferson*, ed. Merrill Peterson (New York: Penguin, 1980), 211.

3. Henry Steele Commager, "The New Year Puts a Challenge to Us," *New York Times Magazine*, January 1, 1939, 1.

4. Leo Marx, letter to author, May 15, 1992.

5. Henry Steele Commager, "To Secure the Blessings of Liberty," *New York Times Magazine*, April 9, 1939, 4, 16.

6. Henry Steele Commager, "The Investigating Power of Congress," *Senior Scholastic*, February 5, 1940, 7, and Commager, "Conduct of the War," *Senior Scholastic*, April 20–25, 1942, 6, 35.

7. Henry Steele Commager, *The American Mind* (New Haven: Yale University Press, 1950), 413.

8. "Commager Decries U.S.-British Tiffs," *New York Times*, October 24, 1945, 21.

9. Henry Steele Commager, "Washington Witch-Hunt," in *Freedom and Order* (Cleveland: Meridian, 1966), 73–74; first published in the *Nation*, 1947.

10. "Forum Criticizes House Committee," *New York Times*, October 21, 1948, 14.

11. "Commager, Berle Score U.S. 'Jitters,'" *New York Times*, March 4, 1950, 9.

12. "Commager Attacks Loyalty Oath Policy as 'Fat-Headed Pattern of American Life,'" *New York Times*, October 10, 1951, 6.

13. "Vigilante Trend in U.S. Is Feared," *New York Times*, May 27, 1952, 23.

14. "Amnesty Is Asked for Reds in Jail," *New York Times*, December 21, 1955, 20; "L.I. School Cancels Talk by Commager," *New York Times*, November 21, 1956, 28.

15. The textbook was probably one of several versions he did in the 1930s and 1940s with Row, Peterson—likely brought into the collaboration by his former professor and mentor William E. Dodd. These included Eugene Campbell Barker, William E. Dodd, and Commager, *Our Nation's Development* (Evanston, Ill.: Row, Peterson, 1934 and 1937); Barker and Commager, *Our Nation* (1941); and Barker, Commager, and Walter P. Webb, *The Building of Our Nation* (1937, 1959, and 1961).

16. G. M. Jones to Henry Steele Commager, March 16, 1950, McCarthyism file, HSCP.

17. "Anti-Red Extremes Feared by Eurich," *New York Times*, April 7, 1951, 17; "Sarah Lawrence Gives 73 Degrees," *New York Times*, May 31, 1952, 37; "Free Discussion Held Restrained," *New York Times*, March 27, 1954, 14; "'Egghead' Label Called Handicap," *New York Times*, April 9, 1954, 25; "Commager Assails Oaths for Teachers," *New York Times*, November 8, 1954, 12; "Red Control Act Scored by Panel," *New York Times*, February 13, 1955, 29.

18. "Denial of Award to Professor Hit," *New York Times*, June 14, 1959, 81; Henry Steele Commager, letter to the editor, *New York Times*, June 23, 1959, 32.

19. Peter Novick, *That Noble Dream* (New York: Cambridge University Press, 1988), 325–32, Ellen Schrecker, *No Ivory Tower* (New York: Oxford University Press, 1986), chaps.

9–10; Lionel S. Lewis, *Cold War on Campus* (New Brunswick, N.J.: Transaction Books, 1988), chap. 9; Jonathan M. Wiener, "Radical Historians and the Crisis in American History, 1959–1980," *Journal of American History* 76, no. 2 (September 1989): 402–4; Henry Nash Smith to Daniel Aaron, December 16, 1944, and February 26, 1945, DAP; Henry Nash Smith, "Legislatures, Communists, and State Universities," *Pacific Spectator* 3, no. 3 (Summer 1949).

20. Commager reminiscences, 306–7, 314–16.

21. Malcolm Cowley, "Matty for One," *New Republic*, April 24, 1950, 21. "What I Have to Do," *Time*, April 10, 1950, 40–43.

22. Thomas Cochran to Henry Steele Commager, April 4, 1950, Thomas Cochran file, HSCP.

23. Commager, "Red-Baiting in the Colleges," in *Freedom and Order*, 78–85.

24. R. M. MacIver to Henry Steele Commager, October 18, 1951, McCarthyism and Anti-communism file, HSCP.

25. Alfred H. Hetkin, letter to the editor, *New York Times Magazine*, November 22, 1953, 78. Susan Faulkner, letter to the editor, *New York Times Magazine*, July 17, 1949, 4. "Five Rights Exponents Win Hillman Prizes," *New York Times*, April 1, 1954, 21. "Sevareid Decries Narrow Teaching," *New York Times*, April 21, 1955, 15. Crane Brinton, "Our Freedoms Have Worked," *New York Herald Tribune Book Review*, May 30, 1954, 9. Claude Fuess, "The Great Danger," *Saturday Review*, May 1, 1954, 38–39.

26. Henry Steele Commager, *Freedom, Loyalty, Dissent* (New York: Oxford University Press, 1954), 31, 18, 23.

27. Michael Young, letter to the editor, *New York Times Magazine*, September 12, 1948, 2. Karl E. Yount Jr. to Henry Steele Commager, June 14, 1954, McCarthyism and Anticommunism file, HSCP; Yount referred to Commager's discussion on page 77 of his book. John P. O'Rourke, letter to the editor, *New York Times Magazine*, July 17, 1949, 4.

28. Commager, *Freedom, Loyalty, Dissent*, 98, 106.

29. Ibid., 108–10, 122.

30. John Oakes, "The Exhilarating Search," *New York Times Book Review*, April 25, 1954, 10.

31. Letters to the editor, *New York Times Magazine*, November 22, 1953, 79.

32. Commager, *Freedom, Loyalty, Dissent*, 144–47, 152–53.

33. Letters to the editor, *Harper's*, November 1947, n.p.

34. Commager reminiscences, 49–50.

35. Ibid.

36. Gregory M. Pfitzer, *Samuel Eliot Morison's Historical World* (Boston: Northeastern University Press, 1991), 230–33.

37. Louis Budenz, "The Plight of the Liberals," *American Mercury*, April 1955, 29–32.

38. Lester Markel to Commager, July 29, 1957, New York Times file, HSCP.

39. Letters to the editor, *Harper's*, November 1947, n.p.

40. Irving Kristol, " 'Civil Liberties,' 1952—a Study in Confusion," *Commentary* 13, no. 3 (March 1952): 229–30. Commager discussed Shura Lewis in his 1947 *Harper's* article "Who Is Loyal to America?" which became chap. 5 of *Freedom, Loyalty, Dissent*.

41. Kristol, " 'Civil Liberties,' " 231–32.

42. Michael Wreszin, *A Rebel in Defense of Tradition* (New York: Basic, 1994), 259.

43. Arthur Schlesinger Jr., letter to author, May 13, 1992.

44. Arthur Schlesinger Jr., *The Vital Center* (Boston: Houghton Mifflin, 1949), pp. 115, 136, 150. Hannah Dorner (executive director of the ICCASP) to Commager, August 2, 1946, and Schlesinger to Commager, January 3, 1947, in Arthur Schlesinger Jr. file, HSCP.

45. Henry Steele Commager, "The Survival of Liberalism in Our World," New York *Herald Tribune Weekly Book Review*, September 11, 1949, 1.

46. Ibid.

47. Schlesinger, *The Vital Center*, 37; Neil Jumonville, *Critical Crossings: The New York Intellectuals in Postwar America* (Berkeley: University of California Press, 1991), chap. 1.

48. On Schlesinger's anticommunist ties to the New York Intellectuals, see Michael Wreszin, "Arthur Schlesinger, Jr., Scholar-Activist in Cold War America: 1946–1956," *Salmagundi* 63–64 (Spring–Summer 1984): 268–69. For his anticommunism generally, see Schlesinger, *The Vital Center*. On his antiabsolutist connections to the New York group, see Neil Jumonville, "The New York Intellectuals' Defence of the Intellect," *Queen's Quarterly* 97, no. 2 (Summer 1990): 290–304, and Arthur Schlesinger Jr., "The Opening of the American Mind," *New York Times Book Review*, July 23, 1989, 1, 23–24. For his debt to Niebuhr, see Marcus Cunliffe, "Arthur M. Schlesinger, Jr.," in *Pastmasters*, ed. Marcus Cunliffe and Robin Winks (New York: Harper and Row, 1969), 363–64, 373–74. Daniel Bell noted that he, Niebuhr, Lionel Trilling, and Richard Hofstadter were all influenced by the winds of irony, complexity, tragedy, ambiguity, capriciousness, and limitation at midcentury. "The thing which put together Niebuhr, Trilling, and Hofstadter," Bell reported, "is the emphasis on the tragic sense of life." Daniel Bell, interview by author, May 20, 1985, and Jumonville, *Critical Crossings*, 124–26.

49. Henry Steele Commager, *The Study of History* (Columbus, Ohio: Charles Merrill, 1966), viii.

50. Arthur Schlesinger Jr., "The Historian as Participant," in *Historical Studies Today*, ed. Felix Gilbert and Stephen Graubard (New York: Norton, 1972), 399–400.

51. Henry Steele Commager, *The American Mind* (New Haven: Yale University Press, 1950), 433.

52. Thomas Jefferson, "A Bill for Establishing Religious Freedom," in *The Portable Jefferson*, ed. Merrill Peterson (New York: Penguin, 1980), 252–53.

53. Schlesinger, *The Vital Center*, 212–17.

54. Henry Steele Commager, "Red-Baiting in the Colleges," in *Freedom and Order*, 83–84; first published in the *New Republic* in 1949.

55. Commager, "What Ideas Are Safe?" in *Freedom and Order*, 86–90; first published in *Saturday Review* in 1949 and reprinted in *Freedom, Loyalty, Dissent*.

56. Commager, "Is Freedom Really Necessary?" in *Freedom and Order*, 97–98; first published in *Saturday Review* in 1953 and reprinted in *Freedom, Loyalty, Dissent*.

57. "American Revival for Freedom Urged," *New York Times*, February 27, 1952, 4.

58. Commager, *The American Mind*, 98–100.

59. Sidney Hook, "Unpragmatic Liberalism," *New Republic*, May 24, 1954, 19.

60. Ibid., 20.

61. Henry Steele Commager, "Does the Klan Ride to Its Death?" *Senior Scholastic*, October 7, 1946, 7.

62. Hook, "Unpragmatic Liberalism," 19.

63. Letter from Henry Steele Commager to Allan Nevins, October 26 (no year, but probably in the 1960s), ANP.

64. Commager, interview by author, Amherst, Mass., August 22, 1988.

65. Commager, *Freedom and Order*, 282.

66. Commager reminiscences, 304.

67. Hook, letter to author, December 19, 1988.

68. *New York Times*, October 23, 1949, 62.

69. Alfred Kazin, letter to author, June 26, 1992.

70. Jacques Barzun, letter to author, July 22, 1993.

71. William F. Buckley Jr. to Henry Steele Commager, September 23, 1959, William F. Buckley Jr. file, HSCP. William F. Buckley Jr., letter to author, May 27, 1992.

72. William F. Buckley Jr. to Henry Steele Commager, October 14, 1959, William F. Buckley Jr. file, HSCP.

73. See, for example, Henry Steele Commager to Hans Duus, January 3, 1925, Hans Duus file, HSCP.

74. Henry Commager, "England and the Oregon Treaty of 1846," *Oregon Historical Quarterly* 28, no. 1 (March 1927): 18–38; Henry Steele Commager, "Struensee and the Reform Movement in Denmark" (Ph.D. diss., University of Chicago, 1928).

75. Mary Powlesland Commager, interview by author, Amherst, Mass., June 4, 1991.

76. For Commager's recognition of his great-grandfather, see the dedication page in his *The Blue and the Gray* (New York: Bobbs-Merrill, 1950). Interestingly, the middle name Henry adopted was not his great-grandfather's Steel (which was Henry's great-great-grandmother's maiden name) but Steele. The first appearance of the final *e* on the end of the name is with his uncle Harry Steele Commager, born in 1878. Henry no doubt adopted the form Steele to distinguish himself from his great-grandfather. Robert F. Commagere, Genealogy of the Commagere Family (unpublished), Los Angeles, 1997; copy in possession of the author.

77. William F. Buckley Jr. to Henry Steele Commager, October 14, 1959, William F. Buckley Jr. file, HSCP.

78. Henry Steele Commager to William F. Buckley Jr., October 27, 1959, William F. Buckley Jr. file. Nevin O. Winter, *A History of Northwest Ohio* (Chicago: Lewis Publishing, 1917), 3:1468–71. Stewart Sifakis, *Who Was Who in the Civil War* (New York: Facts on File, 1988), 136. Mark Mayo Boatner, *The Civil War Dictionary*, rev. ed. (New York: David McKay, 1988), 168.

79. William F. Buckley Jr. to Henry Steele Commager, November 3, 1959, William F. Buckley Jr. file, HSCP.

80. William F. Buckley Jr. to Henry Steele Commager, November 3, 1959, William F. Buckley Jr. file, HSCP.

81. Mary Powlesland Commager, interview.

82. Henry Steele Commager, "Urgent Query: Why Do We Lack Statesmen?" *New York Times Magazine*, January 17, 1960, 21, 65–67; W. F. Rickenbacker, "The Spacious Ideas of Mr. Commager," *National Review*, February 27, 1960, 133–35.

83. John Chamberlain, "Statesmen and the Impossible," *National Review*, March 12, 1960, 167.

CHAPTER 6

1. *New York Times*, Friday, February 8, 1952, 18.

2. Fred L. Schultz, "New Ideas from a Seasoned Historian," *American History Illustrated*, May 1982, 18.

3. Richard Morris, "The View from the Top of Fayerweather," in *Freedom and Reform*, ed. Harold Hyman and Leonard Levy (New York: Harper and Row, 1967), 1–3. Joseph

Deitch, "The Commagers Mined the Gold in 'St. Nick,'" *Christian Science Monitor Magazine*, November 11, 1950, 14.

4. Leonard Levy, letter to author, May 24, 1992.

5. John Thomas, letter to author, October 3, 1992; Linda Kerber, "The Direction of American Studies in the United States," *Nanzan Review of American Studies* 11 (1989): 7; Levy, letter to author.

6. Christopher Lasch, letter to author, September 27, 1992.

7. Levy, letter to author.

8. William Leuchtenburg, letter to author, June 12, 1992.

9. Levy, letter to author.

10. Harold Hyman, letter to author, June 17, 1992.

11. Levy, letter to author. Leuchtenburg, letter to author.

12. Hyman, letter to author.

13. "Allan Nevins," *Political Science Quarterly* 86 (September 1971): 559. Ray Allen Billington, "Allan Nevins, Historian: A Personal Reminiscence," in Allan Nevins, *Allan Nevins on History*, compiled and introduced by Ray Allen Billington (New York: Charles Scribner's Sons, 1975), xv.

14. David Donald, interview by author, Cambridge, Mass., February 21, 1989; William Leuchtenburg, letter to author, June 10, 1996.

15. Billington, "Allan Nevins, Historian," xii–xiii. Levy, letter to author.

16. Nevins reminiscences, 153. Billington, "Allan Nevins, Historian," xiii.

17. Dwight W. Morrow Jr. to Henry Steele Commager, September 28, 1972, Allan Nevins file, HSCP.

18. Henry Steele Commager, Obituary for Allan Nevins, *American Historical Review* 77, no. 3 (June 1972): 870. "Allan Nevins," 559. Billington, "Allan Nevins, Historian," xx.

19. Donald, interview. See also Donald F. Tingley, "Allan Nevins: A Reminiscence," *Journal of the Illinois State Historical Society* 66, no. 2 (Summer 1973): 179, and Mort R. Lewis, "Allan Nevins' Triumph of Will," *American History Illustrated* 11, no. 9 (January 1977): 27.

20. Tingley, "Allan Nevins: A Reminiscence," 179.

21. Meredith Mayer (Nevins's daughter), letter to author, May 28, 1996. The Carroll sisters reportedly thought the incident funny. This is perhaps the most famous story of Nevins, and it has taken on a life of its own, with various characters in attendance. Donald Tingley recounts it as two graduate students. Tingley, ibid., 180–81. "This happened to us in California!" according to Commager's daughter Lisa. Lisa Commager, letter to author, June 30, 1996. William Leuchtenburg heard the story differently: "A young woman came to see his country home for the weekend. He greeted her by saying 'Let me show you around the house. Here is the living room. Here is the dining room. Here is my study. Each morning I come in here and sit down in this chair at this typewriter, roll in paper like this, and start typing.' He demonstrated this by typing away, and, the story goes, that's the last she saw of him for the rest of the weekend." Leuchtenburg, letter to author, June 10, 1996.

22. Jacques Barzun, letter to author, July 22, 1993.

23. Tingley, "Allan Nevins: A Reminiscence." Billington, "Allan Nevins, Historian." Lewis, "Allan Nevins' Triumph of Will."

24. Billington, "Allan Nevins, Historian," xviii–xix.

25. Commager to Hans Duus, September 7, 1925, Hans Duus file, HSCP.

26. Harold J. Laski, *The Rise of European Liberalism* (London: Allen and Unwin, 1936). Bernard Bailyn, *The Ideological Origins of the American Revolution* (Cambridge: Harvard University Press, 1967).

27. Herbert Croly, *The Promise of American Life* (1909; reprint, Cambridge: Harvard University Press, 1965). Charles Forcey, *The Crossroads of Liberalism* (New York: Oxford University Press, 1961), 28–29.

28. Henry Steele Commager, "When Labor Challenged Government," *Senior Scholastic*, May 24–29, 1943, 5.

29. Henry Steele Commager, "Bureaucracy: Is Red Tape Necessary?" *Senior Scholastic*, October 2, 1944, 8.

30. Henry Steele Commager, "Democracy and Planning," *American Mercury*, January 1946, 113–14.

31. Henry Steele Commager, *The American Mind* (New Haven: Yale University Press, 1950), 338.

32. Ibid., 345.

33. Henry Steele Commager, *Freedom and Order* (Cleveland: Meridian, 1966), 189–90, 193.

34. Ibid., 232, 235.

35. On Hoover see Joan Hoff Wilson, *Herbert Hoover: Forgotten Progressive* (Boston: Little, Brown, 1975).

36. Mayer, letter to author.

37. *New York Times*, October 6, 1952, 10. Mark Van Doren, Ernest Nagel, Paul Lazarsfeld, and Robert Merton were among the others who signed the statement.

38. *New York Times*, October 11, 1952, 18.

39. Merle Curti, *American Paradox* (New Brunswick: Rutgers University Press, 1956), 69. Commager reminiscences, 41–43.

40. Gregory M. Pfitzer, *Samuel Eliot Morison's Historical World* (Boston: Northeastern University Press, 1991), 214–15.

41. *New York Times*, January 10, 1956, 25.

42. Allan Nevins to Commager, October 18, 1959, Allan Nevins file, HSCP. Commager to Nevins, October 27, 1959, and February 10, 1960, box 76, ANP.

43. *New York Times*, June 8, 1960, 1, 27; June 9, 1960, 15; June 13, 1960, 1, 19; June 17, 1960, 16, 18.

44. Commager to Allan Nevins, June 17, 1960, box 76, ANP.

45. Commager to Allan Nevins, Thanksgiving Day 1960, box 76, ANP.

46. Henry Steele Commager, letter to the editor, *New York Times*, October 2, 1962, 38; Alfred E. Kahn, letter to the editor, *New York Times*, October 15, 1962, 28.

47. Commager to Hans Duus, September 7, 1925, Hans Duus file, HSCP.

48. Henry Steele Commager, "The U.S. in 1970—Three Forecasts," *New York Times Magazine*, May 17, 1959, 76. For a similar sentiment in 1961, see his "Our Declaration Is Still a Rallying Cry," in *Freedom and Order*, 174–77; first published in the *New York Times Magazine*.

49. Henry Steele Commager, letter to the editor, *New York Times*, May 17, 1960, 36.

50. Commager to Allan Nevins, September 23, 1961, box 76, ANP.

51. Commager to Allan Nevins, October 15, 1961, box 76, ANP. Nevins to Commager, October 17, 1961, Allan Nevins file, HSCP.

52. Commager to Allan Nevins, October 23, 1962, box 76, ANP. Nevins to Commager, October 24, 1962, Allan Nevins file, HSCP.

53. Allan Nevins to Commager, August 19, 1963, Allan Nevins file, HSCP.

54. Henry Steele Commager, letter to the editor, *New York Times*, April 17, 1963, 40.

55. On the League of Nations, see Commager reminiscences, 248–49.

56. *New York Times*, October 16, 1959, 33. Henry Steele Commager, "Brave World of the Year 2000," *New York Times Magazine*, November 1, 1959, 24.

57. Henry Steele Commager, "Conduct of the War," *Senior Scholastic*, April 20–25, 1942, 35; Commager, "Up from Slavery," *Senior Scholastic*, March 15–20, 1943, 7.

58. Commager, "Up from Slavery," 7; Henry Steele Commager, "Nisei: What Future for the Japanese-Americans?" *Senior Scholastic*, January 22, 1945, 7. For similar sentiments, see also Henry Steele Commager, "The Race Problem in America," *Senior Scholastic*, September 25, 1944, 9.

59. Henry Steele Commager, "The States and the Poll Tax," *Senior Scholastic*, February 26, 1945, 9.

60. Henry Steele Commager, "The Negro Problem in Our Democracy," *American Mercury*, June 1945, 751–56.

61. Samuel Eliot Morison and Henry Steele Commager, *The Growth of the American Republic*, 4th ed. (New York: Oxford University Press, 1951), 1:537–39. This section had not changed substantially ("negroes" were now "Negroes") since the original edition in 1930 (415–18).

62. August Meier, *A White Scholar and the Black Community, 1945–1965* (Amherst: University of Massachusetts Press, 1992), 3–7.

63. August Meier, letter to author, May 14, 1992. See also August Meier and Elliot Rudwick, *Black History and the Historical Profession, 1915–1980* (Urbana: University of Illinois Press, 1986), 244.

64. Peter Novick, *That Noble Dream* (New York: Cambridge University Press, 1988), 350 n.

65. Samuel Eliot Morison to Commager, May 1, 1950, and June 1, 1950, Samuel Eliot Morison file, HSCP.

66. Samuel Eliot Morison to Commager, June 12, 1950, Samuel Eliot Morison file, HSCP.

67. Samuel Eliot Morison to August Meier, June 13, 1950 (copy sent to Commager), Samuel Eliot Morison file, HSCP; John Hope Franklin, letter to author, August 14, 1992.

68. Meier, *A White Scholar and the Black Community*, 10–12.

69. Meier, letter to author. Commager reminiscences, 310.

70. Levy, letter to author.

71. Ibid.

72. Ibid.

73. Meier, letter to author. August Meier, "The Racial Ancestry of the Mississippi College Negro," *American Journal of Physical Anthropology* 7 (June 1949): 227–40. Meier, *A White Scholar and the Black Community*, 10 and chap. 1.

74. Meier, letter to author.

75. Ibid.

76. Ibid.

77. Ibid. George M. Fredrickson, letter to author, August 23, 1991.

78. Henry Steele Commager, *Majority Rule and Minority Rights* (1943; reprint, Gloucester, Mass.: Peter Smith, 1958), 55, 64.

79. Franklin, letter to author.

80. Novick, *That Noble Dream*, 507. Richard Kluger, *Simple Justice* (New York: Knopf, 1976), 614–21.

81. Charles S. Johnson to Commager, March 22, 1952, Race and Ethnicity file, HSCP; Mrs. William Thomas Mason to Commager, April 16, 1957, and Senator Paul Douglas to Commager, July 11, 1957, both in Race and Ethnicity file, HSCP; Commager to John Hope Franklin, October 2, 1957, and John Hope Franklin to Commager, November 15, 1957, John Hope Franklin file, HSCP.

82. Commager to Reinhold Niebuhr, September 6, 1958, Race and Ethnicity file, HSCP.

83. Jonathan M. Wiener, "Radical Historians and the Crisis in American History, 1959–1980," *Journal of American History* 76, no. 2 (September 1989): 415. Daniel Joseph Singal, "Beyond Consensus: Richard Hofstadter and American Historiography," *American Historical Review* 89, no. 4 (October 1984): 993.

84. Commager to Nicholas Katzenbach, January 29, 1965, John Doar to Commager, February 1965, and Commager to John Doar, February 19, 1965, Race and Ethnicity file, HSCP.

85. Meier, letter to author.

86. *New York Times*, Tuesday, January 10, 1956, 33.

87. Commager reminiscences, 82–83. David Donald to Commager, April 19, 1959, David Donald file, HSCP.

88. Commager to Hans Duus, July 6, 1926, Hans Duus file, HSCP.

89. Commager to Merle Curti, January 13, 1956, MCP.

90. Allan Nevins to Commager, March 27, 1958, Allan Nevins file, HSCP.

91. Leuchtenburg, letter to author, June 10, 1996.

92. Henry Steele Commager, *Theodore Parker* (Boston: Little, Brown, 1936), 144–49, 98.

93. Ibid., 287.

94. Allan Nevins to Commager, October 18, 1957, Allan Nevins file, HSCP.

95. For stories on these representative events including Commager, see *New York Times*, May 16, 1953, 2; July 27, 1955, 25; December 18, 1955, 41; May 12, 1959, 9; November 13, 1960, 61; September 2, 1970, 36; January 10, 1976, 27; April 29, 1968, 29; and June 13, 1955, 17.

96. Document labeled "spring schedule," probably for 1967, in Miscellaneous Correspondence file, HSCP.

97. Lisa Commager, letter to author.

98. Leuchtenburg, letter to author, June 10, 1996.

99. Carol Newell, "Commager Has Shaped Both Amherst, American History," *Amherst Student*, May 24, 1992, 18. Allen Guttmann, letter to author, October 29, 1992.

100. Theodore Greene, interview by author, Amherst, Mass., June 12, 1991.

101. Leo Marx, letter to author, May 15, 1992.

102. Newell, "Commager."

103. Friederike Dewitz, the American studies secretary at Amherst, who had taken a class from Commager in 1979, interview by author, Amherst, Mass., June 13, 1991.

104. Greene, interview. Lisa Commager, letter to author. Guttmann, letter to author.

105. Dewitz, interview. Gordon Levin, interview by author, Amherst, Mass., June 4, 1991. Greene, interview. Guttmann, letter to author.

106. Newell, "Commager." Guttmann, letter to author.

107. Greene, interview.

108. Henry Steele Commager to Amherst president Plimpton, May 20, 1964, American Studies and American Character file, HSCP. Guttmann, letter to author.

109. Henry Steele Commager to his lawyer in Boston, Mr. Johnson, September 17, 1972, Financial file, HSCP.

110. Newell, "Commager."

111. Henry Steele Commager to Merle Curti, June 24, 1956[?], MCP. Donald, interview.

112. Henry Steele Commager, ed., *The St. Nicholas Anthology* (New York: Random House, 1948), xix–xx. *New York Times*, January 19, 1958, 93; November 7, 1965, 91; July 1, 1956, 53; March 25, 1962, 91. Commager to Curti, June 24, 1956. Lisa Commager, letter to author.

113. Daniel Aaron, interview by author, Cambridge, Mass., May 4, 1990.

114. Christopher Lasch, letter to author.

115. Storm Jameson, *Journey from the North* (London: Collins and Harvill, 1970), 2:238–39.

116. Lasch, letter to author.

117. Ibid.

118. Henry Steele Commager to Hans Duus, September 7, 1925, and August 8, 1925, Hans Duus file, HSCP.

119. Henry Steele Commager to Alexander Meiklejohn, January 18, 1964, AMP. Lisa Commager, letter to author.

120. On Parkman's partial blindness, see William R. Taylor, "Francis Parkman," in *Pastmasters*, ed. Marcus Cunliffe and Robin Winks (New York: Harper and Row, 1969), 3, 10–11.

121. John D. Hicks to Henry Steele Commager, January 13, 1965, Miscellaneous Correspondence file, HSCP.

122. *New York Times*, March 29, 1968.

123. Henry Steele Commager, undated, in Biography file, HSCP. George Santayana, *Poems of George Santayana*, ed. Robert Hutchinson (New York: Dover, 1970), 3.

CHAPTER 7

1. Neil Jumonville, *Critical Crossings: The New York Intellectuals in Postwar America* (Berkeley: University of California Press, 1991).

2. Milton Cantor, interview by author, June 13, 1991.

3. Henry Steele Commager, "An Inquiry into 'Appeasement,'" *New York Times Magazine*, February 11, 1951, 39–40.

4. Commager to Allan Nevins, October 29, 1963, box 76, ANP.

5. Commager to Allan Nevins, October 22, 1963, box 76, and November 4, 1964, box 78, ANP.

6. *New York Times*, January 12, 1965, 36. Commager to Allan Nevins, April 20, 1965, box 81, ANP.

7. J. William Fulbright to Commager, December 15, 1964, and Commager to Fulbright, December 20, 1964, Vietnam War file, HSCP.

8. Commager to Lyndon Johnson, Robert McNamara, George Ball, and J. William Fulbright, February 7, 1965, Vietnam War file, HSCP.

9. Henry Steele Commager, letter to the *New York Times*, February 12, 1965, Vietnam War file, HSCP.

10. Henry Steele Commager, draft of letter to the editor of the *New York Times*, March 7, 1965, Vietnam War file, HSCP.

11. Henry Steele Commager, drafts of letters to the editor of the *Herald Tribune*, March 31, 1965, July 29, 1965, and December 1, 1965, Vietnam War file, HSCP.

12. *New York Times*, December 5, 1965, 13.

13. Ibid., April 5, 1967, 1–2.

14. Ibid., May 11, 1967, 9.

15. "The Week," *National Review*, August 8, 1967, 832. "For the Record," *National Review*, May 16, 1967, 542.

16. Donald F. Tingley, "Allan Nevins: A Reminiscence," *Journal of the Illinois State Historical Society* 66, no. 2 (Summer 1973): 183–85.

17. Commager reminiscences, 51.

18. Allan Nevins to Commager, May 3, 1964, Allan Nevins file, HSCP. Carl Bode and Malcolm Cowley, eds., *The Portable Emerson* (New York: Penguin, 1981), 667.

19. Commager to Allan Nevins, November 17 (no year), February 23, 1965, and April 20, 1965, box 81, ANP.

20. Allan Nevins to Commager, August 29, 1964, Allan Nevins file, HSCP.

21. Allan Nevins to Commager, April 26, 1965, Allan Nevins file, HSCP.

22. Allan Nevins to Commager, April 26, 1965, and April 30, 1965, Allan Nevins file, HSCP.

23. Allan Nevins to Commager, January 22, 1966, Allan Nevins file, HSCP. Mort R. Lewis, "Allan Nevins' Triumph of Will," *American History Illustrated* 11, no. 9 (January 1977): 32.

24. Commager to Allan Nevins, May 10 (no year), box 81, ANP.

25. Gregory M. Pfitzer, *Samuel Eliot Morison's Historical World* (Boston: Northeastern University Press, 1991), 270–71.

26. Commager reminiscences, 52–53.

27. For the split in the liberal intellectual community, see Jumonville, *Critical Crossings*, chaps. 1–3; and William L. O'Neill, *A Better World* (New York: Simon and Schuster, 1982).

28. Henry Steele Commager, "The Last Best Hope of Earth," *Senior Scholastic*, January 5–10, 1942, 13; Commager, "Why the War Came," *Senior Scholastic*, February 2, 1942, 8; Commager, "The Senators and the Peace," *Senior Scholastic*, April 5–10, 1943, 9; Commager, "The Lessons of April 6, 1917," *New York Times Magazine*, April 6, 1952, 13; and Commager, "Maker of History, Writer of History," *Reporter*, January, 19, 1954, 38.

29. Henry Steele Commager, "The Republican Party 'Is a Mess,' " *New York Times Magazine*, January 12, 1964.

30. Henry Steele Commager, letters to the editor, *New York Times*, May 17, 1960, 36, and April 17, 1963, 40. Commager to Allan Nevins, September 23, 1961, October 15, 1961, and October 23, 1962, box 76, ANP.

31. *New York Times*, February 21, 1967, 1, 16.

32. Henry Steele Commager, "Statement by Henry Steele Commager at the Hearings before the Committee on Foreign Relations of the United States Senate, February 20, 1967," Commager's own manuscript of his talk, copy in the Senator J. W. Fulbright and Fulbright Hearings file, HSCP.

33. Walter Lippmann to Commager, February 24, 1967, C. Vann Woodward to Commager, February 22, 1967, and Herman [last name?] to Commager, February 21, 1967, in the

Senator J. W. Fulbright and Fulbright Hearings file, HSCP. Henry Steele Commager, "How Not to Be a World Power," *New York Times Magazine*, March 12, 1967. Jay Gurian, "American Studies and the Creative Present," *Midcontinent American Studies Journal* 10, no. 1 (Spring 1969): 78. "Dr. King Advocates Quitting Vietnam," *New York Times*, February 26, 1967, 10.

34. Alfred Kazin to Commager, February 21, 1967, J. W. Fulbright and Fulbright Hearings file, HSCP.

35. Henry Steele Commager, "Where Are We Headed?" *Atlantic*, February 1946, 57–58.

36. J. William Fulbright to Commager, December 15, 1964, and Commager to Fulbright, December 20, 1964, Vietnam War file, HSCP.

37. Arthur Schlesinger Jr., *The Vital Center* (Boston: Houghton Mifflin, 1949), 221, 230, 240–41.

38. Henry Steele Commager, "The Old, the Poor, the Unemployed," *New York Times*, March 4, 1973, sec. 4, p. 13.

39. Commager to Allan Nevins, April 4 (no year, but probably 1969), box 81, ANP.

40. *New York Times*, October 2, 1969, 46.

41. Ibid., March 6, 1972, 32.

42. Ibid., March 23, 1972, 42.

43. Henry Steele Commager, *Freedom and Order* (Cleveland: Meridian, 1966), 307. Daniel Bell, "The End of American Exceptionalism" (1975), in *The Winding Passage* (New York: Basic Books, 1980), 245–71. Godfrey Hodgson, *America in Our Time* (Garden City, N.Y.: Doubleday, 1976), 16–17, 33–34, 38, 260.

44. Commager, *Freedom and Order*, 312.

45. Ibid., 312–13.

46. Henry Steele Commager, "The Democratic Party 'Is a Mess,'" *New York Times Magazine*, January 12, 1964, 95; Commager, "Is Freedom Dying in America?" *Look*, July 14, 1970, 21; Commager, "The Roots of Lawlessness," *Saturday Review*, February 13, 1971, 63.

47. Henry Steele Commager, "The Defeat of America," in *The Defeat of America* (New York: Simon and Schuster, 1974), 86, 101; essay first published in a slightly different form, as a review of Richard Barnet's *Roots of War*, under the title "The Defeat of America," *New York Review of Books*, October 5, 1972, 7–13.

48. Commager, "Defeat of America," 103–4.

49. Henry Nash Smith to Commager, October 1, 1972, Henry Nash Smith file, HSCP.

50. Jumonville, *Critical Crossings*, chaps. 1, 3.

51. For most of his life Hook thought of himself as a Jeffersonian; in fact, shortly before his death he claimed he was more of a Jeffersonian than was Commager (Hook, letter to author, December 19, 1988). While some might object to Hook's description of himself as a Jeffersonian, the term does underscore basic values shared by Hook and Commager about the benefits of intellectual freedom, open debate, and a marketplace of ideas. True, Hook wasn't a pure Jeffersonian, in the original conception of that term, but then neither was Commager.

52. Sidney Hook, "America Now: A Failure of Nerve?" *Commentary* 60, no. 1 (July 1975): 42.

53. Sidney Hook, "Unpragmatic Liberalism," *New Republic*, May 24, 1954, 19.

54. Leo Cherne, "Why We Can't Withdraw," *Saturday Review*, December 18, 1965, 17.

55. Mary McCarthy, *The Seventeenth Degree* (New York: Harcourt Brace Jovanovich, 1974), 149–55, 171–87. The book contains pieces McCarthy wrote on the Vietnam War as pamphlets or magazine articles. Also included is a reprint of Diana Trilling and Mary McCarthy, "On Withdrawing from Vietnam: An Exchange," *New York Review of Books*, January 18, 1968, 5–10.

56. Max Weber, "Politics as a Vocation," in *From Max Weber: Essays in Sociology*, ed. H. H. Gerth and C. Wright Mills (New York: Oxford University Press, 1946), 120, 126–27.

57. Hook, "Unpragmatic Liberalism." Irving Kristol, " 'Civil Liberties,' 1952—a Study in Confusion," *Commentary* 13, no. 3 (March 1952): 228–36. Roger Baldwin, letter to the editor, *Harper's*, November 1947, n.p.

58. Henry Steele Commager, "Are We Creating a Dictator?" *New York Times Magazine*, March 2, 1941, 3, 23–24.

59. Henry Steele Commager, "Presidential Power: The Issue Analyzed," *New York Times Magazine*, January 14, 1951, 11, 23–24.

60. *New York Times*, January 16, 1951, 10, and January 22, 1951, 16. Arthur Schlesinger Jr., *The Imperial Presidency* (Boston: Houghton Mifflin, 1973), 139.

61. Henry Steele Commager, "The Perilous Folly of Senator Bricker," *Reporter*, October 13, 1953, 12, 17.

62. Schlesinger, *The Imperial Presidency*, 138, 285–86.

63. Henry Steele Commager, "Can We Limit Presidential Power?" in *Defeat of America*, 48–58; first published in the *New Republic*, April 6, 1968.

64. Henry Steele Commager, "Determining on Peace and War" [reprint of Commager's Senate testimony], in *Defeat of America*, 59–81.

65. An example of this is a shift in the outlook of American liberalism, which in the eighteenth and nineteenth centuries was a doctrine defending individuals and which consequently in these centuries opposed the growth of the state, which represented the largest potential threat to the liberties of individuals. But at the beginning of the twentieth century, in the midst of the Industrial Revolution, when corporate power eclipsed that of the state, liberals made a significant change, abandoning their opposition to the state and turning to embrace it as a protector, shield, and countervailing force to that of the new and greater threat from corporations. Although liberals might be accused of having changed, they might argue that they kept the value of individual protection paramount, changing their commitments only to maintain a consistent value system.

66. Henry Steele Commager, "Is Freedom an Academic Question?" *Saturday Review*, June 20, 1964, 54–56.

67. Harvey Shapiro to Commager, March 26, 1964, New York Times file, HSCP.

68. Henry Steele Commager, "The Problem of Dissent," *Saturday Review*, December 18, 1965, 21, 23.

69. Henry Steele Commager, "The Nature of Academic Freedom," *Saturday Review*, August 27, 1966, 14; Commager to Mr. Price (*Herald Tribune*), April 3, 1966, Vietnam War file, HSCP.

70. Henry Steele Commager, "The University as Employment Agency," *New Republic*, February 24, 1968.

71. *New York Times*, November 12, 1969, 37. Among other signatories were Hannah Arendt, Ramsey Clark, F. W. Dupee, John Kenneth Galbraith, David Halberstam, Elizabeth

Hardwick, Richard Hofstadter, Murray Kempton, Robert Lowell, Mary McCarthy, George McGovern, Lewis Mumford, Ernest Nagel, Reinhold Niebuhr, Richard Rovere, Arthur Schlesinger Jr., Allen Tate, Andrew Young, and C. Vann Woodward.

72. "Commager Likens Kent Indictments to Fascist or Communist Reactions," Associated Press article, no paper or date, in Vietnam War file, HSCP. Brooks W. Maccracken to Commager, April 12, 1971, Commager to Maccracken, April 22, 1971, and Maccracken to Commager, April 26, 1971, Vietnam War file, HSCP.

73. *New York Times*, January 30, 1973, 12. Henry Steele Commager, "A Case for Amnesty," an article based on his Senate testimony, originally in *New York Review of Books*, April 6, 1972, reprinted in *Current* 140 (May 1972): 13–15.

74. Nicholas Violante to Commager, March 6, 1972, Mrs. James Gallo to Commager, March 15, 1972, and Joseph Ellis to Commager, March 12, 1972, Vietnam War file, HSCP.

75. Henry Steele Commager, "Why Student Rebellion?," *Current* 97 (July 1968): 14.

76. Commager to Allan Nevins, April 4 (no year, but probably 1969), box 81, ANP.

77. *New York Times*, April 26, 1969, 36, and May 5, 1969, 46.

78. Henry Steele Commager, "Topics: Revolution 1776 and 1969," *New York Times*, July 5, 1969, 18; Louis Lomax, letter to the editor, *New York Times*, July 19, 1969, 24.

79. Leo Marx, letter to author, May 15, 1992; William R. Taylor, "The Liberal Case," *Washington Post Book Week*, October 30, 1966, 2, 14.

80. *New York Times*, July 6, 1967, 18. *National Review*, July 25, 1967, 776. *New York Times*, April 22, 1968, 21, and August 26, 1968, 26. *National Review*, September 10, 1968, 926.

81. Commager to Allan Nevins, August 17 (no date, but probably 1968), box 81, ANP. Judy Oldham (McGovern for President Committee) to Commager, February 24, 1972, Social Issues file, HSCP. Commager to Mr. Oberdorfer, April 2, 1972, Vietnam War file, HSCP.

82. Henry Steele Commager, "Foreign Policy: Telling It Like It Isn't," *New York Times*, September 18, 1972, 25.

83. Henry Steele Commager, "On the Way to 1984," *Saturday Review*, April 15, 1967, 68.

84. Commager, "Is Freedom Dying in America?" 17. *New York Times*, June 18, 1971, 38.

85. Henry Steele Commager, "A Senator's Immunity," *New York Times*, October 15, 1971, 41.

86. Norman Dorsen (chairman of CPJ) to Commager, October 10, 1972, Committee for Public Justice file, HSCP.

87. Arthur Schlesinger Jr. to Commager, November 9, 1972, Arthur Schlesinger Jr. file, HSCP.

88. *New York Times*, January 14, 1972, 21.

89. Commager, "Defeat of America," 96–97.

90. *New York Times*, June 28, 1973, 1, 38. "Creating a New Who's Who," *Time*, July 9, 1973, 19.

91. *New York Times*, March 4, 1973, 1, 47.

92. Ibid., March 9, 1973, 18.

93. Commager, "Defeat of America," 106–8, 114–16.

94. *New York Times*, October 23, 1973, 32; Barbara Tuchman, *Practicing History* (New York: Ballantine, 1982), 297–301.

95. Henry Steele Commager, "The Real Bases for Impeachment," in *Defeat of America*, 141–49; reprinted from *Newsday*, May 12, 1974; Commager, "Five Grounds for Impeaching the President," *New York Times*, June 28, 1974, 33.

96. *New York Times*, July 13, 1974, 22.

1. Although American studies and American intellectual history are overlapping academic areas, I do not address the latter here as that would be too ambitious for one essay. I am aware that many intellectual historians who paid little attention to American studies as an entity still pursued the same questions as American studies scholars about the nature of American identity, mind, character, values, and myths, and I hope that interested readers will make their own connections between the two groups at appropriate points. In this essay I focus only on those historians, literary critics, cultural geographers, and others who wrote on American identity and myths and who are typically thought of as American studies figures.

2. Representative of the articles critical of this midcentury American studies approach are Bruce Kuklick, "Myth and Symbol in American Studies," *American Quarterly* 24, no. 4 (October 1972): 435–50, and Robert Sklar, "The Problem of an American Studies 'Philosophy': A Bibliography of New Directions," *American Quarterly* 27, no. 3 (August 1975): 245–62.

3. There have been several essays tracing the antagonism on the part of a younger generation to what might be called midcentury American studies. Among the best are Gene Wise, " 'Paradigm Dramas' in American Studies," *American Quarterly* 3, no. 1 (Spring 1979): 293–337; Wise, "The Contemporary Crisis in Intellectual History Studies," *Clio* 5, no. 1 (Fall 1975): 55–71; David Stannard, "American Historians and the Idea of National Character: Some Problems and Prospects," *American Quarterly* 23, no. 2 (May 1971): 202–20; and Luther Luedtke, "Not So Common Ground," in *The Study of American Culture: Contemporary Conflicts*, ed. Luther Luedtke (Deland, Fla.: Everett/Edwards, 1977), 323–67.

4. I am not referring to those who are often categorized as the "consensus historians"— Richard Hofstadter, Daniel Boorstin, Louis Hartz, and others. Instead I mean those American studies writers—such as Constance Rourke and F. O. Matthiessen, Henry Nash Smith, and Henry Steele Commager, or R. W. B. Lewis and John William Ward— whose work has focused on intellectual and cultural matters of American identity, mind, and character. Although American studies figures sometimes shared themes and a generational outlook with members of the consensus school, they stood apart from them on many issues. Further, while several of the American studies writers, such as Boorstin and Hartz, are thought of as consensus historians, it is as American studies scholars that I discuss them here.

5. For the connection between the growth of American intellectual history and cultural nationalism, see Robert Spiller, "Unity and Diversity in the Study of American Culture: The American Studies Association in Perspective," *American Quarterly* 25, no. 5 (December 1973): 611.

6. Van Wyck Brooks, *Three Essays on America* (New York: Dutton, 1934), and Claire Sprague, ed., *Van Wyck Brooks: The Early Years* (New York: Harper and Row, 1968); Harold Stearns, ed., *Civilization in the United States* (New York: Harcourt, Brace, 1922).

7. Ralph Henry Gabriel, "Vernon Louis Parrington," in *Pastmasters*, ed. Marcus Cunliffe and Robin Winks (New York: Harper and Row, 1969), 153; Malcolm Cowley, *Exile's Return* (1951; reprint, New York: Penguin, 1976), 27–33; F. O. Matthiessen, *American Renaissance* (New York: Oxford University Press, 1941), xvii.

8. Gabriel, "Parrington," 153. Richard Hofstadter, *The Progressive Historians* (New York: Knopf, 1968), 376–77, 389. Wise, " 'Paradigm Dramas,' " 305.

9. Gabriel, "Parrington," 153. Hofstadter, *Progressive Historians*, 375–76. Robert Berkhofer Jr., "Clio and the Culture Concept: Some Impressions of a Changing Relationship in American Historiography," in *The Idea of Culture in the Social Sciences*, ed. Louis Schneider and Charles Bonjean (New York: Cambridge University Press, 1973), 84. John Higham, *Writing American History* (Bloomington: Indiana University Press, 1970), 48–59.

10. Spiller, "Unity and Diversity," 612.

11. Richard Pells, *Radical Visions and American Dreams* (New York: Harper and Row, 1973).

12. Theodore Hamerow, *Reflections on History and Historians* (Madison: University of Wisconsin Press, 1987), 44.

13. Gabriel, "Parrington," 163.

14. Ibid., 164; Linda Kerber, "The Direction of American Studies in the United States," *Nanzan Review of American Studies* (Nagoya, Japan) 11 (1989): 2; Theodore P. Greene, "Remarks at the Fiftieth Anniversary Dinner for American Studies at Amherst College," June 2, 1989, photocopy provided to the author.

15. Henry Luce, "The American Century," *Life*, February 17, 1941, 61–65; Marcus Cunliffe quoted in Kerber, "Direction of American Studies," 2.

16. Peter Novick, *That Noble Dream* (New York: Cambridge University Press, 1988), 311.

17. The best and most detailed history of the early Harvard program is Joseph Gordon Hylton Jr., "American Civilization at Harvard, 1937–1987" (paper distributed at the Fiftieth Anniversary Celebration of the program at Harvard, May 9, 1987). For the history of other programs, see Wise, " 'Paradigm Dramas,' " 305–6.

18. Carl Bode, "The Start of the ASA," *American Quarterly* 31, no. 3 (Bibliography Issue, 1979): 345–54.

19. Myth-symbol writers searched for the emblematic expressions of American culture in history, literature, technology, or other related areas of thought. Their investigations did not pursue merely an image or metaphor but rather a symbol—an image or metaphor used repeatedly and subscribed to by a large proportion of the culture as a whole. Some of the prominent members and works associated with this outlook were Henry Nash Smith, *Virgin Land: The American West as Symbol and Myth* (Cambridge: Harvard University Press, 1950); Richard W. B. Lewis, *The American Adam* (Chicago: University of Chicago Press, 1955); John William Ward, *Andrew Jackson: Symbol for an Age* (New York: Oxford University Press, 1955); Leo Marx, *The Machine in the Garden* (New York: Oxford University Press, 1964); and Alan Trachtenberg, *Brooklyn Bridge: Fact and Symbol* (New York: Oxford University Press, 1965). Further, many other historians who have never been classified as character or myth-symbol historians might fit there comfortably. C. Vann Woodward, for example, has utilized the concepts of agrarian myth, southern identity, American mind, and American innocence, yet his work is rarely considered in these categories. C. Vann Woodward, *The Burden of Southern History*, rev. ed. (New York: New American Library, 1969), vii, ix–xi, 23–31; Woodward, *Thinking Back* (Baton Rouge: Louisiana State University Press, 1986), 105–18, 137; and Woodward, *The Future of the Past* (New York: Oxford University Press, 1989), 103–5, 112–13, 130–39.

    American character scholars, a much more diffuse group of writers, searched for an overriding American mind, identity, or character and often described it as the product of an innocent and pure New World that had escaped the evil and corrupt European

Old World. Figures and works identified with this approach include Vernon Louis Parrington, *Main Currents in American Thought* (1927; reprint, New York: Harcourt, Brace, 1954); Constance Rourke, *American Humor* (New York: Harcourt, Brace, 1931); Perry Miller, *The New England Mind: The Seventeenth Century* (New York: Macmillan, 1939); Wilbur Cash, *The Mind of the South* (New York: Knopf, 1941); Matthiessen, *American Renaissance*; Denis Brogan, *The American Character* (New York: Knopf, 1944); Henry Steele Commager, *The American Mind* (New Haven: Yale University Press, 1950); Daniel Boorstin, *The Genius of American Politics* (Chicago: University of Chicago Press, 1953); David Potter, *People of Plenty* (Chicago: University of Chicago Press, 1954); Louis Hartz, *The Liberal Tradition in America* (New York: Harcourt, Brace and World, 1955); Daniel Aaron, *Men of Good Hope* (New York: Oxford University Press, 1951) and *Writers on the Left* (New York: Harcourt, Brace and World, 1961); and Allen Guttmann, *The Wound in the Heart* (New York: Free Press, 1962). The two groups shared common roots, friendships, training, and goals, and blended together well enough that they were often indistinguishable.

20. Annette Kolodny, Richard Slotkin, and John Stilgoe are more recent writers who employ a modified myth-symbol approach. Annette Kolodny, *The Land before Her* (Chapel Hill: University of North Carolina Press, 1984); Richard Slotkin, *Regeneration through Violence* (Middletown, Conn.: Wesleyan University Press, 1973); John Stilgoe, *Metropolitan Corridor* (New Haven: Yale University Press, 1983).

21. Robert Spiller, "American Studies, Past, Present, and Future," in *Studies in American Culture*, ed. Joseph Kwiat and Mary Turpie (Minneapolis: University of Minnesota Press, 1960), 209.

22. Henry Steele Commager, "Our Commonwealth: Bryce's Prophetic Vision," *New York Times Magazine*, August 7, 1938, 6.

23. Henry Steele Commager, "Echoes of Marshall," *New York Times Magazine*, June 11, 1939, 10.

24. Henry Steele Commager, "Keystones of Our National Unity," *New York Times Magazine*, November 10, 1940, 3.

25. Henry Steele Commager, "Who Are the American People?" *Senior Scholastic*, September 13, 1943, 8.

26. Unidentified member of the Johns Hopkins history department to Henry Steele Commager, February 17, 1944, and Elspeth V. Davies, "Report on the American Studies Program at Barnard College," November 7, 1941, American Studies and American Character file, HSCP.

27. Henry Steele Commager, draft of a proposal to the Columbia University history department, undated, in American Studies and American Character file, HSCP.

28. David Hackett Fischer, *Historians' Fallacies* (New York: Harper, 1970), 190–91, 265.

29. For some of Commager's subsequent work on American character, see Henry Steele Commager, "The Ambiguous American," *New York Times Magazine*, May 3, 1964, 16; Commager, *Freedom and Order* (Cleveland: Meridian, 1966), 52–68, 246–53; Commager, *The Search for a Usable Past* (New York: Knopf, 1967), ix–xi, 9–13, 26–27; Commager, "Science, Learning, and the Claims of Nationalism," *American Heritage* 23, no. 3 (April 1972): 78–80; Commager, *The Defeat of America* (New York: Simon and Schuster, 1974), 19–47, 99–104; Commager, *The Empire of Reason* (New York: Oxford University Press, 1977), 162–64; John Garraty, ed., *Interpreting American History: Conversations with Historians*, pt. 1 (New York: Macmillan, 1970), 95–98, 107–10, 114–15;

Fred L. Schultz, "New Ideas from a Seasoned Historian," *American History Illustrated*, May 1982, 18.

30. Greene, "Fiftieth Anniversary Dinner." Commager to President Plimpton of Amherst College, May 20, 1964, American Studies and American Character file, HSCP. For more on the Amherst program, see Allen Guttmann, "American Studies at Amherst," *American Quarterly* 22, no. 2, pt. 2 (Summer 1970): 433–48.

31. Richard W. B. Lewis to Commager, February 15, 1951, Salzburg Seminar in American Studies file, HSCP. Commager to unidentified correspondent, January 3, 1978, American Studies and American Character file, HSCP.

32. Lee Coleman, "What Is American?" *Social Forces* 19, no. 4 (May 1941): 492–99; David Riesman, *The Lonely Crowd*, abridged ed. (New Haven: Yale University Press, 1973), 307.

33. Commager, *The American Mind*, 247–76. Harvey Breit, "Talk with Mr. Commager," *New York Times Book Review*, March 12, 1950, 27.

34. Lionel Trilling, *The Liberal Imagination* (1950; reprint, New York: Harcourt, 1978), 3–4, 7–12; Lionel Trilling to Commager, October 7, 1950, Lionel Trilling file, HSCP.

35. Hofstadter, *Progressive Historians*, 350; William Leuchtenburg, letter to author, June 12, 1992.

36. C. Vann Woodward, letter to author, June 20, 1992. C. Vann Woodward, ed., *The Comparative Approach to American History* (New York: Basic Books, 1968), 3–17.

37. Potter, *People of Plenty*, 11, 51.

38. Ibid., 27–28; Potter, "The Quest for the National Character," in *The Reconstruction of American History*, ed. John Higham (New York: Humanities Press, 1962), 209.

39. Ralph Linton, for example, theorized that there is a basic prevailing national personality, on which are grafted other traits that result from the overlapping affiliations we have with other groupings—such as class, race, gender, ethnicity, religion, occupation, and interest. By this approach, no two personalities receive the national culture identically, because there are different classes, status groups, and subcultural experiences. National character is not fixed, then, but diverse and changeable—within a larger pattern of shared culture. This vision of overlapping identities, of course, reflected the political theory of liberal pluralism that also became current in the 1950s. Ralph Linton, *The Cultural Background of Personality* (New York: Appleton Century Crofts, 1945). For other approaches to character studies, see Murray Murphey, "An Approach to the Historical Study of National Character," in *Context and Meaning in Cultural Anthropology*, ed. Melford Spiro (New York: Free Press, 1965); Philip Gleason, *Speaking of Diversity* (Baltimore: Johns Hopkins University Press, 1992), chap. 5; Stannard, "American Historians," 213–19; and Potter, *People of Plenty*, chap. 2.

40. Cecil Tate, *The Search for a Method in American Studies* (Minneapolis: University of Minnesota Press, 1973), 127. See also Wise, "Contemporary Crisis," 55–71; Wise, " 'Paradigm Dramas,' " 314–19; Kerber, "Direction of American Studies," 5; and Sklar, "The Problem of an American Studies 'Philosophy.' "

41. Laurence Veysey, "Intellectual History and the New Social History," in *New Directions in American Intellectual History*, ed. John Higham and Paul Conkin (Baltimore: Johns Hopkins University Press, 1979), 3.

42. Kuklick, "Myth and Symbol in American Studies."

43. Sklar, "Problem of an American Studies 'Philosophy,' " 255, 258–60.

44. Wise, "Contemporary Crisis," 58–61.

45. Lasch quoted in ibid., 59.

46. Luedtke, "Not so Common Ground," 332; Allen F. Davis, "The Politics of American Studies," *American Quarterly* 42, no. 3 (September 1990): 355.

47. Sacvan Bercovitch, ed., *Reconstructing American Literary History* (Cambridge: Harvard University Press, 1986), vii–viii.

48. Giles Gunn, *The Culture of Criticism and the Criticism of Culture* (New York: Oxford University Press, 1987), 149.

49. For a useful discussion of the concept of conservatism and its treatment by American historians, see Alan Brinkley, "The Problem of American Conservatism," *American Historical Review* 99, no. 2 (April 1994): 409–29.

50. For the impact of anthropology on American studies in the postwar period, see Berkhofer, "Clio and the Culture Concept," and Murray Murphey, "American Civilization in Retrospect," *American Quarterly* 31, no. 3 (Bibliography Issue, 1979): 402–6.

51. Hofstadter, *Progressive Historians*, 429–30. Trilling, *Liberal Imagination*, 3–10, 20. For a recent discussion of Parrington's place within the American studies movement, see John Thomas, "The Uses of Catastrophism: Lewis Mumford, Vernon L. Parrington, Van Wyck Brooks, and the End of American Regionalism," *American Quarterly* 42, no. 2 (June 1990): 223–51. On Constance Rourke, see Joan Rubin, *Constance Rourke and American Culture* (Chapel Hill: University of North Carolina Press, 1980), 119–20; Arthur Wertheim, "Constance Rourke and the Discovery of American Culture in the 1930s," in *Study of American Culture*, ed. Luedtke, 52–53; and Thomas, "Catastrophism," 225.

52. Thomas, "Catastrophism," 223. According to Leo Marx, Matthiessen called himself a Christian *and* a Socialist, but not a "Christian Socialist," because of the specifically European associations of the latter.

53. Commager said he voted for La Follette in 1924 and voted straight Democratic thereafter. Henry Steele Commager, interview by author, Amherst, Mass., August 22, 1988.

54. Daniel Aaron, "Cambridge, 1936–39," *Partisan Review* 51 (Double Issue, 1984): 833–36.

55. See Alan Wald's introduction to Daniel Aaron's *Writers on the Left* (New York: Columbia University Press, 1992).

56. Henry Nash Smith to Daniel Aaron, September 30, 1940, February 16(?) and June 13, 1941, DAP.

57. Henry Nash Smith to Daniel Aaron, December 16, 1944, and February 26, 1945, DAP.

58. Henry Nash Smith to Daniel Aaron, May 30, 1947, October 11, 1948, and April 19, 1949, DAP.

59. Henry Nash Smith, "Legislatures, Communists, and State Universities," *Pacific Spectator* 3, no. 3 (Summer 1949): 334. See also Smith's review of George R. Stewart's *The Year of the Oath* (1950) in *American Quarterly* 2, no. 4 (Winter 1950): 372–75.

60. Henry Nash Smith, "Symbol and Idea in *Virgin Land*," in Sacvan Bercovitch and Myra Jehlen, eds., *Ideology and Classic American Literature* (New York: Cambridge University press, 1986), 21, 32 n.

61. Arthur Schlesinger Jr., "Richard Hofstadter," in *Pastmasters*, ed. Marcus Cunliffe and Robin Winks (New York: Harper and Row, 1969); Christopher Lasch, foreword to *The American Political Tradition*, by Richard Hofstadter (1948; reprint, New York: Vintage, 1974); Bernard Sternsher, *Consensus, Conflict, and American Historians* (Bloomington: Indiana University Press, 1975); Daniel Joseph Singal, "Beyond Consensus: Richard

Hofstadter and American Historiography," *American Historical Review* 89, no. 4 (October 1984): 976–1004.

62. Leo Marx, "The Harvard Retrospect and the Arrested Development of American Radicalism," in *A Symposium on Political Activism and the Academic Conscience: The Harvard Experience, 1936–1941*, ed. John Lydenberg (Geneva, N.Y.: Hobart and William Smith Colleges, 1977), 31–33. Copy of book provided to the author by Robert Skotheim.

63. Leo Marx, "Thoughts on the Origin and Character of the American Studies Movement," *American Quarterly* 31, no. 3 (Bibliography Issue, 1979): 399.

64. Leo Marx, letters to author, May 15, 1992, and November 18, 1993.

65. Philip Bennett, Obituary, *Boston Globe*, September 15, 1985, 1, 24.

66. Elizabeth Dilling, *The Red Network* (Kenilworth, Ill.: Published by Elizabeth Dilling, 1935), 331.

67. George Rogers Taylor, ed., *Hamilton and the National Debt* (Boston: D. C. Heath, 1950); Gail Kennedy, ed., *Democracy and the Gospel of Wealth* (Boston: D. C. Heath, 1949).

68. Greene, "Fiftieth Anniversary Dinner."

69. Mulford Sibley and Philip Jacob, *Conscription of Conscience* (Ithaca: Cornell University Press, 1952).

70. Allen Guttmann, letter to author, September 10, 1991.

71. Allen Guttmann, *The Conservative Tradition in America* (New York: Oxford University Press, 1967), 180.

72. Alan Trachtenberg, "Myth and Symbol," *Massachusetts Review* 25, no. 4 (Winter 1984): 669–71.

73. Michael Denning, " 'The Special American Conditions': Marxism and American Studies," *American Quarterly* 38, no. 3 (Bibliography Issue, 1986): 357–62. See also Warren Susman, *Culture as History: The Transformation of American Society in the Twentieth Century* (New York: Pantheon Books, 1984), chap. 5.

74. Jonathan Wiener, "The Odyssey of Daniel Boorstin," *Nation*, September 26, 1987, 305–7.

75. Matthiessen, *American Renaissance*, viii–ix, xiv–xv, xvii, 633.

76. Commager, *The American Mind*, 433–34.

77. Daniel Aaron, *Writers on the Left* (1961; reprint, New York: Avon Books, 1969), 401–5.

78. Henry Nash Smith, *Virgin Land* (1950; reprint, New York: Vintage, 1957), 139, 156, 178–79, 221.

79. Henry Nash Smith to Daniel Aaron, May 30, 1947, DAP.

80. Marx, *Machine in the Garden*, 30, 150, 219, 325, 365.

81. Guttmann, *The Wound in the Heart*, ix, 211.

82. Myra Jehlen, "Introduction: Beyond Transcendence," in *Ideology and Classic American Literature*, ed. Bercovitch and Jehlen, 2–3.

83. See, for example, Peter Clecak, *Radical Paradoxes* (New York: Harper and Row, 1973); Maurice Isserman, *If I Had a Hammer* (New York: Basic Books, 1987); Neil Jumonville, *Critical Crossings: The New York Intellectuals in Postwar America* (Berkeley: University of California Press, 1991); and Paul Buhle, ed., *History and the New Left: Madison, WI, 1950– 1970* (Philadelphia: Temple University Press, 1990).

84. Steven Watts, "The Idiocy of American Studies: Poststructuralism, Language, and Politics in the Age of Self-Fulfillment," *American Quarterly* 43, no. 4 (December 1991): 640.

85. Kiklick, "Myth and Symbol in American Studies."

86. Constance Rourke, *American Humor: A Study of the National Character* (1931; reprint, Tallahassee: Florida State University Press, 1986), 98–99. Wertheim, "Constance Rourke," 58.

87. On socialists and high culture, see Jumonville, *Critical Crossings*, chap. 4.

88. Robert Dawidoff, in his assessment of *The American Mind*, complained that Commager scorned "popular culture in all its vital forms." But Dawidoff also acknowledged the great diversity of material that Commager addressed, the positions from "proletarian" to "conservative" he adopted toward literary works, and his openness to blacks, women, and workers. See Dawidoff, "Commager's *The American Mind*: A Reconsideration," *Reviews in American History* 12, no. 3 (September 1984): 456–58.

89. Henry Steele Commager, draft of an article on the American people for *Senior Scholastic*, in Senior Scholastic file, HSCP. Probably printed later in an altered form as "Who Are the American People?" *Senior Scholastic*, September 13, 1943, 8.

90. For example, see Daniel Aaron, *American Notes* (Boston: Northeastern University Press, 1994), pt. 2. Daniel Aaron, letter to author, November 16, 1993.

91. Richard Dorson, "The American Studies Type," *American Quarterly* 31, no. 3 (Bibliography Issue, 1979): 369. On the cultural radicalism of both Smith and Leo Marx, see Guenter H. Lenz, "American Studies and the Radical Tradition: From the 1930s to the 1960s," *Prospects* 12 (1987): 41–51.

92. Allen Guttmann, letter to author, November 2, 1993.

93. Kerber, "Direction of American Studies," 3–5.

94. Allan Megill, "Fragmentation and the Future of Historiography," *American Historical Review* 96, no. 3 (June 1991): 693–94.

95. Doris Friedensohn, "The Mid-Life Crisis of American Studies," *American Quarterly* 31, no. 3 (Bibliography Issue, 1979): 374–75. See also Werner Sollors, "A Critique of Pure Pluralism," in "*Reconstructing American Literary History*," ed. Bercovitch, 250–79.

96. E. H. Carr quoted in Fischer, *Historians' Fallacies*, 103.

97. For the suggestion of this argument, see Michael Zuckerman, "Myth and Method: The Current Crises in American Historical Writing," *History Teacher* 17, no. 2 (February 1984): 229–30.

98. Spiller, "Unity and Diversity," 613.

99. There are many representative works of the past several decades that utilize the concepts of identity, mind, or character. A notable example is David Hackett Fischer, *Albion's Seed* (New York: Oxford University Press, 1989). Historians who have been particularly influenced by E. P. Thompson often write about the creation of a "mind" or consciousness of a class. Examples are Herbert Gutman, *Work, Culture, and Society in Industrializing America* (New York: Knopf, 1976), and Sean Wilenz, *Chants Democratic* (New York: Oxford University Press, 1984). Similarly, some historians describe the creation of a mind or consciousness within an ethnic group such as African Americans. Consult, for example, Philip Morgan, "Work and Culture: The Task System and the World of Lowcountry Blacks, 1700–1880," *William and Mary Quarterly* 39, no. 4 (October 1982): 563–99, and Charles Joyner, *Down by the Riverside* (Urbana: University of Illinois Press, 1984). Ethnocultural political historians have talked about the mind or character of ethnically or religiously based political groups. See Lee Benson, *The Concept of Jacksonian Democracy* (Princeton: Princeton University Press, 1961), and Ronald Formisano, *The Birth of Mass Political Parties: Michigan, 1827–1861* (Princeton: Prince-

ton University Press, 1971). In some approaches to women's history there is an attempt to formulate a mind of women at a particular time without falling into an essentialism. Those who have written about republican motherhood are useful examples. Consider Linda Kerber, *Women of the Republic* (Chapel Hill: University of North Carolina Press, 1980), and Nancy Cott, *The Bonds of Womanhood* (New Haven: Yale University Press, 1977). Works representing "studies in" and the "voices of" are too voluminous to list but may be found by a quick computer check, using the appropriate keywords. The point is not to criticize these historians but to show how difficult it is to banish the concept of mind, identity, or character even when we say we want to.

100. Luedtke, "Not So Common Ground," 360.

101. David Hollinger, *In the American Province* (Bloomington: Indiana University Press, 1985), 92–94; Hollinger, "How Wide the Circle of the 'We'? American Intellectuals and the Problem of the Ethnos since World War II," *American Historical Review* 98, no. 2 (April 1993): 318–22.

102. Jumonville, *Critical Crossings*, chap. 5.

103. Ibid. Daniel Bell, *The End of Ideology* (Glencoe, Ill.: Free Press, 1960); Irving Howe, *Twenty-Five Years of "Dissent"* (New York: Methuen, 1979); Michael Harrington, *Decade of Decision* (New York: Simon and Schuster, 1980); Sidney Hook, *Political Power and Personal Freedom* (New York: Criterion Books, 1959); Seymour Martin Lipset and Earl Raab, *The Politics of Unreason* (New York: Harper and Row, 1970).

104. Cited in Theodore Roszak, *The Making of a Counter Culture* (Garden City, N.Y.: Doubleday, 1969), 22; see also 49, 55.

105. For example, see Clayborne Carson, *In Struggle: SNCC and the Black Awakening of the 1960s* (Cambridge: Harvard University Press, 1981); Sara Evans, *Personal Politics* (New York: Knopf, 1979); Godfrey Hodgson, *America in Our Time* (Garden City, N.Y.: Doubleday, 1976); and Christopher Lasch, *The Agony of the American Left* (New York: Knopf, 1969).

106. James Miller, *Democracy Is in the Streets* (New York: Simon and Schuster, 1987).

107. Of course this is an oversimplification of the differences between the Old and New Left. The Frankfurt school, which had close ties to the Old Left, was drawn to alienation. Many New Leftists remained organizers and pragmatists. But despite the exceptions and without the space to make this part of the argument more nuanced, this is a useful and defensible separation for the purposes of this discussion.

108. Russell Jacoby, *The Last Intellectuals* (New York: Basic Books, 1987); Watts, "Idiocy of American Studies"; Eric Alterman, "Making One and One Equal Two," *Nation*, May 25, 1998, 10.

CHAPTER 9

1. John Higham, "American Historiography in the 1960s," in *Writing American History* (Bloomington: Indiana University Press, 1970), 165.

2. Richard Hofstadter, *The American Political Tradition* (1948; reprint, New York: Knopf, 1965), vii–x. Hofstadter later identified his book as the opening voice in the consensus chorus; Richard Hofstadter, *The Progressive Historians* (New York: Knopf, 1968), 444 n. 3. A sampling of others who regard Hofstadter as the earliest articulator of consensus history include Peter Novick, *That Noble Dream* (New York: Cambridge University Press, 1988), 333; and J. R. Pole, "Daniel J. Boorstin," in *Pastmasters*, ed. Marcus Cunliffe and Robin Winks (New York: Harper and Row, 1969), 211.

3. Note how Perry Miller has many of the same complaints about Vernon Parrington's assumptions as a historian that Hofstadter, in *The Progressive Historians*, wields against Parrington. Miller, "Thomas Hooker and the Democracy of Connecticut," in *Errand into the Wilderness* (Cambridge: Harvard University Press, 1956), 16–47. See also Novick's characterization of Miller as a consensus historian in *That Noble Dream*, 380–82.

4. John Higham, "The Cult of the 'American Consensus': Homogenizing Our History," *Commentary*, February 1959, 93–100. Higham, *Writing American History*, 138, 144, 195 n. 9.

5. John Higham points out that Ralph Henry Gabriel's *The Course of American Democratic Thought* (New York: Ronald Press, 1940) also presaged the consensus viewpoint (*Writing American History*, 195 n. 9).

6. Henry Steele Commager, "Can Roosevelt Draw New Party Lines?" *New York Times Magazine*, September 4, 1938, 3, 15.

7. Ibid., 15. See also *New York Times*, September 4, 1938, sec. 4, p. 8.

8. Allan Nevins, "The Strength of Our Political System," *New York Times Magazine*, July 18, 1948, 31.

9. Ibid.

10. Henry Steele Commager, "Keystones of Our National Unity," *New York Times Magazine*, November 10, 1940, 3. Frederick Jackson Turner, *The Frontier in American History* (1920; reprint, Tucson: University of Arizona Press, 1986).

11. Daniel Boorstin, *The Genius of American Politics* (Chicago: University of Chicago Press, 1953), 8, 23; Commager, "Keystones of Our National Unity," 3; Alexander Hamilton, "The Federalist No. 9," in Hamilton, John Jay, and James Madison, *The Federalist* (New York: Modern Library, 1941), 51.

12. Henry Steele Commager, *Majority Rule and Minority Rights* (1943; reprint, Gloucester, Mass.: Peter Smith, 1958), 60–61, 63.

13. Commager, "Keystones of Our National Unity," 30.

14. Hofstadter, *American Political Tradition*, vii–x.

15. Ibid.

16. Boorstin, *Genius of American Politics*.

17. Louis Hartz, *The Liberal Tradition in America* (New York: Harcourt, Brace, World, 1955), 74, 85.

18. Ibid., 106, 108.

19. Higham, *Writing American History*, 144.

20. Ibid., 146.

21. Novick, *That Noble Dream*, 323–25.

22. Louis Hartz, "Seth Luther: The Story of a Working-Class Rebel," *New England Quarterly* 13, no. 3 (September 1940): 403, 405, 407, 411.

23. Several observers have noted Hartz's critical edge. John Higham, for example, explained that Hartz's book, "the most fertile of the several consensus interpretations," actually "was built on class analysis." See Higham, "Changing Paradigms: The Collapse of Consensus History," *Journal of American History* 76, no. 2 (September 1989): 465–66.

24. Daniel Joseph Singal, "Beyond Consensus: Richard Hofstadter and American Historiography," *American Historical Review* 89, no. 4 (October 1984): 980. Novick, *That Noble Dream*, 245.

25. David Noble, "The Reconstruction of Progress: Charles Beard, Richard Hofstadter, and Postwar Historical Thought," in *Recasting America*, ed. Lary May (Chicago: University of Chicago Press, 1989), 68–69.

26. Quoted in Novick, *That Noble Dream*, 323.

27. Hofstadter, *Progressive Historians*, 105, 149.

28. Ibid., 444 n. 3.

29. Ibid., 451.

30. Arthur Schlesinger Jr., "Richard Hofstadter," in *Pastmasters*, ed. Cunliffe and Winks, 459 n. 37.

31. William Leuchtenburg, *The FDR Years* (New York: Columbia University Press, 1995), 233; this section of Leuchtenburg's book was first published in John Garraty, *Interpreting American History* (New York: Macmillan, 1970).

32. Hofstadter, *Progressive Historians*, 454, 458.

33. Quoted in Schlesinger, "Richard Hofstadter," 291.

34. Henry Steele Commager, *The American Mind* (New Haven: Yale University Press, 1950), 408, 422.

35. Ibid., 416, 421.

36. Henry Steele Commager, "Why Almost Half of Us Don't Vote," *New York Times Magazine*, October 28, 1956, 74.

37. Ibid., 76.

38. David Trask, letter to the editor, *New York Times Magazine*, November 11, 1956, 6.

39. Henry Steele Commager, "Brave World of the Year 2000," *New York Times Magazine*, November 1, 1959, 30, 32.

40. Commager, *The American Mind*, ix.

41. Singal, "Beyond Consensus," 997.

42. John Higham, "Changing Paradigms," 464.

43. Christopher Lasch, "Consensus: An Academic Question?" *Journal of American History* 76, no. 2 (September 1989): 458.

44. Christopher Lasch, letter to author, September 27, 1992.

45. Hofstadter, *Progressive Historians*, 350.

46. Theodore Hamerow, *Reflections on History and Historians* (Madison: University of Wisconsin Press, 1987), chap. 2. David Levin, *History as Romantic Art* (1959; reprint, New York: AMS Press, 1967). Peter Novick, *That Noble Dream*.

47. Henry Steele Commager, *The Study of History* (Columbus, Ohio: Charles E. Merrill, 1966), 3, 6–8, 38, 77–78.

48. Henry Steele Commager, interview by author, Amherst, Mass., May 27, 1991.

49. Dominick LaCapra, *Rethinking Intellectual History* (Ithaca: Cornell University Press, 1983), 14, 20–21, 35.

50. Ibid., 26–27, 40, 18.

51. Hayden White, *Tropics of Discourse* (Baltimore: Johns Hopkins University Press, 1978), 90. See also White, "The Value of Narrativity in the Representation of Reality," *Critical Inquiry* 7, no. 1 (Autumn 1980): 5–27.

52. Randall Jarrell, "The Age of Criticism," *Partisan Review* 19 (March–April 1952): 185–201.

53. Commager, *Study of History*, viii.

54. Ibid.

55. Ibid., 37, 40, 89.

56. Henry Steele Commager, *Theodore Parker* (Boston: Little, Brown, 1936), viii. For a discussion of the reviews of the book, see Chapter 3.

57. Quoted in Hofstadter, *Progressive Historians*, 33.

58. Bernard Bailyn, "The Challenge of Modern Historiography," *American Historical Review* 87, no. 1 (February 1982): 1–24.

59. Commager, *Majority Rule and Minority Rights*, 4–5, 85 n. 3; Commager, *The American Mind*, 337.

60. Wilbur Jacobs, "In Memory of Allan Nevins," *Pacific Historical Review* 40 (May 1971): 254.

61. Robert Skotheim, in his seminal account of American intellectual historians, suggested that the Progressive historians (especially Beard, Parrington, and Curti) emphasized the deterministic nature (economically and socially) of the ideas that they *disagreed* with but thought that the ideas they *supported* were rationally determined. But Skotheim suggested that intellectual historians after World War II (such as Commager, Stow Persons, and Daniel Boorstin) behaved in a manner just opposite that of the Progressives and described ideas that they *supported* as determined by surrounding conditions. But Skotheim, by omitting Frederick Jackson Turner from the list of the Progressive historians he discussed, miscast the "environmental" relationship between the Progressives and the postwar intellectual historians. Commager and Boorstin, like Turner, described *most* ideas as environmentally determined. Robert Skotheim, *American Intellectual Histories and Historians* (Princeton: Princeton University Press, 1966), 276, 279. Skotheim has noted correctly that his book was about intellectual historians, and he excluded Turner on that criterion. Robert Skotheim, letter to author, July 3, 1992.

62. Vernon Louis Parrington, *Main Currents in American Thought*, vol. 1, *The Colonial Mind* (1927; reprint, Norman: University of Oklahoma Press, 1987), 37, 42, 47, 50, 54, 195. James Madison, "The Federalist No. 10," in Hamilton, Jay, and Madison, *The Federalist*, 53–62.

63. Ibid., 74–75.

64. Skotheim, *American Intellectual Histories and Historians*, 261–62.

65. Novick, *That Noble Dream*, 26.

66. Henry Steele Commager, "Struensee and the Reform Movement in Denmark" (Ph.D. diss., University of Chicago, 1928), 39.

67. Commager, *Study of History*, 50.

68. Ibid., 53.

69. Ibid., 59.

70. For Nevins's views, see Allan Nevins, *The Gateway to History* (Boston: D. C. Heath, 1938), 38–44; Nevins, *Allan Nevins on History*, ed. Ray Allen Billington (New York: Scribner's, 1975), 131–50; Nevins, "Should American History Be Rewritten?" *Saturday Review*, February 6, 1954, 7–9; Harvey Wish, *The American Historian* (New York: Oxford University Press, 1960), 338, 344–45; and Novick, *That Noble Dream*, 259, 290.

71. Commager, *The American Mind*, 309.

72. Commager, *Study of History*, 52.

73. Nevins, *Allan Nevins on History*, 22.

74. For a slightly longer discussion of the distinction between scholars and intellectuals, see Neil Jumonville, *Critical Crossings: The New York Intellectuals in Postwar America* (Berkeley: University of California Press, 1991), 3–13.

75. Henry Steele Commager, *The Empire of Reason* (New York: Oxford University Press, 1977), 236–37.

76. Henry Steele Commager to Merle Curti, January 1, 1955, MCP.

77. Henry Steele Commager to Merle Curti, June 24, 1956, MCP.

78. Henry Steele Commager, "The Heart against the Head," *New York Times Book Review*, September 5, 1965, 5.

79. R. G. Collingwood, *The Idea of History* (New York: Oxford University Press, 1946), 282–302.

80. Cunliffe and Winks, *Pastmasters*, xiii.

81. Nevins, *Allan Nevins on History*, 24, 38.

82. Merle Curti, letter to author, December 18, 1991.

83. Commager, *The American Mind*, 280.

84. William Leuchtenburg, letter to author, June 12, 1992; Leo Marx, letter to author, May 15, 1992.

85. Singal, "Beyond Consensus," 993; Novick, *That Noble Dream*; Jonathan Wiener, "Radical Historians and the Crisis in American History, 1959–1980," *Journal of American History* 76, no. 2 (September 1989): 399–434; Michael D. Bess, "E. P. Thompson: The Historian as Activist," *American Historical Review* 98, no. 1 (February 1993): 18–38.

86. Nevins, *Allan Nevins on History*, 42.

87. Henry Steele Commager to Merle Curti, November 29, [1943 or 1944?], and Commager to Curti, January 10, [1955?], Merle Curti file, HSCP.

88. C. Vann Woodward, letter to author, June 20, 1992; Leuchtenburg, letter to author; John Garraty, letter to author, July 12, 1992.

89. Leonard Levy, letter to author, July 1, 1992.

90. Commager, on the television program, claimed that Churchill was one of the great historians of the twentieth century. "The Dialogues of Allan Nevins and Henry Steele Commager," CBS Public Affairs television broadcast, Wednesday, July 31, 1963 (videotape in author's possession). See also Henry Steele Commager, "Maker of History, Writer of History," *Reporter*, January 19, 1954, 34–38.

91. Howard Lamar, "Frederick Jackson Turner," in *Pastmasters*, ed. Cunliffe and Winks, 102.

92. This observation was made by William Leuchtenburg in his letter to the author of June 12, 1992.

CHAPTER 10

1. Mort R. Lewis, "Allan Nevins' Triumph of Will," *American History Illustrated* 11, no. 9 (January 1977): 26–33.

2. Henry Steele Commager to Joseph Hazen, December 20, [1975?], Miscellaneous Correspondence file, HSCP.

3. Henry Steele Commager to Mary Nevins, March 16, 1971, Allan Nevins file, HSCP.

4. Ibid.

5. Quoted in Richard Hofstadter, *The Progressive Historians* (New York: Knopf, 1968), 389.

6. Henry Steele Commager, interview by author, Amherst, Mass., August 22, 1988.

7. Carol Newell, "Commager Has Shaped Both Amherst, American History," *Amherst Student*, May 24, 1992, 18; Israel Shenker, "A 'Theoretically Retired' Commager Teaches On," *New York Times*, Monday, September 27, 1971, 70.

8. Henry Steele Commager to George Kennan, September 12, 1978, and to Professor Woolf, November 26, 1978, Financial file, HSCP.

9. Commager, interview.

10. Theodore Greene, interview by author, Amherst, Mass., Amherst College, June 12, 1991. Milton Cantor, interview by author, Amherst, Mass., June 13, 1991. Henry Steele Commager, "Why Student Rebellion?" *Current* 97 (July 1968): 13; first published in the *New York Post*, June 1, 1968.

11. Fred L. Schultz, "New Ideas from a Seasoned Historian," *American History Illustrated*, May 1982, 18–19. Henry Steele Commager, "The Roots of Lawlessness," *Saturday Review*, February 13, 1971, 18.

12. Abraham Lincoln, in *Abraham Lincoln: A Documentary Portrait*, ed. Donald Fehrenbacher (Stanford: Stanford University Press, 1977), 156.

13. Commager, "Roots of Lawlessness," 63; Henry Steele Commager, "Our Father and Mother," letter to the editor, *New York Times*, October 29, 1983, 26.

14. John Garraty, letter to author, July 12, 1992; William Leuchtenburg, letter to author, June 10, 1996.

15. Henry Steele Commager to William Leuchtenburg, November 11, 1974; copy in possession of the author.

16. Arthur Schlesinger Jr., "Writing, and Rewriting, History," *New Leader*, December 30, 1991, 12–14. See also Arthur Schlesinger Jr., *The Disuniting of America* (New York: Norton, 1992). For an attempt to bridge the gap between the competing visions of a diverse and a unified culture, see David Hollinger, "How Wide the Circle of the 'We'? American Intellectuals and the Problem of the Ethnos since World War II," *American Historical Review* 98, no. 2 (April 1993): 317–37.

17. C. Vann Woodward, *The Future of the Past* (New York: Oxford University Press, 1989), 122–24.

18. Samuel Eliot Morison to Henry Steele Commager, January 20, 1971, Samuel Eliot Morison file, HSCP.

19. Schultz, "New Ideas from a Seasoned Historian," 19.

20. Alfred Kazin, letter to author, June 26, 1992.

21. Henry Steele Commager to Julian Boyd, April 19, [no year], in Miscellaneous Correspondence file, HSCP; Hofstadter, *Progressive Historians*, 434.

22. J. H. Plumb, "Hymn to the Republic," *New York Times Book Review*, August 14, 1977, 10, 30.

23. Jack C. Thompson, "Ideas and the American Enlightenment," *American Quarterly* 30, no. 2 (Summer 1978): 244–46.

24. Henry Steele Commager, *Jefferson, Nationalism, and the Enlightenment* (New York: George Braziller, 1975), 3.

25. Ibid., xviii–xx.

26. This and the following material, unless indicated otherwise, is from "Democracy in America: A Conversation with Henry Steele Commager," transcript from *Bill Moyers' Journal* (Educational Broadcasting Service, 1979). Public Broadcasting System air date: April 16, 1979.

27. See Henry Steele Commager, "Where Are We Headed?" *Atlantic*, February 1946, 54–59. Again in the *Atlantic* in 1982, three years after his interview with Moyers, Commager maintained that it was wrong to assume that any of our serious problems "can be resolved within the framework of the nation-state system." Actually, he reported, "nationalism as we have known it in the nineteenth and much of the twentieth century is as much of an anachronism today as was States Rights when Calhoun preached it and

Jefferson Davis fought for it." The real problems that humanity faced—energy; pollution; the destruction of oceans and agricultural and forest lands; famine, disease, terrorism, and war—all needed to be resolved through some one-world mechanism. Henry Steele Commager, "Outmoded Assumptions," *Current* 242 (May 1982): 37. First published in the *Atlantic*, March 1982.

28. Henry Steele Commager, "Tocqueville's Mistake," *Harper's*, August 1984, 70–74.

29. Henry Steele Commager, *Commager on Tocqueville* (Columbia: University of Missouri Press, 1993), xii, 27, 44–49, 69.

30. *New York Times*, November 21, 1975, 17, March 2, 1976, 32, and September 12, 1976, 53.

31. Henry Steele Commager, "Political Experience and the Presidency," *New York Times*, September 5, 1976, sec. 4, p. 13; *New York Times*, December 2, 1979, sec. 4, p. 20.

32. *New York Times*, March 6, 1977, sec. 4, p. 16; Henry Steele Commager, "Nations Aren't Innocent," *New York Times*, sec. 1, p. 23; Commager, "Reagan Just Loves to Send Troops," *New York Times*, sec. 4, p. 29; Herbert Mitgang, "A Bouncing, Zestful Commager Turns 80 Today," *New York Times*, October 25, 1982, sec. 3, p. 15.

33. Henry Steele Commager, "Ideology's Dangers," *New York Times*, April 12, 1980, 23.

34. Henry Steele Commager, "No Place for CIA," letter to the editor, *New York Times*, December 23, 1986, sec. 1, p. 20.

35. Henry Steele Commager, "Public Morality, Not Religion," *New York Times*, September 16, 1984, sec. D, p. 23.

36. See also Neil Jumonville, "Diversity among Evangelicals," *New York Times*, May 12, 1981, sec. A, p. 15.

37. Commager interview; Alfred Kazin, letter to author.

38. Quoted in Peter Novick, *That Noble Dream* (New York: Cambridge University Press, 1988), 451.

39. Henry Steele Commager, *The Study of History* (Columbus, Ohio: Charles Merrill, 1966), 26; Daniel Bell, *The Cultural Contradictions of Capitalism* (New York: Basic Books, 1978), xi.

40. Quoted in Novick, *That Noble Dream*, 404.

41. Hofstadter, *Progressive Historians*, 345–46.

Index

rights, 64–68; on common values to bind society, 65–66, 68, 82, 201, 209, 217, 227–29, 231–34, 242–44, 259, 260, 262–67, 274; on importance of dissent, 72–74, 90, 101–19, 122–23, 184–86, 220, 228, 230, 234, 240–42, 259, 260, 274–75; as optimist, 74, 88–89, 99, 117–18, 122, 163, 241, 244, 277; work on behalf of Allies in World War II, 81–89, 95–97; and presidential politics, 83, 84, 140–44, 168, 180–83, 187–92; as Anglophile, 93–95, 250; opposed to double standards, 97, 98, 143, 152, 166, 167, 172, 176–77, 274; moderation of, 100, 128, 276; work on behalf of the United States during cold war, 103; on moral decay, 118, 151, 175–77, 182, 190–92, 265, 274; in Amherst, 153–63, 167–68, 263–64, 271, 274, 275–76; and American exceptionalism, 175–76, 207, 225; alleged political conservatism of, 195, 205–10, 221–25, 227–29, 237, 240; pluralism of, 223, 227; relativism of, 252–53, retirement, 262–63, 273–74; on women, 265–66, 272; death, 275
Commager, Henry Steele, Jr. (Steele), 5, 27, 159–60
Commager, James William, 6
Commager, Lisa, 5, 27, 159
Commager, Mary Powlesland, 124, 263–64
Commager, Nell. *See* Lasch, Nell (Commager)
Commagere, Gerard Jean, 6
Commager(e), Henry Steel, 6, 10, 125
Commager on Tocqueville (Commager), 271–72
Committee for Public Justice, 189–90
Committee on Public Information (Creel Committee), 12
Committee on Un-American Activities (U.S. House), 102, 110, 210
Committee to Defend America by Aiding the Allies, 82–83, 85
Communism, 15, 34, 96, 104, 109, 111, 112, 113–14, 121–22, 124–25, 128, 142, 147, 152, 172, 178–79, 188, 189, 210–11, 217, 220, 238
Congress of Industrial Organizations, 210

Consensus history, 206–11, 213, 218–19, 230–44, 248, 259, 260, 274, 304 (n. 4)
Coolidge, Calvin, 32
Coser, Lewis, 52
Cotton, John, 33, 45–46, 250
Cowley, Malcolm, 5–6, 15–16, 24, 49, 69, 156, 196, 225, 277
Croly, Herbert, 35–36, 54, 137
Crossman, Richard, 119
Cuba, 97, 143–44, 166, 171, 173, 176
Cultural Left, 208, 226–29, 264–67, 277
Culture wars, xi, 195–96, 205–8, 214–15, 219, 222–29, 260–61, 264–67, 276–77
cummings, e. e., 204
Cunliffe, Marcus, 199
Curti, Merle, 37, 40, 47, 52–53, 54, 69, 84–85, 95–96, 140, 153, 200, 237–38, 254–55, 257, 270

Dahl, Robert, 223
Dan, Adam, 7–9, 11, 16–17, 25, 36, 38, 39, 49–50, 98, 126, 161, 200, 255
Danish Lutheran Evangelical Church in America, 7–8, 36, 255
Darmstadter, Paul, 13–15
Davies, Elspeth, 202
Davis, Allen, 207
Davis, Jefferson, 175
Davis, John A., 150–51
Davis, John W., 32
Dean, John, 190
Defeat of America (Commager), 50, 210, 257
Denning, Michael, 214
Dennis, Eugene, 152
Depew, Chauncey, 184
Derrida, Jacques, 246
DeVoto, Bernard, 56, 85
Dewey, John, 9, 28, 35, 51, 73, 108, 113, 117, 120–22, 213, 252, 277
Dies, Martin, 203, 210
Dilling, Elizabeth, 213
Diversity. *See* Multiculturalism
Doar, John, 152
Dodd, William E., 10–13, 16–17, 18, 25, 36, 49–50, 98, 134, 139, 200, 251, 255

Gruntvig, N. F. S., 7–8, 16, 36–38
Gunn, Giles, 207
Guttmann, Allen, 212, 213–14, 218, 221–22

Hamilton, Alexander, 32, 33, 37, 47, 63, 234
Hamiltonianism, 33, 35–36, 48, 137–39, 163, 174, 180, 272
Harrington, Michael, 156, 226, 227
Hartz, Louis, 231, 232, 236–38, 243
Hayek, Friedrich, 138
Heffron, Edward, 110
Heidegger, Martin, 246
Henry, Patrick, 90
Hersey, John, 140, 141
Hesseltine, William, 84
Hicks, Granville, 210, 215
Higham, John, 152, 231, 232, 237, 242–43
Hiss, Alger, 111
Historical Branch Advisory Committee, War Department, 86–87
History: theory in, 4, 48, 117, 230, 247–48; narrative in, 26, 27, 29–31, 39, 43–44, 46, 89–93, 229, 230, 245–47, 267, 269–70, 277; interpretation in, 40–42, 44, 74; partisanship in, 44–50, 95–97, 252–57; as literature, 46, 48, 68–69, 89–93, 98, 200, 202, 217, 219, 244–48, 259, 267–70, 277–78; as public dialogue, 57, 59–60, 88, 91–92, 98, 111, 128, 130, 153, 154–56, 158, 162, 163, 167–68, 230, 252–60, 262–63, 267–69, 273, 277–78; contextualism in, 69, 200, 202, 219–20, 226, 229, 245–55, 270; specialization and generalization in, 198–200, 202, 223–25, 245, 253–59, 262, 267–70, 277–78; social, 208, 222–25, 245, 267; conflict in, 232–43, 259; as language and texts, 245–47; as theory, 247
Hitler, Adolf, 96, 121, 177, 190
Hodgson, Godfrey, 175
Hoffman, Stanley, 168
Hofstadter, Richard, 73, 152, 200, 217; on Parrington, 48, 204, 209, 243, 269; historical outlook different from Commager's, 49, 53–54, 113, 243, 254; at Columbia, 53–54, 107, 129, 131, 140, 161;

on Commager, 66, 204–5; and New York Intellectuals, 113, 117; and consensus history, 211, 231–32, 235–40, 243; on Beard, 277–78
Holism and unity, 221–29, 233–34, 244, 259, 264–67, 274, 276, 277
Hollinger, David, 224–25
Holmes, Oliver Wendell, Jr., 69, 73, 121, 261, 274
Hook, Sidney, 9, 66–68, 83, 113–26 passim, 178–79, 226, 301 (n. 51)
Hooker, Thomas, 232, 250
Hoover, Herbert, 35, 139, 170, 235
House Committee on Un-American Activities (HUAC). See Committee on Un-American Activities (U.S. House)
Howe, Irving, 9, 113, 114, 123, 126, 219, 226
Howells, William Dean, 238
Hull, Cordell, 13
Hutchinson, Thomas, 45–46
Hyman, Harold, 132–34, 149, 152, 258

Independent Citizens Council for the Arts, Sciences, and Professions, 115
Intellectual freedom, 48, 68, 72, 99–123, 128, 137, 148, 153, 183–86, 189–92, 209, 211, 215, 220, 234, 241, 256, 272, 278, 301 (n. 51)
Intellectuals as historians, xii–xiii, 11, 13, 23, 25, 37–38, 50, 55–56, 75–76, 88, 98, 99, 111, 112, 128, 152, 154–56, 158, 162, 163, 167, 168, 192, 230, 253–63, 273, 277–78, 279 (n. 1), 282 (n. 76)
Interventionism, 83–85, 98, 171–74, 181–83
Isolationism, 83–85, 87, 98, 171–74, 181

Jackson, Andrew, 235
James, Henry, 95, 206
James, William, 73–74, 120, 122
Jameson, J. Franklin, 10, 91
Jameson, Storm, 161
Jarrell, Randall, 247
Jefferson, Thomas, 12, 16–17, 25, 31–33, 36, 37, 63, 64, 68, 82, 89, 90, 125, 177, 218, 235, 236, 248, 269, 270–71, 274
Jeffersonianism, 13, 34–36, 44, 48, 49, 72,

McDowell, Tremaine, 69, 199–200, 212, 221

McGovern, George, 177, 188, 226

McKinley, William, 273

McLaughlin, Andrew, 10–12, 18, 25, 49–50, 85, 98, 134, 255

MacLeish, Archibald, 82, 85, 86, 141, 263

McMaster, John Bach, 261

McNamara, Robert, 166, 168

Madison, James, 117, 248, 250

Majority Rule and Minority Rights (Commager), 62–68, 76, 88

Malone, Dumas, 54, 86, 129, 140

Mao Tse-tung, 143

Markel, Lester, 57, 112–13, 125

Marshall, John, 65–66, 201

Marshall, Thurgood, 150

Marx, Karl, 34, 100, 117, 213, 227, 239, 276

Marx, Leo, 95, 106, 157, 187, 196, 211–12, 213, 218, 220, 221, 256

Marxism, 47, 206, 214, 225, 238, 239, 249, 250

Matthiessen, F. O., 69, 89, 107, 196, 199, 209, 212, 214, 215

May, Henry, 84

Megill, Alan, 222

Meier, August, 56, 146–50, 152

Mencken, H. L., 63

Merk, Frederick, 59

Metzger, Walter, 107

Miller, Perry, 68, 73, 89, 199, 212, 232, 254, 257

Mills, C. Wright, 52–53, 227

Modern Language Association, 197, 198

Monaghan, Frank, 85

Monroe, James, 182, 248

Montesquieu, Charles, 234

Monthly Review, 212

Moral Majority, 275

More, Paul Elmer, 20, 70

Morgan, Edmund, 199, 232

Morgan, Helen, 232

Morgenthau, Hans J., 168

Morison, Samuel Eliot, 24, 26–30, 40, 44, 58, 59, 85, 91–93, 140–41, 257, 258, 267; collaboration with Commager, 57, 71, 98, 124, 200; and McCarthyism, 111; and race, 146–48; and Vietnam, 170

Morris, Richard, 54, 55, 129, 130, 140, 149

Morse, Wayne, 167, 181–82, 188

Moscow Trials, 84

Mowrer, Edgar Ansel, 120

Moyers, Bill, 271–72

Multiculturalism, 153, 195, 201–2, 204–8, 212, 215, 219–29, 259, 260, 264–67, 276

Mumford, Lewis, 82, 85, 104

Murdock, Kenneth, 69, 199

Muste, A. J., 104

Myrdal, Gunnar, 145

Namath, Joe, 190

Nation, 12, 20–21, 83, 113, 116, 128, 171, 189, 276

National Association for the Advancement of Colored People, 147, 150–51

National Committee for an Effective Congress, 187–88

National Council of Negro Women, 151

National Institute of Arts and Letters, 129–30

National Lawyer's Guild, 111

National Review, 123–27

Nazism, 41, 83, 96, 114, 121, 184, 186, 272, 275

Nazi-Soviet Pact, 66, 83, 84

Nevins, Allan, xii, 69, 154, 155, 257–59; early life, 19–25, 27, 122, 162, 261; hurried schedule, 20–22, 56, 62, 134–37, 262, 295 (n. 21); collaboration with Commager, 29, 57–58, 88–93, 98, 168–70, 200, 287–88 (n. 68); and New Deal, 34, 36; and historical narrative, 44, 90–93, 244–45, 248; on Parrington, 47; at Columbia, 52, 58–59, 129, 134, 261–62; and *American Heritage*, 59, 261; and Society of American Historians, 59–60; organizational projects, 59–60, 261–62; and Columbia Oral History Project, 60, 261; and business history, 60–62, 90, 140; on *The American Mind*, 70–72, 287–88 (n. 68); conservatism of, 71–72, 90, 168, 243; and World War II, 85, 86, 93–94, 97, 261; and Vietnam, 110, 165, 168, 170–71; and

Ranke, Leopold, 251–52
Rauh, Joseph L., Jr., 141
Read, Conyers, 59, 86
Reagan, Ronald, 262, 272, 274–75
Rhodes, James Ford, 92, 261
Ribicoff, Abraham, 142
Richardson, Seth, 102
Rickenbacker, William Frost, 127
Riesman, David, 204, 254
Robinson, Edward Arlington, 204
Robinson, James Harvey, 51, 73, 197, 198
Rockefeller, John D., 140
Rockefeller, Nelson, 144, 165
Romney, George, 165
Roosevelt, Eleanor, 104
Roosevelt, Franklin, 12, 32–35, 87, 125, 141,
    164, 168, 169, 180–81, 188, 217, 232–33, 273
Roosevelt, Theodore, 12, 35–36, 138, 171, 273
Root, Elihu, 171
Ross, Edward A., 73
Rossiter, Clinton, 232
Rourke, Constance, 209, 220–21, 259
Rusk, Dean, 166, 168
Russell, Bertrand, 24

Salzburg Seminar in American Studies,
    150, 203
Sandburg, Carl, 141
Santayana, George, 163, 198
Saturday Review, 57
Schlesinger, Arthur, Jr., xii, 59, 86, 103, 113,
    123, 172, 256; on *The American Mind*, 75;
    and Kennedy, 141; on presidential power,
    181–83; and Nixon, 190; and consensus
    history, 211, 239; and multiculturalism,
    266–67
Schlesinger, Arthur, Sr., 24, 54
Schmidt, Bernadotte, 86
Schorr, Daniel, 273
Schuman, Frederick, 83
Schumpeter, Joseph, 117
Senior Scholastic, Commager's column in,
    57–58
Seymour, Horatio, 170
Shannon, Fred, 84
Shapiro, Harvey, 184

Sherman, Stuart, 20, 168
Shils, Edward, 223
Sibley, Mulford, 213
Singal, Daniel, 211
Sklar, Robert, 206
Skotheim, Robert, 251, 314 (n. 61)
Slotkin, Richard, 212
Smith, Al, 142
Smith, Henry Nash, 69, 177, 196, 199, 210,
    213, 214, 217–21, 231
Smith Act, 104
Socialism, 34, 38, 49
Society of American Historians, 59–60, 69,
    91
Southeast Asia Treaty Organization, 166
Soviet Union, 97, 101–2, 113, 116, 118–20,
    124, 128, 144, 166–67, 176, 272, 275
Spaulding, Oliver, 86
Spencer, Herbert, 117, 138
Spiller, Robert, 68–69, 197, 200, 212, 224
Spingarn, Joel, 147
Squires, J. Duane, 86
Stalin, Joseph, 124, 126–28, 190
Stearns, Harold, 196
Steel, Abigail, 6
Steiger, Rod, 188
Steinbeck, John, 141
Sternsher, Bernard, 211
Stevenson, Adlai, 110, 139–42, 144, 168
Stevenson, Coke, 211
Story, Joseph, 63, 156, 257, 258
Stowe, Harriet Beecher, 96
Streisand, Barbra, 190
Struensee, Johann Friedrich, 13–14, 17–18,
    36, 51, 100, 251, 269
Student radicalism, 181, 183–87, 274–75
Sumner, William Graham, 63
Sweezy, Paul, 212
Symington, Stuart, 141

Taft, Robert, 140, 181–82
Taft, William, 273
Taine, Hippolyte, 45
Tate, Cecil, 205
Taylor, A. A., 149
Taylor, George Rogers, 212, 213